WAR AND PEACE

War and Peace
Ireland since the 1960s

Christine Kinealy

REAKTION BOOKS

To Ivan Cooper, and all those who campaign for social justice in Ireland.

Published by Reaktion Books Ltd
33 Great Sutton Street
London EC1V 0DX
www.reaktionbooks.co.uk

First published 2010

Printed and bound by CPI/Antony Rowe, Chippenham, Wiltshire

British Library Cataloguing in Publication Data
Kinealy, Christine
   War and peace : Ireland since the 1960s.
   1. Ireland – History – 20th century. 2. Ireland – History –
   21st century. 3. Ireland – Politics and government – 1949–
   4. Ireland – Social conditions – 1922–1973. 5. Ireland –
   Social conditions – 1973–
   I. Title
   941.5'0824–DC22

ISBN 978 1 86189 779 4

Contents

Irish Phrases and Abbreviations

An Garda Síochána	Police force of the Republic
Áras an Uachtaráin	Official Residence of the Irish President
Ard Fheis	Main festival or gathering, usually annual conference
Dáil Uladh	Ulster Assembly
Dail Éireann	Irish parliament based in Dublin
Fianna Fáil	Political party founded in 1926, and associated with Éamon de Valera
Fine Gael	Political party founded in 1933, and identified with Michael Collins
Oireachtas Éireann	Irish Legislature
Seanad Éireann	Upper House of the Legislature
Sinn Féin	Republican political party
Teachta Dála (TD)	A Member of the Dáil
Taoiseach	Prime Minister of the Republic

Abbreviations

DUP	Democratic Unionist Party
GFA	Good Friday Agreement
HMG	Her Majesty's Government
HMSO	Her Majesty's Stationery Office
INLA	Irish National Liberation Army
IRA	Irish Republican Army
IRSP	Irish Republican Socialist Party Political wing of the INLA
MLA	Member of Legislative Assembly (Northern Ireland)
MTF	Margaret Thatcher Foundation

NAE	National Archives, England
NICRA	Northern Ireland Civil Rights Association
NIO	Northern Ireland Office
OIRA	Official Irish Republican Army
PRIA	Provisional Irish Republican Army
PSNI	Police Service of Northern Ireland
PUP	Progressive Unionist Party
RTÉ	Radio Telefís Éireann
SAS	Special Air Service
SDLP	Social Democratic Labour Party
UAC	Ulster Army Council
UDA	Ulster Defence Association
UDP	Ulster Defence Party
UDR	Ulster Defence Regiment
UFF	Ulster Freedom Fighters
UKUP	United Kingdom Unionist Party
UPNI	Unionist Party of Northern Ireland
UUAC	United Unionist Action Council
UUC	Ulster Unionist Council
UUP	Ulster Unionist Party
UUUC	United Ulster Unionist Council
UWC	Ulster Workers' Council
WP	Workers' Party

Introduction

In 1960 the total population of Ireland was 4,300,000: the North accounted for 1,400,000 and the South for 2,900,000.[1] The area covered by the Republic was 70,273 km², making it a little larger than the state of West Virginia in the USA. Northern Ireland covered 13,843 km², making it similar to the size of Connecticut.[2] Yet this small, divided country on the edge of Europe was to dominate news headlines in many parts of the world in the decades that followed, largely as a result of the violence taking place within its borders. Yet, regardless of the conflict and despite the smallness of the population, Irish writers, musicians, actors and dancers – and even Irish pubs – were evident in all parts of the world. Ireland enjoyed a presence on the international cultural landscape that was disproportionate to its size.

By 1960 partition had been in place for less than 40 years. It had resulted from the Government of Ireland Act of 1920. Without prior discussion or consent, Ireland had been divided into two states; Southern Ireland, which quickly changed its name to the Irish Free State, had been forced to remain in the British Commonwealth, although it unilaterally removed itself in 1948. The Northern state gained its own parliament in Belfast, but remained within the United Kingdom and thus linked directly to Westminster.[3] The early years of both states were violent, punctuated by anti-Catholic pogroms in the North and a civil war in the South. Internal violence preoccupied the new governments in both the North and the South, and left little time for cross-border conflict or cross-border cooperation. The Government of Ireland Act had provided for a Council of Ireland:

> with a view to the eventual establishment of a Parliament for the whole of Ireland, and to bringing about harmonious

action between the parliaments and governments of Southern Ireland and Northern Ireland, and to the promotion of mutual intercourse and uniformity in relation to matters affecting the whole of Ireland.[4]

The Council never met. The partition, which had been conceived as a temporary expedient, became further embedded as the two Irish governments shaped their respective states in ways that made the creation of a single, inclusive parliament both impracticable and improbable.

Attitudes to Irish republicanism, the flag-bearers of a united Ireland, were also changing. When Éamon de Valera, a hero of the 1916 Rising and the founder of the Fianna Fáil Party, decided to ban the IRA in 1936, the move was widely welcomed.[5] Yet the aspiration to a united Ireland was foregrounded in the new Constitution that was introduced in 1937. This Constitution replaced the original Constitution of the Irish Free State that had been in use since 1922, and therefore was viewed as tainted by British input. De Valera used the abdication crisis in Britain to replace it, and thus to create an Irish Constitution that conformed more to his vision. Hence the Catholic Church was assigned a 'special position' (repealed in 1973) and the claim to a united Ireland was enshrined in Articles 2 and 3:

Article 2: The national territory consists of the whole island of Ireland, its islands and the territorial seas.

Article 3: Pending the reintegration of the national territory, and without prejudice to the right of the parliament and government established by this constitution to exercise jurisdiction over the whole territory, the laws enacted by the parliament shall have the like area and extent of application as the laws of Saorstat Éireann and the like extra-territorial effect.[6]

Members of the Ulster Unionist Party, who had controlled the government of Northern Ireland since its inception, were angry, one member asking, 'does not the new Constitution of the Free State propose to wipe out this Parliament, with execution deferred?' He was reassured that the affairs of a 'foreign country' could have no impact on the constitutional status of Northern Ireland, and that 'the Free State Government have no jurisdiction over us of any kind or shape'.[7]

Regardless of the aspirations of the Irish Constitution, for much of the decades after 1921 the Southern government ignored Northern Ireland and its internal workings. Moreover, this lack of interest was mirrored by the British government, despite having a constitutional responsibility for the affairs of the six counties. Instead they let successive Unionist governments have a free rein to do what they chose, which meant passing legislation that guaranteed their position of ascendancy would continue. In other ways, Northern Ireland seemed to be hermetically sealed from the outside world. The suave travel writer Alan Whicker, following a visit there in 1959, commented that: 'No country deserves the Government you have here. This is the only place in the world you cannot report honestly without silly people kicking up about what is only the truth.'[8] Politically, Northern Ireland was situated in a no-man's-land; British political commentators and analysts tended to leave it alone, thus reinforcing the idea that it was separate and different.[9] In the Republic, economic isolation and the search for an 'Irish' identity had produced a society that was both Catholic and conservative.[10] Surprisingly – or perhaps because of this seclusion – cultural activities on both sides of the border flourished.

By the 1960s the sectarian nature of the Unionist government led to it being challenged both by nationalists and liberal Protestants, radicals and moderates, under the broad umbrella of the Civil Rights Association. Some have speculated that if the British Labour government under Harold Wilson had intervened in the 1960s and developed a policy to meet what had become a fast-deteriorating situation, the subsequent decades of violence could have been avoided.[11] According to the historian Peter Berresford Ellis, who first visited Belfast in the 1960s: 'Northern Ireland was a festering boil that had either to be lanced or erupt. The UK parliament steadfastly refused to apply the lance to the boil. The eruption was inevitable.'[12] The consequence of non-intervention was that after 1969 Northern Ireland was engulfed in an internecine war, which spilled over into the Republic and into Britain.

In what follows, the island of Ireland is viewed largely through the prism of the unfolding conflict in Northern Ireland, and how divisions and conflict within the six counties often shaped developments elsewhere. Some political fault lines had been present since partition in 1921. However, the fluidity of political alliances and allegiances in the decades after 1960 were greater than is generally assumed. Beneath the political posturing, regrouping and reconciliations were often taking place, which allowed progress to be made. The complexity of the situation was evident even in the main strands of relationship: the political relationships within the Republic; within Northern Ireland; between the Republic and the North; between the North and Britain; between the Republic and Britain; and between the United Kingdom and the Republic. The borders may have stayed the same, but political loyalties and associations did not. Moreover, the political structure of the United Kingdom changed following devolution and the creation of a Welsh Assembly and a Scottish Parliament in 1999. If, as some wish, Scottish independence were granted, this would have unknown significance for the constitutional future of the United Kingdom and Northern Ireland's position within it.

Ireland, helped by its geographic position at the edge of Europe, and the first point of contact with the United States, had often provided a stepping stone between the two continents.[13] In the eighteenth century and the early nineteenth, Ireland looked to France as its political ally against Britain. In the 1840s, even before the mass emigration associated with the Great Famine, groups within the United States were organizing to help the nationalist struggle in Ireland.[14] Unionism, traditionally, had less support. Relationships between America and Ireland remained strong after 1960, helped by continuing emigration, the political influence of Irish-America, and the personal involvement of successive presidents. The election of John Kennedy in 1960, the first President of Irish Catholic descent, through to the election of Barack Obama in 2008 – who was found to have ancestors from County Offaly – gave Ireland a presence in the White House that was unchallenged.[15]

Throughout this period Ireland's relationships with Europe strengthened, helped by the joining of the European Economic Community in 1973. People in the Republic embraced the opportunities offered by being a member. It brought substantial benefits to Irish farmers, giving them access to new markets and guaranteed prices.[16] This meant that they were no longer dependent on low-priced United Kingdom markets. It thus marked an important step in the changing economic relationship between Britain and the

Republic. The rejection of the Lisbon Treaty in 2008 temporarily put this closeness to Europe in jeopardy. A second referendum in 2009, however, voted yes.[17] In addition to the economic benefits, European Directives also played a major role in standardizing employment practices and in removing discrimination regarding sexual orientation throughout Ireland.[18]

The changing cultural landscape is an integral part of the story of Ireland since 1960. The transformations taking place in Ireland, particularly in regard to politics, issues of gender, the economy and religion, all found an outlet in works of literature, in art, music, celluloid and dance, which found audiences throughout the world. The conflict in Northern Ireland had a significant impact on popular culture: both John Lennon and Paul McCartney were moved to write songs on Bloody Sunday, which merited being banned by the BBC. In regards to high culture, according to the literary critic Michael Parker: 'The terror and dislocation of the Northern Ireland Troubles have left a legacy of anger, but they have also stimulated writing of the highest order: powerful, searching and painfully candid.'[19] The chapters that follow tell the story of terror and dislocation as the search for social justice and peace unfolded in all parts of Ireland. They also tell the story of determination and achievement, frequently set against a background of poverty and social conservatism. Above all, they tell the story of wasted years, and of lives that were lost or were shattered, as men and women of vision and courage were outmanoeuvred by those who put prejudice and personal gain above peace and social justice.

As Chapter One shows, in a number of ways the swinging sixties bypassed Ireland. People on both sides of the border remained insulated from many external changes, their main contact with other countries being as a result of high levels of emigration. The spread of television and the growth of tourism, though, exposed Ireland increasingly to outside cultural influences. Nonetheless, the influence of the Catholic Church in the South, and the Presbyterian Church in the North, remained strong. The attempts by politicians in both the North and the South to modernize their economies met with mixed results. In the Republic, seeds were sown that paved the way for the economic miracle of the 1990s. The political conflicts that erupted at the end of the 1960s started as a peaceful demand for civil rights for the Catholic minority population in Northern Ireland. Mishandling by both the Unionist and the British governments turned the campaign into a war, during the course of which the very existence of the six-county state was challenged.

Chapter Two explores the consequences of sending British troops to Northern Ireland in August 1969, initially to protect the Catholic minority. Their arrival is sometimes regarded as marking the beginning of the period known as 'the Troubles'. From an early stage Britain realized that they were fighting a propaganda war, and from the outset the military campaign was accompanied by 'psychological operations'. For writers such as Seamus Heaney, the renewed conflict presented the dilemma: should the situation be addressed or ignored. As the subsequent years were to prove, culture was at the forefront of this ideological struggle.

Chapter Three shows how the early years of the conflict dominated politics within Ireland on both sides of the border. By the early 1970s patterns of violence had been established in Northern Ireland that, depressingly, remained in place for more than two decades. An aspect of the hostilities that was frequently overlooked was the activities of loyalist paramilitaries. Moreover, as was later proved to be the case, they often acted in collusion with the security forces. The introduction of internment in 1971 signified the draconian way in which the law was to be marshalled to support the flagging Unionist government. A protest march in January 1972, remembered as Bloody Sunday, marked the demise of the Northern Ireland Civil Rights Association and a parallel increase in support for the Provisional IRA. The ruthless actions of the British soldiers precipitated not only a loss of life, but a loss of the political middle ground. Initially there was widespread sympathy in the Republic for the plight of the Catholic minority, but as the violence spilled into the South, and as the IRA extended its military struggle, this dissipated.

In 1973 both the UK and the Republic joined the European Economic Community. While people in the Republic embraced their role as Europeans, and benefited economically from the connection, the United Kingdom's involvement remained more ambivalent and, occasionally, confrontational.[20] However, as Chapter Four demonstrates, the violence in Northern Ireland overshadowed other developments. There were some hopes of progress towards a constitutional solution made in the mid-1970s, largely represented by the Sunningdale Agreement. It was a false dawn. In the eyes of militant unionists, any agreement that involved the government of the Republic was a form of 'creeping nationalism' – summed up in the slogan 'Dublin is just a Sunningdale away'. Bombs in the Republic, especially those planted in Dublin and Monaghan in May 1974, were a lethal reminder of the human cost of not reaching an agreement. An intensified campaign of bombings in England also took its toll, while hardening attitudes against the IRA. The wider context was that Britain was facing its own internal problems. High inflation, industrial strikes and large-scale unemployment occupied and weakened the attention of successive governments. British Prime Ministers faced industrial unrest in Britain and civil unrest in Northern Ireland.

The failure to find a power-sharing solution created a political vacuum that militant unionism sought to fill. The cycle of bloodshed continued and became ever more gruesome and gratuitous. Chapter Five examines the emergence of a new loyalist paramilitary group, known as the Shankill Butchers, who took the violence to new depths of depravity. Against the brutal backdrop there were realignments and attempts to find peace. Poetry and music sometimes provided a catharsis for what was taking place, although a solution remained elusive.

The 1981 hunger strike attracted international attention for the republican cause. At the same time, the ruling Conservative Party was criticized for its handling of the situation. Chapter Six shows how, like Bloody Sunday, the preventable deaths of a group of young men had a profound, long-term impact. The backdrop was economic stagnation, unemployment and emigration. Economic stagnation was mirrored by social conservatism on both sides of the border. In 1986, U2 performed at a concert in Dublin on behalf of the unemployed. Undoubtedly, though, the concert of the decade – again for humanitarian purposes – was 'Live Aid' in 1984. It was the brainchild of an Irish musician, Bob Geldof. Constitutional politics in the Republic and Britain were dominated by Charles Haughey and Margaret Thatcher respectively. They were each controversial in their style of leadership and both divided opinions within their own parties. The decade also witnessed the rise of Gerry Adams and Ian Paisley as major figures in Northern Irish politics. Paisley finally lost power in 2008, brought down by his own party, but Adams showed a unique ability to survive the vicissitudes of Irish politics, which was unmatched by any of his contemporaries.

By the beginning of the 1990s international politics were changing. In February 1990 anti-apartheid campaigner Nelson Mandela was freed from prison in South Africa after 27 years' imprisonment. It marked the ending of racial segregation by the South African government. The fall of the Berlin Wall led to the unification of Germany. It also heralded the end of the Cold War. As the political map of Europe adjusted to this change, Northern Ireland became of less geographical significance to Britain in the post-Cold War world.[21] Tellingly, in a speech made by the Secretary of State for Northern Ireland in November 1990, Peter Brooke declared that Britain had 'no selfish strategic or economic interest' in Northern Ireland.[22] It was a landmark declaration and paved the way for secret talks between John Hume and Gerry Adams.[23] However, partition remained in place and the divisions, both between and within nationalism and unionism, appeared to be as great as ever. As Chapter Seven shows, however, attempts were taking place, usually covertly, to initiate peace talks. The election of Mary Robinson as President of Ireland in 1990 suggested that some things were changing in a positive way. Her Presidency witnessed the start of a decade of economic and social change in the Republic.

Chapter Eight outlines the various moves to find peace in the mid-1990s. A ceasefire by the IRA and by loyalists in 1994 appeared to augur a new dawn of peace. It was short-lived, but it paved the way for the more lasting Good Friday Agreement of 1998. These years also marked the emergence of the Celtic Tiger, which transformed the economy of the Republic and ended decades of emigration. Ireland may not have been exporting its people overseas, but it was exporting its culture. The Irish presence on the international stage was felt in other ways – particularly through music, poetry, film and dance. *Riverdance* gave a positive image of Ireland and its culture was transmitted throughout the world. Economic change inevitably brought social change in its wake. Throughout the 1990s the dominant position of the Catholic Church was challenged, especially over issues to do with women's rights, such as divorce, abortion and contraception. This coincided with mounting accusations of endemic abuse of children in the care of the Catholic Church. The supremacy of the Church in the Republic finally appeared to have ended.

Chapter Nine looks at the final years of the twentieth century in Ireland. In the North, they were dominated by the Good Friday Agreement and the attempts to re-establish a power-sharing Assembly. Political changes were also taking place in Britain, largely as a result of devolution. For many people in the Republic, these years were prosperous. Inward migration was one outcome of the thriving economy, but an unpalatable aspect of this was racism towards the new arrivals. Helped by the peace process, the Northern economy was also showing signs of economic recovery. Actually achieving peace and political cooperation with Northern Ireland, however, was proving to be slow and arduous.

The Epilogue brings together some of the main developments in Ireland since 1960. It also explores some of the challenges faced in the twenty-first century, especially in regard to sustaining the peace process. Despite the challenges and setbacks, enormous progress had been made. In 1960 the three governments had operated in distinct political zones, with little interaction or cooperation. Forty years later, this had changed – although much had been lost in the intervening period. In the twenty-first century the peace process in Northern Ireland was being held up as a model for other entrenched conflict zones. Ireland had found peace, but the country remained partitioned. In the Republic, one of the greatest challenges facing the people was the implosion of the Catholic Church, which had led to the publication of the Ryan report into child abuse in 2009. The backdrop to this was a deepening economic crisis, which revealed that beneath the patina of the success of the Celtic Tiger, the Irish economy was highly sensitive to global financial changes.

Finally, language carries a particular political meaning within Ireland. An obvious nationalist/unionist divide is whether or not to use Derry/Londonderry. Some of the divisions within nationalism are more complex. Is Northern Ireland a state? Some nationalists prefer the designation 'Six Counties'. Similarly, when referring to the Great Famine of the 1840s, some prefer to use the Great Hunger, or *an Gorta Mór*. In a book largely concerned with politics, especially recent politics, and especially recent Irish politics, it is impossible not to offend somebody. Language has become a tool of politics and a book concerned with Irish politics is bound to cause offence to somebody. The alternative is, in the words of Seamus Heaney, 'Whatever you say, say nothing.'

A further note of caution and a pre-emptive warning. The recent history of Ireland – especially the peace process – is unfinished business. A number of interpretations offered in this book might be modified or even be reversed as more evidence is revealed. The last few years have exposed the extent to which collusion and deception have been part of Irish politics. Undoubtedly, more will be revealed as leading protagonists move from the centre stage or government records are made available. It will be many more years before the full story of Ireland since 1960 is revealed.

ONE

Fault Lines

In 1960 Northern and Southern Ireland remained politically divided, separated by an artificial partition imposed in 1920 as a result of the passing, by the British Parliament, of the Government of Ireland Act. During the intervening four decades, the physical divide, although unprecedented and imposed without majority consensus, had become embedded in the everyday life of the Irish people and the psychological reality of Irish politics. Consequently, demands for reunification were low on the political agenda on both sides of the border. The IRA, however, who remained the torchbearers of the pre-Partition demand for a united, independent Ireland, had been involved in a guerrilla, border campaign since 1956 (referred to as 'Operation Harvest'). It demonstrated the lack of support for the IRA and their tactics. By 1962 the campaign was over, and the IRA had been discredited and weakened.

Yet, while the republican struggle had little support in reality, in memory it was being lionized. On 5 February 1960 the epic documentary *Mise Eire* ('I am Ireland') was put on general release in the Irish Republic. The title was derived from a poem by Patrick Pearse, the rebel leader executed in 1916. It presented an idealized view of Ireland's revolutionary fight for independence. It contained a montage of events, including original footage of 'The birth of the Irish nation'.[1] A follow-up, *Saoirse* ('Freedom'), was made eleven years later.

Ireland's republican past was also remembered in 1965 when the British government, under the Labour Party leader, Harold Wilson, agreed that the remains of Roger Casement could be returned to the Republic, on the condition they were not taken to the North, where Casement had asked to be buried. Casement, an executed hero of 1916, was thus given a state funeral and burial in the

Republican Plot in Glasnevin Cemetery, with full military honours. Despite ill-health and against medical advice, Éamon de Valera, the only surviving Commander from the Rising, attended. The following year marked the fiftieth anniversary of the Easter Rising. On 8 March, Nelson's Column, which had dominated the Dublin skyline in O'Connell Street for almost 150 years, was blown up, probably by former members of the IRA.[2] Its demise marked a symbolic break with Ireland's colonial past. The anniversary was also commemorated officially by the Irish government. The state-sponsored memorial, which was overseen by Seán Lemass, the Taoiseach and a veteran of the Rising, provided a platform for glorifying Ireland's republican struggle. Yet, only a few years later, the Southern state was distancing itself from all associations with republicanism, past and present, refusing to get involved with any further commemorations and even banning one planned to be held in Dublin in 1976.

July 1966 marked the fiftieth anniversary of the Battle of the Somme, one of the most violent conflicts of the First World War. Thousands of Irishmen had been killed in the first few days of fighting, including members of the 36th Ulster Division, many of whom had been former members of the original UVF. Traditionally, this anniversary was ignored by the Southern State, some believing that Irishmen who supported Britain in the First Word War were traitors. In 1966, however, the Irish Taoiseach, Seán Lemass, acknowledged their sacrifice:

> In later years it was common – and I was also guilty in this respect – to question the motives of those men who joined the new British armies formed at the outbreak of the war, but it must in their honour and in fairness to their memory be said that they were motivated by the highest purpose.[3]

For Northern Ireland unionists, honouring the men who died at the Somme was regarded as an important part of their history. To mark the fiftieth anniversary, the Prime Minister, Terence O'Neill, travelled to France. His visit ended abruptly when he had to return to deal with sectarian violence on the streets of Belfast.[4] Ironically, a revived UVF had declared war on the IRA. Fifty years after both the Easter Rising and the Battle of the Somme the same groups were still fighting the same battles within Ireland, suggesting that partition had done little to resolve political differences.

Juxtaposed against this imagined, heroic, and idealized, view of Ireland and her political struggle as shown in *Mise Eire* was the fact that in the 1960s Ireland (north and south) remained poor, socially conservative and economically underdeveloped. The Republic also remained tied to the Catholic Church, but a Catholic Church that proved unwilling to embrace many of the changes heralded by the Second Vatican Council. Censorship had been part of the Irish Free State for most of its brief existence. The censorship of publications, including books, had been introduced in 1929. In 1942, when most of the world was involved in fighting the Second World War, there was a debate in the Irish *Seánad* (Upper House), concerning the recent banning of the innocuous, and now classic, *Tailor and Anstey*. Sir John Keane, the speaker who objected to the ban, pointed out that since the censorship laws had been passed, 1,600 books had been banned. Mr O'Donovan, who opposed him, answered by saying,

> Since our last meeting, I have seen references to the fact that we, the Irish people, by adopting this so-called high standard, or assumption of a higher standard than other peoples, would make ourselves ridiculous to the people of the world. I think that we should demonstrate by our votes that we have the greatest confidence in the members of the Censorship Board in the magnificent work they are doing. Although it does not come within this motion, if possible we should look for extended powers to enable the board to stop vulgarity as well as indecency.[5]

Senator O'Dwyer, agreeing with these sentiments, pointed out:

> We know that conditions in the outside world are very bad at the moment. In Europe, America and all countries there is an increasing tendency towards immorality and lawlessness. The literature from these countries portrays the lawlessness and degeneracy into which the masses of people there have sunk. It is by such literature they are endeavouring to destroy the youth of this country, just as the youth of these other countries have been destroyed by evil literature.[6]

Despite these fears, the censorship of publications was liberalized in 1946. However, the reaction to Edna O'Brien's semi-autobiographical novel *The Country Girls*, about two young women who escaped to Dublin to find freedom, suggested that this vision of purity extended into the 1960s. *The Country Girls* was the first part of a trilogy published between 1960 and 1964. Shortly afterwards, it was banned by the government of the Irish Republic. Three of her other books written in the 1960s were also banned.

O'Brien had been born in County Clare in 1930. Like other Irish writers before her, she sought refuge and literary freedom in exile. She had moved to London in the late 1950s, and the reception of her books informed her decision to remain there. When interviewed, she admitted: 'James Joyce lived all his life away and wrote obsessively and gloriously about Ireland. Although he had left Ireland bodily, he had not left it psychically, no more than I would say I have.'[7] O'Brien did return to Ireland periodically, though, to speak out against censorship, often carrying copies of her banned books with her.[8]

The continuation of censorship into the 1960s suggested that the dream of Éamon de Valera (and, clearly, of many other people) of creating 'a really Irish Ireland', by which was meant a monolithic, Catholic, Ireland, had been realized.[9] But what was the economic and social cost of realizing this aspiration? For some writers, such as O'Brien, it was not an Ireland that she could live in. Furthermore, where did Northern Ireland, or indeed the Protestant minority in the Republic, fit into this exclusive vision of Irishness? And for how long could the Irish Republic remain hermetically sealed from an increasingly secular western world that had discovered the 'beat generation', 'angry young men' and 'teenagers' in the 1950s? How would Ireland, north and south of the border, cope with the move into the swinging sixties? A significant change to the censorship laws was made in 1967 when the period for which a book could be banned for being indecent or obscene was limited to twelve months – although any book could subsequently be re-banned. Nonetheless, the impact of this legislation was immediate with thousands of books being unbanned.[10]

Throughout the 1960s Ireland was being exposed to external influences in a number of ways. Large-scale emigration in the 1950s meant that links between Ireland and the outside world were inevitable. Even more importantly, the advent of television changed Ireland in the 1960s, exposing the population to an outside world that itself was changing at a rapid rate. An Irish state radio broadcasting service had begun in January 1926, with the foundation of a public radio station, Radio Éireann, based in Dublin. Those who worked for this new service were employed directly by the government and hence were civil servants, which inevitably limited the opportunity for critical or truly independent broadcasting. In 1960 a new service, also known as Radio Éireann, was established and an Irish television service was launched on the last day of 1961. The popularity of this medium was evident from the rapid increase in the number of homes that possessed a television. In 1963 there were 237,000 homes; by 1971 this had increased to 536,000. Almost half of these homes were able to receive British channels in addition to Irish transmissions.[11] In 1966 the broadcasting service was renamed Radio Telefís Éireann (RTÉ). Its first Chairman was Dublin-born Éamonn Andrews, who achieved fame on British television with the popular shows *What's My Line?* (1951–63 and 1984–7) and *This is Your Life* (1955–87).[12] Ultimately, responsibility for the new service lay with the Minister for Posts and Telegraphs and the 1960 legislation made clear his ability to censor any material under what was to be referred to simply as 'Section 31'. The advent of 'the Troubles' later in the decade was to result in some of the most controversial uses of this ability to censor material, primarily directed against those sympathetic to the Republican movement.

During the summer of 1962 RTÉ launched a programme intended to fill the summer, low season slot. It was known as *The Late Late Show*. Unusually, it combined entertainment with social discussion and, in the suffocating environment of Ireland, often provided the forum for introducing topics previously not considered suitable for public debate. At the same time, it combined specifically Irish topics with those of international relevance. The time slot allotted – two hours on a Friday evening – also appealed to the viewing public. Within a few years, *The Late Late Show* had become an institution, interviewing not only politicians and musicians, but anybody in the news in Ireland, and also interviewing celebrities and guests from around the world, ranging from Elton John to Mother Teresa to U2. The first host and the person indelibly associated with *The Late Late Show* was Gay Byrne, who went on to achieve iconic status within the Irish media. With the exception of one season when he chose to work in London, Byrne hosted the show for 37 seasons and was consequently one of the most recognized, and influential, figures in Ireland. In September 1999, following Byrne's decision to retire, Pat Kenny became the new host. In May 2009 RTÉ announced that *The Late Late Show* was to have a new host, Ryan Tubridy, only the third since the show's origin.[13]

John F. Kennedy

Within a few months of its introduction the new television station was presented with a challenge that propelled it to the centre of international media. In June 1963 John Fitzgerald Kennedy, the great-grandson of an Irish emigrant from County Wexford, became the first serving American President to visit Ireland. He spent four days in the country, visiting Dublin, Wexford, Cork, Galway and Limerick. Telefís Éireann broadcast more than fourteen hours of the visit live, while Radio Éireann provided similar coverage for its listeners.[14] Kennedy's visit was all the more special because not only was he the first Catholic President of the United States, he made it clear that he regarded Ireland as his 'ancestral homeland', his family having left there during the Great Famine. The visit was made both personal and emotional by Kennedy's declaration that 'I am coming home'. While in Limerick, he declared, 'This is not the land of my birth but it is the land for which I hold the greatest affection.'[15] At his family home in New Ross, County Wexford, a banner declared 'Welcome home, Mr President'.[16] As a special honour, he was invited to address both Houses of the *Oireachtas*.[17] Kennedy's speeches about Britain's historic role in Ireland proved to be controversial. Furthermore:

> The visit was unpopular in the United States, proved a security nightmare, and provoked much discussion amongst the political leadership in Belfast, Dublin and London over Kennedy's attitude to partition. The visit marked a major development in the history of Irish-American relations as it eased tensions over Ireland's neutrality, marked a shift towards White House activism in Irish affairs, boosted Irish tourism, and fostered increased trading and cultural links between the two countries.[18]

Just months later, on 22 November 1963, President Kennedy was shot dead in Dallas, Texas. The Irish people mourned his death. The *Dáil*, as a mark of 'sympathy and respect', adjourned. Speaker Dillon said, 'Our grief here in Ireland is mingled with pride in the knowledge that through the veins of the leader of the free world flowed the blood of Fitzgeralds and Kennedys.'[19]

Church and State

The 1937 Constitution had recognized 'the special position' of the Catholic Church in the Southern state. At this time, approximately 93 per cent of the population were Catholic and observant, but de Valera was persuaded from making the links between Church and Southern state too clear. For Éamon de Valera, this assertion represented a compromise, attained with a view to not alienating Protestants in the North or in Britain.[20] A Vatican Council held from 1962 was only the second one ever convened. Seán Lemass, the Taoiseach, attended its official opening on 11 October 1962.[21] Bishops from Ireland were present, but they represented just over 1 per cent of all bishops attending. The Vatican Council introduced many changes that brought about a liberalization in church practices. A further purpose had been to promote better relations with the various Protestant churches. The Council also directed that the Mass should be conducted in vernacular languages rather than in Latin, and it encouraged everybody to study the Bible. The Irish bishops, however, identified themselves with a conservative group from Italy, Spain and Portugal, who proved to be staunch opponents of change.[22] Famously, despite three years of intense deliberations and having attended every session, Archbishop John Charles McQuaid of Dublin returned from Rome saying that there would be no changes in church practices. McQuaid achieved further notoriety when he forbade Catholics from attending Trinity College Dublin.[23]

The Catholic Church in Northern Ireland also exerted wide-ranging influence on the everyday lives of the minority community. Overall, this gave the Catholic Church a power base within the 32 counties of Ireland that was unsurpassed by any other church or political party. For this reason alone, the Irish Protestants had reason to be apprehensive that a united Ireland would become a Catholic state for a Catholic people. Vatican Two clearly paved the way for a more liberal approach in Ireland. The Belfast-born Cardinal William Conway, who served as Archbishop of Armagh and Primate of All Ireland from 1963 until his death in 1977, showed himself to be open to ecumenical ideas and willing to work with Irish Protestants throughout Ireland, but especially those in Northern Ireland. During a debate in 1969 about the proposed removal of Clause 44 of the 1937 Constitution, which had banned divorce, he professed that he 'would not shed a tear if the relevant sections of Article Forty Four were to disappear'.[24] The clause was not removed until 1972, by which time relations between Protestant and Catholics in the north of Ireland had deteriorated.

The Catholic Church was extremely visible throughout the Republic with approximately three priests to every parish, due in large part to an exceptionally high number of vocations between 1920 and 1960 – even higher than it had been in the nineteenth century.[25] Additionally, the Catholic Church controlled much of the educational and welfare provision in the country and through institutions such as the Magdalen Laundries and the Industrial Schools that acted as moral guardians of Ireland's youth. The fact that a portion of Catholic priests and nuns abused this power was not fully appreciated or acknowledged until the 1990s.[26]

The ethos of Catholic teaching permeated the culture of the Republic in various other ways. Pope Pius XII declared 1950 to be a 'Holy Year', that is, one of pilgrimage, penitence and forgiveness. Officials at Radio Éireann wanted to mark the year and decided to do so by playing a gramophone recording of the Angelus Bell at 6 pm every evening. The Angelus is a Catholic prayer of devotion said three times daily: at 6 am, noon and 6 pm. The first recording was broadcast on the Marian Feast of the Assumption on 15 August 1950. The accompanying blessing was attended by virtually the entire management of Radio Éireann. In 1962, when the Angelus was first broadcast on Irish television, the bell was from a taped recording, while 'Old Master Paintings' of the *Annunciation* provided the visual background.[27] Regardless of debates about the appropriateness of this message, the Angelus remained part of the RTÉ service. Showcasing the Angelus in this way, on the state radio and television services, indicated that Catholicism was an important part of the identity of the Southern state.

In both the North and South of Ireland, political stability had been achieved through the unusual longevity of those in power. In the South, Éamon de Valera, a hero of 1916, an opponent of the Anglo-Irish Treaty and a founder of the Fianna Fáil Party, dominated politics in the pre- and post-Partition period. Moreover, he was Taoiseach from 1937 to 1948, between 1951 and 1954, and again from 1957 to 1959. He then served two consecutive terms as President of

Ireland, from 1959 to 1973. Even after his death, his imprint cast a shadow over Irish politics.

Similar longevity was shown by the early Prime Ministers in Northern Ireland. The Government of Ireland Act of 1920 had omitted to provide for such an office; the Lord Lieutenant rectified this omission, however, by establishing an Office of the Prime Minister. In the first fifty years of its existence, Northern Ireland had only four Prime Ministers: James Craig (1921–40), John Andrews (1940–43), Viscount Brookeborough (1943–63) and Terence O'Neill (1963–9). The onset of the Troubles contributed to holding this office up to public scrutiny in a way that had not happened previously. Ironically, it was the actions of hard-line unionists that led the British government to bring down this symbol of Protestant ascendancy. As a consequence, the office of Prime Minister, together with the whole Stormont government, was abolished in 1972 when Direct Rule was imposed from London.

In 1959 Seán Lemass was elected as Fianna Fáil Taoiseach. Despite his republican background, he demonstrated that he was willing to foster friendlier relations with Protestant politicians in Northern Ireland. To this end, he agreed to visit his counterpart, Captain Terence O'Neill. The visit was controversial, but cautiously welcomed, on both sides of the border. Upon his return, Lemass was asked to disclose the contents of his discussion and, more pointedly, Seán Brady demanded that he 'make a statement to the *Dáil* on his meeting with Captain O'Neill and on events subsequent to this meeting; and if he will deal in particular with the suggestion that his visit to Belfast involved recognition of the constitutional status of the Northern Ireland Government'.[28] Mr Barron asked if

> in his recent discussion with Mr O'Neill at Stormont he sought any assurance that equal voting rights and equal opportunities in employment, housing and education will be afforded the nationally-minded people in the Six Counties; and, if not, if he intends to raise these matters in future discussions to be held with Mr O'Neill?[29]

Within Stormont, similar questions were being asked of the Prime Minister and he was able to reassure the ministers that the Taoiseach's visit to the North was a recognition of the status of Northern Ireland and that no discussions had been made regarding the internal politics of either state.[30] Significantly, a month following Lemass's visit, O'Neill visited Dublin. These visits did not appear to damage Lemass politically. He called a General Election in April 1965 and the Fianna Fáil Party increased its number of seats by two, which was sufficient to give it an overall majority.[31] Regardless of this victory, in November 1966 Lemass announced that he was stepping down as Taoiseach. He was replaced by Jack Lynch, the first leader of the Southern state not to have been personally involved in the 1916 Rising and its aftermath.

Lemass's legacy was impressive. His attempts to open up education facilitated the introduction of free secondary schooling in 1967. His reaching out to Northern Ireland was particularly remarkable given his own involvement in the 1916 Rising. Moreover, his economic vision for the development of Ireland, working closely with the economist T. K. Whitaker, ended the protectionist policies so beloved by De Valera and opened the way for free trade. In October 1962, following his attendance at the Vatican Council in Rome, Lemass visited five other capital cities in an attempt to win support for Ireland's entry to the European Union. He was warmly treated wherever he went.[32] Lemass failed in his attempt to get Ireland admitted in 1963 but he saw the advantage of working with the nearest economy, Britain, which paved the way for the signing of the 1965 Anglo-Irish Trade Agreement. Additionally, Lemass correctly believed that this agreement would ease the way for the Republic's eventual entry into the European Union.[33] It was not until 1973, however, that the Republic, alongside the United Kingdom and Denmark, joined the original six member states.

No-Man's-Land?

The Census of 1961 revealed that the population of Northern Ireland was 1,426,000, while the population of the Republic of Ireland was 2,818,000. This meant that one in every three people on the island lived in the six northern counties that had remained part of the United Kingdom after 1921. When the Northern Ireland state had been created, it had been described as 'A Protestant state for a Protestant people'. In reality, what did this mean, especially in regard to identity? By the 1960s this question had become even more charged, leaving the Protestant writer Stewart Parker to muse:

I cannot sink my identity in Dublin, nor in New York, or Toronto, or London, or Glasgow either, for it is skulking somewhere in the fierce, drab, absurd streets of Belfast which was once Beal Féirste . . .

The taig [a pejorative term for a Catholic] gazes over his shoulder at the *Dáil* while the prod [Protestant] turns his face towards Buckingham P., but they both know secretly that their heart is in No Man's Land.[34]

As Parker explained, while many Protestants in Northern Ireland regarded themselves as British, it was a variety of Britishness that would have been little recognized by many people living in Britain; meanwhile, those in the North who regarded themselves as Irish would not have been recognized (or even welcomed) as such by many people in the Republic.

The two states in Ireland had developed along different lines since Partition. Yet, while differences were real and deep, in some ways the two states were mirror images of each other and out of step with developments in most advanced economies. Since Partition, both sides of the border had experienced high levels of unemployment and emigration. In the North, the economic decline largely resulted from the decline in traditional, heavy industries such as shipbuilding. In the 1960s, just as Lemass had laid a foundation for economic development of the South, in the North Prime Minister Terence O'Neill attempted to regenerate the local economy and move it away from its high dependence on British subventions. To this end, he sought American investment and was successful in getting some US companies to base themselves in Northern Ireland.[35] One of the purposes of his meetings with Lemass in 1965 was to foster more cross-border cooperation, especially in areas such as tourism.[36]

Both Northern and Southern Ireland shared a high level of religious observance: in the South, the Roman Catholic Church reigned supreme, while in the North, this took the form of a powerful Protestant fundamentalist Christian lobby. In Southern Ireland, Sunday was the day in which weekly Mass was attended. In Northern Ireland, the Sabbath was observed by engaging in no social activities: virtually nothing was open on Sundays, sports were not played, playgrounds were locked, and shops, restaurants and pubs were closed. This situation was not to change until the 1990s, or even later.[37]

In the North also, a different, although no less pernicious, form of censorship was evident. It was less concerned with issues of morality and 'obscenity' than with issues relating to religion. In 1959 a production of *Over the Bridge*, a play written by Sam Thompson exposing the lethal effects of sectarianism in the Belfast shipyards, was cancelled at the last minute by Ritchie McKee, a prominent unionist and Director of the Ulster Group Theatre.[38] The rest of the theatre group disagreed with this decision and resigned. The next year an independent company performed the play and attracted a non-traditional audience, including the future playwright Stewart Parker. It ran with full houses for six weeks.[39] Thompson, born in 1916 in working-class Ballymacarret in Belfast, had been employed in the Harland and Wolff Shipyard at the age of fourteen. His later writings, especially *Over the Bridge*, exposed Northern sectarianism even before the civil rights movements and the events of 1969 brought it to global attention. According to a biographer of Thompson, 'The play and the controversy surrounding it became a landmark in the cultural history of Northern Ireland and were later seen as prophetic of the Troubles to follow.'[40] For Michael Parker, a Professor of English, the play 'anticipates the apprehensiveness of many subsequent "Troubles" writers over direct representations of violence'.[41] As early as 1960, then, the arts had become a battleground for wider ideological and religious tensions, with which successive Unionist governments had neither the desire nor the political will to deal. One of the casualties of the subsequent conflict was Thompson, a radical, liberal Protestant of a type that seemed more difficult to find after the events of 1969 destroyed much of the middle ground in Northern politics.

The seeds of a move to more religious and political conservatism and exclusion by hard-line Protestants had been sown in the 1950s. On 17 March 1951 a young Protestant minister, Ian Paisley, had founded the Free Presbyterian Church. Paisley had been ordained in the Ravenhill Evangelical Mission Church in Belfast in 1946. Although the ecclesiastical authority of the ministers who performed this act was questioned subsequently, he had sufficient authority and following to help found a breakaway church in 1951, the Free Presbyterian Church, and to become a Moderator in it – a position that he held until 2007. Paisley did not create divisions within Protestantism, but he knew how to exploit them for political ends. In this way, he was to make his mark in Northern Irish society.

The revival of IRA activity in 1956, although evoking relatively little support from the Catholic community, had an immediate effect on the Protestant community. Paisley, then a young Protestant evangelical minister known for his anti-Catholic rhetoric, was invited to address a meeting of unionists in Belfast. Similar to the actions of Protestants in County Armagh in 1795, who had formed the Orange Order as a way of defending Protestant interests against an imagined Catholic threat, this group decided to defend their modern-day interests by forming a group calling itself Ulster Protestant Action, which operated on similar lines to a vigilante group. Paisley, a vehement supporter of this action, controlled the Ravenhill branch of the UPA. Even when it was clear that the IRA border campaign had limited support and was achieving little, the UPA kept up its activities.[42] In 1966 it reformed itself as the Protestant Unionist Party.

Paisley's interests were not confined to the religious arena. In 1971 he was a co-founder of the Democratic Unionist Party – a party he led until 2008. Uniquely, for more than 50 years he combined religious and political conservatism, all underpinned by his deep-rooted anti-Catholicism. For most of his long career he has been a controversial figure, but his ability to garner popular support and to outlast both his allies and his foes has been unprecedented. His nickname, 'Dr No', had its roots in the 1960s, although his negative, uncompromising stance lasted far beyond this date. His obdurate and populist tactics became evident in January 1965 when Prime Minister Terence O'Neill invited Seán Lemass, the Fianna Fáil Taoiseach and a former member of the IRA, to visit Stormont.

Paisley was vehemently opposed to any softening in the relationship between the two states. For security reasons, this historic visit was kept secret for as long as possible. Nonetheless, when the Taoiseach arrived, Paisley threw snowballs at him and allegedly shouted, 'No mass! No Lemass!' Even Paisley's actions, however, could not detract from the significance of this meeting, especially as Lemass invited O'Neill to Dublin on 9 February. Within Stormont, O'Neill's actions were generally hailed as 'courageous' and having provided public recognition that the Dublin government finally recognized the constitutional status of Northern Ireland.[43] David Little, the Unionist MP for West Down, pointed out:

> as well as our own Prime Minister being courageous I think that An Taoiseach, as I think he is called down South, was

even more courageous, because he was the Prime Minister who crossed the Boyne and the Border and came up here to the very seat of our Government.[44]

Gerry Fitt, the leader of the Nationalist Party, believed the meeting could do only good for all citizens of the country, and as a result of it his party had voted to accept the role of official Opposition – thus giving recognition to the Stormont government.[45] A dissenting voice was raised by the unionist MP for Shankill in Belfast, Desmond Boal, who believed that the visit had damaged the constitutional integrity of Northern Ireland. He also castigated O'Neill for acting like a dictator in not consulting his Cabinet before the meeting took place.[46] A few years later Boal, together with Ian Paisley, founded the Democratic Unionist Party. For liberals and moderates, however, these meetings signalled a new era in North/South relationships.[47] Such views proved to be short-lived as hardliners, initially a minority, sought to foster divisions within the unionist community and win the ideological battle for Protestant hearts and minds.

Paisley's opposition was not confined to the activities of nationalists. He also opposed liberal unionists. In 1968, when Prime Minister O'Neill showed himself willing to acquiesce to some of the demands of the Civil Rights leaders, he denounced this as a betrayal. A few months later, in April 1969, O'Neill resigned. Thus traditional Unionism found itself being attacked both internally and externally. According to the historian Graham Walker, 'From within the pro-Union community, moreover, the turmoil created by Paisley was on a markedly greater scale – commensurate with the Civil Rights protest than anything hitherto contrived by disaffected Independent and maverick Unionists.'[48] From this point Ian Paisley was not only proving to be the scourge of nationalist and republican aspirations, he was to be a thorn in the side of any Protestant who deviated from uncompromising unionist orthodoxy. Paisley also opposed the next two Prime Ministers of Northern Ireland, James Chichester-Clark and Brian Faulkner, on similar grounds.

Although generally styled 'Dr' Ian Paisley, the title was an honorary designation only. In 1954 he had been awarded a dubious degree from the outlawed American Pioneer Theological Seminary in Illinois, known for its fundamentalist, conservative evangelicalism and its advocacy of creationism. In 1966 Paisley received an honorary Doctor of Divinity degree from Bob Jones University, also a fundamentalist Christian college in South Carolina. Bob Jones University was at that time a segregationist, unaccredited, Christian college that banned black students from its campus. Despite being unaccredited, this seminary and other similar institutions were renowned for awarding 'degrees' to many evangelical ministers and pastors.[49] Paisley's association with the university continued with his returning more than fifty times to lecture there.[50]

Paisley proved to be a powerful and persuasive demagogue and his words did not fall on deaf ears. A group of hard-line, working-class Belfast Protestants, alarmed by the alleged sell-out by their unionist leaders and angered by the 1916 commemorations, revived the Ulster Volunteer Force. Throughout spring 1966 they petrol-bombed Catholic homes, shops and schools. In early May an elderly Protestant woman, who lived beside a Catholic pub, died following its petrol bombing. A few days later, the UVF shot a Catholic man dead.[51] On 22 May the UVF issued a statement officially declaring war on the IRA, regardless of the fact that it was now a largely defunct group. In reality, they were declaring war on Catholics. During the summer the UVF killed a number of Catholics indiscriminately, although claiming that their targets were members of the IRA. O'Neill publicly criticized 'Paisleyites' for fuelling sectarian divisions and he banned the UVF under the terms of the Special Powers Act.[52] This action appalled many unionists, who viewed the legislation as something to be deployed against Catholics, not Protestants. Nationalists, however, believed that the Unionist government was turning a blind eye to the collusion between the security forces and the UVF, with the former continuing to supply the latter with weapons.[53] The Northern state was showing signs of strain as unionism started to implode.

Culture

Against the backdrop of increasing civil dissatisfaction, Northern Ireland displayed a cultural vibrancy that cut across religious divides. Despite its sectarian political structures, Northern Ireland proved a fertile ground in terms of culture and sports personalities, many of whom achieved international acclaim. Their achievements were all the more remarkable given the poverty and high levels of unemployment that had been a feature of the Northern economy since its foundation, and the small size of the population. One of the most glittering personalities, both on the national and international stage, was a poet who was born in County Derry in 1939. Seamus Heaney's first book, *Eleven Poems*, was published in November 1965 for the Queen's University Festival. It was followed the next year by *Death of a Naturalist*, which won several awards and propelled Heaney into the national limelight. The first poem in this collection, 'Digging', showed his commitment to his rural past and to honour the life of his forebears, while acknowledging that his own life would be very different. While working as a lecturer in Modern English Literature at Queen's University, Belfast, he published *Door into the Dark* (1969). Heaney left Northern Ireland in 1972, spending the rest of his life mostly between the Republic and America. Following his departure, Heaney attempted to 'address the social unrest in Northern Ireland by taking the stance of commentator rather than participant'.[54]

A musician also achieved international acclaim. Van Morrison was born in 1945 on the Orangefield Estate in Belfast, a working-class, Protestant district. He lived in Belfast until 1966, when he signed a new musical contract and moved to New York. He remained in the United States for over ten years, following which he returned to the United Kingdom, but settled in England. Yet, like many artists, Ireland continued to influence his work. His acclaimed 1968 album *Astral Weeks* was an early example of 'Celtic Rock', while his 1982 album *Beautiful Vision* suggested a more overt return to his Irish roots; this move was consolidated with the 1988 release, with the Chieftains, of *Irish Heartbeat*.[55] Significantly, he named his own record company Exile Productions. Another Belfast musician who achieved international recognition and admiration, although in a different genre, was the flautist James Galway, who had been born in the city in 1939. Throughout his long career he played with many of the world's finest orchestras and conductors. Galway, who latterly described himself as a 'Celtic Minstrel', was knighted by Queen Elizabeth in 2001.[56]

A young Protestant man from Belfast was to become one of the most celebrated footballers ever to play in the English Football League. George Best joined Manchester United in 1963, making his debut when aged only seventeen. The following year Manchester United won the League title. In 1968 he played a pivotal role when they won the European Cup, with Best named as the European Footballer of the Year. His good looks, fashion sense and celebrity lifestyle resulted in him being named 'the fifth Beatle'. Being a football superstar, however, also proved to be a distraction and his reputation for gambling, drinking and dating glamorous women disrupted his playing career. In 1974 he left Manchester United and then played for a number of football clubs in England and elsewhere. Increasingly, though, his notoriety was based on his glamorous celebrity lifestyle rather than his footballing skills. Nonetheless, in Northern Ireland his achievements continued to be summed up in the ditty 'Maradona good; Pelé better; George Best'.[57] Best died prematurely in 2005. The following year, Belfast City Airport was renamed in his honour, which proved controversial in light of his alcoholism.

Discrimination

Since its inception the Northern Ireland state had been distinguished by widespread discrimination against the Catholic minority. Discrimination was most evident in electoral politics (through gerrymandering, plural voting that favoured wealthy people); education (which favoured state, that is, Protestant schools); housing (whereby Catholic families, whatever their needs, were automatically placed at the bottom of the waiting list for public housing) and employment (whereby the best jobs, especially in the shipbuilding industry and the civil service, were given to Protestants). The continuation of the Special Powers Act meant that a system of law prevailed in Northern Ireland unlike that in any other part of the United Kingdom. Although Section 75 of the 1920 Government of Ireland Act had given the Westminster government ultimate responsibility for the governance of Northern Ireland, in reality successive British governments had chosen not to interfere.

For Catholics who lived in Northern Ireland there was a sense that all of the state structures, but especially the law, were used to keep them in a subordinate position. The Flags and Emblems (Display) Act of 1954, which forbade the public display of any flag or emblem that could cause a breach of the peace, was an example of the partisan use of legislation. The fact that the Union Flag was specifically excluded angered the nationalist community who felt that they were being surreptitiously targeted. At the same time, failure to enforce this legislation angered some unionists. This was evident in 1964 when Ian Paisley demanded that an Irish tricolour be removed from Divis Street (a Catholic enclave in west Belfast). When the RUC did remove it, rioting ensued.[58] In the same year Paisley demanded that the tricolour be removed from the Sinn Féin

Office in Belfast, and another from the nationalist Falls Road in West Belfast. On both occasions the removal resulted in rioting. It was not until 1987 that the Westminster Parliament finally repealed the Flags Act.[59]

Political tensions within Northern Ireland often overshadowed the social deprivation suffered by many of the population, exacerbated by high levels of unemployment and poor quality and inadequate housing. A report by the Northern Ireland Housing Trust in 1964 confirmed that thousands of people were either homeless or living in squalor. The Labour MP for Belfast Woodvale, William Boyd, believed this situation contributed to delinquency in the province. He estimated that an additional 150,000 houses were required and he called on the Stormont government to 'have a crash programme of building'.[60] For the poor in Northern Ireland, but especially the Catholic poor, the housing issue was a major concern. Although a limited amount of public housing was available, it was under the control of local authorities who gave priority to Protestant families, regardless of their need. Only householders, and their wives, had the vote for local elections and many local authorities had been 'gerrymandered' (their electoral boundaries redrawn) to ensure unionist control even in majority nationalist areas. Thus the city of Derry had a Protestant/unionist controlled council, even though two-thirds of the population were Catholic. Consequently houses were not just homes, they represented votes. Denying Catholics housing was also denying them votes.

An early protest about housing polices took place in Dungannon in County Tyrone in the early 1960s. Unusually, it was initiated by Irish Catholic women who were triply disadvantaged – by their class, their religion and their gender. A number of young mothers established the Homeless Citizens' League. In 1963 it organized for families to move into empty houses that were about to be demolished. Despite the electricity supply being cut off, and threats of eviction and imprisonment, the women held firm, organizing marches and pickets. The council reluctantly agreed to rehouse them. The League was quickly taken over by a middle-class couple, Dr Conn McCluskey and his wife Patricia, who used it as a springboard from which to establish the Campaign for Social Justice.[61] Initially the group focused on collecting statistics about discrimination in housing. They then tried to raise awareness outside the province by sending their findings to the British Labour Party.

The actions of these community groups and the increasing focus on social justice led to the formation of the Northern Ireland Civil Rights movement on 29 January 1967 in Belfast. NICRA was not the first organization to focus on civil rights as a political issue. In 1962 a Northern Ireland Council for Civil Liberties had been established, but shortly afterwards it had disappeared from political view.[62] Although all parties had been invited to attend NICRA's founding meeting, the Ulster Unionist Party representative had withdrawn over a disagreement about capital punishment. The National Party of Northern Ireland remained aloof from the new organization. The committee, though, did include representatives from communist, republican, trade unionist, liberal and social justice organizations. Its main demands were for the repeal of the Special Powers Acts of 1922, 1933 and 1943; the disbandment of the B Specials, a paramilitary police force; an end to the gerrymandering of local electoral districts, which ensured unionist control over local government even in towns with a nationalist majority; an end to discrimination in the awarding of local authority housing; and an end to discrimination in government employment. The tactics of the organization were to be peaceful – mainly marches, sit-ins and pickets, similar to the tactics used in Dungannon a few years earlier and employed by the American Civil Rights movement. The demands were no longer confined to housing, however, but extended to protest about discrimination in voting, jobs and education.

However, discrimination in housing allocation continued. This was evident in Caledon in County Tyrone in 1967 when, out of fifteen newly built council houses, only one was allocated to a Catholic family. Two Catholic families responded by occupying the houses. One of the families, the Goodfellows, had three small children, aged four, two and ten weeks. Eight months later they were forcefully evicted from the house.[63] A newly formed Housing Action Committee in Derry was organizing similar housing protests. In Caledon, the Civil Rights Association together with local activists organized what was to be the first civil rights march from Coalisland to Dungannon on 24 August 1968. When NICRA organized a second march to take place in Derry on 5 October, the local Apprentice Boys announced that they would be marching at the same time. The Minister for Home Affairs, William Craig, responded by banning the NICRA march from going into the city centre. When the civil rights marchers defied the ban, they were attacked by the RUC.[64] Scenes of unarmed marchers being baton-charged and beaten were captured by RTÉ and transmitted across the world. Suddenly, what had begun as a small, localized protest against housing policies had transformed into a civil rights issue that captured world attention.[65]

The actions of the RUC proved to be a trigger for civil unrest and violence. Some young people in Derry immediately responded to the attack by breaking shop windows in the city. A protest was held in Dublin, when about 300 demonstrators, bearing a petition protesting about Protestant discrimination in the North, burned a Union flag before marching to the British Embassy in Merrion Square, where about 100 policemen prevented them from entering the building. There were some clashes before the protesters were dispersed.[66] For the most part, the follow-up to the Derry march was to organize further peaceful protests – generally sit-ins, parades and mass meetings. The protests in Derry were organized by two local businessmen, Ivan Cooper, a Protestant, and John Hume, a Catholic. The protests had extended beyond those of just community activists. At Queen's University, Belfast, a college generally known to be conservative and Protestant, students from both sides of the religious divide came together in October in a left-of-centre group known as People's Democracy that wanted to support the civil rights protestors. Republicans were also involved in the movement. Since the end of the IRA campaign in 1962, intellectuals in the movement, especially those associated with the Wolfe Tone Societies, had been developing strategies for linking civil rights with the national question. According to the historian Bob Purdie, the republicans were 'keen to push the civil rights agitation further and to use it to build a radical coalition which would set its sights, eventually, on a united Ireland'.[67]

External events were also informing and encouraging what was happening in Northern Ireland. The civil rights movement in the United States and the words of Martin Luther King were seen as an inspiration to Irish protesters: one placard carried in County Tyrone in 1963 read 'Racial discrimination in Alabama hits Dungannon'.[68] Developments in Europe in 1968, when students agitated for political change, also seemed a harbinger of the end of old-style politics and the emergence of a new generation of political leaders. Events closer to home were also regarded as positive. In both 1964 and 1966 Labour governments were elected in Britain and it was hoped by nationalists that they would intervene in Northern Ireland affairs. As early as August 1966 the British government had asked Terence

O'Neill, the Unionist Prime Minister, to speed up reforms in the Province.[69] Direct British intervention, however, was brought about by the violence that followed the civil rights marches, notably the march on 5 October 1968. Only at this stage did the British Prime Minister, Harold Wilson, make it clear that discrimination against Catholics had to end, intimating that Britain would withdraw financial support from the province unless changes were made.[70] Involvement in the affairs of Northern Ireland was regarded as undesirable by all political parties in Britain, but, 'after fifty years of trying to avoid even discussion of the Irish issue, Westminster was now confronted with the real possibility of having to take direct control of Northern Irish affairs'.[71]

As O'Neill had realized, pleasing all sides was virtually impossible. The fury of unionists had been aroused when Jack Lynch, the new Irish Taoiseach, recommended at the end of October that partition should be ended as a way of resolving the conflict in the North. Although he subsequently seemed to backtrack on this statement, this comment inflamed unionist anger.[72] To appease his own base of support, in early November 1968 O'Neill announced that there would be no transfer of the Northern state to the Republic without the consent of the Northern Ireland Parliament. At the end of the month, however, knowing that the eyes of the western world – and of the government in London – were on him, O'Neill announced a reform package that would help alleviate the housing situation. Significantly, housing was to be taken out of the hands of the local authorities and future allocation was to be based on an objective points system. Moreover, in Derry, 9,600 new houses and 10,000 jobs were to be created by 1981. In a city that had a population of 56,000 and only 10,000 existing homes, many of which were of poor quality, the impact of these reforms would be immense. Moreover, a Commission was to be appointed to oversee the administration of these changes and to implement them impartially. In a political move, O'Neill promised that he would consider removing the power of detaining people without trial, which inevitably was used against Catholics.[73]

For the civil rights movement, O'Neill's reforms represented an important victory, but for many they constituted only the first step in reforming Northern Ireland. Significantly, the reforms did not extend to giving 'one man, one vote'. Nonetheless, they marked a radical departure by a Unionist government. O'Neill, aware of the spirit that had been unleashed in the previous months, wanted to go further but was tempered by his more conservative colleagues such as William Craig. He was also aware that many ordinary unionists would feel betrayed by his actions. He was right. Ian Paisley, who was emerging as the leader of hard-line Protestants, announced that he would be organizing a protest demonstration in Armagh. He and his followers attacked a civil rights march taking place in the city, which resulted in rioting and street fighting on a larger scale than any previous unrest. O'Neill was swift and fulsome in his condemnation of the actions of the Protestants in Armagh, referring to them as 'bully boys' and 'lunatics'. He rejected their call for an independent Northern Ireland that would cut all political ties with Britain, pointing out that the local economy depended on British subsidies for its survival.[74]

While O'Neill's words and actions were praised in London, in Belfast his own government had split, the opposition being led by William Craig. By the end of 1968, therefore, Unionism, which had been the main beneficiary and defender of the Northern Ireland state, was in disarray. Mainstream unionism, which had attempted to reform itself internally, was under attack from its own traditional base of support. Even more worryingly, a more serious challenge was coming from 'new political forces outside, in particular those centred on Ian Paisley'.[75]

Nationalist politics were also changing. The National Party and Sinn Féin, which had traditionally represented the nationalist community, were in decline. The Civil Rights movement in contrast, appeared strong and focused, bringing together a variety of groups under its umbrella, and they responded to O'Neill's appeal for calm by offering to hold no further marches for a month. After decades of stability, Northern Ireland politics appeared to be heading in a new direction, and street politics had replaced Stormont as the vehicle for political change. A new party, made up largely of students, had also emerged: People's Democracy. A few days before Christmas, they announced that they would be holding a civil rights march in January 1969, from Belfast to Derry. As the previous few months had indicated, however, many of the marches had ended in violence despite the peaceful intentions, and the demand for social justice was becoming subsumed beneath the traditional fault lines of conflict between Catholics and Protestants.

TWO

Troubles

The period of conflict known as 'the Troubles' is sometimes dated from 1969. During the preceding years there had been an escalation of violence and sectarian tensions, largely due to two peaceful initiatives: the emergence of the civil rights movement and the attempts by some politicians in the North and South to foster better cross-border relations. Neither of these initiatives had sought to end the partition, instead they aimed at improving conditions for people living on the island. The outcome, however, was to destabilize both states in Ireland and to force a reluctant British government to intervene in Irish politics. Since 1920 the British government had largely ignored the affairs of Northern Ireland. Following the events of 5 October 1968 in Derry, when peaceful civil rights demonstrators had been attacked, this was no longer possible. Under pressure from London, on 3 March 1969 the Northern Irish government announced the appointment of an official inquiry to examine the events that led up to, and resulted from, the violence on 5 October. It was to be headed by Lord Cameron, assisted by Professor Sir John Biggart and James Joseph Campbell. The Commission's findings were published in September 1969.[1] By this time the situation in Northern Ireland had deteriorated further and British troops were on the streets.

In other ways the year began inauspiciously. On 1 January 1969 People's Democracy, a new radical grouping within the civil rights movement, organized a march from Belfast to Derry. It was a distance of 75 miles and was expected to take four days. About 40 people were in the original group, mostly students – both Protestant and Catholic – and supporters of People's Democracy. The leaders included Bernadette Devlin and Michael Farrell, both of whom were students at Queen's University. The protest was inspired by

Martin Luther King's march from Selma to Montgomery, Alabama. The march was breaking the civil rights 'truce' that had been agreed a few weeks earlier. Their placards suggested that their aims were the same as those of the civil rights groups, including 'One man. One vote'. Even before the march left Belfast, there were indications that hard-line unionists were not going to let it proceed easily. Major Ronald Bunting, a founder of 'The Loyal Citizens of Ulster', organized a demonstration on the other side of the road and declared that his 70-strong group was intent on 'harassing and harrying' the marchers.[2] Significantly, there were more people protesting against the march than there were taking part in it.

The decision to march was clearly provocative in the existing tense climate. Even some supporters of civil rights doubted the wisdom of holding the march, which inevitably would pass through Loyalist and Orange strongholds. In the preceding days meetings had been held in Queen's University and other colleges, where the overwhelming feeling had been against the march going ahead.[3] Roy Johnson, a leading IRA strategist, believed that the effect would be to polarize politics in Northern Ireland and to drive sympathetic, liberal Protestants out of the civil rights movement. A further consequence would be to ghettoize the movement as being of concern to Catholics and nationalists only.[4] Nonetheless, the march went ahead and it ended in violence – violence that was clearly disproportionate to the anxiety that existed within the unionist community. Consequently this march proved to be one of the many turning points in the descent towards open conflict.

Events at the beginning of the march provided a foretaste of what would take place subsequently. Banners were seized and the marchers were physically attacked; despite the heavy police presence, little was done to protect the marchers or punish the perpetrators. The slogans shouted by Bunting's followers included 'Paisley, Paisley, Paisley' and 'Ask the Pope to let you have a pill'.[5] These calls suggested that Ian Paisley was already being regarded as a champion of unionist values, and that the marchers were being categorized as Catholic. On the fourth day of the march, as it reached Burntollet, near Derry, the marchers were ambushed by loyalists. The attack was vicious and, again, members of the RUC either stood by or participated. Thirteen marchers required hospital treatment.[6] The images of young, peaceful, marchers being attacked were shown across the world, which resulted in much criticism of O'Neill and his government. He responded, however, by augmenting the existing police force with B Specials.[7] These were a part-time and unpaid part of the police force whose duties were required only in times of emergency.[8] They had been brought into existence at the time of the partition in 1920 and they were overwhelmingly Protestant in composition. According to their official historian, 'the B Specials came to occupy a unique place of mythic proportions within the unionist community'; their disbandment was a key demand of the civil rights movement.[9] Their deployment was inflammatory. The completion of the march was followed by rioting in Derry and the creation of what became known as 'no go' areas, from which the police and other members of the security forces were banned.

For the Dublin government, events in Burntollet and their aftermath could not be ignored. They protested to the British government and pointed to the historic role of the B Specials in suppressing Catholics following the creation of the Northern Ireland state. At this stage it appears that the Irish government wanted the British government to play a more active role in the internal affairs of Northern Ireland, as a way of ensuring that reforms took place swiftly.[10] For most of the 1960s a focus of Irish politics had been on increasing cooperation between the Southern and Northern governments. Following Burntollet, much of this goodwill was dissipated.

Increasingly, the British government put pressure on the Stormont government to introduce reforms that would include a reorganization of the voting system. The majority of unionist politicians were opposed to any change. Moreover, O'Neill, faced with revolt in his own party and the re-emergence of Protestant paramilitary groups, had little remaining political authority. He threatened to resign if reforms were not introduced. The resignation on 24 January 1969 of Brian Faulkner, an influential member of the Unionist Party, was a further blow to O'Neill. In February, in an attempt to regain control, O'Neill called a surprise General Election for 24 February. Although he won with a majority of eleven seats, the election revealed his unpopularity: he had almost lost his own constituency seat to Ian Paisley, and he had been largely unsuccessful in winning the Catholic middle-class vote. The election, however, brought some of the leaders of the civil rights movement into the Stormont Parliament, namely John Hume, Ivan Cooper and Paddy O'Hanlon.[11]

It was not just the Unionist Party that was fracturing internally. The civil rights movement was concerned with some of the activities of the People's Democracy, who were bringing left wing politics into the movement. They tried to counter this by co-opting two leading PDs, Michael Farrell and Kevin Boyle, onto the executive committee of the Northern Ireland Civil Rights Movement This move backfired. In March four founding members of NICRA – Fred Heatley, Raymond Shearer, Betty Sinclair and John McAnerney – resigned over the proposal by People's Democracy that there should be a march from Belfast city centre to Stormont in east Belfast. Eight members of the Omagh Association resigned in protest.[12] The march never took place but the resignations damaged the civil rights movement, just at a time that some of its demands, including for universal suffrage, were being met by the Stormont government.

While much media attention was on the role of nationalists, in 1969 the UVF resumed its activities. Its main focus was no longer the IRA, but O'Neill, whose government they were determined to topple. To this end, in March and April public buildings and utilities were attacked, including a reservoir, which left Belfast without water. The RUC immediately pronounced these acts to be the work of the IRA. This allegation was repeated in the Westminster Parliament by James Chichester-Clarke, a Unionist MP.[13] In fact, the bombs had been laid by the UVF.[14] The explosions were used by O'Neill's opponents to further weaken his premiership. The British government responded by sending 1,500 troops to Northern Ireland to guard public installations. The Dublin government was alarmed by escalating violence on its doorstep. Jack Lynch informed the Dáil that he would be seeking an urgent meeting with Harold Wilson. He wanted to ask the London government to intervene on behalf of the Catholic minority and to urge that the civil rights demands should be granted immediately. When three months later no meeting had taken place, and none had been scheduled, the Taoiseach was criticized for his failure to act as he had promised. His justification was that 'I wish to ensure that any action I shall take is not counter-productive and that it will not in any way add to the troubles or the problems with which we are now faced'.[15] Lynch's failure to act indicated that he had no clarity about the role of the Dublin government in the escalating conflict. However, the Irish government did send representatives to New York to speak at the

United Nations and thus bring international pressure to bear on the situation.[16] While their message to the British government was that more intervention was necessary, in America their focus was to condemn partition and its effects. The Republic's interventions in Northern Ireland proved particularly annoying to Ted Heath, the leader of the British Conservative Party. At a private meeting he allegedly told the Irish Minister for External Affairs that 'Eire' had no right to interfere in the affairs of the United Kingdom.[17]

Amidst a background of confusion, violence and political regrouping, O'Neill announced that universal suffrage would be allowed in local elections. The significance of this concession was lost amongst the political fallout in the Unionist Party. James Chichester-Clark, the Minister for Agriculture, resigned on the grounds that this concession 'might encourage militant Protestants even to bloodshed'.[18] This comment was disingenuous given that many of the peaceful civil rights demonstrations were already ending in carnage. On 19 April NICRA organized a sit-in in Derry; Ian Paisley responded with a counter-demonstration and attacked the protesters. This provided a trigger for the RUC to mount an assault on the Catholic Bogside area, during which 79 civilians were brutally attacked. The RUC also broke into the home of Samuel Devenney, a 42-year-old Catholic, and beat him viciously. He died in hospital three months later of his injuries. An inquest announced that he had died of 'natural causes'. A few months later Scotland Yard was brought in to investigate the actions of the RUC, but met with a wall of silence.[19] Shortly afterwards, the new Conservative government in Britain announced that this matter was the responsibility of the Northern Ireland government.[20]

On 28 April 1969 O'Neill announced his resignation as Prime Minister and as leader of the Unionist Party. He was the first, but not the last, major political casualty of the Troubles. He was replaced in both positions by Chichester-Clark. Ultimately, O'Neill had been brought down by fellow unionists, who had shown that their loyalty to their party leader, to the British government and to constitutional politics was conditional. Although O'Neill was regarded by some as a loss to liberal Unionism and the politics of reconciliation, only days after this resignation he gave an interview to the *Belfast Telegraph* in which he revealed how deep-rooted his unionist prejudices were, summed up in this now-famous quote:

It is frightfully hard to explain to Protestants that if you give Roman Catholics a good job and a good house they will live like Protestants, because they will see neighbours with cars and television sets; they will refuse to have eighteen children. But if a Roman Catholic is jobless, and lives in the most ghastly hovel, he will rear eighteen children on National Assistance. If you treat Roman Catholics with due consideration and kindness, they will live like Protestants in spite of the authoritative nature of their Church.[21]

The change of administration in Northern Ireland did not end the tension and violence. This was not helped by Chichester-Clark's tardiness in implementing any reforms. In frustration, on 1 June NICRA announced it would again be protesting on the streets as a way of forcing the reforms to be put in place. But the movement was riven by internal divisions that sometimes spilled into public view. In July most of the committee of the Armagh Civil Rights Association resigned, largely because it did not like the direction in which the PD was attempting to take the movement.[22]

A major success for the radical element of NICRA had been achieved with the election of Bernadette Devlin to the Westminster Parliament after she won the Mid-Ulster by-election on 18 April, standing on a socialist programme as candidate for 'Unity'. Aged only 21, she was the youngest woman ever to be elected to the British Parliament. Her maiden speech was, according the Conservative MP, Norman St John Stevas, 'electrifying'.[23] In a break with convention, she spoke on her first day in Parliament, and on a controversial issue – 'the oppressed people of Northern Ireland'. The *New York Times* reported that she held the House of Commons 'spellbound . . . with a speech of quiet eloquence and powerful emotion'.[24] A representative of the BBC described it as 'a speech for human freedom, illuminated by poetry'.[25]

As the Protestant 'marching season' approached, more trouble on the streets of Northern Ireland appeared inevitable. On the days surrounding 12 July there were on-going clashes in the streets of Derry, Belfast and a number of other towns. The violence seemed to be getting out of control, and again the RUC were at the forefront of the attacks on Catholics. In Dungiven, police baton charges left 66-year-old Francis McCloskey dead, while in Belfast's Disraeli Street a Catholic house was burned down. Chichester-Clark's government responded by banning civil rights marches. NICRA decided to defy the ban and held a meeting in Armagh on 14 August. The RUC used this as an opportunity to attack Catholics indiscriminately; the dead victims included a nine-year-old boy in Belfast's Divis flats.[26] Yet the Stormont government inflamed feelings further by interning 24 republicans under the controversial Special Powers Act. Deaths were becoming commonplace and the RUC seemed to be out of control, adding to rather than containing the violence. To ease the situation NICRA suggested that the police should vacate the Bogside and that the interned prisoners should be released. The advice was ignored.

The situation was also getting out of hand in Derry. On 12 August the RUC fired tear gas at the Catholic protesters, the first time that this deterrent had been used. It marked the beginning of what became known as 'the Battle of the Bogside', which lasted for more than two days. The latest riots had been triggered by a march by the Protestant Apprentice Boys around the perimeter of this area. Stormont had been asked in advance not to allow this provocative march to go ahead. Bernadette Devlin and Eamon McCann, both members of People's Democracy, emerged as leaders within the Bogside. The trouble also spilled over into the city centre. According to a BBC report, 'Protestants who gathered near the barricade in Rossville Street were egged on by police, as they aimed catapults armed with stones at the Roman Catholics on the other side.'[27] Nonetheless, Catholics were subsequently blamed for the rioting. Bernadette Devlin, who only a few months earlier had been the darling of the House of Commons, received a nine-month prison sentence for taking part in the riots in Derry.

Following this summer of violence, the British government was forced to intervene. There were already 1,500 British troops in the North, who had been sent there to protect public buildings. A request for more troops had been made by the Northern Ireland Prime Minister, Major Chichester-Clark, to prevent the total breakdown of law and order and to give some respite to the RUC. The British government now made the decision to send troops to Northern Ireland, this time to protect Catholics. On 14 August 1969, 400 soldiers of the 1st Battalion, The Prince of Wales's Own Regiment of Yorkshire, were deployed on the streets of Derry. It was hoped that their stay would be short. The troops were welcomed by NICRA who believed that only a security force controlled from Westminster could be impartial. Initially they were welcomed by Catholics in

Derry, with some chanting, 'We've won, we've won. We've brought down the government.'[28] This optimism and goodwill proved to be short-lived as the British Army increasingly came to be regarded as a tool of the Unionist government.

For some, the arrival of the troops on the streets of Derry marked the real commencement of 'the Troubles'. In reality, sectarian conflict, violence and deaths were already taking place on the streets of Northern Ireland months before the arrival of the British Army. However, the deployment of British troops to prop up the Unionist government was a further indication of the failure of the Northern Ireland state. Despite the wide-ranging coercive powers of successive Unionist governments, they had proved unable to contain these protests; moreover, these protests had initially been peaceful and sought the same civil rights as people living in the rest of the United Kingdom.

The Republic

The worsening situation in Northern Ireland caused concern for the people and the government south of the border. Throughout 1968 the relationship between Jack Lynch and Terence O'Neill had been deteriorating. Lynch, with an eye to appeasing the more republican supporters of the Fianna Fáil Party, on a number of occasions publicly blamed the situation in Derry on partition and unfair electoral practices. At one point, he suggested that the British government no longer had any interest in supporting the partition. Inevitably, unionists were furious, especially O'Neill and Faulkner, who had been most involved in the North-South discussions about economic cooperation. O'Neill responded by issuing a measured public statement though the Northern Ireland Public Information Service that said:

> I am afraid that relations between Belfast and Dublin have deteriorated in the last few days since Mr Lynch made his statement based on recent events in Londonderry. However, we can all hope that time will restore the former good relations that existed between Mr Lynch and Captain O'Neill and indeed also that we will be able to restore the steady progress which we were making towards better community relations in Northern Ireland itself.[29]

Events in the following twelve months did nothing to improve relations between the two governments. During the summer of 1969, as violence erupted on the streets of Derry and elsewhere, Lynch's actions became increasingly provocative. On 13 August he stated:

> It is evident that the Stormont Government is no longer in control of the situation. Indeed the present situation is the inevitable outcome of the policies pursued for decades by successive Stormont Governments. It is clear, also, that the Irish Government can no longer stand by and see innocent people injured and perhaps worse.[30]

As a way of winning popular support, Lynch announced that he was establishing 'field hospitals' and would be sending Irish troops to the border. On 21 August the Irish government set up a fund of £100,000 to give 'relief' to the people of the North, which was to be administered by the Red Cross. This money was subsequently put in the care of Charles Haughey, a member of the Cabinet and son-in-law of Seán Lemass. The government also announced it would finance a number of publications to provide up-to-date information about what was happening. Lynch also called for a United Nations Peacekeeping Force to be sent to the province and for Anglo-Irish talks on the situation, which many unionists described as 'outrageous interference'.[31]

Lynch, who was not from the hard-line republican wing of his party, quickly appeared to draw back from some of his earlier statements. In September he made a speech in Tralee, County Kerry, stating that he did not seek a violent overthrow of the Stormont government, but that unity should be achieved through consent.[32] Nevertheless, in February 1970 the Cabinet issued a directive to the Defence Forces to prepare contingency plans to defend nationalists in the event of disintegration in Northern Ireland.[33] Unknown to Lynch or other members of the government at the time, Charles Haughey was holding his own meetings with British government officials in an attempt to bring about a resolution to the situation. In early October 1969 he summoned the British Ambassador, Sir Andrew Gilchrist, to his home and proposed that, in return for British support for a united Ireland, Britain or NATO could have access to the former Treaty Ports in the Republic (three Irish ports retained by Britain after 1921). Some of the details of this meeting were revealed only in 2000: Gilchrist had said of Haughey that there was 'nothing he would not sacrifice, including the position of the Catholic Church, to achieve a united Ireland'.[34]

Around this time Gilchrist was also having secret meetings with the Chief Executive of the *Irish Times*, Major Thomas B. McDowell. McDowell had already offered his services to the British Prime Minister to help the troops in Northern Ireland. Both men were concerned about the newspaper's sympathetic portrayal of the situation of the Catholics in the North, especially that of the editor, Douglas Gageby. On 2 October 1969 Gilchrist explained:

> McDowell is one of the five (Protestant) owners of the *Irish Times*, and he and his associates are increasingly concerned about the line the paper is taking under its present (Protestant, Belfast-born) Editor, Gageby, whom he described as a very fine journalist, an excellent man, but on the northern question a renegade or white nigger. And apart from Gageby's editorial influence, there is difficulty lower down, whereby sometimes unauthorised items appear and authorised items are left out.[35]

This episode demonstrated that, even at this early stage in the conflict, the media had become an ideological battleground. The Dublin government was experiencing its own internal problems with republicans, whose activities tended to be overshadowed by events in the North. On 3 April 1970 Richard Fallon, a member of the Garda Siochána, was killed by Saor Éire (Free Ireland), shot during an armed raid on the Bank of Ireland at Arran Quay, Dublin.[36] The Irish government had no solution to these attacks or to those caused by other republican groups. However, the Republic's bellicose approach to events in Northern Ireland in 1969 and 1970 had consequences that were to divide the Fianna Fáil government and the country for many years. In 1970 the so-called 'Arms Crisis' took place. It commenced with the sacking on 6 May of two prominent Fianna Fáil government ministers, Charles Haughey and Neil Blaney, for being involved in a failed attempt to smuggle guns into Dublin airport. During the subsequent trial they were accused of using some of the £100,000 that had been set aside as aid money for Northern Ireland to fund arms for the Provisional IRA. Lynch had been totally unaware of this.[37] Both ministers were found innocent. Following his acquittal, Haughey made a speech on behalf of himself and his fellow 'patriots' in which he made it clear that Lynch should resign.[38] Lynch remained in place and, in the short term, his position was strengthened as a result of the trial. Neither Haughey nor Blaney ever escaped from suspicion that they had knowingly tried to smuggled arms into Ireland. Haughey was, however, later elected as Taoiseach.

Regardless of the economic and political problems of the Republic, it maintained its tradition of producing writers and artists of international stature. By the 1960s the Dublin-born artist Francis Bacon was recognized as one the most important figurative painters in Europe.[39] In the field of poetry Eavan Boland, Brendan Kennelly and Paul Durcan were prominent. Ireland's literary achievements were further honoured when Samuel Beckett was awarded the Nobel Prize for literature in 1969. Like many successful writers he had chosen to live for most of his adult life outside of Ireland. Also in 1969, and in a bold and imaginative move that was lauded and envied by artists elsewhere, the Fianna Fáil government announced that creative artists, writers and musicians would receive tax concessions.[40]

International recognition also came in a different way in 1970 when Dana, an eighteen-year-old schoolgirl from the Bogside in Derry, representing the Republic, won the Eurovision Song Contest. Ireland had first entered the competition in 1965 and this was the first success. The winning song was 'All Kinds of Everything'. As was the case with most of the contestants, Ireland's entries were sung in the English language: Ireland's 1972 entry, *Ceol an Ghrá* ('The Music of Love'), was an exception. Music quality was, however, often secondary to providing a showcase for potential tourists.[41] The lyrics of Dana's song, in which she sang about flowers, butterflies and bees, amongst other things, gave no sense of the turmoil that was being played out on the streets of Derry. For Irish people throughout the world, it was a jubilant occasion. According to the *RTÉ Guide*:

There we were, all 200 million of us, watching 26 stations strung across the globe from Russia to South America, giving the schoolgirl from Derry our full attention and admiration as she sang her way out of the classroom and into stardom. For Irish viewers there hasn't been an occasion to compare since Ronnie Delaney won the Olympic 1,500 metres in Melbourne in 1956, and at that time we had to depend on radio or foreign television stations.[42]

'All Kinds of Everything' achieved international success, topping both the Irish and the United Kingdom 'pop' charts. In 1971, as was the custom, the previous year's winner hosted the show. The show was held in Dublin and was RTÉ's first outside broadcast in colour. This time, the on-going conflict north of the border did influence the outcome. The British government, apprehensive of audience reception to the British entrant, selected Clodagh Rodgers, a popular singer from Ballymena in the North of Ireland, to represent the United Kingdom. She later claimed to have received death threats from the IRA for agreeing to appear.[43] Rodgers came fourth in the competition.

Ireland's close ties with the United States continued through the 1970s, helped by a visit of the American President Richard Nixon in October 1970. When he landed at Shannon Airport, the Taoiseach, Jack Lynch, welcomed Nixon by saying: 'The ties between our two countries have been very, very close over very, very many years. Your coming on this occasion will make these ties even more close.' Nixon responded by referring to the fact that he and his wife had Irish heritage; in his case, it came from his great-great-great-great-great-great-grandparents. Perhaps prophetically, he also claimed that 'As a matter of fact, I can't find anybody in Ireland that will claim me.'[44] He went on to say:

> I can assure you that we in the United States are very appreciative of the enormous contribution that has been made of those Irish backgrounds to all of American life, not just in the field of politics but in the field of business, in the field of the arts, in any area that you choose. The Irish have added a warmth to the American diverse personality, a sense of humour, a spirit, a courage, character for which we will be eternally grateful.[45]

While pleasantries were being exchanged in the west of Ireland, a demonstration against the Vietnam War was taking place outside the American Embassy in Dublin. The thousand demonstrators, many of whom were students or supporters of the IRA, carried a coffin for the dead of Vietnam and burnt an effigy of Nixon.[46]

It was hoped that Nixon's visit would help to counterbalance negative news reports from the North, and that trade and tourism with the United States would increase in its wake. In a number of other ways the Republic was changing and laying foundations for its subsequent economic development. In 1969 the first Regional Technical College was opened in Waterford, which marked a major step in the development of tertiary education in the provinces. In the same year other colleges were opened in Athlone, Carlow, Dundalk and Sligo. A less obvious, but equally significant, change came in June of that year when Catholic bishops meeting at Maynooth College decided to lift the ban on Catholics attending Trinity College, Dublin. Educational provision was also expanding in the North. In September 1970 a Royal Charter was granted for the establishment of a third-level college, to be known as 'The University of Ulster'. The location of this new university caused bitter debate. Many nationalists believed it should be located in Derry, the major city in the west of the province. For political reasons, though, it was decided to place the university near the small and relatively inaccessible town of Coleraine, which, unlike Derry, had a predominantly Protestant population.[47] Education, like so much else in Northern Ireland, was a contested ground in such a highly charged political atmosphere, and once again Catholics' claims appeared to have lost out to those of Protestants.

While attitudes in Northern Ireland regarding politics and religion appeared to be getting more entrenched and polarized, there were some attempts in the South to modernize its conservative, Catholic approach to matters. At the Fianna Fáil *Ard Fheis* in February 1971, Jack Lynch talked about the Republic's Constitution and attitude to issues such as divorce and contraception (which were both banned) and how these matters might affect northern thinking. He wondered if 'a new kind of Irish society may be created agreeable to North and South . . . if this means that we must grasp some nettles which sting our pride then we will readily do so if the result be a just and lasting peace throughout our island'.[48] His vision for Ireland's future had little support. Moreover, it had fierce opposition in the figure of the Catholic Archbishop of Dublin, Dr John Charles McQuaid, who equated Lynch's ideas with a loosening of sexual mores. He warned that this 'would indeed be a foul basis on which to attempt to conduct the unity of our country'.[49]

Fall of the Unionist State

The sending of troops to Northern Ireland may have given respite to the battle-weary RUC and brought temporary calm on the streets, but it resolved nothing politically. Faced with this unstable situation, the British Prime Minister, Harold Wilson, cut short his summer vacation to hold urgent talks with Chichester-Clark.[50] On 19 August Chichester-Clark had nine hours of talks with Wilson in London. The talks resulted in the Downing Street Declaration, a joint statement that commenced by unequivocally declaring Northern Ireland's position within the United Kingdom. It went on to say that the situation in Northern Ireland was regarded as a domestic problem. Two significant developments were announced: firstly, that two senior civil servants, Oliver Wright and Alec Baker, were appointed as liaison officers between Westminster and Stormont; secondly, that the Commander of the British Army in Northern Ireland would take control of all security issues, including the B Specials.[51] Overall, the Declaration was an admission that the Stormont government was unable to govern Northern Ireland.

In the wake of the summer riots, on 26 August the British Home Secretary, James Callaghan, established a committee under Baron Hunt, a former army officer, to look at policing in the province.[52] While the Hunt Commission was making its investigations, the Cameron Commission, which had been appointed in March to investigate the disturbances on and since 5 October 1968, made its report. The investigators had invited a number of people to give evidence. This included a number of key figures on the unionist side, namely:

the Rt. Hon. Mr. William Craig, M.P. (N.I.), former Minister of Home Affairs, the Rev. Dr Ian Paisley, Major R. T. Bunting, the Rev. J. Brown of Magee University College, Londonderry and Mr. Douglas Hutchinson of Armagh.

Dr Paisley is chairman of the Ulster Constitution Defence Committee which avowedly controls the Ulster Protestant Volunteers of which Major Bunting is Commandant. The Rev. Mr. Brown is District Commandant of the Ulster

Special Constabulary in Londonderry, a County Grand Master in the Orange Order and prominent in the Apprentice Boys organisation. Mr. Hutchinson (prominent in the Ulster Protestant Volunteers) was charged with and convicted of offences arising from the disturbances in Armagh on 30th November.

We had hoped for their help, though we are of course aware that they were all perfectly entitled to refrain from being witnesses in this Enquiry. We regret to record that all refused to give us the benefit of their assistance. Mr Craig's refusal was couched in the following terms: 'The appointment of the Commission of Enquiry was the act of a weak inept Government and cannot be justified. I do not wish to have any part in it.'

The report identified 'opposing sentiments' within Northern Ireland. This meant that, while grievances had been 'long unadmitted and therefore unredressed by successive Governments', there also existed 'sentiments of fear and apprehension sincerely and tenaciously felt and believed, of risks to the integrity and indeed continued existence of the state'.[53] The report suggested that many of the grievances of the minority community did have some foundation and would have been exacerbated by the fact that those who opposed the Unionist government had no possibility of acquiring political power. It pointed out that the wide-ranging powers of the police and B Specials under the Special Powers Act were an aberration. This legislation had been born out of the conflict in 1921/2 and its continued existence gave the IRA an excuse to engage in its activities. Allowing these powers to exist outside a period of emergency was 'in their nature at variance to the common law right of the citizen, [which] is contrary to a fundamental principle of English law'.[54]

The Commissioners suggested that the decision to re-route the civil rights parade in Derry on 5 October, and the decision announced on 13 November to ban marches in Derry, had arisen from the fact that 'in many influential quarters' an 'erroneous estimate' was made that the civil rights movement was a cover for more sinister republican activities. However, the report pointed out that the rise of a Catholic middle class in Northern Ireland had changed the face of nationalist politics for the better. In what amounted to a defence of the movement it stated:

> We were impressed by the number of well educated and responsible people who were and are concerned in, and have taken an active part in, the Civil Rights movement, and by the depth and extent of the investigations which they have made, or caused to be made, to produce evidence to vouch their grievances and support their claims for remedy.[55]

They did point out that some more militant elements, including representatives of the republican movement and of the PD, had joined the civil rights movement and wanted to give it a more militant, left-wing flavour. The report concluded that while the civil rights protests had at all times sought to be peaceful, the same could not be said of those who opposed them. The UVF was described as 'a clandestine and provocative ultra Unionist force', while individual loyalists were criticized:

> We are left in no doubt that the interventions of Dr Paisley and of Major Bunting in Londonderry and Armagh and the threatened marches of Major Bunting elsewhere, e.g., Newry, were not designed merely to register a peaceful protest against those engaged in Civil Rights or People's Democracy activities, however much they profess the contrary . . . their true purpose was either to cause the legal prohibition of the proposed Civil Rights or People's Democracy demonstrations by the threat of a counter-demonstration, or, if this move failed, to harass, hinder and if possible break up the demonstration. It must have been quite apparent to Dr. Paisley at least, that, in the existing state of the law and having regard to the available strength of the police, and to political realities in Northern Ireland, it would not be practicable to prevent congregation or concentration of 'loyalists' or to disperse them once gathered together on the route or in the vicinity of a proposed Civil Rights demonstration meeting or march.

The report was unequivocal in stating that the use of force had been 'contemplated or expected and prepared for both in Armagh on 30 November and in Londonderry on 4 January by loyalists'. Despite being aware of this, Paisley and Bunting had held a meeting in the Guildhall in Derry on 3 January, which served to inflame existing tensions. The Report condemned the meeting as 'an act of the great-est irresponsibility', leading them to conclude that:

> Both these gentlemen and the organisations with which they are so closely and authoritatively concerned must, in our opinion, bear a heavy share of direct responsibility for the disorders in Armagh and at Burntollet Bridge and also for inflaming passions and engineering opposition to law-ful, and what would in all probability otherwise have been peaceful, demonstrations or at least have attracted only modified and easily controlled opposition.[56]

While the language used in the Cameron report was balanced and temperate throughout, its overall message was clear and hard-hitting, with its main criticism directed at militant Unionists rather than militant nationalists. The Unionist government accepted the report, although it was disliked by some unionists, even by those who had not been supporters of Paisley previously. When intro-ducing the report in Stormont, the Prime Minister, Major Chich-ester-Clarke, requested that his colleagues would 'not pursue this debate like two lines of ostriches, facing in opposite directions but with our heads equally deep in the sand'.[57] He urged his colleagues to use the report as a way to move forward and improve Northern Ireland.[58] Some nationalist MPs, however, viewed the findings in the report as an indictment of unionist government, John Carron declaring that:

> For 50 years this Government have had the direction of affairs and today what have we to show? Only a population in revolt; the name of this part of Ireland flung across the face of the world as a byword for intolerance and a denial of citizens' rights. The Prime Minister, I am sure, is not very proud of that; none of us would be; none of us should be. Does he now admit, in the face of the Cameron findings, that this Government have been thoroughly bad servants of the public; that they have committed illegalities and wrongs upon a large section of the people; that they have brought these counties to their lowest depth for many years?[59]

Opposition to the report's conclusions was led by the Unionist MP Norman Laird, who rejected its findings. He accused it of containing 'omissions, opinions expressed in the language of fact, instances of vital subjects dismissed in a few words or completely ignored, occasions where opinions are expressed unsupported by facts or even contrary to the facts'.[60] In a subsequent debate, he described the report as 'merely an expression of opinion of three men. It did not prove anything'.[61]

The Hunt Committee reported on 3 October 1969, having sat for less than six weeks. The speed with which the enquiry was completed suggested the urgency with which the British authorities viewed this matter.[62] In a pre-emptive comment the report said, 'Our principal recommendations are framed with a view to enabling both the police and the citizens of Ulster to move towards a better relationship with one another in order to achieve this common need and purpose'.[63] Regarding accusations of police brutality, it averred:

> We have been most concerned by the harm which, during the disturbances in the past twelve months, has been done to the image of the Royal Ulster Constabulary, not only in the Province but in the eyes of the world, resulting in some lowering of morale among members of the force, and loss of public esteem. Allegations against some police officers, albeit mainly in circumstances of severe stress and provocation, at times under attack from that appalling weapon, the petrol bomb, against which they had no defence, are not a matter for comment by ourselves.[64]

Harsher criticisms were reserved for the media as:

> coverage of these events has resulted in magnifying, in the minds of readers and viewers, the actual extent of the disorders, in generalising the impression of misconduct by the police and of bad relations between police and public, while sometimes failing correspondingly to illustrate the calm which has prevailed in most parts of Ulster, or the degree of deliberate provocation, the danger and the strain under which the police, frequently and for long periods, tried to do their duty, as well as the fact that the great majority acted not only with courage but with restraint.[65]

The Hunt report recommended that the RUC should be reorganized and that the B Specials should be disbanded. In breaking with an historic tradition, the report suggested that it was 'in our opinion essential that individual police officers should perform their duties without carrying firearms other than for a particular purpose, at a particular time and in a particular locality'.[66] Essentially, the report's recommendations were attempting to make the RUC into a civil police force, more on the model of police in the rest of the United Kingdom; their paramilitary functions would be taken over by the army, if they proved to be necessary.[67] Although Chichester-Clark accepted the report, hard-line unionists opposed it. Ian Paisley called on the Northern Irish Prime Minister to resign, declaring the findings to be 'an absolute sell-out to the republicans and the so-called civil rights movement which is only a smokescreen for the republican movement'.[68] The cracks within unionism were deepening.

By the time the Cameron and Hunt reports were completed, British troops were being welcomed on the streets of Derry and reforms of the police were in process. Moreover, a further Commission had been appointed, under the northern industrialist Patrick Macrory, to recommend reform of local government. Northern Ireland, after fifty years of political inertia and invisibility, was now being held up for public scrutiny and investigation. The Macrory report was made public in June 1970. It recommended that the local government services (libraries, health and education) should no longer be controlled by government appointment, and thus in the gift of the Unionist Party. Even before the report was published, however, rumours and criticisms abounded, which the Commissioners felt necessary to address in the preamble to the report:

> To avoid any misunderstanding, we should add that after you [Brian Faulkner] had addressed us you left the meeting, and have taken no further part in our proceedings. We say this because there have been rumours to the effect that before you appointed us your mind had already been made up as to the direction in which we must go and that the report had in effect been written for us before we had even begun to study the problem . . .

> At an early stage of our review the charge was made in the press and elsewhere that we were operating with undue secrecy. 'Dangerous Secrecy' was the headline favoured by

one newspaper and such phrases as 'sessions in camera' and even 'Star Chamber methods' were freely bandied about.[69]

The report resulted in brief unity amongst the various factions of unionism; they all hated it.[70] The Unionist government did not formally accept the report's finding until December 1970.

Violence Resumes

Following the arrival of troops, there was a brief respite in the period of inter-communal warfare. Some, including the IRA, believed it was only a matter of time before loyalist forces regrouped and again went on the offensive. As some of the promised reforms were implemented, even moderate Protestants were feeling that their traditional rights were being taken from them. In March 1970 the Police Act came into effect, providing for an unarmed, civilian police force. The following month the B Specials were disbanded, although on 1 April a new force, the Ulster Defence Regiment, came into existence. Initially, 18 per cent of the UDR were Catholic, but this number fell sharply as the newly formed security forces proved to be just as partisan as their predecessors. Nevertheless, these changes were an affront to Protestant sensibilities and increased their sense of insecurity.

There were early indications of this hardening of attitudes in two April by-elections, which resulted in Ian Paisley and his fellow-minister in the Free Presbyterian Church, William Beattie, being elected to the Stormont Parliament.[71] Paisley won the seat by a margin of over 1,000 votes. Both Paisley and Beattie had campaigned on a platform of opposing any reforms for the Catholic minority. A contemporary BBC news report predicted that 'Their wins could spell problems for the reform programme currently under discussion in the Northern Ireland parliament at Stormont'.[72] Paisley and Beattie's election even alarmed their fellow unionists, who feared that the inclusion of such hardliners would fragment the parliament further, and this would herald the end of Stormont.[73] Within parliament Paisley proved to be as fiery as he had been outside it. He insisted that unless the government took more stringent action against the IRA, the Protestant people had a right to defend themselves. This was particularly important, he believed, because 'this country has to the south of it an unfriendly Government, some of whose members were engaged in subversive activity and are now being tried, it is time the Protestant people had the protection they rightly deserve. All the Government's assurances will not allay loyalists' fears.'[74] John Hume, the Independent nationalist MP, responded that government ministers should not be making such inflammatory statements.[75] A new dimension had entered Stormont politics and the fissures and fault lines within unionism were deepening.

Violence throughout the early months had been intermittent. There had been clashes in Derry in March following attacks on a parade to commemorate the Easter Rising. There were also riots in Belfast in the wake of an Orange parade that resulted in serious clashes between the army and local Catholic youths, in which 38 soldiers were injured. The army responded by using, for the first time, large amounts of tear gas.[76] This conflict suggested that the honeymoon period was over for the British Army. A hardening of attitude was evident a few days later when the Commanding Officer, Ian Freeland, warned that those throwing petrol bombs could be shot dead if, after a warning, they did not stop.

A General Election was held in the United Kingdom on 18 June 1970. It was a resounding success for the Conservative Party, led by Ted Heath. In their Election Manifesto the references to Northern Ireland had been perfunctory:

> We reaffirm that no change will be made in the constitutional status of Northern Ireland without the free consent of the Parliament of Northern Ireland.
>
> We support the Northern Ireland Government in its programme of legislative and executive action to ensure equal opportunity for all citizens in that part of the United Kingdom. We will provide the military and other aid necessary to support the Royal Ulster Constabulary in keeping the peace and ensuring freedom under the law; with the Ulster Defence Regiment as a strong and efficient reserve force capable of playing a significant role in maintaining peace and security.[77]

The election results in Northern Ireland reflected shifting political allegiances: the Unionist Party held only eight of the twelve seats; Ian Paisley gained North Antrim, Frank McManus won as a Nationalist Unity candidate, taking Fermanagh-South Tyrone,

Gerry Fitt held West Belfast, and Bernadette Devlin held Mid-Ulster. The new Home Secretary for Northern Ireland was to be Reginald Maudling.

Only a week following the General Election, nationalist anger was aroused when, on 26 June, Bernadette Devlin, an elected MP, was imprisoned for her part in the rioting in Derry in the previous year. She had appealed against the judgement but was unsuccessful. Devlin had been due to address a meeting in Derry, before handing herself to the police. News of her early arrest and removal to Armagh Gaol resulted in rioting throughout the city. This development was regarded with alarm by the British Army who had to control the violence. The Commander of the Eighth Brigade, Brigadier Alan Cowan, was reported as saying 'it is very sad indeed. There have been many weeks of quiet and now things are going backwards again instead of going forwards.'[78] The timing of Devlin's imprisonment coincided with the build-up to the marching season. The Stormont government was anxious that they should be seen to be in control and on 5 July 1970, following a special Cabinet meeting by the Northern government, they banned parades for six months and called for all civilians to disarm. Regardless of the ban, the annual Boyne commemorations took place on 13 July. In late July the Stormont government announced a further ban on all parades until January of the following year.

The summer of 1970 was marked by increasingly violent clashes on the streets between Catholics and Protestants, and Catholics and the British Army. A particularly violent conflict that took place in Belfast, when the Catholic community was defended against a Protestant mob that set out to destroy it, became known as 'the battle of Short Strand'.[79] The IRA played an important role during this and other clashes, suggesting that they were increasingly being regarded as the defenders of the Catholic community. The IRA also appeared to be preparing to recommence a bombing campaign. Early victims of this were their own supporters when a bomb that was in the process of being prepared went off prematurely. Five people were killed, including the bomb-maker (a member of the IRA) and his two daughters, aged nine and four – these children were the first female victims of the 'Troubles'.[80] The British Army responded with ever-more stringent measures. At the beginning of July a curfew was imposed on the Falls Road area of Belfast, so that the houses could be searched for weapons and members of the IRA.

The curfew lasted 36 hours, during which three Catholics were killed by the army. A Polish photographer was also shot and killed when taking pictures of the British Army. The curfew was only brought to an end when 3,000 Catholic women, on hearing reports of families not having enough to eat, marched on the lower Falls to bring them food. Apart from the attacks on people, many homes had been destroyed gratuitously during the curfew period. Three hundred 'republicans' had been arrested.

The day after the curfew ended, Patrick Hillery, Irish Minister for External Affairs, paid an unofficial visit to the Falls Road area of Belfast. The visit was criticized by Chichester-Clarke and by the British government. The Civil Rights Association called for a public inquiry into the conduct of the soldiers. This was not granted. Instead, the British Defence Minister, Lord Balniel, defended the action of the Army stating, 'I am deeply impressed by the impartial way they are carrying out an extremely difficult task.'[81] For those who lived through the curfew, it proved to be a turning point in relationships between nationalists, republicans and the British Army.

Shortly after coming to office, the new Home Secretary held talks with the Unionist government. He visited Belfast on 30 June, staying for just one night. Upon boarding the plane back to London he was alleged to have demanded a 'Scotch' and exclaimed, 'What a bloody awful country.' When hearing this, the IRA's response was 'Who made it a "Bloody awful county?"'[82] Regardless of his distaste for his new role, Maudling warned the Stormont government that unless it proved to be in control of Northern Ireland, direct rule would be imposed.

In August 1970 rubber bullets were introduced into Northern Ireland, and these gradually replaced plastic bullets. Despite assurances that they were a safe alternative to real bullets, between 1970 and 1999 at least sixteen people died as a result of this ammunition, and many more were seriously injured.[83] The sensitivity of the British government to criticism on this topic was demonstrated when they intervened to limit the airplay of a song named 'Rubber Bullets' by the pop group, 10cc. According to one of its members, the BBC 'limited its airplay, because they thought it was about the ongoing Northern Ireland conflicts', although the band claimed it was in fact about a prison riot in the United States.[84] In general, while the British government under Labour had responded to the conflict in the previous two years by pushing the reform agenda and by holding enquiries, the new Conservative government showed that it would respond to violence by introducing even more draconian measures against the perpetrators.

Political Regroupings

The arrival of British troops in Northern Ireland and the granting of many of the demands of the civil rights movement inevitably contributed to a number of reconfigurations and regroupings in local politics, both on the unionist and nationalist sides. After 1969 protests that had initially only been seeking more civil rights for Catholics in Northern Ireland developed an increasingly nationalist tinge and, by doing so, made the eventual collapse of the Northern Ireland government inevitable. Both constitutional and republican nationalists had been involved in the civil rights movement and they now played a part in challenging the existence of the unionist state. Since the end of Operation Harvest in 1962 the IRA had been seeking a role for itself in the ever-changing political situation. The ceasefire that it had declared at that time remained in existence in 1969. The arrival of British troops and their welcome by the Catholic communities, together with a reform of policing insisted on by the British government, seemed to be heralding a new era in community relations. Barricades in the Bogside district of Derry and Catholic areas of Belfast were dismantled and troops were allowed to 'police' these areas. The role of the IRA and Sinn Féin in this changed world clearly had to be rethought.

Secretly, talks were being held by the IRA that revealed deep divisions. These came to a head in December 1969. One section, which included Gerry Adams, held that it was of primary importance to force the British government to impose Direct Rule, which they believed was a crucial step towards a united Ireland.[85] This could only succeed if the existing leadership was challenged. This was made possible at the December meeting when the Dublin-based Cathal Goulding suggested, among other things, that Sinn Féin should end its traditional policy of absentionism, thus allowing it to sit in the Dublin, London and Belfast parliaments. Led by Sean MacStiofain, a breakaway group formed themselves into what became known as the Provisional IRA, while those who supported Goulding were referred to as the Official IRA (or, colloquially, the 'Stickies', a reference to the gum they used to affix labels to their clothes).[86] In the following months, as news of the split became public, the Provisionals increased their support base in Belfast and Derry. Under MacStiofain's leadership, they prepared for what they believed was an inevitable attack by Protestants, and for the time when the warm relations between the Catholic community and British troops had cooled off.[87]

In August 1970 the Social Democratic and Labour Party (SDLP) was founded. From the outset it rejected violence, supporting non-sectarian, non-violent, constitutional methods to attain its goals of civil rights and social democracy. The goal of a united Ireland was to be achieved through majority consensus. The SDLP brought together people from earlier labour and nationalist parties, although it was also heavily influenced by the civil rights movement. Its founders included six Stormont MPs (Gerry Fitt, John Hume, Paddy Devlin, Austin Currie, Paddie O'Hanlon and Ivan Cooper) and one Senator. The party's first leader was Fitt, with Hume as his deputy. In the 1972 policy document 'Towards a New Ireland', the SDLP made proposals for an agreement that addressed the three core sets of relationships: between nationalists and unionists in the North, between the North and the South, and between Britain and Ireland.[88] Inevitably, there was internecine conflict between the two main republican groups and the SDLP as to who was the true torchbearer for Irish nationalism. The verbal attacks were frequently vicious.[89] Even working as distinct entities, these groups proved to be a powerful force against the Unionist government, with the modernizing constitutional nationalism of the newly formed SDLP contributing to the defeat of Stormont by refusing to accept the limited reforms on offer. The traditional militant nationalism of provisional republicans did so by creating an insoluble security problem.[90]

Realignments were also taking place among loyalist and unionist groups. The Ulster Defence Association was formed in September 1971 to provide an umbrella group for various loyalist groups. One of these was the Shankill Defence Association, which had been formed in 1968 by John McKeague to defend the Lower Shankill against republican violence. As had been the case in nationalist areas like the Bogside, the Shankill Association set up checkpoints and patrolling interfaces.[91] As its name suggested, defence was regarded as an integral part of the new association, to defend Protestants against nationalist encroachments. Reform of the RUC and the disbanding of the B Specials added to the feeling of vulnerability and anger among loyalist communities. The motto of the UDA was 'law before violence', but violent acts were alleged to have been carried out by the Association's paramilitary wing, the Ulster Freedom Fighters. Moreover, when parading in public, members of the UDA wore 'dark glasses with masks, bush hats, combat jackets or balaclavas', while their activities, according to the political commentator Tim Pat Coogan, also extended 'to welfare, to extortion, thuggery, murder, and . . . helping to bring down a government'.[92] At the height of their power, membership of the UDA reached 50,000.

In October 1971 Ian Paisley and Desmond Boal formed a new political party for militant Protestants, known as the Democratic Unionist Party (DUP). It promised to be 'on the right' on constitutional issues, but 'on the left' regarding social issues.[93] The party evolved out of the Protestant Unionist Party, in which Paisley had played a leading role. Not surprisingly, the philosophy of the new party was also underpinned by evangelical religious fundamentalism. In addition to being bitterly opposed to Sinn Féin and the IRA, the DUP also sought to challenge the Ulster Unionist Party for its position as the largest Protestant Party. The Unionist Party was continuing to have its own internal wrangles, one of which had resulted in the expulsion of five Unionist Members of Parliament, including William Craig and Harry West. In 1972 William Craig founded Vanguard, comprised of militant unionists who wanted a semi-independent Northern Ireland.[94] One of the chief strategists of the party was David Trimble, who subsequently led the Unionist Party.[95]

A counter to the increasing polarization between nationalist and unionist parties was creation of the Alliance Party in April 1970, largely to provide an alternative to the entrenched form of unionism offered by the Ulster Unionist Party. The party sought to go beyond characterizing the conflict simply as one between two different religious groups, preferring instead to bridge any existing divisions.[96] Unusually, it also appealed to Northern Ireland's small Jewish, Asian and non-religious groups. Although it supported the unionist principle of remaining within the United Kingdom, it wanted this to be achieved on a principle of consent rather than conflict. In 1970, demonstrating its dislike of extreme unionism, the Alliance Party called for the Shankill Defence Association to be charged under the Incitement to Hatred Act of 1970. The appeal fell on deaf ears.[97]

Culture and Propaganda

The onset of the 'Troubles' in Northern Ireland created issues for artists and writers that have still not been resolved: namely, to what extent should arts and culture inform and reflect on the conflict in the six counties? For many, the solution lay in ignoring what was happening. Moreover, according to Ronan Bennett, 'On the rare occasion that the conflict penetrates the arts, its treatment tends to be apolitical, disengaged, sceptical.'[98] Bennett, a successful writer and screenwriter, had himself been imprisoned twice for his alleged political activities, although on both occasions his convictions were overturned.[99] For the sociologist Bill Rolston, the reasons for this lack of engagement were politically driven as artists and writers were actively encouraged *not* to become involved with the politics of Northern Ireland, but to distance themselves from political engagement.[100] The poet Seamus Heaney, when musing about his own failure to engage directly with the atrocities being perpetrated in his country, explained 'somehow language, words, didn't live in the way I think they have to live in a poem when they were hovering over that kind of horror and pity. They became, they just became inert, strangely, for me anyway.'[101] Overall it appeared that playwrights, poets and others who tried to explore and understand what was happening, through their chosen medium, could lay themselves open to charges of being naive spectators or, far worse, sympathetic witnesses.

Yet, for others, the Troubles inevitably contributed to the emergence of 'resistance theatre':

> the theatres of Ireland and Northern Ireland are alive with productions that have little, if any, overt reference to the Troubles. However, whether by obligation, lived experience, or obsession, the Troubles and its haunting centuries of prehistory strongly inform the focus and reception of much recent Irish, Northern Irish, and Anglo-Irish and even British drama.[102]

For a while it seemed that the Northern conflict was being addressed by mainstream theatre companies in the South. The Abbey Theatre in Dublin, which had emerged during an earlier period of nationalist struggle, decided that the 1970–71 programme would feature plays that examined the role of the artist during a period of political unrest. The opening production was 'A State of Chassis' by Eugene Watters, John D. Stewart and Tomás MacAnna, who was also the theatre director. It parodied both civil rights protestors and northern loyalists, but targeted in particular Bernadette Devlin as a figure of fun. In the second half of the play, Eamon McCann and another civil rights activist mounted the stage to protest at the way the Catholic minority in the north were being portrayed. This protest evinced little sympathy, with the audience commencing a slow hand-clap, and some even helping to remove the protestors physically from the stage. The press, on both sides of the border, were equally unsympathetic, the *Irish Times* going as far as to describe what happened as 'a riot'.[103]

As the civil rights movement was replaced with sectarian violence, and as the various paramilitary groups embarked on inter-necine conflict, sympathy for the situation in Northern Ireland started to dissipate in both the Republic and in Britain. The British government welcomed this situation. In addition, as the paramilitary campaign got under way, a different type of war commenced – a propaganda war. This arose largely because of the belief that, in spite of the wide-ranging powers of the security forces, the IRA could not be defeated by legal methods.[104] Consequently a covert and dirty war took place. A key figure in this struggle was Brigadier Frank Kitson, a British Army intelligence officer. His main function, and that of his colleagues, was to keep public opinion on the side of Britain.[105] Kitson arrived in Belfast in April 1970 and was put in charge of the 39th Infantry Brigade. His earlier experiences were an indication that he was no ordinary soldier. In 1960 he had written *Gangs and Counter-Gangs* about his experiences fighting the Mau Mau in Kenya. It became the 'manual of counter-insurgency'. In 1971 Kitson published a further book entitled *Low Intensity Operations: Subversion, Insurgency, Peacekeeping*, in which he argued that, as the nature of conventional warfare was changing, so too should the army's methods of fighting it. The new approach should include 'deviousness, patience, and . . . determination to outwit their opponents by all means'.[106] One of the tactics that Kitson recommended was the use of 'counter-gangs', which were to be attributed to the opposition, in order to discredit them.[107]

Kitson's stay in Belfast was brief. Before he left in April 1972 he had developed 'a system of intelligence gathering, of penetrating the IRA and of exploiting propaganda'. He may also have been responsible for some of the illegal interrogation techniques used during the early days of internment.[108] Clearly influenced by Kitson, the British Army Manual in 1971 talked about the use of censorship and non-obvious tactics in defeating the enemy, which at this stage generally meant the IRA. One of its recommendations was to 'keep the resistance movement physically and psychologically from [its] civilian base'.[109] Even after Kitson departed from Northern Ireland, his writings provided the basis for intelligence gathering and counter-insurgency operations that damaged the IRA campaign throughout the course of the conflict.[110]

Kitson's approach dovetailed neatly with work being carried out by Colin Wallace, who since 1969 had been employed by the Ministry of Defence as Information Officer for the British Army. Wallace was himself from Northern Ireland, which made him invaluable for local knowledge and undercover work. Wallace played a key role in the Army's Information Policy Unit, often referred to as 'Psy Ops' or psychological operations. This unit provided information to the RUC and the Northern Ireland Office. It was also responsible for counter-propaganda, or 'dirty tricks', giving stories to the press that were distorted or not true. The aim was to win popular support for the security forces, while discrediting the paramilitaries and causing dissent among them.[111] Wallace was later joined by Captain Fred Holroyd, who worked in British Army Intelligence, which some alleged was a cover for MI6. Holroyd resigned his commission in 1976. In his book *War Without Honour* (1989) he later outlined cases of collusion between the security forces and loyalist paramilitaries, and of other underhand tactics.[112] Despite repeated questioning in the House of Commons by Ken Livingstone and Tam Dalyell, the government continued to deny the use of dirty tricks or any illegal activity by the security forces in Northern Ireland.[113]

By the end of 1970, therefore, not only was a military war underway in Northern Ireland, but a more subtle, though no less pernicious, propaganda war had commenced. The final months of the 1970s were marked by more murder and mayhem, establishing patterns of violence and sectarian hatred that were to be a feature of the next two decades. In September the 100th explosion of the year went off, and the RUC voted to be re-armed. The turmoil was so extensive that in October it was decided to cancel local government elections. None were to take place until 1973, by which time a system of proportional representation would be introduced. Three nights of rioting in October in the Ardoyne district in Belfast resulted in more emergency meetings between Chichester-Clark and Maudling. The violence overshadowed other changes in Northern Ireland, including the establishment of the Northern Ireland Housing Executive in November 1970. Housing discrimination, which had been the initial focus of all the civil rights protests, had been displaced from the political agenda and replaced by the question of who should govern Northern Ireland. Throughout 1970 there had been 24 murders as a direct result of the political conflict in Northern Ireland: ten Protestants and fourteen Catholics. The youngest victim was aged only four.[114] The year had started with the hope that the worst of the conflict was over and that Northern Ireland was being reformed internally. The first death had not taken place until June, but by the end of the year the political system was in tatters, there was violence on the streets, the IRA was reinvigorated and the government in power in London appeared less interested in reform and reconciliation than in imposing increasingly repressive security measures. Many of the demands of the original civil rights movement had been met, but in the space of a few years the political context had changed totally.

THREE

War

Violence in Northern Ireland in 1971 followed patterns that had been established in the previous year, namely, communal strife, sectarian killings and increasing repression by the security forces. To this cauldron of violence were added new ingredients: revenge and reprisal killings and punishment attacks. The nature of the violence also changed when, on 6 February, Gunner Robert Curtis became the first British soldier to be killed in the conflict. Four other soldiers were injured in the ambush by the IRA in North Belfast.[1] Curtis was twenty years old and his wife was pregnant. Poignantly, his father commented 'I do not even know what my son died for.'[2] His observation would have applied to many people in Britain, who had little idea what the conflict was about. On 15 May the British Army shot dead Billy Reid, the man who had killed Curtis. Reid had been a member of the Belfast Brigade of the Provisional IRA. He was aged 32 and left behind four children.

While support for the Provisional IRA on the streets of Northern Ireland was increasing, Unionists and the mainstream British and Irish media became increasingly critical. The murder of three off-duty soldiers by the IRA on 10 March created outrage. Two days later, thousands of Belfast shipyard workers marched to the headquarters of the Unionist Party demanding the introduction of internment for members of the Irish Republican Army. Chichester-Clark, preferring to have more troops on the streets and an enhanced security role for the RUC, refused.[3] By doing so, he alienated many of his supporters and placed another nail in his political coffin.

Early in 1971 the precarious status of Chichester-Clark's position became evident when 170 delegates from the Ulster Unionist Council called for his resignation. The murder of the three off-duty soldiers raised further questions about the efficacy of his leadership.

Chichester-Clark flew to London to ask for 3,000 additional troops and for some control of the security forces to revert back to Stormont. Increased troop presence in Northern Ireland would anger nationalist opinion further, but Chichester-Clark argued, with justification, that Stormont could not survive without military intervention. The Conservative Party, despite its impatience with some unionists, did not want to take over the government of such a fractured, war-torn society. Nonetheless, they did provide troops although the level of support requested by the Unionist Prime Minister was never granted, despite growing violence on the streets: he was offered only 1,300 troops. Two days later he resigned, despite attempts by Lord Carrington to persuade him otherwise. The Conservative government asked him not to criticize them directly in his resignation speech and he complied.[4] Chichester-Clark was both gracious and pragmatic in defeat. However, he stated that resigning was the only way that he had of 'bringing home to all concerned the realities of the present constitutional, political and security situation'.[5]

Chichester-Clark's premiership had lasted only two years. During those years the failure of previous unionist administrations became more evident. Moreover, he had multiple masters with conflicting aims, and he had been unable to bridge the divide between paramilitaries on the streets of Northern Ireland and remote politicians in the halls of Westminster. His own party, which had propelled him to power, rejected him. Chichester-Clark retired to his estate in Moyola, County Derry. He was rewarded by being appointed a life peer later in the year, adopting the title Lord Moyola. In this capacity he spoke in the British House of Lords on matters relating to Northern Ireland.[6] His resignation marked the end of an era in a different way. Since its foundation, Northern Ireland had been governed by the upper-class elite of Protestant society. Chichester-Clark was regarded as, 'The last of the "big house" landed gentry to be prime minister'.[7]

Although Northern Ireland appeared ungovernable, Brian Faulkner took over the Premiership on behalf of another Unionist administration. He had defeated William Craig in the leadership contest. Initially Faulkner appeared to have the support of the various sections of the Unionist Party. He stressed 'positive government' and asked all members of his party to support him.[8] This reassured the Conservative Party, which had been privately debating whether or not the time had come to impose Direct Rule. Faulkner and

Heath also enjoyed a close personal relationship, which the *Sunday Times* described as 'The closest links ever between a British and a Northern Ireland Prime Minister were established with the two men in constant touch on the phone.'[9] The honeymoon period was short. During the following months, violence and deaths became a feature of everyday life in Northern Ireland. Reluctantly, the British government was forced to send more troops to the province. The fact that Faulkner could not control even his own supporters became evident when, in June and July, the Orange Order openly defied the ban on marching. At a prayer meeting that preceded a march through the Catholic town of Dungiven in County Derry in June, the Rev. Dickinson said, 'if we do not carry out our parades this year then we are finished'. He added, 'the PM is the person responsible for banning the parades'.[10] An outcome was that the British Army and the RUC were involved in a fight with Protestant militants. This did not augur well for the approach of 12 July.

On 8 July the British army shot dead two men in Derry. Their friends claimed that they had been unarmed. The killings resulted in the worst rioting in the city for three years. It also marked the beginning of a summer of violence. The Ministry of Defence announced that an extra 500 men (from The First King's Own Scottish Borderers) would be deployed: this brought to 1,200 the total that had been sent to Northern Ireland over a period of ten days.[11] The funerals provided a trigger for more rioting. When the British government refused to hold an inquiry into the deaths, six members of the moderate Social Democratic and Labour Party withdrew from Stormont. An unofficial inquiry was held on 21 and 22 July in the Guildhall in Derry, chaired by a Labour Peer, Lord Gifford. He was assisted by Paul O'Dwyer, an American lawyer, and Albie Sachs, a South African lawyer. The Ministry of Defence and the Royal Ulster Constabulary refused to participate. The report that followed commented that the weeks of violence that followed the murder of these two men would not have happened if an official inquiry had been held. It demonstrated 'how quickly public anger is aroused when army claims lack credibility'. Prophetically, in light of what was to take place over the subsequent two decades, it warned:

> The old maxim, that the law should not be silent amidst the clash of arms, has been borne out anew in Northern Ireland. The position of the army there is politically

controversial and constitutionally obscure: martial law has not been declared, yet the supremacy of the civil authorities is more nominal than real.[12]

The report concluded that neither dead man had been armed. By the time it was made public, internment had been introduced and even more violence was to follow.

Over the summer violence appeared to be getting out of control, with multiple bombings, shootings, arrests and killings. Ironically, in the midst of this mayhem most of the Orange Order parades went off peacefully. Nothing else was peaceful. Like his predecessors, on 5 August Faulkner flew to London for emergency talks with the British Prime Minister. Internment was declared under the terms of the Special Powers Act on 9 August 1971. It gave the authorities the power to detain suspected terrorists indefinitely without trial. Those who were not released within 48 hours would be taken to special detention centres for an indefinite period. Although there was a right to appeal to an Advisory Council, none had been set up when this measure was enforced. Internment had last been used ten years previously, resulting in 200 IRA men being detained for an average period of two years. The new measure was clearly on a far larger scale. In a series of surprise, dawn raids, 342 suspects were arrested. The main target of internment was declared to be the IRA, but as its early implementation showed, it was used indiscriminately against Catholics. The information upon which arrests were made was out of date and defective and, according to the journalist Tim Pat Coogan:

> included people who had never been in the IRA, including Ivan Barr, chairman of the NICRA executive, and Michael Farrell. What they did not include was a single Loyalist. Although the UVF had begun the killing and bombing, this organization was left untouched, as were other violent Loyalist satellite organizations such as Tara, the Shankill Defenders Association and the Ulster Protestant Volunteers. It is known that Faulkner was urged by the British to include a few Protestants in the trawl but he refused.[13]

In an official statement justifying these actions, Faulkner said that Northern Ireland was 'quite simply at war with the terrorist'. Ted

Heath, however, privately admitted that internment was an explicitly 'political act', intended to shore up the government of Northern Ireland's Ulster Unionist Prime Minister, Brian Faulkner, in the face of 'the rising tide of IRA violence'.[14] The BBC pointed out that the Special Powers Act 'was one of the most powerful anti-terrorist measures on the statute books of any Western democracy but Mr Faulkner said he could not give any guarantees it would bring an end to the campaign'.[15] They added that 'The decision to reactivate the powers goes against the Convention for the Protection of Human Rights of the Council of Europe to which Great Britain signed up in November 1950, although a let-out clause states the measures can be used if a state of war exists'.[16]

Within Westminster, the opposition parties asked if parliament could be convened to discuss the issue, but this was refused, although a debate did take place in September. Many concerns were raised and 68 Labour MPs voted against the government, but Callaghan rejected a call to censure their actions. He did not want to be viewed as giving support to extreme nationalists, and he wanted to maintain the bipartisanship that had become customary in regard to Northern Ireland.[17] Consequently the rights of Catholics in the province were made secondary to wider political exigencies that had little to do with social justice.

The events that followed suggested that Northern Irish society was indeed at war. According to the historian Paul Bew, internment had been 'a desperate gamble' and one that 'visibly failed'.[18] It had been strenuously opposed by, amongst others, leading members of the military. Lieutenant General Sir Harry Tuzo, head of the army in the province, had warned privately against introducing this measure, as had civil servants in Whitehall. Even those who initially supported internment came to regard it as 'one of the biggest mistakes of the troubles'. Tuzo had advised that 'The view of the GOC, with which the defence secretary entirely agrees, is that the arguments against resorting to internment remain very strong and that other possibilities for disrupting the IRA should certainly be tried first.'[19] Faulkner had been Minister for Home Affairs during the Republican border campaign of the late 1950s, when internment had been used on both sides, and he was convinced of its efficacy.[20] He had persuaded Heath that this would be a way to smash the IRA and, significantly, Heath had chosen to back Faulkner against the advice of the army.[21] Both Prime Ministers were quickly proved wrong.

After the disaster of internment, the relationship between Heath and Faulkner and between the Conservative Party and the Ulster Unionist Party deteriorated.

A week after internment was introduced it was revealed, at a secret Cabinet meeting in London, that 'The political and social consequences have been serious – more serious than many people in Northern Ireland expected.'[22] In the 48 hours that followed its introduction, seventeen people were killed, ten of whom were Catholics killed by the British Army. This included a Catholic priest, Father Hugh Mullen, who was shot while giving the last rites to a wounded man. He was one of eleven people killed that day in the small Ballymurphy estate in Belfast.[23] A further seven people were killed in the following 24 hours. Whole communities were disrupted. Two thousand Protestants moved out of the predominantly Catholic Ardoyne area of Belfast, but before leaving they set fire to their homes so that they would not be occupied by Catholics. Approximately 2,500 Catholics fled Belfast and set up refugee camps in the Republic. They were joined by 500 people from Derry. In total, an estimated 7,000 Catholics fled their homes in the days that followed the introduction of internment.[24] There was a marked increase in bombings in the province, which continued to rise. British troop activity on the border also increased, with many roads being cratered to render them impassable. Reports of frequent incursions into the Republic (some 40 since August 1969) inflamed existing tensions along the border areas.[25] The British Cabinet's private assertion that the political and social consequence of internment had been 'serious' gave no idea of the devastation that this single measure had caused.

In a statement in the Dáil, the Taoiseach, Jack Lynch, described internment as resulting from 'the political poverty of the policies that had been pursued in that area for some time'. He blamed the Unionist government for not standing up to extreme elements within the Protestant community. More controversially, he repeated an earlier threat that 'if the existing policy of attempting military solutions were continued I intended to support the policy of passive resistance being pursued by the non-unionist population'.[26] Clearly, however, Lynch was hoping that there would be a political solution. Although he was not invited to the emergency meeting that took place between Heath and Faulkner on 19 August, he sent them a communiqué saying that 'military operations then in progress were a failure and that solutions would have to be found by political means'. Lynch was included in meetings with Heath (6 and 7 September) and Faulkner (27 and 28 September). He subsequently informed the Dáil that he had made it clear that, ultimately, a united Ireland was the only solution.[27]

In public statements, the British government was disingenuous about the impact of internment. In 1972 the Northern Ireland Government Information Service published a graph that showed a sharp decline in security incidents between August and October 1971.[28] This was far from the case. Internment had been introduced to destroy the IRA, but it had the opposite effect by giving an enormous boost to recruitment.[29] Consequently the Provisional IRA became the main beneficiary from the introduction of internment. Regardless of the palpable failure of this measure to achieve its main objectives, internment continued in use until 5 December 1975. During this period a total of 1,981 people were detained; 1,874 were Catholic/nationalist, while 107 were Protestant/unionist.

The treatment of the people arrested caused further anger among the nationalist communities. Although this was denied at the time, some of the arrested men were subjected to several techniques that served as pre-interrogation procedures. These included:

> placing a black bag over their heads ('hooding'); being made to stand against a wall with their hands held high above their heads and legs apart for up to 16 hours at a stretch and being deprived of sleep for the first two or three days. In addition, the rooms where the men were left had recorded 'white noise' played in them and the men were made to wear boiler suits (perhaps to reduce tactile stimulation). It was also alleged that the men's diets were severely restricted to occasional administrations of dry bread and cups of water.[30]

The army referred to the five techniques used as 'interrogation in depth' and the government argued that they were essential for security reasons. They were widely criticized outside Britain, however, and the Irish government initiated the process of taking the British government to the European Commission of Human Rights in Strasbourg. At this point, Heath agreed that the use of these techniques would cease. In 1978 the European Court ruled that the techniques used in 1971 had been 'inhuman and degrading', but did not amount to torture.[31]

Internment was the subject of a song written by Paddy McGuigan, a member of the Barleycorn folk band from the Falls Road in Belfast. It referred to 'armoured cars and tanks and guns' taking away the youth of the area, but added defiantly that the community would 'stand behind the Men Behind the Wire'.[32] A recording was issued by the Andersonstown Civil Resistance Committee in 1971. It was banned by the BBC but it held the number one spot in the pop charts in the Republic for three weeks in 1972.[33] The song continued to be recorded by other nationalist groups, including the Wolfe Tones, and Barleycorn gained a reputation as one of Ireland's best traditional folk groups.[34]

During the final months of 1971, attention was focused on the increasingly violent and deadly campaigns waged by both the Provisional IRA and the British Army. However, other violent forces were coming into play. At the beginning of September William Craig and Ian Paisley spoke in Belfast before a crowd of approximately 20,000 people and called for the establishment of a 'third force' to defend Ulster – in effect, an army of Protestant vigilantes. In the same month, a number of loyalist paramilitary groups, including the Shankill Defence Association, came together and formed the Ulster Defence Association (UDA). Its first leader was Charles Smith. After 1973, members of the UDA used the cover name of Ulster Freedom Fighters (UFF) to claim responsibility for the indiscriminate killing of 'Catholics'. The UDA quickly became the largest loyalist paramilitary organization in Northern Ireland, attracting many thousands of members: at its peak the estimated membership was 50,000. It was particularly strong in working-class areas of Belfast.[35] Despite its activities, and indiscriminate targeting of Catholics, the UDA was not proscribed until 10 August 1992.

Against the backdrop of violence and social upheaval, there were some attempts to find a peaceful solution. On 5 September the Army Council of the Provisional IRA proposed a five-point plan to bring about peace and at the same time to reassure unionists about their future. They suggested that Stormont be abolished and replaced by a nine-county Ulster Assembly (*Dáil Uladh*). It was to be one of four regional Assemblies covering the whole of the island. These measures would be accompanied by an immediate ceasefire and the release of all internees. This set of constitutional proposals

was reported in *Republican News* on 11 September 1971.[36] They proved
to be less newsworthy than the violent activities of the IRA. Moreover, the latest round of violence meant that Unionists, even moderate ones, were not willing to enter into discussion, never mind
government, with their enemies. Instead, the IRA resumed an even
more vicious campaign, which was no longer confined to military
or economic targets.[37] In October, at the Sinn Fein *Ard Fheis*, the
President stated that Northern Ireland had to be made ungovernable, as the way to bring about a united Ireland.[38] Shortly afterwards,
they bombed the Post Office Tower in London – a symbol of the
technological progress of the 1960s. Nobody was hurt, although the
structural damage was extensive.[39] The IRA was taking its tactics to
the heart of the United Kingdom.

Following internment, constitutional nationalists mounted a
campaign of civil disobedience. The SDLP withdrew from all public
offices; in Derry, more than 8,000 workers went on strike in protest
against internment; and the Executive of NICRA called for financial
non-cooperation with Government departments. Within weeks, an
estimated 30,000 households were withholding an estimated £80,000
per week. The protests were the largest ever to have taken place in
Northern Ireland and the leaders of the campaign were the women.
On 7 September NICRA issued a statement asking for all sides to end
their killing and bombings, arguing that violence would only lead to
more violence.[40] On 26 October NICRA set up its own parliament in
Dungiven, which they ironically referred to as 'a Catholic parliament for a Catholic people'. In reality, they regarded it as 'a symbolic gesture of defiance and frustration'. Part of their frustration
had arisen from a Green Paper on the future of Northern Ireland
government produced by Faulkner, which gave no indication of
making any further reforms.[41]

The violence on the streets overshadowed the publication of a
report into police brutality in November. The report of an inquiry
chaired by Sir Edmund Compton did find instances of ill-treatment
of internees, but concluded that it was not systematic brutality. In the
Introduction to the report, blame for the introduction of internment
was placed firmly at the feet of the IRA, with no reference to the
wider demands for civil rights. Instead, it stated:

At the beginning of February this year the I.R.A. began to
increase the ferocity of their well-established campaign of

violence. A marked increase in intensity occurred in July, and has been maintained up to the present time.

The aims of the I.R.A. are to intimidate the population by brutal terrorism and so to prevent any co-operation with the Government, the police and the courts of law; to inhibit normal political activity and constitutional progress, and to cause the public in Great Britain to become so sickened by the ceaseless bloodshed and destruction that the Army's withdrawal will come to be seen as the lesser of two evils. No responsible Government can afford to yield to pressures of this kind.[42]

Political discussions were also taking place at the highest levels. On the same day that Paisley was calling for a third force, Jack Lynch was having talks with Ted Heath at Chequers in England. The involvement of the Republic in discussions to do with Northern Ireland was opposed by a number of unionists. On 16 September 1971 a number of them resigned over the proposed tripartite talks involving Northern Ireland, Britain and the Republic of Ireland. Nonetheless, tripartite talks did take place at the end of the month in England. The following month a further 1,500 troops were sent to Northern Ireland.

Events in Northern Ireland were being followed by the media throughout the world, but especially in the United States. On 20 October 1971 Edward Kennedy, then a Senator in the United States Congress, called for the withdrawal of British troops from Northern Ireland and for all-party negotiations to establish a united Ireland. He made this call repeatedly over the subsequent years. The involvement of Kennedy was deeply resented by the Conservative government.[43] Nearer to home, other politicians offered their solutions to this situation. In November 1971 Harold Wilson, who opposed internment, issued his own fifteen-point plan for British withdrawal and a united Ireland.[44] Politically, Northern Ireland had reached an impasse.

Civilians, both Catholic and Protestant, were increasingly the victims of the vicious cycle of reprisal killings. On 29 September a large bomb exploded in the Four Step Inn in the loyalist Shankill Road. Two men died in the explosion. The bomb signalled that the Provisional IRA was now directing its campaign at non-military targets. As the end of the year approached, one of the worst single incidents of the year took place. Fifteen Catholic civilians were killed when loyalist paramilitaries exploded a bomb at McGurk's Bar in North Queen Street, north Belfast. The pub was frequented by Catholics but had no IRA connections. The bomb had been planted by the Ulster Volunteer Force. Four of those killed were women, including the owner's wife and fourteen-year-old daughter. The BBC reported that, 'Police suspect the IRA planted the bomb, although it remains a mystery why the attack should have been carried out in a Catholic area. One theory is that the bomb went off by mistake.' Although the IRA vigorously denied having any part in this bombing, they continued to be held responsible until 1997, when a member of the UVF admitted his part in what had happened.[45]

On 23 December 1971 Pope Paul VI condemned the use of force in Northern Ireland, but went on to say that Irish peace was dependent on full political and economy rights for the Roman Catholic minority.[46] On the same day, Edward Heath visited troops serving in Northern Ireland and expressed his determination to end the violence. It was a hollow gesture. The death count in 1971 had been high: before internment there had been 34 deaths in the North; following internment there were 139.[47] Yet in December of that year Reginald Maudling had described what was happening in Northern Ireland as being at 'an acceptable level' of violence.[48]

Bloody Sunday

Internment had revived the civil rights movement. In August, Faulkner's government announced that it was extending the ban on marching for a further 12 months. NICRA, however, had decided to revive their campaign in the streets by holding peaceful marches. On 22 January an anti-internment march took place in Magilligan in County Derry. Members of the Green Jackets and Parachute Regiment used rubber bullets and tear gas to disperse the march. They also beat up a number of the protesters.[49] This was an ominous foretaste of what was to happen just over a week later, when NICRA organized an anti-internment march to take place in Derry on 30 January 1972. Speakers were to include Bernadette Devlin, MP, Ivan Cooper, MP, and Eamon McCann. The local IRA was asked to stay away from the march. The civil rights movement hoped to reclaim the political high ground and transform the violence of 1971 back into peaceful protests. This did not prove to be the case. The march on 30 January, which became known as Bloody Sunday or 'The

Massacre at Derry', proved to be another brutal watershed in the violent history of Northern Ireland. In the words of those who organized it:

> 13 people were murdered in cold blood by members of the Parachute Regiment [and a fourteenth died several weeks later of wounds he sustained that day]. Jackie Duddy, Kevin McElhinney, Paddy Doherty, Bernard McGuigan, Hugh Gilmore, William Nash, Michael McDaid, John Young, Michael Kelly, Jim Wray, Gerard Donaghy, Gerald McKinney and William McKinney were among the 20,000 who marched down William Street demanding an end to internment, the introduction of proportional representation, the complete abolition of the Special Powers Act, legislation to guarantee the rights of all political groupings including those opposed to the existence of the state, an end to discrimination, the establishment of an impartial and civilian police force . . . They were demanding basically the same reforms which had been demanded on the road from Coalisland to Dungannon in August, 1968. They were demanding the same rights as those who had been beaten off the streets of Derry in October, 1968, and now, four years later they were met not with batons but with bullets, and when the guns were silenced the thirteen lay dead. Brian Faulkner and Edward Heath had given their response to the demand for civil rights.[50]

The events in Derry on that single day in January 1972 became the most investigated and yet controversial episode of the whole of the Troubles. Seven of those murdered were aged only seventeen. No soldiers died on the day. Faulkner believed that Bloody Sunday would damage his party, saying, 'This is London's disaster, but they will use it against us.'[51]

The Conservative Party was quick to defend the behaviour of the soldiers. Reginald Maudling told a packed House of Commons that the government was setting up an inquiry into the events. He went on to say that the troops had 'returned the fire directed at them with aimed shots and inflicted a number of casualties on those who were attacking them with firearms and with bombs'. Bernadette Devlin challenged him on a point of order. She was the only Westminster MP to have been present on the day. When her objection was dismissed by the Speaker, she shrieked, 'Is it in order for the Minister to lie to the House?' She was supported by a Labour member, Hugh Delargy, who shouted that the paratroopers would go down in history 'with the same odium' as the hated Black and Tans of the 1920s. When Maudling tried to continue, Devlin again interjected by saying, 'Nobody shot at the paratroopers, but somebody will shortly', adding that Maudling was a 'murdering hypocrite'. Ignoring attempts by the Speaker to restore order she attacked the Home Secretary physically, punching, scratching and spitting at him. When she was pulled away from Maudling and escorted from the chamber she defiantly shouted, 'I did not shoot him in the back, which is what they did to our people!' The following day, Devlin was allowed to give her account of events to the House, which she did in a quiet voice. She reiterated that the Army had fired first. She added, 'It was a sight I never want to see again: thousands and thousands of people lying flat on their faces on the ground. I was lying on my mouth and nose.'[52]

Anger extended into the Republic. On 1 February Jack Lynch commenced proceedings in the Dáil by saying:

This is the saddest occasion on which I have ever addressed this House. We share with the people of Derry the tragedy which has befallen them.

Derry has a special place in the history of Ireland. It was there that Columcille founded a church and it was from there that he carried his torch to Iona. Columcille is claimed as much by Protestants as by Catholics as one of the great Irish pilgrims of Christianity.

Derry has been magnificent also in other ways. It has been fought over, been attacked and defended heroically. Derry is a city which could be beautiful. Its people have the desire, the ability and, above all, the pride to make it so. To have misunderstood this about Derry's character is the most ignoble thing of all.

The madness that brought death to Derry last Sunday will never be forgotten. In time it will be forgiven – out of charity. I can say no more about this and nothing better than Columcille said:

Is aire charaim Doire ar a réide, ar a gloine;
ar is iomlan aingel finn on chinn co n-ice ar-oile.

Which translated, means 'This is why I love Derry, it is so calm and bright; for it is all full of white angels from one end to the other'.

Lynch went on to outline a proposed course of action that had the support of the opposition parties: an immediate withdrawal of British troops from Derry and Catholic ghettos elsewhere in the North and cessation of harassment of the minority population; an end to internment without trial; and a declaration of Britain's intention to achieve a final settlement of the Irish question and the convocation of a conference for that purpose. He concluded with the statement that: 'The Government are satisfied that nothing less can bring about peace. We also believe that these proposals will put an end to violence.'[53]

Furious crowds in Dublin besieged the British Embassy. The leaders, carrying coffins draped in Union flags, were allowed to march around the building. On the third day the crowd, between 20,000 and 30,000 strong, set the Embassy on fire while a number of the demonstrators prevented the fire brigade from getting through. The burning of the Embassy took place on the same day as the funerals of those who had died. A number of companies with British connections were also attacked. When the British government made a formal protest over the attack on the Embassy, the Irish government expressed its regret and said it would pay for damages. On the day of the funerals, however, the Republic observed a day of mourning, with many businesses closing down. Special church services took place throughout the country. The President, Eamon de Valera, and the Taoiseach attended services in Dublin. Demonstrations also took place at which effigies and pictures of Ted Heath and Brian Faulkner were burned.[54]

Public opinion in other parts of the world was shocked by what had taken place in Derry. In February 1972 a hearing was convened in Washington to give evidence against Britain's policies in 'Ulster' and to ask the Nixon administration to take a strong stand against them. Edward Kennedy opened the testimony with what was described as 'his bitterest attack yet on British policy'. He described Bloody Sunday as 'Britain's Mylai' [sic]. Kennedy was referring to the massacre of civilians by the US Army during the Vietnam War. He also criticized Heath for his recent comment that the absorption of Northern Ireland into the Republic made no more sense than

Spain absorbing Portugal. Kennedy's comments drew some criticism, notably from Republican Congressman Peter Frelinghuysen of New Jersey.[55] Events in Northern Ireland were no longer just dividing politicians in Ireland and Britain.

On 1 February Ted Heath announced that the inquiry into Bloody Sunday would be carried out by Lord Widgery, the Lord Chief Justice. Unionists were opposed to the investigation, with one Unionist member of Stormont declaring:

> I am not opposed to an inquiry, but if the same evidence is given as was given by the clerics on television then it will be a waste of everyone's time. I have heard people talking time after time about the decent Roman Catholics who are no part of the IRA. Let me here and now say that the Roman Catholic clergy have been soaked in it from the very start.[56]

Ian Paisley was more forceful, arguing that:

> We have heard that protest before. We have heard these same voices raised before . . . When one analyses what is said by every one of those journalists and those personnel in the media and also by the voice of protest that has been raised one finds that they are all inherently against this state and what it stands for.[57]

Years later, it was revealed that privately the British Prime Minister had dispatched a note to Widgery reminding him that 'we were in Northern Ireland fighting not only a military war but a propaganda war'.[58] Pressure was put on the Irish Taoiseach to hold an Irish Inquiry or to call for an international one to be held. Lynch was sceptical, though, fearing that Britain would participate in neither. He urged that they should wait and see the outcome of the Widgery Inquiry before acting.[59] On 6 February, defying the government ban on marching, civil rights supporters gathered in Newry. The poets Seamus Heaney and Michael Longley were among those who marched.[60] Again, on 26 February, they marched, this time following the route taken four weeks earlier.[61] The political pendulum, however, had swung away from the civil rights movement.

More violence followed the sorrow and mourning. On 22 February the Provisional IRA planted a bomb at the Aldershot army barracks in England, which they claimed was revenge for Bloody Sunday. It killed five female kitchen staff and a Roman Catholic army chaplain, Padre Gerry Weston. It marked the first of a series of revenge bombings of army barracks in Britain by the Provisional IRA.[62] Three days later, an assassination attempt was made on John Taylor, the hard-line Minister for Home Affairs in the Stormont government.[63] The Official IRA claimed responsibility. Bloody Sunday had ushered in a new phase of violent warfare. According to Devlin, Bloody Sunday changed the rules of engagement in Northern Ireland. She believed:

> That was when the civil rights movement ended and the armed struggle began . . . That was the point of realisation for me that the penalty for demanding equal rights in your society was that your government would kill you. Then you say, 'If it's OK for the government to declare war on the people, the people have a right to declare war on the government'.[64]

Events in Derry had a profound effect on those who lived through them. Two of Northern Ireland's greatest poets, the veteran John Hewitt and the relative newcomer Seamus Heaney, wrote of them in 'Bogside, Derry' and 'Casualty', respectively. The playwright Brian Friel also explored Bloody Sunday in *The Freedom of the City*. Friel had been present at Bloody Sunday and so was able to provide eyewitness testimony. The play first opened in Dublin in February 1973 and was generally disliked by critics for being too political and too critical of the British government. Less commented on was the fact that it criticized both unionist and nationalist politicians for their historic failure to resolve the problems of Northern Ireland. Although Friel was later to say that the play's failings resulted from the fact that he had written it in 'some kind of immediate passion', Michael Parker has argued that 'much of its power is in fact derived from the immediate passion'.[65] Friel was doing with his pen on stage what Devlin was doing with her fists in Westminster.

Sympathy for Bloody Sunday came from unexpected quarters – pop and rock idols. The Beatles, who were probably the most critically acclaimed band of the period, had broken up in 1970. Two former members, Paul McCartney and John Lennon, had Irish roots and each wrote a song protesting about what had happened in Derry. McCartney and his band Wings rush-released 'Give Ireland back to the Irish'. Its lyrics were placatory, referring to Britain as 'tremendous', and then posing the question, 'But REALLY, what ARE you doing?', which led one music critic to describe it as 'more polite interruption than protest song'.[66] 'Give Ireland Back to the Irish' marked a rare incursion into contemporary politics by McCartney. It was instantly banned by every media outlet in the United Kingdom, although it reached the No. 1 position in the Irish charts. The brother of the Wings guitarist Henry McCullough received a vicious kicking in Belfast as a loyalist protest against the song.[67] In the following months some Wings concerts were picketed by anti-IRA protesters.[68]

The musical response from John Lennon was more in keeping with his reputation as a political radical and his professed sympathy for Irish nationalism. In August 1971 he had attended an anti-internment rally in London. From his home in New York he wrote two songs, 'Sunday Bloody Sunday' and 'The Luck of the Irish'. The royalties for the latter were donated to Northern Aid, which looked after the families of interned prisoners. While some of the lyrics for 'Luck of the Irish' were anodyne, such as 'Let's walk over rainbows like leprechauns', both it and 'Sunday Bloody Sunday' were hard-hitting, with the latter referring to thirteen 'martyrs', while pointing out that not one soldier had been injured.

On 5 February Lennon spoke at a rally in Manhattan to show solidarity with the civil rights movement. He and Yoko sang 'The Luck of the Irish', the lyrics of which averred that Ireland had suffered a thousand years of 'torture and hunger'. They also referred to Britain's involvement in Ireland as 'rape'.

Following Bloody Sunday, Lennon became an open supporter of the Troops Out movement. The FBI and MI5 opened files on him, nervous about him becoming involved with republican activists in New York.[69] A later allegation by an MI5 agent that Lennon had given thousands of pounds to the IRA was denied by Yoko and his biographer, John Steiner.[70]

The songs written by Lennon and McCartney about Bloody Sunday were banned by the BBC in 1972 and largely forgotten. In 1983 the Irish rock band U2 released *War*, one of the most successful albums ever. It included the track 'Sunday Bloody Sunday', which won both popular and critical acclaim throughout the world. Ten years after the actual event, there was no need to ban it. Moreover, Bono repeatedly made it clear that his song was a call for peace.[71]

1972 and Direct Rule

Bloody Sunday provided a grim prelude to a year that was marked by even more violence and death in Northern Ireland. While the murder of fourteen unarmed men in Derry had united the Catholic community in its grief, constitutional unionism seemed in crisis. An outcome was that the political middle ground shrank further, allowing extremists on both sides to determine the course of events. In February William Craig, previously Minister for Home Affairs, launched Ulster Vanguard, an umbrella organization for hard-line unionists and loyalists. David Trimble and Reginald Empey were members. At a rally held in Belfast on 18 March, attended by an estimated 60,000 people, Craig warned that 'if and when the politicians fail us, it may be our job to liquidate the enemy'.[72] Despite the ban on marching, Craig and his supporters were allowed to parade in military formation to Stormont.

The popularity of Vanguard contrasted with the weakening position of the Unionist Party. On 22 March Brian Faulkner travelled to London where Ted Heath informed him that the Stormont Parliament was being prorogued and Direct Rule was being imposed. It appears that there was little consultation with the Stormont government. Heath made an official announcement on 24 March. Following the prorogation of Stormont at the end of the month, the Northern Ireland Office (NIO) was created and William Whitelaw was appointed the first Secretary of State for Northern Ireland. The role of the Northern Ireland Office was described as supporting the Secretary of State in securing a lasting peace.[73]

Both unionists and nationalists disliked this latest political move. Anger was particularly intense among Unionist MPs, who still believed that their party was an integral part of the Conservative Party. The Unionist MP John Taylor (later Lord Kilclooney) believed that Heath did not have a favourable perception of Northern Ireland. Moreover, the relationship between the Ulster Unionist Party and Heath was not good as the British Prime Minister's 'perception of Northern Ireland was one of distaste and he did not look kindly upon Ulster Unionists'. Taylor regarded the decision to introduce Direct Rule as 'traumatic for the unionist population' and 'the first step towards the British government giving Dublin executive powers within Northern Ireland'.[74] Ulster Vanguard responded to the news by organizing a two-day industrial strike that resulted in the stoppage of public transport, cuts in power supplies and many firms closing. It was an early indication of what a powerful player it had become in Northern Ireland politics.

Direct Rule did not have the full support of the Conservative Party. Sir Alec Douglas-Home, the Foreign Secretary, wrote:

> I really dislike Direct Rule for Northern Ireland because I do not believe that they are like the Scots or the Welsh and doubt they ever will be. The real British interest would, I think, be served best by pushing them towards a united Ireland rather than tying closer to the UK.[75]

While the decision to impose Direct Rule proved to be controversial in Ireland and Britain, it was welcomed by critics of British policy in the US, including Senator Edward Kennedy, who suggested that it be followed up with the release of 800 internees, respect for civil rights, withdrawal of British forces and steps towards the reunification of Ireland. Paul O'Dwyer, a trustee of the American Committee for Ulster Justice, commented that it was tragic that so much blood had been lost before the Westminster government intervened.[76]

The imposition of Direct Rule overshadowed the publication of yet another inquiry about violence in Northern Ireland, this time examining the breakdown of law and order in the summer of 1969. The tardiness in publishing the report resulted in questions in the House of Lords about the delay. The Minister of State for Home Affairs responded that 'the Inquiry had very complex terms of reference. It covered seven different sets of incidents in 1969'.[77] The Scarman Tribunal, like the earlier Cameron Commission, made serious criticisms of the way in which the RUC and the B Specials had conducted themselves in 1969. Regarding the incident at Burntollet, it stated, 'there is no doubt that some breakdown of police discipline did occur on 4/5 January'.[78] The report confirmed that the bombing of public installations that year had been the work of 'Protestant Extremists', not the IRA.[79] The Commissioners, in rejecting the various conspiracy theories about the events, suggested that the riots had not been part of a wider plot to overthrow the government and that they did not believe that the riots were planned by the IRA or by any Protestant organization. Similarly, they believed that 'NICRA did not plan the rioting but it did help to spread the disturbances'. Rather, they regarded them as 'communal disturbances arising from a complex political, social and economic situation. More often than not they arose from slight beginnings: but the communal tensions were such that, once begun, they could not be controlled.'[80] They were more critical of Bernadette Devlin, saying:

> Although her participation was limited, her principal activity being associated with the building and the manning of the Rossville Street barricade in Londonderry, she must bear a degree of responsibility, once the disturbances had begun, for encouraging Bogsiders to resist the police with violence. Yet her role was a minor one, and we have no evidence that she was a party to any plot to subvert the state or stir up insurrection.[81]

The Inquiry had received submissions blaming Ian Paisley for his role in provoking violence, but he was also exonerated, on the grounds that:

> Dr Paisley's spoken words were always powerful and must have frequently appeared to some as provocative: his newspaper was such that its style and substance were likely to rouse the enthusiasm of his supporters and the fury of his opponents. We are satisfied that Dr Paisley's role in the events under review was fundamentally similar to that of the political leaders on the other side of the sectarian divide. While his speeches and writings must have been one of the many factors increasing tension in 1969, he neither plotted nor organized the disorders under review and there is no evidence that he was a party to any of the acts of violence investigated by us.[82]

The role of the police was a central part of the inquiry. Although on six occasions their actions were ruled to have been at fault, ultimately they were judged not to have been a partisan force. Rather, Scarman praised them for the fact that, despite insufficient numbers, they 'struggled manfully to do their duty in a situation which they could not control'. On occasions, however, the Ulster Special Constabulary (USC) was deemed to have acted 'without proper discipline'. Overall, the Scarman Report was a chilling reminder of how out of control the violence was, especially violence directed against Catholics, before the Army were called in. Yet, for the most part, the heavy-handedness of the security forces was exonerated, and attributed to the fact that 'many of the police, including senior officers, believed that they were dealing with an armed uprising engineered by the IRA'.[83] The reasons why they believed this so firmly were not addressed by the Tribunal. Throughout, it was made clear that the Catholic community had lost faith in the security forces, although the reasons for this were never fully examined.

The publication of the Widgery report on 18 April attracted more attention. The report had been completed in only eleven weeks. It concluded that the soldiers had been fired on first. It also averred that there would have been no deaths in Derry on 30 January if there had not been an illegal march, which had created 'a highly dangerous situation' given the presence so many 'hooligans'. The fourteen dead men were thus judged to have been the guilty ones. Given Ted Heath's secret intervention in the process, it was unlikely that any other conclusion could have been reached.[84] The term generally used by nationalists to describe it was 'whitewash'. Its crude defence of the actions of the soldiers unleashed more hurt and fury within the nationalist community.[85] The riots marked the beginning of a summer of more violence. In August it was announced that no legal action would be taken against the soldiers involved in the murders on Bloody Sunday.

A literary response to the Widgery report was provided by the Dublin poet Thomas Kinsella. In 'Butcher's Dozen: A Lesson for the Octave of Widgery', he gave the victims a voice, something that the Report had failed to do, while emphasizing the lack of honesty that had followed the deaths. The anger of the poet was undisguised. Kinsella not only condemned the dishonesty of Widgery, but he accused England of both lying and murder, While walking amidst the dirt and decay of the Bogside, he located the place where the thirteen men had died and stated, 'it shrivelled up my heart'.[86]

In a society where gratuitous death had become commonplace, the victims were increasingly reduced to statistics, rather than individuals. Some gruesome firsts transpired, however. The first death from a plastic bullet occurred on 22 April: the victim was Francis Rowntree, an eleven-year-old Catholic boy. On 5 July 1972 two Protestant brothers were found shot dead outside Belfast; it was widely accepted that they had been killed by loyalists because they had Catholic girlfriends. Sectarianism appeared to have reached new depths of hatred. In the midst of this carnage John Johnson, who had been shot twice on Bloody Sunday, died on 16 June, thus bringing the death toll to fourteen.

As the escalating conflict showed no signs of abating or disappearing, the interned republicans became concerned that they should not be viewed or treated as ordinary prisoners. In spring 1972 a hunger strike, led by Billy McKee, had commenced in Crumlin Road Prison to force authorities to grant political or prisoner of war status to IRA prisoners. In June the IRA invited the Secretary of State, William Whitelaw, to meet them in 'Free Derry'. He refused, saying 'The disrespect for law rooted there tends to spread like a cancer to other places. I will take the sternest measures to stop the spread of that cancer elsewhere.' Secretly, though, the SDLP was involved in negotiations with the IRA and was trying to bring them into talks with the government. Confronted with McKee's deteriorating health and possible death, the British government agreed to a secret meeting with a member of the Provisional IRA to negotiate a settlement. The latter agreed to call a ceasefire and to meet with Whitelaw, if two conditions were met: to release Gerry Adams from jail, so that he could participate in the talks, and to grant the internees special political status.

On 19 June Whitelaw announced the introduction of Special Category Status for political prisoners; on 22 June the IRA called a ceasefire. What was not made public was the fact that on 20 June a secret meeting had taken place between members of the British government, including Whitelaw and Franck Steele (an MI6 official), and of the IRA, including Gerry Adams, who had been released from jail for this purpose.[87] Further secret talks were held on 7 July. This time the IRA delegation included Seán MacStiofáin and Martin McGuinness. The talks failed when Whitelaw rejected their demands for withdrawal, 'saying they were not only naive but politically impossible'.[88] Shortly afterwards, he revealed his involvement in these talks. On 18 July Harold Wilson, then leader of the Opposition, also met with the Provisional IRA. Joe Cahill, who was among the republican delegation, remembered the meeting as a 'waffling session' and 'complete waste of time', also noting that Wilson was 'disappointed that none of us took a drink'.[89]

Following the failed talks, the IRA ceasefire ended, triggered by a confrontation between the British Army and homeless Catholic refugees. On 21 July, a day that was to be known as 'Bloody Friday', the IRA detonated more than twenty bombs in Belfast, killing nine and injuring 130. It proved to be one of the most violent single days of the conflict. Ten days later the British government responded with 'Operation Motorman', when the British Army entered no-go areas in Belfast and Derry. The operation commenced at 4 am on 31 July. It involved almost 22,000 soldiers, 27 infantry and two armoured battalions aided by 5,300 UDR men. Tanks had been specially shipped in for this purpose. Two young men were shot and killed during the operation. One of them had IRA connections and the other, fifteen-year-old Daniel Hegarty, was described by the Army as being a 'terrorist' and armed. In 2007 the Army apologized for both statements, which they admitted were 'inaccurate'.[90]

What was not known at the time was that, only days earlier, the Prime Minister had secretly authorized new rules of engagement for British troops serving in Northern Ireland. These included, 'Soldiers may fire *without warning* . . . a company commander may order the firing of heavy weapons (such as Carl Gustaf [84 mm recoilless rifle])'.[91] The IRA was not strong enough to engage in a direct fight with the British Army, but they responded later in the day with a bomb that killed nine people in the village of Claudy in County Derry.

Regardless of the bloodshed and carnage, some were hopeful that a political solution could be found. In September, the SDLP published a policy document, *Towards A New Ireland*, which included a Declaration that:

> Britain must not again attempt to impose a settlement on this country. The key to her role now lies in her making an immediate declaration that she believes that it would be in the best interests of all sections of the Communities in both Islands, if Ireland were to become united on terms which would be acceptable to all the people of Ireland. Such declaration should contain no hint of coercion but should make it abundantly clear that this is Britain's view and it is the one that she will positively encourage.[92]

Later in the month, a meeting was held in Darlington in England to talk about devolution. Whitelaw was present, as was the Ulster Unionist Party, the Alliance Party and the Northern Ireland Labour Party. Hard-line Unionists refused to attend, as did the SDLP, the latter as an objection to the continuation of internment. In October the Northern Ireland Office published a document entitled 'The Future of Northern Ireland'. Although it reassured unionists about Britain's commitment to the Union, it also talked about the 'Irish dimension' in any future changes.

In the latter months of 1972, loyalist activities were increasing. The talks between Whitelaw and the IRA had alarmed and angered many in the Protestant community. In the following few months, Loyalist paramilitaries were involved in a number of raids on Ulster Defence Regiment bases, stealing their weapons and ammunition. Clearly they did not believe that the violence was nearing an end. Furthermore, following the killing of two UDA members (one of whom was aged only fifteen) by the British Army, the UDA issued a statement in September stating that the British Army and the British Government was 'now their enemy'. In October, William Craig of Vanguard warned that, if the British government did anything that hurt the Protestant community, he could mobilize 80,000 men who were willing to kill if necessary. A secret document from the Ministry of Defence to the British Prime Minister in November talked about links between the UDA and the UDR, but was willing to tolerate them as 'an important function of the UDA is to channel into a constructive and disciplined direction Protestant energies which might otherwise become disruptive'.[93]

Privately, while the war continued, negotiations were going on to reach a different settlement for Northern Ireland. Heath believed that Bloody Sunday had strengthened his hand politically. When briefing the Queen, he informed her that he was hopeful that the day had 'created a climate in which there was a prospect of making a political initiative which could be acceptable to majority opinion and to a great body of moderate Catholic opinion on both sides of the border'.[94] He and his advisers believed it had provided an opportunity to place a cleavage between moderate and republican Catholics in Northern Ireland. Senior civil servants were also briefing him about the legality of sending British troops over the border in pursuit of IRA members. Just as controversially, a redrawing of the border was being secretly considered. The document, known as

'Redrawing the Border and Population Transfer', envisaged that, if this were done, as many as one-third of the Catholic population in the North would relocate to the Republic.[95] If the Republic acted against Britain's interest, sanctions would include 'penurious tariffs on Irish exports to Britain and severe restrictions on free movement of Irish citizens between the Republic and all parts of the United Kingdom including the North'.[96] Consideration of these measures was only fully abandoned when both the Republic and the United Kingdom signed up to the Treaty of Rome, as a prequel to entry to the European Economic Community.

By the end of 1972 a political solution for Northern Ireland was as elusive as ever. During the year, there had been 467 deaths as a result of the conflict. The British government, however, was suggesting that the military war was being won. In November 1972, when questions were raised in the House of Commons about the impact of Operation Motorman, the Secretary of State for Northern Ireland responded that it had:

> put an end to the no-go areas, and as a military operation with that objective it was a total success.
>
> Since that day the security situation in Northern Ireland has improved. The evidence for this is the marked decline in the number of shooting and bombing incidents; the increasing number of arrests of known Provisional IRA officers, of whom more than 150 have been arrested since Motorman; and the very large finds of firearms, ammunition, and explosives made by the security forces. The security forces will continue their operations against terrorism until the violence ends.[97]

Information and Misinformation

From early on in the Troubles, control of information had been regarded as a crucial part of the war. As violence increased in the early 1970s, so did the role of army intelligence. The role of 'dirty tricks' particularly expanded. After 1969 Colin Wallace became a central figure in the army's Information Policy Unit, also known internally as 'psychological operations'. In that year Wallace had been assigned as a public relations officer to Thiepval Barracks in Lisburn, the headquarters of the British Army in Northern Ireland.

Wallace had been born in County Antrim, so had a local knowledge that proved invaluable when the army first arrived on the streets of Northern Ireland. One of his jobs was to brief the press about what was going on and he proved to be a mastermind of misinformation and counter-propaganda. Secretly his role extended beyond this to the area of 'dirty tricks', working on the model established by his colleague Frank Kitson. Wallace later claimed that he had pretended to be a barrister in the Widgery tribunal on Bloody Sunday.[98]

The main target of the Information Policy Unit was the IRA. In addition to running false information about their activities, spies and informers were used extensively. In this operation, the Army was helped – and sometimes hindered – by the involvement of both MI5 and MI6.[99] According to Wallace:

> our task was to use psychological methods to support the army's operations. We dealt largely in black intelligence more than operational intelligence. My job was to study individuals and organizations. We looked at their weapons, their tactics, where they were getting money from and any supporters and links they had outside the United Kingdom. My role then was to use that information offensively against specific targets.[100]

On 2 October 1972 the IRA smashed a British intelligence operation that was using a laundry business as a cover in west Belfast. This was regarded as a tremendous victory by the republicans, but even they could not have realized how embedded the dirty tricks campaign had become.[101] By 1974:

> the security forces had established a fairly effective intelligence system throughout Northern Ireland. The Army had a number of agencies. In addition, there were also the two main civilian intelligence organizations, the Secret Intelligence Service and the Security Service, MI5, as well as the RUC special branch. We produced intelligence reports on a daily basis on all terrorist activity throughout the province. In addition, there were weekly intelligence summaries looking at the activities of the past week.
>
> By 1974, it is true to say that probably most terrorist organizations were fairly well infiltrated by the intelligence services by one means or another and it was very unusual

that we did not know, certainly within a week of the activity at the outside, who was responsible.[102]

Wallace claimed that in 1972 and 1973 he was involved in an operation known as 'Clockwork Orange', aimed not at republicans, but at elected politicians. The Conservative Party was politically weak and, in order to prop them up, similar tactics were used to discredit the Labour Party, notably Harold Wilson and Tony Benn. In the context of Northern Ireland, leverage to persuade politicians to support the Conservatives was provided by the Kincora Boys' Home, where some Northern politicians had allegedly been involved in homosexual activities.[103] Wallace was removed from Northern Ireland in 1975 and shortly afterwards he was accused by the Ministry of Defence of leaking classified documents, which he denied.[104] In 1980, shortly after he began talking to the press about his work in Northern Ireland, he was convicted on a charge of manslaughter. Again he claimed his innocence and later it was revealed that MI5 had framed him for this murder.[105]

Information flow was controlled in other ways. The arrival of British troops in Northern Ireland changed the way in which both the British and Irish media provided coverage. Both were subject to censorship, but whereas in the Republic it was overt, in Britain it was just as stringent according to Lance Pettitt, more 'insidious', especially as it operated as a form of self-censorship.[106] After 1969, both the BBC and the IBA introduced new codes of practice regarding reporting of the conflict. In 1971 a system of 'Reference Upwards' was introduced, whereby clearance from various people within the management structure had to be sought for programmes dealing with Northern Ireland.[107] Moreover, both the Irish and British states had wide-ranging powers to force a journalist not to use sensitive information, and to reveal their sources if they did.[108] News reporting was especially difficult as it was immediate. In the frenzied and increasingly violent climate of Northern Ireland, it was hard to be dispassionate or to find words and explanations that would not offend any of the protagonists – or the British government. On 19 August 1971, for example, shortly after internment was introduced, the BBC was accused of political bias by the then British Minister of Defence, Lord Carrington.[109]

An incident in early 1972 further demonstrated not only how sensitive the British government was on matters to do with Northern Ireland, but how sensitive certain sections of the local population had become on this topic. On 5 January 1972 the BBC broadcast a three-hour television special, *The Question of Ulster: an Inquiry into the Future*. The programme had already caused friction between the BBC and the Home Secretary, Reginald Maudling, who had urged that it be banned, and the Stormont government, then led by Brian Faulkner. The Ulster Unionists and the Home Secretary refused to take part but Harold Wilson, then leader of the Opposition, did. The conservative media were appalled that this programme was going ahead. On the day that the programme was transmitted the *Belfast News Letter* led with the portentous headline 'The Full United Kingdom is Now in Peril'. The advance publicity ensured a large audience. Seven and a half million viewers were tuned in to BBC1, including nearly two-thirds of the population of Northern Ireland. Telefís Éireann showed the programme simultaneously. The programme began at 9.20 pm but by the end almost half of the viewing audience had switched off. According to the Controller of BBC Northern Ireland, what the viewers saw was 'a cool, at times laborious, examination of eight different solutions to the problems of Ulster'. The general consensus was that the programme was dull and, according to the historian Asa Briggs, 'several right-wing politicians admitted in private that the Ulster unionists had misjudged the whole thing and should have been represented officially at a senior level'. The most positive outcome of the programme was that the streets of Northern Ireland were quieter than they had been for weeks.

The Republic

In the early years of the 1970s there were signs that the hegemony of the Catholic Church was being challenged in the Republic. An area of ongoing difference with the North lay in the position of the Catholic Church within the Republic, which the 1937 Constitution had defined as 'special'. Holding on to this clause was regarded by many as an impediment to unity. In a debate in the Dáil in November, Dr Noel Browne, the radical libertarian TD, asked the Taoiseach:

> whether in order to reduce to the minimum those differences
> in the freedom available to citizens which at present help to
> impede progress towards the unity of the Irish people he
> will introduce legislation to delete Article 41 of the Consti-

tution which prevents those citizens who conscientiously accept the right to divorce from exercising that right?[110]

Lynch responded by saying that 'The Government have been considering the constitutional, economic, social and other aspects of Irish unity', although he refused to provide any more details on these topics.[111] In November 1972 Fianna Fáil introduced a bill to remove this clause from the Constitution. A referendum on the voting age and the Constitution agreed to remove it, with the Church itself showing little opposition.[112] However, it would be many years before divorce was allowed.

In other ways the Catholic Church exerted its influence over the lives of people in the Republic, especially over women. The liberalizing intentions of Vatican Two did not extend to birth control. In 1968 a papal encyclical, *Humanae Vitae*, banned artificial contraception. In the Republic, where the Catholic Church exerted both moral and legislative influence over such matters, an early response to this dictum by feminists was to establish a Family Planning Clinic in 1969. More followed. They provided advice on contraception, despite the fact it was illegal to do so under the terms of the 1935 Criminal Law (Amendment) Act. Both the Catholic Church and the Fianna Fáil Party were implacably opposed to any change in the law. For many years, the Irish Labour Party was the only group in the Dáil to support a reform.[113]

In 1970 the Irish Women's Liberation Movement was founded in Dublin, bringing together some of the most dynamic writers and commentators of the day, including Máirín de Burca, Nell McCafferty, Mary Maher, Moira Woods, Máirín Johnston and Mary Kenny.[114] On 22 May 1971 the organization decided to challenge the legislative ban on contraception and 47 women took the train to Belfast in order to purchase contraceptives, which were legal in Northern Ireland. On their return home, they challenged the customs officials in Dublin to arrest them. Although their actions were illegal, the officials allowed the women to continue on their journey. One of the protestors described their reception: 'The customs men were mortified and quickly conceded they could not arrest all of us, and let us through, waving the banned items.' Later that evening, some of the women appeared on the 'Late Late Show' and Mary Kenny held up the contraceptives.[115] By the summer, the Irish Women's Liberation Movement had disbanded. Nevertheless, the

'contraceptive train' gained enormous public attention and thus provoked public discussion about the issue. Legal challenges to the ban
were also being made. Mary Robinson raised the need for reform of
the law in the *Seanad* on a number of occasions, but she was unsuccessful. As usual, the Catholicism of the majority of the population was cited against any change.[116] It was not until 1993 that all
restrictions on the sale of contraceptives would be lifted.

While Bloody Sunday had evoked much sympathy in the Irish
Republic, the escalating violence north of the border became a source
of alarm rather than concern. The conflict was also having an impact on the tourist industry both north and south of the border. In the
Republic, where tourism provided an important source of revenue,
this development was particularly worrying as it was expected to
extend into 1973.[117] As the violence in the North spiralled out of control, a further consequence was to 'have convinced policy makers that
this form of nationalism was actually subversive of the state; through
their efforts, but also as a consequence of other social changes, the
intensity of irredentism gradually diminished in the last quarter of
the century'.[118] The long-cherished goal of political unification,
which had been constitutionally defined, was disappearing from the
political agenda in the Republic, just at a time when it had been
reawakened in the North. In summer 1972 the Official IRA, which
since the split in the republican movement had been stronger in the
South, announced that it was withdrawing from the military campaign.[119] This decision was made following public outrage at their
killing an off-duty soldier who was visiting his family in Derry.

A new stringency regarding republican activities was evident
when, in May 1972, a Special Criminal Court was reinstituted in
Dublin to deal with crimes arising out of the Northern Ireland conflict. As part of the measure, trial by jury was suspended. Challenges
to the constitutionality of this court were unsuccessful.[120] What its
establishment suggested was that the government of the Republic
was willing to suspend normal legal safeguards – something they
had criticized the British government for doing. A new tougher
stance in regard to republicans was also evident in late 1972 when
the Sinn Féin offices in Dublin were forcibly closed down and a
number of leading republicans, including Maire Drumm, then Vice-
President of Sinn Féin, and Seán MacStiofáin were arrested in the
Republic. MacStiofáin was subsequently sentenced to six months in
prison. The arrest of Ruairi Ó Brádaigh and Martin McGuinness

later in the year showed how far the government of the Republic had come over three years, when it had surreptitiously provided money to help fund the Provisional and Official IRA.[121]

Northern violence, however, was spilling into the South. A bomb placed near a cinema in Dublin on 26 November 1972 was thought to be a republican response to this crackdown: 40 people were injured. On 1 December two car bombs exploded in Dublin city centre: two people were killed and 131 were injured. The IRA was blamed, although it was later found to be the work of the UVF.[122] The bombings provided a small and unpalatable taste of what was occurring daily north of the border. Later that day, the Dáil passed a bill that would enable members of paramilitary groups to be sentenced on the word of a senior police officer in front of three judges, so giving the Irish state much greater powers against the IRA. The bill had been opposed by Fine Gael but, following the bombings, they changed their mind and it was passed with an overwhelming majority. Two decades later, an Inquiry suggested that: 'It is quite possible that the bombs were planted in order to influence the debate on the Bill.'[123] Only a few weeks following the Dublin bombs, on 20 December, the British government published the Diplock Report, which suggested that political crimes should be heard by a Judge of the High Court, or a County Court Judge, sitting alone with no jury. In terms of legal procedures against the republicans, it appeared that the South and the North were moving closer together.

On 28 December a car bomb exploded without warning in Belturbet, County Cavan, killing two teenagers, Geraldine O'Reilly, aged fourteen, and Patrick Stanley, aged fifteen.[124] Later that day, bombs exploded in counties Monaghan and Donegal. The Taoiseach, Jack Lynch, publicly stated that he believed they could be the work of British intelligence. His statements soured relationships between the two governments. There were calls for the British Minister of Defence, Lord Carrington, to resign. However, relationships were already fraught as a result of a trial in Dublin of the Littlejohn Brothers for carrying out a robbery in Dublin, allegedly on behalf of the Provisional IRA. In court they claimed that they were British spies who had infiltrated the organization.[125] Their claim was later shown to be true: they had been recruited by MI6 and paid to act as spies and agents provocateurs within the Provisional IRA.[126] Both of these events in the Republic indicated that the war in the North was confusing boundaries between honesty and deception, between victim and aggressor, and these distortions went to the highest level of office.

By the end of 1972 there were signs that relationships were softening between the British and the Irish governments. The Conservative Party had conceded that there had to be an 'Irish dimension' to finding a solution for Northern Ireland. In turn, Lynch said that he was willing to consider cooperating with Britain to enable security issues to be dealt with on an all-Ireland basis.[127] Lynch's receptiveness to this idea may have been prompted by the bombs in Dublin and Cavan in November and December. Clearly, the attitude of some members of the Irish government and of the Irish population to the conflict in Northern Ireland was changing. The year had commenced with concern for the situation of the minority population in the North, especially following Bloody Sunday. The activities of the IRA, however, had diminished that sympathy as the Republic increasingly sought to ensure that the violence would not spread into the 26 counties.

This political and legal distancing was also evident in relation to the media, where the government used the powers granted by the 1960 broadcasting legislation, notably Section 31, to 'gradually erect a broadcasting *cordon sanitaire* in an attempt to insulate the Republic from the Troubles'.[128] This was never going to be fully possible given that many people in Ireland, particularly the towns and cities on the east coast, had access to British television and radio and to overseas newspapers. In November 1972, though, a forceful message had been sent by the government to Irish journalists when the whole RTÉ Authority had been dismissed for having sanctioned an interview with a Provisional IRA spokesman. Furthermore, the reporter, Kevin O'Kelly, was convicted for refusing to identify his source.[129] Even more insidiously, however, members of the Official IRA had positioned themselves within RTÉ in such a way that they could control news coverage, especially regarding the North. They were vehemently opposed to their former colleagues in the Provisional IRA, therefore they deliberately manipulated debates on republicanism or on anything that they perceived to be 'too green'. The Officials maintained their influential position in Irish broadcasting up to the 1990s.[130]

The distancing between the Republic and Northern Ireland that was evident at the end of 1972 was to become more embedded in the following year. Ironically at a time when the British government admitted that there had to be an 'Irish dimension in resolving the conflict', other viewpoints were hardening. At the Annual Party Conference at the beginning of December, the Northern Ireland Prime Minister had steered his party clear of a clash between moderates and hardliners.[131] As events in the early months of 1973 demonstrated, this unity was to be short-lived.

FOUR

Implosion

In December 1972 William Whitelaw, the British Secretary of State for Northern Ireland, told Orangemen at Stormont that 'he had never equated the UDA with the IRA in the viciousness of their activities'.[1] Over the next twelve months, this assertion proved to be empty. The killing and bombings patterns that had been a feature of 1972 continued in the following year. While members of the security forces continued to be targeted, increasingly the violence became centred on the conflict between the Provisional IRA and the Ulster Defence Association and their affiliates in the Ulster Freedom Fighters. Many civilians were killed or injured as a result. Internment continued, but a new element became apparent on 3 February when two loyalists were detained under this provision, as they were suspected of having killed a Catholic. It was the first internment of Protestants. Approximately 2,000 outraged sympathizers marched to the RUC headquarters in Castlereagh in Belfast to protest. On 7 February the United Loyalist Council (which represented Ulster Vanguard, the Loyalist Association of Workers, the Ulster Defence Association and Loyalist Defence Volunteers) called for a one-day general strike in protest.[2] The Council was led by William Craig, an upper-class lawyer who was increasingly referred to by Protestants as 'King Billy';[3] Catholics had nicknamed him 'Adolf Craig'.[4] Craig, like Paisley, had been a constant critic of Catholics, pointing to their allegiance to Rome rather than the Northern Ireland government. He warned Ulster Protestants: 'the Roman Catholic community has quite different standards of democracy than we have, because their religious faith dictates that it must be that way'.[5]

These actions confirmed the belief that the loyalist community was not afraid to defy the law to defend their interests. Moreover, the strikes resulted in power cuts and disrupted public transport.

Barricades were erected by the UDA and by loyalist groups known as 'Tartan Gangs'. A 'mob' of 1,200 in East Belfast destroyed a Catholic church and a priest's house. There was a surge in rioting and shootings on the day, leading to five deaths, one of the victims being an on-duty fireman. In a debate in the House of Lords, Lord Shackleton noted in regard to the UDA that, 'What was at one time a peaceful body is rapidly becoming less peaceful.'[6] Not all Protestants supported the strike, but it provided a foretaste of the power of loyalist groups within Northern Ireland.

Loyalist groups were also challenging British policy. On 17 February William Craig held a rally in the Ulster Hall in Belfast on behalf of the United Loyalist Council. He was responding to a government Green Paper entitled 'The Future of Northern Ireland'. It cited the Cameron Commission to prove instances of sectarian malpractice within the province, allegations denied by Craig. The Green Paper reiterated the government's promise that there would be regular plebiscites in Northern Ireland regarding the border. Craig followed up the meeting with the production of a pamphlet in which he suggested that 'Ulster is for sale' and that the Green Paper was 'a recipe for civil war'. Craig warned:

> The United Kingdom Government's Green Paper entitled 'The Future of Northern Ireland' further confirms the worst fears of Ulster Loyalists who cherish and seek to maintain their British Heritage. Gently, but with great clarity, the United Kingdom Government has declared that it has no interest in maintaining the Union of Great Britain and Northern Ireland and would favour the unification of Ireland as an independent Republic if the Ulster people would or could be prevailed upon to give their consent. The policies favoured in the document appear to be more concerned with weakening the political power of the loyalist majority and sapping their will to resist.[7]

Craig believed that holding a plebiscite would be flouting the terms of the Ireland Act (1949) and the Downing Street Declaration (1969), which had both guaranteed there would be no tampering with the constitution without the consent of the Northern Ireland Parliament. Thus, he believed, the suspension of Stormont was unconstitutional. Furthermore, he rejected the conclusions of both the Cameron and other tribunals, together with the assertions made in the Green Paper, regarding the onset of conflict. Craig totally ignored the issue of civil rights as a trigger, but attributed the conflict to 'the plans and preparations of the violent republican minority to overthrow the constitution'.[8] The Dublin government was castigated for:

> their part and that of their party in the formation and equipment of the Provisional I.R.A., the subversive operation of Eire Army Officers within the boundaries of Northern Ireland, the stockpiling of weapons for use by insurgent elements in Northern Ireland. All so very relevant, rendering the so-called reform programmes, political initiatives and political solutions not only irrelevant but dangerous.[9]

The British Army was also criticized, for spending 'as much time spying on the police as it did on the I.R.A.'. Further, he believed that the police had been 'sacrificed' to meet 'Republican demands'.[10] Craig was scathing of the claim that the Northern Ireland state could only exist thanks to British grants and subsidies. Rather, he argued, British economic interventions and farming quotas had hindered the development of the Northern Irish economy. He suggested that while 'Ulstermen' preferred to have a future within the United Kingdom, 'they are ready to do it without the United Kingdom if Westminster so wills it'. If the British government refused to restore Stormont, Northern Ireland should seek the status of independent dominion. Craig concluded that Northern Ireland should demand to again be treated as an 'inviolable and integral part of the United Kingdom', which would be proven by 'a shift of power from London to Belfast so as to give the majority the legal and physical power to resist attack or betrayal'.[11]

Craig's vocal responses to the Green Paper suggest that he was positioning himself as the leader of the dissident unionist opposition. However, while other militant leaders, including Ian Paisley, were arguing for more integration within the United Kingdom, he was suggesting more independence for Northern Ireland. His proposals attracted attention, even in North America. In an interview with *Time* magazine the following year, Craig stated that Ulster 'faces a takeover by the Catholic-dominated Republic of Ireland and this can be prevented only if Ulster's Protestants band together in political and military opposition to union'.[12] Unexpectedly, Craig's arguments found favour with the SDLP who had been debating the viability of an independent Northern Ireland, seeing it as the first step to Irish unification. Craig's overt opposition to Brian Falkner resulted in his expulsion from the Unionist Party.[13]

Craig need not have worried about the referendum, which was held on 8 March. Two questions were asked: 'Do you want Northern Ireland to remain part of the United Kingdom?' and 'Do you want Northern Ireland to be joined with the Republic of Ireland outside the United Kingdom?' Almost 99 per cent of voters voted yes to the first question; only one per cent voted yes to the second one. The outcome was resoundingly in favour of keeping the existing border and remaining in the United Kingdom. The SDLP, however, had organized a boycott of the referendum and less than 1 per cent of Catholics had voted. Nonetheless, unionists used the result to bolster their position. Brian Faulkner averred that 'this removes any argument about our constitutional position from the lips of politicians for good and all, not just for five or ten years'.[14] The Provisional IRA marked the day of the referendum by detonating two car bombs in London. Gerry Kelly was one of those convicted for this action. On the same day there were also bombs in Belfast and Derry.

Two weeks following the referendum, the British government produced a White Paper that proposed a 78-member, devolved power-sharing assembly in Northern Ireland. It was to be put in place as quickly as possible with elections taking place on 28 June. Voting was to be by proportional representation, using the single transferable vote, which was the system used in the Republic. The issue of law and order was a major concern of the White Paper:

(xv) Since the Government has no higher priority than to defeat terrorism and end violence, Parliament will be asked to approve specific emergency legislation for the more effective combating of terrorism, including giving effect to the recommendations of the Report of the Diplock Commission. This will make possible the repeal of the Special Powers Act and the re-enactment by the United Kingdom Parliament of those provisions which are regarded as essential.[15]

The document confirmed that all matters relating to law and order were to remain under the control of the United Kingdom government because of 'the current security situation'. An integral part of these measures, which suggested a new stringency in dealing with the violence, was the establishment of Diplock Courts, thus abandoning the principle of trial by jury and replacing it with trial by a single judge. This measure was disliked by the nationalist community. The White Paper proposed a Council of Ireland to promote cross-border links with the Republic and facilitate consultation and cooperation between the North and the South, which was even less palatable from the unionist perspective. It also included a 'Bill of Rights', as a way of ending religious discrimination within Northern Ireland.

On 27 March the Ulster Unionist Party voted on whether or not to accept the White Paper. The result was 381 to 231 voting to accept it, a victory for Faulkner. The Ulster Unionist Council voted by 281 by 131 to accept it. Opposition centred on William Craig. A number of disaffected members of the UUP and of the UUC joined with him to form the Vanguard Unionist Progressive Party, which supported an independent Northern Ireland. Martin Smyth, the Grand Master of the Orange Order, also rejected many of the precepts of the White Paper, demanding instead that internal security should lie with the Northern Ireland Parliament, and that its focus should be the total destruction of the IRA. Like many unionists, both moderate and militant, he was opposed to having a Council of Ireland.[16]

The White Paper won the approval of Liam Cosgrave's new government in the Republic. In the preceding months there had been evidence that the conflict was spreading to the South. On 1 January two men, Briege Porter and Oliver Boyce, were found dead in Burnfoot in County Donegal, killed by loyalists. On 20 January a car bomb in the centre of Dublin killed one person and injured seventeen others. It was suggested by Sinn Féin that these and other bombs were the result of collusion between the Ulster Defence Association (UDA) and British security forces.[17] The accusation of collusion was to be repeated many times. At the time, however, these incidents were a grim start to another violent year and suggested that the bloodshed would not respect borders and could not be contained within the six counties.

Cosgrave, who was an implacable enemy of the IRA, had been leader of the Fine Gael Party since 1965. On 1 March 1973 he led a

Fine Gael/Labour Coalition into power, thus ending the sixteen years of government by the Fianna Fáil Party. Cosgrave had been an early opponent of what he regarded as 'terrorism' and had been instrumental in exposing the role of some senior members of Fianna Fáil in providing arms to the IRA. Bombs in Dublin and elsewhere in the Republic had won support for his stance.[18] His Cabinet included Garret FitzGerald and Conor Cruise O'Brien of the Labour Party, both of whom shared his uncompromising views about the republican struggle in the North. Two weeks after the Coalition took office, the *Claudia*, a ship from Libya carrying arms for the Provisional IRA, including anti-tank weapons and large amounts of Semtex, was seized off the coast of Waterford. Joe Cahill, a veteran member of the IRA, was on board. Ted Heath was delighted with the action of the new government, believing it augured well for future cooperation in security matters: he wrote to Cosgrave saying, 'I should like to express my personal congratulations to you in the successful interception of the *Claudia*'.[19]

In May 1973, in a Dáil debate on the British White Paper on Northern Ireland, the new Taoiseach appealed for the Opposition to put their sympathy for Catholics in the North and political opinions aside, in order to find the way to peace and stability. Regarding the 'Irish dimension', which was so disliked by many unionists, he explained:

> The full measure of the problem of Northern Ireland is that reconciliation between its communities cannot be brought about successfully in isolation from the larger issue of reconciliation within the island as a whole. The two issues are inseparable – since hope for a coming together of North and South is an essential part of the aspiration of one of the two communities in the area . . .
>
> But this does not mean, and I emphasise this very strongly, that we see a council as a Trojan horse to deceive the North, or as a device to lure it towards an eventual unity which it does not accept. We do not deny our aspirations. But I believe I speak for a wide range of opinion here when I say that we are more anxious to see a process of co-operation, of growth towards reconciliation, get under way than to set a time-table or try to determine in advance exactly what the end result would be.

Cosgrave was clear in his support for this initiative, stating, 'Overall the aim of the paper is to establish in Northern Ireland a broader consensus than has hitherto existed so that its people may enjoy the benefits of good Government and social and economic justice', adding:

> they [the British government] accepted that there is no quick or easy solution to the many problems of Northern Ireland. In that statement we said that we saw in the White Paper proposals which could help towards a solution . . . We are ready to play our part in this process and to put forward concrete proposals to that end at the forthcoming Conference to which the British Government proposes to invite the Government here and representatives of Northern Ireland opinion.[20]

The Fianna Fáil Party had already given 'cautious approval' to the White Paper, but Jack Lynch used the debate as an opportunity to again call for the ending of internment and to suggest that the brutality used by the security forces should be halted.[21] Overall, the White Paper appeared to herald a new phase of cooperation in the affairs of Northern Ireland by the Irish and British governments.

Local elections took place in Northern Ireland on 30 May. The UUP won over 41 per cent of the vote, which showed it was still overwhelmingly the largest unionist party, despite the Democratic Unionist Party and Vanguard also fielding candidates. The SDLP won the majority of the nationalist vote. Constitutional politics remained overshadowed by the violence. The day following the election, the UFF and the UVF attacked Catholic-owned public houses, killing two men. The Provisional IRA was carrying out similarly indiscriminate and sectarian attacks: on 12 June 1973, six Protestant civilians, aged between 60 and 76, were killed when a car bomb exploded in Railway Road, Coleraine. Those murdered included three holidaymakers.[22] On 9 June the Dublin-based *Sunday World* published a statement from the UDA justifying their tactics. It accused former Unionist governments of mishandling the civil rights protests, and criticized both the Irish and British governments for failing to understand their perspective. It suggested that within Britain people of Scots-Irish descent were viewed as '*second* class Englishmen and half-caste Irishmen', while the Dublin government was accused of 'tacitly' supporting the bombing campaign. It believed that it had no alternative but to intensify its campaign of bloodshed, because 'the Scots-Irish are fighting for their survival'.[23] A few days later the UFF announced that it was going to intensify its attacks on Catholics.[24] On 26 June Paddy Wilson, then a Social Democratic and Labour Party Senator in Stormont, and 29-year-old Irene Andrews, a Protestant friend, were found dead in a quarry in Belfast. Wilson had been stabbed 32 times, Andrews nineteen.[25] Shortly afterwards, two members of the UFF 'brigade staff' gave an interview to an Irish and a British reporter. One of the men declared, 'Wilson and Andrews was a ritual killing. It was a godsend to get rid of vermin like that.'[26]

The increasing violence of the UDA and UFF, and their continuing links with the Ulster Defence Regiment, was a source of concern for the British government. In August 1973 a top secret document entitled 'Secret. UK Eyes. Subversion in the UDR' was prepared by British military intelligence. It suggested that the main source of weapons for loyalist paramilitaries was raids on UDR barracks. The UDR was 96 per cent Protestant and in the document it was suggested that between 5 and 15 per cent of that number were affiliated to loyalist paramilitaries:

> Subversion will not occur in every case but there will be a passing on of information and training methods in many cases and a few subversives may conspire to 'leak' arms and ammunition to Protestant extremist groups. The presence within the UDR of members of extremist groups does, however, contain within it the danger that at some future stage, if HMG's [Her Majesty's Government] actions were perceived to be unfavourable to 'loyalist' interests, those men could act as a source of information, training and weapons for their fellows and might even work within the UDR to make it unreliable.[27]

The report acknowledged that 'the first loyalties of many of its members are to a concept of "Ulster" rather than to HMG, and that where a perceived conflict in these loyalties occur, HMG will come off second best . . . disquieting evidence of subversion is available'. The report foresaw two scenarios in which the level of subversion would become dangerous: if the Assembly failed, or if the government made any moves that could be viewed as supporting a united Ireland. A likely outcome would be that a loyalist party, with the support of the UDR, would declare unilateral independence.[28]

Against the background of increasing loyalist activity, elections to the Assembly took place on 28 June. The turn-out was over 72 per cent. Those who supported the White Paper won 52 seats; those opposing it, 26. The Ulster Unionist Party remained the largest party, holding 24 seats; the second largest was the SDLP with nineteen seats. Other seats were won by Unionists (eight), Democratic Unionist Party (eight), Vanguard Unionist Loyalist Coalition (seven), Belfast West Loyalist Coalition (three), Alliance Party (eight) and Northern Ireland Labour Party (one). In the North Antrim Constituency, two hard-line unionists won seats: Ian Paisley for the Democratic Unionist Party and William Craig for the Vanguard Unionist Loyalist Coalition. Paisley topped the poll, winning over 6,000 more votes than Craig.[29] The election showed how finely balanced support for traditional unionism and militant unionism had become. At the same time, it confirmed the SDLP as the overwhelming voice of the nationalist community. Privately, Whitelaw was disappointed with the results, writing to Heath, 'It is encouraging that the extremists on the whole fared badly. But an uncomfortably large number of seats have been won by dissident loyalists of one kind or another.'[30]

The new Assembly met on 31 July in Stormont. The two-hour meeting was disrupted by a group of 27 hardliners, calling themselves the Loyalist-Unionists Alliance. They were led by Ian Paisley who declared, 'I should like those members of the British Government who are here and the Westminster members who are skulking in the galleries to know that Ulstermen are free people and we are not going to be bullied.' The actions of the protesters were criticized by both Faulkner and Gerry Fitt, the leader of the SDLP, who said, 'We have come here today with a clear commitment to make this assembly a fair and just system of administration for the people of Northern Ireland.'[31] It was an inauspicious start to the attempt to restore democratic politics in Northern Ireland.

The creation of the Assembly made little difference to the activities of the paramilitaries. During a riot in August the RUC tried out plastic batons (bullets) and these gradually replaced the rubber ones. They were intended to be less lethal but in practice, especially if misused, they proved just as destructive and deadly. In November Jamie Flanagan was appointed head of the RUC, thus becoming the first Catholic to hold this position. Flanagan had joined the RUC in 1934 and had had a successful career, receiving a CBE earlier in 1973. He was known to be non-political in his dealings.[32] His two years in office coincided with even more political turmoil. Secretly the British Army was requesting more powers in the event of a complete breakdown of law and order in Northern Ireland. The discussions were referred to as 'Operation Folklore'. In addition to augmenting powers to stop and search and arrest, more controversially they wanted the ability to shoot, without fear of legal retribution. As the Head of Defence in London explained to the Northern Ireland Office:

> We feel strongly that in the wholly abnormal situation envisaged it would be essential for a soldier to be able to open fire without fear of legal penalty in certain circumstances where under the present law a court would consider that he had acted unlawfully. The situations we envisage include:
> a. opening fire without warning on persons merely 'carrying firearms (i.e. without having to be satisfied that they were about to use them etc);
> b. opening fire at persons breaking a curfew who failed to halt when challenged; and
> c. opening fire in certain other situations, e.g. at persons who fail to halt when challenged, in areas designated by the s of s [Secretary of State for Northern Ireland] or, perhaps, the GOC [General Officer Commanding the British Army in Northern Ireland] as 'special areas', which would, typically, be exceptionally 'hard' areas in which the Army needed to regain control and which might or might not correspond with areas under curfew.[33]

The Provisional IRA's bombing campaign in England intensified in 1973, with explosions in Solihull and the Harrods store in London on 29 August, in Manchester and London on 8 September, in various London train stations on 10 September, and in Birmingham on 23 September. Although there were no civilian deaths, there were extensive injuries, and in Birmingham a soldier had been killed trying to detonate the bomb. Moreover, as the IRA had intended, their campaign brought fear and disruption within England, which was not helped by the multiple hoax bomb warnings received by Scotland Yard.[34] In November nine men were arrested for their part in the London bombings.

The Provisional IRA achieved a major publicity coup in late October when, using a stolen helicopter, they freed three of their members from Mountjoy Prison in Dublin. Apparently some of the prison officers, upon seeing a helicopter land in the compound, believed they were getting a surprise visit from the Minister of Defence. At that point there were 1,400 members of the Provisional IRA in various prisons and this audacious escape was viewed as a boost to their morale. Those who escaped were Séamus Twomey, Chief of Staff of the IRA, Joe O'Hagan, Quartermaster of the IRA, and Kevin Mallon, an IRA activist since the 1950s. Despite a massive police hunt in the Republic, the men remained free. Sinn Féin later claimed that, 'The primary purpose was to embarrass Liam Cosgrave, his Fine Gael Party, and the Labour Party with Conor Cruise O'Brien, who had boasted in September that their government was having greater success than the British in crushing the Republican Movement.'[35] Further embarrassment was to come. A nationalist group, The Wolfe Tones, released 'The Helicopter Song', which was immediately prohibited from being played on RTÉ stations. Notwithstanding this ban, it sold more than 12,000 copies within a week, propelling it to the top of the Irish charts, where it remained for four weeks.[36]

Cooperation

Following the election of the Fine Gael-Labour Coalition, more collaboration took place, both privately and publicly, between London and Dublin. On 2 April Heath secretly contacted Cosgrave seeking further cooperation between security forces in Northern Ireland and those in the Republic of Ireland, which was granted.[37] Two days later the Head of the British Defence Secretariat sought the support of the Irish government in clearing an area of woodland along the border from where the IRA was making attacks on the RUC base in Belleek.[38]

On 17 September Ted Heath met Liam Cosgrave at Baldonnel, near Dublin, to discuss security. It was the first visit by a British Prime Minister to the South since Independence. The Army's Chief of Staff had warned that Baldonnel was 'wide open' from a security point of view, but no problem occurred. However, no progress was made in the nine hours of talks.[39] Security was not the only topic discussed. Since its founding in 1970, the SDLP had emerged as the strongest nationalist party in the North. The relationship between Cosgrave and John Hume, deputy leader of the party, however, had proved to be thorny, with the latter criticizing the Irish government's inaction. At the Baldonnel meeting Cosgrave confided in Heath of his 'impatience' with the SDLP's 'inexperience'. Heath, in turn, warned that the SDLP were in danger of 'overplaying their hand', and that could result in toppling the Unionist leader, Brian Faulkner.[40] Their comments underlined the fragility of constitutional politics in Northern Ireland. Later that day Heath made a statement to the BBC in which he warned the new Northern Ireland Assembly that if they failed to establish a power-sharing Assembly by March 1974, the alternative would be further integration of Northern Ireland into the United Kingdom. His statement alarmed both nationalists and unionists. The following day, however, he made it clear that integration was not, in fact, envisaged.[41]

Regardless of the public cooperation between the two leaders, privately Heath remained frustrated with Cosgrave's unwillingness to tackle the Provisional IRA directly. The British government had given Cosgrave's government a highly sensitive dossier on members of the Provisional IRA, which they had failed to act on.[42] Instead, Cosgrave seemed to be pinning his hopes on the success of the new Assembly in bringing peace to Northern Ireland.

A joint communiqué was issued following the meeting between Heath and Cosgrave, but the content of the Baldonnel meeting was not made public. In October, almost four weeks later, it was raised in the Dáil by Jack Lynch, the former Taoiseach, amongst others, who asked for a full statement. Cosgrave refused, on grounds of security. Increasingly the Taoiseach was excluding Fianna Fáil from developments in Northern Ireland, an approach that annoyed the more republican members of the party. During the debate, Cosgrave was asked by Neil Blaney, of Independent Fianna Fáil, for 'details of the co-operation which exists between the peacekeeping forces of the State and the security forces in the Six Counties'.[43] The Taoiseach refused to answer the question directly. Despite being called to order by the Speaker, Blaney persisted and asked Cosgrave if he was aware that:

contrary to past procedure, members of our peacekeeping forces are, in fact, being used by the occupation forces in the Six Counties on identification parades to identify political offenders in order that they may be prosecuted and put into concentration camps at Long Kesh. Is the Taoiseach aware of this? Is it common practice or is it a new procedure?[44]

Blaney returned to the issue repeatedly, finally asking: 'can the Taoiseach say whether during the course of his discussions with Mr. Heath he, as Taoiseach, made it known to the British Prime Minister that we wish to have the British out of this country?' Cosgrave, refusing to be drawn, simply responded, 'The British Government are fully aware of our views on this matter.'[45]

Security issues were again raised in the Dáil the following day. On 16 September the *Sunday Times* had revealed that British helicopters had been given permission to fly over the border into the Republic. This had been done without the knowledge or consent of either the Dáil or the Irish Army. Again, the Opposition questioned the government on its relationship with the British government. Thomas Meany, the member for Mid-Cork, repeatedly questioned the Minister of Defence on this matter:

because I believe it is the duty of the Irish Army authorities to carry out all patrol duties that are necessary in the twenty-six Counties. The Minister and his Department may quibble about the use of words; they may argue whether it is 'fly-over', 'patrol', or 'surveillance' but in this context they all mean the same and lead to the same thing. I submit the Minister should not have taken this action . . . I am raising this matter in the hope that the Minister will say that that permission to the British authorities is cancelled for ever.

Meaney pointed out, 'We have an excellent Army which are well able to carry out their duties'.[46]

The Coalition government's refusal to inform Fianna Fáil of its activities regarding Northern Ireland was a deliberate strategy. According to the historian Richard Bourke, 'the Cosgrave administration, assailed on its flank by Fianna Fáil in opposition, was "pathologically" determined to keep any co-operation with their British counterparts secret'.[47] The debates revealed the fluidity of allegiances as the conflict continued and an increasing determination by the Dublin government to contain the situation without the six counties of the North.

Sunningdale

In the final months of 1973 some progress had been made by the Northern Ireland Assembly, mostly on economic and social issues. This had resulted from cooperation between the Ulster Unionist Party, the SDLP and the Alliance Party. Internment, policing and the proposed Council of Ireland all proved to be much harder to agree upon. Unionists opposed to the Assembly continued to put pressure on it, calling for Faulkner's resignation in October. Clearly his power base was shrinking within his own party. In October a vote to support a policy that would allow UUP members to take part in any future power-sharing executive was passed by 132 to 105 votes. A few weeks later, the UUC voted (albeit by a narrow margin) to reject power-sharing.[48]

On 21 November William Whitelaw announced on the steps of Westminster that the various political parties had agreed to establish a power-sharing executive to govern Northern Ireland. Brian Faulkner was to become the Chief Executive and Gerry Fitt his Deputy. The Assembly was opposed by both militant unionists and the IRA. The Irish and British governments were jubilant, however. Significantly, no agreement had been reached on the role of the Council of Ireland. Unexpectedly, on 3 December, just as crucial talks were about to commence, Whitelaw was replaced by Francis Pym. The *Daily Telegraph* described Pym as 'a man of outstandingly clear mind, precise thoughts and firm purpose' – all qualities that would be called upon immediately in his new role.[49] On the same day that Pym was appointed, Harry West and other 'unpledged' unionists announced the setting up of a new group called the Ulster Unionist Assembly Party. West had been a minister in the O'Neill government, but his latest move suggested that he was positioning himself as leader of the anti-power-sharing unionists.

To work out details of the power-sharing executive, a conference was held in Sunningdale in England between 6 and 9 December. The day before the conference, members of the Northern Ireland Assembly had been physically beaten by those opposing them. Sunningdale was attended by representatives of the Irish,

Northern Irish and British governments. The British Labour Party had not been invited to attend. The conference was boycotted by representatives from the unionist parties opposed to the Executive and, even more bitterly, to the Council of Ireland. Despite knowing how unpopular the Council would be, the SDLP, supported by the Dublin government, pushed for a commitment to this body.[50] Faulkner was pressurized by British representatives to agree to the Council; however, British civil servants doubted privately that he could convince even his supporters.[51] In general, those attending the conference had shown insensitivity to the fears and aspirations of the unionist community who were not represented.

Sunningdale appeared to end in consensus, but both unionists and nationalists came away from the conference with different interpretations of what had been agreed. Moreover, substantial differences remained: nationalists wanted a strong all-Ireland dimension that could pave the way for eventual reunification – unionists wanted the removal from the Irish Constitution of all references to a united Ireland; nationalists desired a reform of the RUC and internment to be ended – unionists wanted increased security, including extradition from the South.[52] The BBC described the outcome of Sunningdale as a 'historic agreement', but warned, 'The agreement is expected to enrage anti-power sharing parties who were excluded from the talks'.[53]

Sunningdale had other enemies. Not all politicians in the Republic approved of the conference. Kevin Boland of Fianna Fáil believed that it had ignored the territorial aspirations laid down in the Constitution. His legal challenge was not upheld by the Irish High Court, which ruled that the Republic's territorial claims remained intact.[54] Shortly after Sunningdale, Francis Pym was criticized in the House of Commons by Ian Paisley for not offering full membership of Sunningdale to loyalist parties who were opposed to the White Paper. Paisley also accused the government of endorsing anti-Catholic policies, demanding of Pym:

> Will he also confirm that when an application goes before the Health Services Board in Belfast the question is asked 'Are you a Protestant?' and if the answer is 'Yes' the applicant is told that he will not be employed? Can that be taken as the right hon. Gentleman's attitude to Protestants?[55]

Paisley, at this stage, was arguing for fuller integration of North-ern Ireland into the United Kingdom, but his behaviour in Parlia-ment suggested that he had little respect for its institutions.

The end of 1973 brought some glimmers of hope that things were improving in the Six Counties: the death toll for the year was 253, approximately half that in the previous year. In November the UVF had called a ceasefire. It lasted more than a month and provided an interlude in the increasingly violent campaign against Catholics.[56] The new government in the Republic seemed to have reached an accommodation with the British government and was working closely with the SDLP on the Sunningdale Agreement. When he addressed the Dáil on 12 December, the Taoiseach claimed, 'The Sunningdale agreement opens out a new prospect of hope for peace and reconciliation and co-operation in this island', and he asked for consensus within the Dáil for the agreement. He warned that 'vio-lent men on two sides' would seek to destroy it, but he was hopeful that, 'They will not succeed because there is at last coming into being, on a firm basis, a working understanding of the centre, rep-resenting the united strength of the sensible elements in this island, drawn from both communities and both traditions of allegiance.'[57]

Heath's government was less sanguine about the new agree-ment. From their perspective, Dublin had not done enough to reassure unionists of their good faith. The British Ambassador in Dublin, Sir Arthur Galsworthy, scathingly commented on the shal-lowness of thinking by the Cosgrave government and their parochial and 'timorous' approach. He believed that 'the Republic had conceded hardly anything'. He was also dismissive of Garret Fitzgerald's repeated demands that he chair the Sunningdale con-ference.[58] Regardless of the posturing by both the British and Irish governments, following Sunningdale, the key player was Brian Faulkner. Faulkner, cajoled by Heath, had accepted the Council of Ireland, but then had to sell it to unionists within Northern Ireland. In the words of the historian Alvin Jackson, Faulkner's 'faltering con-trol over unionist opinion collapsed' after Sunningdale, an occur-rence that jeopardized constitutional unionism.[59]

Opposition to Sunningdale, before and after, gave anti-Assembly forces a chance to regroup. On 3 December the Orange Order organized a meeting at the Ulster Hall, together with the Vanguard movement, led by William Craig, Ian Paisley's Democratic Union-ist Party and the anti-power sharing faction of the Ulster Unionist

Party.[60] They came together in a loose alliance known as the United Ulster Unionist Council. The day after Sunningdale ended, loyalists announced the establishment of the Ulster Army Council (UAC) to resist the proposed Council of Ireland, which they regarded as a form of 'creeping unification'. The main aim of the group was to set up a loyalist army of around 20,000 men to take control of Northern Ireland, if necessary, to prevent any attempt at the reunification of Ireland. The leader was Andy Tyrie, who was also the commander of the UDA. In addition to the UDA, the UAC comprised the UFF, Orange Volunteers, Down Orange Welfare, Ulster Special Constabulary Association, Ulster Volunteer Service Corps and Red Hand Commandos.[61] These groups were to play a major role in the defeat of the 1974 power-sharing executive.

For Ted Heath's Conservative government, the on-going problems of Northern Ireland were of less immediate concern than those facing him in Britain. Since his election in 1970, Heath had sought to expand the British economy and make it more efficient, without having to rely on wage and price controls.[62] This aspiration proved increasingly ephemeral. In a desperate attempt to counter growing unemployment in 1971, he cut bank interest rates. Initially he appeared to be successful, but inflation started to rise and the value of the pound to fall. This coincided with a strike by coalminers, which commenced in January 1972, over a pay increase. Although the miners' strike lasted for only a few weeks, it resulted in power cuts in both homes and businesses. Some factories and businesses had been forced to close, resulting in an estimated 1.2 million people losing their jobs.[63] The government's determination to impose a pay freeze resulted in millions of other workers coming out on strike. In November 1973 the miners announced a ban on working overtime. Electricity workers declared a similar ban. The Yom Kippur War in October had triggered an international oil crisis, leading to massive price increases. This strengthened the miners' hands as energy became more expensive. Heath responded by declaring a State of Emergency. A three-day week began on New Year's Eve 1973. Electricity supplies were again restricted and people had to rely on candles, lamps and extra clothing. Even more devastating for some, television transmissions were to end at 10.30 pm each evening. There was an immediate increase in unemployment.[64] The announcement of a new miners' strike in February led Heath to call a General Election: he labelled it 'Who Governs Britain?' The question of who governed Northern Ireland had temporarily faded into the background. On 1 March 1974 the flailing government of Heath was replaced by Labour, under Harold Wilson. Wilson inherited an economy in distress, a society in strife, and a Northern Ireland Assembly that was on the brink of collapse.

'The Year of Reconciliation'?

The new power-sharing Executive officially took over control of government on 1 January 1974; on 28 May it collapsed and direct rule was again imposed. The intervening period was marked by civil unrest and violence. During this period Britain also experienced civil unrest, triggered by strikes, power cuts and large-scale unemployment, forcing Ted Heath to declare a State of Emergency. The General Election in March was deliberately framed to pit the government against the trade unions. Labour won most of the parliamentary seats, but not an overall majority, and came into power at the head of a 'hung' parliament. They were immediately confronted with two problems: industrial chaos in Britain and political turmoil in Northern Ireland.

For a few days at the beginning of 1974 there was some optimism that a political solution had been found to the problems of Northern Ireland. The Executive had actually met on the last day of December at Stormont to be sworn in. The ceremony was deliberately low key, the recommendation being that 'there should be no church leaders, no wives, and no champagne'.[65] On that day, the new Executive issued a statement:

> We have undertaken to serve in the interests of Northern Ireland and all its people. This is the spirit in which we shall always act, both individually and collectively.
>
> We want the New Year to see the beginning, not just of a new system of Government, but of a new spirit. Let 1974 be The Year of Reconciliation.[66]

On 3 January the Secretary of State reported, 'The Northern Ireland Executive had entered into office on 1 January. They had made a good start and so far they were working well together.'[67] Clearly, Faulkner and Fitt, two traditional adversaries, were capable of cooperating. However, even by Northern Ireland standards, the honeymoon period of the Executive was brief. On 4 January the Ulster Unionist Council voted, by 427 votes to 374, to reject the 'Council of Ireland', which effectively meant it rejected the Sunningdale Agreement. Three days later Faulkner resigned as leader of the Ulster Unionist Party. He was replaced by his former ally, Harry West.[68] Heath partially blamed the Dublin government for Faulkner's weak position. In a confidential letter to Cosgrave he asserted:

> If I may in this situation be perfectly frank, some of the remarks attributed by the press to you and some of your colleagues have been interpreted as meaning that the Republic is maintaining its claim that Northern Ireland is now part of the Republic and that there is no prospect of a change in the law on extradition which is still a burning issue in the North. This has seriously reduced the value to Faulkner of the Sunningdale agreement.[69]

The Dublin High Court's ruling about Irish territorial aspirations had been inflammatory at such a critical time, but this only gave additional ammunition to militant unionists, as did Faulkner's visit to Dublin on 16 January to have a meeting with Cosgrave. Any positive impact Faulkner may have had was undone 24 hours later when Hugh Logue, an SDLP Assemblyman, gave a speech at Trinity College, Dublin, in which he said that the Council of Ireland was 'the vehicle that would trundle Unionists into a united Ireland'. Logue later denied that he had said this, though following up with a warning to unionists that Britain was in the process of withdrawing from Northern Ireland.[70]

The protests against the Assembly continued in the early months of 1974; at the first official meeting of the Assembly on 22 January, eighteen loyalist protesters had to be forcibly removed from the front benches. The *Orange Standard* called the power-sharing experiment 'the first Western example of Iron Curtain treatment of a satellite'.[71] On 1 February unionist anger was further aroused when the first meeting of the Council of Ireland took place. While power-sharing had the support of moderate unionists, the Council of Ireland was almost universally detested by them. In agreeing to the Council meeting, Faulkner had signed his own political death warrant.[72]

Despite the unpopularity of the Executive, and against the advice of Pym, Heath decided to call a General Election in the United Kingdom for 28 February. The backdrop was large-scale industrial unrest in Britain and a Conservative Party in crisis. Those who opposed the Sunningdale Agreement coordinated their electoral strategy to put up only one candidate in each constituency. The plan was masterminded by the United Ulster Unionist Council who adopted the slogan 'Dublin is just a Sunningdale away'. The election was a massive victory for the opponents of Sunningdale, who won eleven out of the twelve available seats. The result was humiliating for Faulkner and worrying for all those who had reached agreement in Sunningdale less than three months earlier. The election also gave a democratic mandate to militant unionists who opposed Sunningdale.

An unwelcome outcome of the election for many unionists was the fact that the Conservative Party had lost the election by a narrow margin and Labour, led by Harold Wilson, was back in power. The Coalition government in the South was equally dismayed. They had been wary of Wilson since his meetings with IRA leaders in 1971. They did not know this at the time, but upon his return to office, Wilson had asked for the consequences of British withdrawal from Northern Ireland to be investigated.[73] On 5 March Merlyn Rees became the first Labour Secretary of State for Northern Ireland. Rees acquired a reputation as somebody who genuinely cared about Northern Ireland and was pained by the cycle of violence. He not only impressed civil servants in Stormont with his interest in and knowledge of Northern Ireland, but hardline loyalists found him easy to talk to.[74] These cordial relations were short-lived. In accordance with Labour policy, Pym was determined to end internment. On 4 April he announced that internment would be phased out; he also de-proscribed both the UVF and Sinn Féin. Following the lifting of the ban, the UVF developed a political wing, the Ulster Volunteer Party.[75]

The Northern Ireland office was concerned about how Faulkner would handle the disastrous election results and a private memo was prepared for the government that warned:

Mr Faulkner was somewhat shaken and somewhat fearful . . . Everyone was shattered by the extent of the feeling against a Council of Ireland . . . Faulkner ended by saying that 'he was no quitter'. He is clearly, however, a worried man and will need a good deal of comfort during the next few weeks.[76]

Faulkner and his supporters in the Assembly responded by suggesting that Sunningdale should not be ratified unless clauses two and three (which mentioned territorial aspirations) were removed from the Irish Constitution. Faulkner followed this up by demanding that the government of the Republic agreed to extradition and gave full recognition to the state of Northern Ireland. For the SDLP, this was a betrayal of all that had been agreed to. Serious divisions were appearing in the new Executive.

On 13 March Liam Cosgrave announced in the Dáil that the position of Northern Ireland within the United Kingdom could not be changed except with the consent of a majority of the people of Northern Ireland. When questioned by Neil Blaney about his stance on Northern Ireland, Cosgrave replied 'that verbal patriotism is no substitute for realism as a solution to the complex problem of the North of Ireland'.[77] Blaney responded that:

> the reality must surely be that before any question of giving what is given in the Declaration at Sunningdale – that of the right of the majority in part of our country to opt in or out – until the British Government takes its presence out of this country that Declaration is not dealing with realities in any shape or form?

This drew no answer from the Taoiseach.[78]

In the early months of 1974 a new political grouping of anti-Sunningdale loyalists had formed, calling itself the Ulster Workers' Council (UWC). In its opening statement it announced that it was willing to fight for the existence of Northern Ireland, but 'the future of Northern Ireland will no longer be decided behind closed doors between rival groups of politicians, each jockeying for the best advantage to himself and to hell with the workers'. These comments, and the fact that its founders were trade union officials, suggested there was also a class dimension to the struggles within unionism. The UWC called for new elections to the Northern Ireland Assembly. On 23 March the UWC threatened civil disobedience in the form of a general strike unless the Executive was dissolved.[79] Two weeks later Merlyn Rees met with the UWC, suggesting that within a short space of time they had become a force within loyalist politics. Nothing was agreed at the meeting; the UWC insisted the Executive was undemocratic and demanded fresh elections, while Rees was adamant that the new Executive needed four years to prove itself.[80]

Two days later Rees reported to the British Cabinet on what he perceived to be 'loyalist intransigence', especially in relation to the Council of Ireland. At the same time, he was concerned that if the Council of Ireland was abandoned, both the SDLP and the Dublin government would withdraw from power-sharing.[81] There was no middle ground. On the same day, the Cabinet discussed a report that warned: 'The security situation was cause for great concern. The pattern of violence had changed and consisted largely of attacks with fire bombs prepared and placed by women, and the placing of car bombs by civilians who were not themselves terrorists but who were acting under extreme duress.'[82] The British government viewed the power-sharing Executive as critical to the political future of Northern Ireland and urged Faulkner to ratify the Sunningdale Agreement. Faulkner was pessimistic about the impact this would have on both himself and on the province, warning that 'if he went ahead and "ratified" Sunningdale now, he would have no political following left; there would also be a strong possibility of civil war'.[83] The seriousness with which the situation was viewed was evident when the British Prime Minister attended a meeting with the Executive at Stormont on 18 April. A secret note of the discussion gave little cause for optimism:

> The Prime Minister therefore came back to the point at which he began: that it was vitally important to make the Executive and power-sharing a success. In discussions about the consequences of its possible failure the words civil war had been used, he feared with reason. Hence there was an absolute determination on the part of the British Government not to give in, or pull out. He recognised however that if our troops were caught in cross-fire between rival terrorist groups the pressure for withdrawal would be very strong.[84]

For loyalists, the Executive had become a symbol of betrayal that had to be brought down. On 26 April the UUUC called for the establishment of a Northern Ireland regional parliament in a federal United Kingdom. On 8 May the UDA gave its official support to the aims of the UUUC. The anti-Sunningdale forces were uniting. On 14 May the UWC announced that a strike was to commence the following day. It was a bold strategy and the UWC was not sure that it would be successful. Initially the strike had little support. By midday, however, people were starting to leave their workplaces – intimidation playing a large part in persuading them to do so. On the first day, the UDA and the UVF closed down the port of Larne, but the leaders of the strike remained privately apprehensive about how successful their actions would be.[85] That evening, an emergency meeting was held between Stanley Orme, the Minister of State at the Northern Ireland Office, and supporters of the strike, the latter including three unionist politicians (Ian Paisley, William Craig and John Laird), representatives from the UWC and from some loyalist paramilitary organizations. Orme took a hard line on the day's events, warning that, 'The workers would not get what they wanted by attempting to intimidate the Government by a political strike of this nature. If the strike continued the workers would leave the government with no alternative but to carry out essential services by the use of the army.'[86]

The meeting achieved nothing except to intensify the strike action. In the following days road blocks manned by loyalist paramilitaries increased, petrol stations closed, rubbish was not collected, public houses closed and there were power cuts for up to eighteen hours. Initially there had been widespread intimidation, but after a few days the Protestant community generally supported the strike. Harsh criticism by Harold Wilson, who accused the strike of being sectarian, only served to increase solidarity. In contrast, the opposite side was split and it became apparent that 'The Northern Ireland Office was folding its arms and waiting to see if the executive would survive'.[87]

The British government did not want to use either the Army or the RUC to confront the strikers. Secretly, they were considering sending a nuclear submarine to Belfast to generate power but decided against it on practical grounds.[88] On 20 May Rees declared a state of emergency in Northern Ireland. Four days later, Rees, Wilson and Faulkner held a crisis meeting at Chequers. Faulkner observed that:

With every hour that passed . . . it became increasingly evident that the administration of the country was in fact in
the hands of the Ulster Workers' Council.

The issue was now not whether the Sunningdale agreement would or would not survive. The outcome which the
Protestant extremists sought was without question an
independent, neo-fascist Northern Ireland.[89]

A few days later, as the strikers held firm, Faulkner suggested that
the Council of Ireland should be watered down, if not abandoned.
Both publicly and privately, Wilson was losing patience with the
strikers. In a personal letter to Cosgrave, his despair was evident:

As this holiday weekend begins Northern Ireland faces the
gravest crisis in her history. And it is a crisis equally for all of
us who live on this side of the water . . .

The people on this side of the water – British parents –
have seen their sons vilified and spat upon and murdered.
British taxpayers have seen the taxes they have poured out
almost with regard to cost – over £300 million a year this
year with the cost of the army operations on top of that –
going into Northern Ireland. They see property destroyed
by evil violence and asked to pick up the bill for rebuilding it.
Yet people who benefit from this now viciously defy Westminster, purporting to act as though they were an elected
government, spend their lives sponging on Westminster and
British democracy and then systematically assault democratic methods. Who do these people think they are?[90]

As the strike continued, it was clear to the British government
that the Executive had become a liability. On 27 May Rees informed
Wilson that:

While the Northern Ireland Executive remain in being,
there can be no real movement. But the situation changes if
they go. From our point of view the most desirable situation
now is that they should go of their own accord, in view of
the intervention. They cannot make any plausible complaints that they have not received full support from HMG.[91]

On the fourteenth day of the strike, Brian Faulkner and his colleagues in the Unionist Party resigned. Faulkner had resigned from O'Neill's administration in 1969 to side with unionist hardliners. Five years later he was himself brought down by unionist hardliners, who included Harry West, Ian Paisley and David Trimble. The resignations effectively marked the end of the Executive, although officially the Northern Ireland Assembly was prorogued for a period of four months. Direct Rule was reintroduced. Kenneth Bloomfield, a leading civil servant and Secretary to the Executive, described his reaction to Faulkner's resignation:

> I wept for the success of the hard men with dark glasses, the balaclava helmets and the pickaxe handles; I wept for the inevitability of a sweeping British judgement that we were all hopeless cases, doomed to an endless conflict in an inferno of our own creation; I wept for the eclipse of local democracy.[92]

Following Faulkner's resignation, the Ulster Workers' Council called off the strike. It had been an outstanding victory for militant unionism and for extra-parliamentary tactics, while moderation and compromise – along with Brian Faulkner – had been sacrificed.

Privately, Wilson was making contingency plans for a withdrawal from Ireland. In a secret memo he suggested:

> We have also got to consider what, if any, preparations we can make against resumption of a strike . . . In Doomsday terms – which means withdrawal – I should like this scenario to be considered.
>
> It is not the only one by any means, and it is open to nearly all the objections set out in the document – outbreak of violence and bloodshed, possible unacceptability to moderate Catholics, ditto to the Republic, the United Nations and the possible spread of trouble across the water, to name but a few.[93]

At this point it appeared that the actions of unionists were the greatest threat to the future of the union with Britain.

The success of the workers' strike contributed to a further cooling in relations between the Dublin and London governments. Some members of the coalition government, including Garret Fitzgerald, blamed Rees's refusal to use the Army against the strikers as the reason for the failure.[94] The South was at this time facing its own internal security issues. Just as the impact of the workers' strike was starting to be felt, there were bombs in the Republic. On 17 May three bombs exploded in Dublin and one in Monaghan, all at rush hour. No warnings were given. Thirty-three civilians and one unborn child were killed, making it the most violent single day of the conflict. In a television interview later that day, Liam Cosgrave said, 'I do not know which evil men did this but everyone who has practised violence or preached violence or condoned violence must bear his share of responsibility. It will bring home to us what the people of Northern Ireland have been suffering for five long years.'[95] Both the IRA and the UDA denied responsibility for the bombs. The Provisional IRA called the explosions 'vile murder'. The UDA Press Officer, Samuel Smyth, declared 'I am very happy about the bombings in Dublin. There is a war with the Free State and now we are laughing at them.'[96]

Regardless of their denial of responsibility, in the public mind the bombs were linked with the Provisional IRA. Only two months earlier they had murdered the most prominent Protestant member of the *Oireachtas*, Senator Billy Fox, at his home in County Cavan. Some members of the Irish government used the latest bombings as a vehicle to condemn IRA violence, even suggesting that what had happened was an inevitable part of a republican plot to bring down Cosgrave's government.[97] Republican sympathizers were also condemned. In the Dáil, the Taoiseach asked:

> What do they hope to gain? What does any man of violence in these islands hope to gain? For the blood of the innocent victims of last Friday's outrage – and of the victims of similar outrages in the North and in England – is on the hands of every man who has fired a gun or discharged a bomb in furtherance of the present campaign of violence in these islands – just as plainly as it is on the hands of those who parked the cars and set the charges last Friday. In our times, violence cannot be contained in neat compartments and justified in one case but not in another.[98]

The coalition government, however, played down the brutality of the atrocity, suggesting that they were seeking to distance themselves from the conflict:

Only in a few instances did politicians visit the families or wounded. There was no national day of mourning as there had been for Bloody Sunday. A decision was even taken, but quickly reversed, that the National Flag should not be flown at half-mast. (In the event, the National Flag flew at half-mast in Dublin and Monaghan town on Wednesday, 22 May.) There was no Government initiative to set up a fund for the dependants of those murdered. There was no consultation with the families and no counselling provided. No progress reports on the investigation were provided by the Gardaí to the families.[99]

The consequence of this distancing was to cause further anguish for the families of the victims and the injured.[100]

Two decades later the UVF and the UDA claimed responsibility for having planted the bombs. Collusion with members of British Intelligence and the RUC was also suggested.[101] In the short term, the Irish government used the bombs to justify a further crackdown on republicanism within the state. At this stage a major fear of the Coalition government was that Wilson might decide to withdraw from Northern Ireland, which, according to Garret Fitzgerald, the Minister for Foreign Affairs, might 'be followed by full scale civil war and anarchy in Northern Ireland, with inevitable disastrous repercussions for our state as well as for the North – and possibly also for Great Britain itself'.[102] On 28 November the Irish government introduced legislation allowing people to be tried for offences committed outside the jurisdiction of the Republic of Ireland. This coincided with the passing of the Prevention of Terrorism Act by the British Parliament.

Following the fall of the Northern Ireland Assembly, there were a number of attempts to find a political alternative to the Executive. In July 1974 a White Paper, *The Northern Ireland Constitution*, written by Rees, was published. It outlined plans for a Constitutional Convention to be elected to consider the most effective ways by which Northern Ireland could be governed. The over-arching theme of this paper was on the need for consensus:

History has caused divisions within the Northern Ireland community. Events of the past few years have amply demonstrated that no part of that community can, let alone should, be coerced into accepting the others' view. Events have also shown that a consensus can be obtained on the basis of serving the interests of the whole community. There must be some form of power-sharing and partnership because no political system will survive, or be supported, unless there is widespread acceptance of it within the community. There must be participation by the whole community.[103]

Around the time of publication of the White Paper, there was dialogue between various political groupings: the UDA offered to meet with the Provisional IRA; Sinn Féin offered to hold talks with the UWC; and the SDLP held talks with the UDA. Unofficially, the Northern Ireland Office was encouraging meetings between what they referred to as 'extremist groups'. Rees informed Wilson that:

Since then [12 July 1974] moves to promote contacts between loyalist and republican paramilitary groups have continued. They were instigated initially by Andy Tyrie, Chairman of the UDA (without the knowledge of many of his supporters), and now involve a part at least of the leaderships of the Official and the Provisional IRA.

[At] A recent conference of the three groups, attended by over 60 of their members . . . there was a certain amount of camaraderie . . .

We are keeping ourselves well informed and providing modest unattributable support.[104]

Political regroupings were taking place elsewhere. In September the Unionist Party endorsed Enoch Powell, a brilliant but controversial member of the Conservative Party, as a candidate. Brian Faulkner, in an attempt to revive his political career, launched his own party, the Unionist Party of Northern Ireland. Changes were also occurring within republicanism. On 8 December the Irish Republican Socialist Party was formed following a split within Official Sinn Féin. Its leadership included Bernadette McAliskey (formerly Devlin).

On 10 October 1974 Harold Wilson called a General Election in the United Kingdom in an attempt to bolster support for his party within Parliament. Labour gained eighteen seats. In Northern Ireland the United Ulster Unionist Council won ten of the twelve seats.

Enoch Powell was returned for South Down. The Social Democratic and Labour Party held the seat of West Belfast and an Independent Nationalist took the seat from Harry West in Fermanagh/South Tyrone. In both 1974 General Elections the Unionists refused to support the Conservative Party Whip, as had traditionally been the case.

Violence

As usual, the backdrop to the attempts to find a political solution was violence. With each death resulting from the conflict that Rees reported to Parliament he became more optimistic, believing that 'London and Dublin were never going to solve anything and that the eventual solution could only be found in the North. He believed that the changed nature of the violence which had started with Bloody Sunday meant that terrorism was institutionalised.'[105] From the republican perspective, however, state violence was just as reprehensible. A report released in May responded to the Irish government's complaints to the European Commission of Human Rights regarding the British government's treatment of internees in the North. The hearings, which had been held in private, concluded that the treatment of internees was inhuman, but did not constitute torture. Nationalists regarded this verdict as arising from the desire not to inflame tensions in the North further.[106]

There was also some concern about the treatment in British jails of republican prisoners, who did not have the same rights as those in prisons in Northern Ireland. A number responded by going on hunger strike to demand an end to solitary confinement, education instead of prison work and a date for transfer to a prison in Ireland. On 3 June Michael Gaughan, a member of the PIRA from County Mayo, died in Parkhurst Prison after refusing food for 64 days. He had been repeatedly force-fed. His body was returned to Mayo for burial and thousands turned out to pay their respects to him, a fact that alarmed the Coalition government.[107] Five days after Gaughan's death, the Price sisters, also republican prisoners, ended their hunger strike in Brixton Prison: this had lasted six months, during which time they had been force-fed by the prison authorities. Neil Blaney had·raised the matter of republican prisoners in England in the Dáil, pointing to the length of their sentences and the way in which they were treated once in prison. He asked for them to be repatriated. The ensuing debate revealed the attitudes of the Coalition government to anybody expressing sympathy with the IRA. Blaney was accused by Garret Fitzgerald of having 'selective sympathy'. In a heated discussion, Fitzgerald repeatedly referred to Blaney as an 'armchair republican'. Despite multiple interruptions (mostly from Blaney), Fitzgerald concluded his statement by saying that any campaign to support prisoners in England would postpone the prospect for peace because it would allow:

> the Provisional IRA to continue a little longer their lethal campaign against the Irish people and also postpones it by giving the impression to the suffering people of Northern Ireland that many in the Republic care more for the voluntary sufferings of guilty prisoners than they care for the involuntary sufferings of innocent people in the North.

He went on to say:

> the prisoners themselves are victims, victims in part of our unhappy history, victims of the distortions by the myth-makers who for so long have plagued our country; victims of the armchair Republicans who encouraged and aided the emergence of the Provisional IRA.

He also accused the 'armchair republicans' and 'myth-makers' of staying 'secure and well cushioned in this Republic and indeed in the seats of Dáil Éireann'.[108]

Within Britain, anger towards the IRA increased as their bombing campaign there intensified in 1974. A brutal incident took place on 4 February when a coach, carrying mostly off-duty soldiers and their families from Manchester to an army base in Yorkshire, was blown up on the M62 motorway. Eleven people, including two children, were killed; four days later the toll increased when an eighteen-year-old soldier died from his injuries. An ambulance official said, 'You can't imagine a thing like this on a British road. How could it have happened?'[109] In November Judith Ward received twelve concurrent life sentences for the bombing. She had also confessed to two other bombing incidents. The IRA denied her involvement in the bombing and her friends described her as a fantasist and an 'IRA groupie'.[110] Ward was released in 1992, her conviction overturned when the Appeal Court ruled that government forensic scientists had withheld information that could have changed the course of her trial.

On 17 June a bomb exploded at Westminster Hall in London; eleven people were injured. The following month there were bombs in Manchester and Birmingham, and a lethal one at the Tower of London. A major attack took place on 5 October 1974 when the Provisional IRA planted bombs in two public houses in Guildford, Surrey. Five people died and 65 were injured. The pubs, the Horse and Groom and the Seven Stars, were targeted because they were frequented by off-duty British soldiers. David Howell, former Minister for Northern Ireland, described his horror at the injuries caused by the bombs, 'I'm afraid I thought I'd seen the last of this in Belfast. It's quite clear that we must hunt down the maniacs and the animals who would do this kind of thing.'[111]

Despite public outrage in England against the IRA, the bombing campaign continued. On 21 November bombs planted in pubs in Birmingham killed 21 and injured almost 200. The dead and injured were primarily teenagers. Although a warning had been given, the police had had insufficient time to clear the area.[112] The Home Secretary, Roy Jenkins, described the carnage as 'a different order of casualties from anything we previously had known'. Public opinion was enraged, and the anger was not directed only towards the IRA. *The Sun*, the British tabloid newspaper, had a headline saying, 'It's War'. A number of Irish-owned pubs, shops and homes were attacked with firebombs. A traveller was man-handled by other passengers in a subway near Charing Cross station, London, when it was discovered he was Irish.[113]

Under pressure to act against the IRA, on 25 November the group was declared illegal in the United Kingdom. Furthermore, 180 hours after the Birmingham bombs had been detonated, the government rushed through the Prevention of Terrorism Act, initially for a period of only six months, but it continued in force for decades.[114] In the opinion of the Home Secretary, such a 'draconian' measure was 'unprecedented in peace time'. One of its provisions allowed for people from Northern Ireland to be excluded from Britain, thus denying them rights of citizenship. The American magazine *Time* commented that 'Some of the measures may be more effective in placating public opinion than in dealing with the I.R.A.'[115] But even this measure was not enough to satisfy some and, under duress, Jenkins agreed to a parliamentary debate on introducing the death penalty for terrorists, although the motion was defeated. A few months after the Birmingham bombings, six men were convicted for this offence. The convictions were overturned in 1991.[116]

As legislation was being implemented to outlaw the Provisional IRA, their representatives were involved in secret meetings with leading Protestant clergymen in Feackle in County Clare. The clergymen had prepared a policy document that, according to Tim Pat Coogan, had been cleared by the British government in advance. The meeting ended abruptly when the IRA received news that the Irish police were about to arrest them. This initiative was not universally welcomed. Paisley referred to the ministers as 'those fickle, Feackle clergy'.[117] Nevertheless, an outcome of the meeting was an IRA ceasefire over Christmas.[118]

In the run-up to Christmas, however, train stations, pubs and the Harrods and Selfridges department stores in London were bombed. On 22 December a bomb was thrown at the London home of Ted Heath; he was not present at the time. Wilson sent him a note saying, 'This attack will only strengthen our united resolve to bring these things to justice.'[119] The following day Heath visited Northern Ireland to show his support for a revival of power-sharing. The IRA Christmas truce came into effect at midnight on 22 December. It lasted until January and during that time the IRA had secret talks with the Labour government. The latter was guarded when referring to these meetings, saying, 'while there was no negotiation with Provisional IRA we did not rule out an exchange of views. We did not want a propaganda campaign . . . If the truce held HMG could take some definite steps . . .'[120] After meeting with the IRA, Wilson had discussions with four religious leaders, Archbishop Dr Simms, Dr Temple Lundie, Rev. Harold Sloan and Rev. Donald Fraser. Wilson's note of their meeting recorded: 'The Church leaders had planted a fragile tree (which one might call a Christmas tree) in the desert of terrorism and we must consider how this tree could be watered.'[121]

The talks were a peaceful ending to a violent year. But as the events that led to the fall of the Executive showed, militant unionists were a powerful force in the province and peace was not possible without their cooperation.

Poets and Myth-Makers

The role of artists and writers as chroniclers of the troubles remained ambiguous. According to one professor of literature, 'As violence increasingly devastated public spaces and private lives, amongst writers and critics debate over the intersection of literature and politics, the responsibilities of artists and the function of art became ever more pressing.'[122] For the poet Michael Longley the responsibility of the artist arose from the fact that: 'To write carelessly and self-indulgently in a place like Northern Ireland could have terrible consequences. I do speak occasionally on radio and television in a measured way, mindful of how much some fellow-citizens have suffered.'[123]

In 1975 Seamus Heaney published *North*, which was an attempt to come to terms with the outbreak of violence in the North and the ongoing cultural crisis.[124] At this stage, Heaney had relocated to County Wicklow in the Republic. His collection included 'Whatever you say, say nothing', which was a poem based on an imagined interview with a journalist who wanted a quick insight into 'the Irish thing'. The poem also described the fears and the silences that were permeating society in Northern Ireland, where so much remained unsaid and where minds remained closed. This literary reticence was explored by the editors of the Belfast-based journal *Threshold*:

> Being political, they say
> Is not poetical
> Neither is it practical
> And does not rhyme
> At this time.[125]

The silence identified in these poems was mirrored in the halls of academia, especially in the writing of Irish history. Many Irish academics, in fact, denied that Northern Ireland had a colonial relationship with Britain, which distorted their interpretation of the reasons for the conflict.[126] Yet, according to David Miller, 'The colonial dimension is a fundamental part of the conflict in Ireland and this has been ignored by the vast majority of academics writing on Northern Ireland'.[127] Since the 1930s, the writing of Irish history had been dominated by an orthodoxy know as 'revisionism'. Helped by the small number of universities in Ireland, they were able to stamp their authority on higher education. Initially, revisionism had sought to write a value-free account of Irish history, one that destroyed the myths of nationalist narrative.[128] The onset of the Troubles, however, provided a political impetus to destroy a coherent nationalist narrative of Irish history, which they feared would give support to the 'armchair republicans' and 'myth-makers' identified by Garret Fitzgerald. One of the topics of contestation for revisionists and their opponents was the Famine, discussion of which, they argued, would give 'ideological bullets' to the IRA.[129] As Miller concluded, 'the writing on Northern Ireland has been fundamentally distorted by the colonial relationships which are of major importance in the origins and current form of the conflict in Ireland'.[130] Revisionism, however, had many supporters on both sides of politics, and it provided a scholarly basis for not engaging with the violence in the North, or seeing it as part of a longer-term struggle. Censorship within the Irish media, therefore, was accompanied by self-censorship by many writers and scholars regarding the conflict in Northern Ireland.

FIVE

Stalemate

The year 1975 commenced relatively peacefully in Ireland and Britain. On 2 January the Provisional IRA announced that it would be extending its ceasefire. Secretly it was involved in talks with Harold Wilson's government, a meeting brought together by the intervention of Protestant clergymen. As a gesture of goodwill, and in order to keep the ceasefire in place, the government released twenty internees and paroled 50 prisoners at the beginning of January.[1] However, the peace talks initiated by the church leaders proved to be fragile: the ceasefire ended on 16 January. The bombings and shootings in Northern Ireland and England resumed. The year 1975 was also the year in which the Vietnam War came to an end and the Conservative Party elected its first woman leader. Labour had won two elections in 1974, but inflation and unemployment had continued to rise in Britain – the latter passing the symbolic one million mark in autumn 1975. It was not until 1977 that the British economy started to improve, helped by the flow of North Sea oil and a bail-out by the International Monetary Fund.[2] The problems of Northern Ireland for many British people were, therefore, a major and unwanted distraction that was not only a drain on lives, but also on financial resources.

When the Democratic Unionist Party leadership learned of these talks they protested about the government meeting with the IRA. Personal relations between Ian Paisley and Merlyn Rees had become so acrimonious that at one point the mild-mannered Secretary of State had hidden under a table to avoid a further confrontation with the leader of the DUP.[3] Unionists were not the only ones unhappy about these secret talks. In the Republic the Taoiseach feared that, if this became known, it would have a 'traumatic effect' throughout Ireland.[4] The SDLP also disliked the fact that Sinn Féin was playing such a pivotal role in political discussions.[5]

Despite the ceasefire ending, secret talks continued, leading to a second ceasefire on 10 February. One of the IRA's demands was for a bilateral truce with the British Army. Whereas the government was willing, if there was peace, to reduce the army to 'peacetime levels', the IRA wanted complete withdrawal.[6] While the Provisional IRA was involved in high-level negotiations, a deadly feud began between the Official Irish Republican Army and the Irish Republican Socialist Party and its military wing, the Irish National Liberation Army. During the ceasefire, violence continued between loyalists and republicans, with many civilians losing their lives. There was also inter-community conflict. The hostilities between the Official IRA and the INLA intensified. A bloody feud also developed between the UDA and the UVF, while in the two weeks between 29 October and 12 November eleven people died in warfare between the Official IRA and the Provisional IRA.[7] Internecine conflicts amongst paramilitaries were just as lethal as their attacks on other groups.

Inevitably the Troubles had had a negative impact on the economic development of Northern Ireland. This coincided with a decline in heavy industries such as shipbuilding and linen production, two of the province's traditional staple industries. International economic problems, which had a severe impact on the British economy, were exacerbating the situation, with escalating inflation and high oil prices in many parts of Europe. These were having a detrimental effect on the economy of the Republic, where unemployment had reached 90,000, out of a population of over three million. The largest employer in Belfast was the shipbuilder Harland and Wolff. Since 1967 the British government had provided £80,000 in subsidies to keep it solvent. At the beginning of 1975 it became clear that the company's financial difficulties were so severe that the government was considering nationalizing it. Protestant employees had played a key role in the workers' strike in the previous year; only 500 of the workforce, out of a workforce of 10,000, were Catholic. Fearing major political fallout if the shipyard closed, however, the government stepped in with further financial support. Wilson wryly commented, 'We may need to play a very strong unionist card.'[8] It was not just Harland and Wolf that was placing a financial burden on the British taxpayer. Prior to 1970, the level of public service provision in Northern Ireland was far lower than in the rest of the United Kingdom. After 1970 public expenditure grew rapidly, overtaking that of Britain. Because not all of it could be financed from tax revenue raised in the six counties, part of the burden fell on British taxpayers; British subvention grew from less than 10 per cent of Gross Domestic Product in 1970 to 27 per cent in the mid-1980s.[9] It was not just in human lives that years of ignoring Northern Ireland was taking its toll.

As a distraction from the gloomy political news and to take advantage of the IRA ceasefire, in spring a number of civil servants came up with an idea that they named 'Brighten Up Ulster'. Its purpose was to 'inject a brighter mood into the province, highlight the "sunny side of life" in Northern Ireland, bring back mass entertainment and create a "post-war atmosphere and spirit"'.[10] One member of the committee advised that, 'It would be important to think really big. For example, why not have big variety stars – Morecambe and Wise? Frank Sinatra?' Another idea was that 'the Northern Ireland Sports Council could organize an inter-town "It's a Knock-Out" competition with a big name such as Eddie Waring to act as compere'.[11] Other proposals included a beauty pageant – 'Miss Good Cheer' – and the hosting of a number of 'Good Cheer Conferences'. This idea was never implemented, but it suggested that, 'Having tried internment, military might, power sharing and even secret talks with the IRA, the government considered one last desperate measure to dig themselves out of the escalating war in Northern Ireland – Morecambe and Wise.'[12] While trying to introduce normality to life in Northern Ireland, the same civil servants were carrying out a propaganda war against the IRA based on 'a concerted PR/information campaign aimed at isolating the Provisional leadership and movement from the remainder of the Catholic community'.[13]

At the end of January 1975 the Gardiner Report had been published. Its remit had been to look at how to deal with terrorism 'in the context of civil liberties and human rights'.[14] The report noted, 'In Northern Ireland memories are long, and past oppression serves to colour present experience.'[15] It criticized some Irish communities overseas for helping sustain violence by supporting paramilitary organizations.[16] It also had harsh words to say of 'terrorists' in Northern Ireland:

> they command the support of only a small fraction of either the minority or the majority community in Northern Ireland. Because they are attempting to destroy Northern

Ireland as a political society, terrorists who break the law – which in Northern Ireland gives greater protection to the accused than in most disturbed communities – are not heroes but criminals; not the pioneers of political change but its direst enemies.[17]

The report recommended a number of significant changes, in respect of internment and Special Category Status. In regard to the former, it deemed, 'it creates a myth of oppression which is part of the terrorist legend'.[18] It regarded the introduction of Special Category Status as 'a serious mistake', and recommended that it should be brought to an end as quickly as was practicable.[19] High-ranking officers in the Army agreed that it should be ended. Lieutenant General Sir Frank King, the Commanding Officer in Northern Ireland, said that 'Special Category Status was objectionable from the point of view of security. It was an aid to the recruitment of terrorists.'[20] On 4 November 1975 Merlyn Rees announced that anybody convicted of terrorist crimes after 1 March 1976 would not be granted Special Category Status. This viewing of paramilitaries as criminals was to be a key part of government policy in Ireland in the following decade.

Elections for the Constitutional Convention were held on 1 May. The Convention's purpose was to recommend 'what provisions for the government of Northern Ireland is likely to command the most widespread acceptance throughout the community there'. The election was a victory for the United Ulster Unionist Council (UUUC), an umbrella group for three unionist parties, all of whom were anti-power-sharing. They won 46 of the 78 seats. The elections revealed the weakness of Faulkner's own position within unionism, as his Unionist Party of Northern Ireland won only five seats. Ian Paisley's Democratic Unionist Party, in contrast, won twelve seats and possibly could have won more if they had fielded more candidates.

Carrying on a trend evident in Northern Irish politics, only four women were elected to the Convention, and they were all unionist: Anne Dickson (UPNI, South Antrim), Eileen Paisley (DUP, East Belfast), Jean Coulter (UUP, West Belfast) and Sheena Conn (UUP, Derry). All four had also been elected to the Assembly in 1973.[21] The Convention held its first meeting on 8 May. A confidential memo by the British government noted that there was 'a good deal of scope for agreement' between the UUUC and the SDLP, although they realized that this was largely because they had skirted around significant constitutional issues.[22] This cooperation appeared to offer some hope when William Craig made a suggestion that there should be a Voluntary Coalition between the UUUC and the SDLP. Privately some members of British government suspected his motives, warning:

> Mr Craig appears to some as a knight in shining armour. The fact is that his aims were – and still are – simple: to get a devolved government which would control security policy as quickly as possible, on the basis of a gentleman's agreement that the SDLP would participate in government for a year or two.[23]

On 8 September the UUUC rejected the proposed package by 37 votes to one – the single vote in favour being cast by William Craig. The report produced by the Convention inevitably reflected the UUUC policy. A memo written by a senior political adviser highlighted the frustration of the Wilson government when he warned that 'a permanent Protestant regime would certainly have many unpleasant characteristics', moreover, 'more of the Catholic population might be driven actively to sympathise with the IRA; it is not a risk but a bloody certainty'.[24] The Convention reported on 20 November, but it was effectively dead and had achieved nothing. Northern Ireland was again governed by direct rule. At this stage the British government appeared to be running out of options and ideas. William Craig paid the price for his suggestion of an alliance with the SDLP. On 12 October he was expelled from the UUUC and the Vanguard Party went into rapid decline. The last ten years had demonstrated that unionists who showed that they were willing to compromise with Catholics were no longer welcome in the Party. Craig's demise also reinforced the ascendancy of Ian Paisley as the voice of uncompromising unionism.

Once again, attempts to find a constitutional solution took place against a backdrop of violence. A feature of the conflict in 1975 was the increase in attacks by the UVF and other loyalist groups, although in part this was internecine as a deadly feud developed between the UDA and the UVF. Both on the streets and in Stormont, unionism was showing how fractured it had become. On 31 July a particularly vicious killing took place when a coach carrying the popular Miami

Showband was stopped at a false checkpoint; three members of the band were shot dead and the others wounded. The murders were gratuitous: the lead singer, Fran O'Toole, was shot in the face 22 times. It was speculated that the band were targeted in revenge for the recent killing of Protestants who had attended a dog show. Initially, however, their deaths were ascribed to a splinter group of the IRA.[25] There seemed to be no end to tit-for-tat killings; clearly the ceasefire had not stopped the violence. On 1 September five Protestant civilians were killed in an attack on an Orange Hall in Newtownhamilton by a group calling themselves the South Armagh Republican Action Force. On 2 October twelve people died as a result of UVF activity: eight civilians and four members of the UVF were blown up by the bomb they were transporting. The following day the government responded to the increase in loyalist activity by banning the UVF.[26]

On the same day that the UVF was proscribed, Dr Tiede Herrema, chief executive of the Dutch-owned Ferenka factory in County Limerick, was abducted and held hostage in Monasterevin, County Kildare.[27] It made international headlines. In return for his release, the IRA wanted three republicans to be freed from jail. This was refused. Secretly the Dutch government believed that action by the Irish police was thwarting any rescue plan and they pleaded with the Irish government to allow more negotiations, including using a leading Irish trade unionist as an intermediary.[28] Herrema was released on 6 November after 27 days' imprisonment and his kidnappers were arrested. Despite his trauma, Dr Herrema looked 'calm and collected' at his news conference. He described his captors, Eddie Gallagher and Marion Coyle, as 'children with a lot of problems'.[29] He also believed that their sentences of 25 and 20 years imprisonment were too long. Garret Fitzgerald, the Minister of Foreign Affairs, however, explained that 'if the kidnapping had not been successfully resolved, Ireland's industrial development could have been badly damaged'.[30]

Although the IRA ceasefire did not officially end until January 1976, seventeen bombs were detonated across Northern Ireland on the morning of 22 September 1975. The Belfast Provisional IRA claimed responsibility. A statement from the Republican Press Centre explained that the bombs were reprisal for the actions of the security forces. Rees described the ceasefire declared seven months earlier as a 'travesty and mockery'.[31] In England, also, Provisional

IRA activity had continued intermittently throughout the ceasefire. In August 1975 there had been a cluster of IRA bombings in the south of England that intensified following the collapse of the IRA's ceasefire. At the forefront of the renewed campaign was a four-man group who became known as the Balcombe Street Gang. They detonated ten devices in just five days. In November they killed Ross McWhirter, a founder and co-editor of *The Guinness Book of Records* and sup- porter of the Conservative Party. He had recently offered £50,000 for information leading to the arrest of members of the IRA. He was shot at close range in the head and chest.[32] Following a failed attack on a Mayfair restaurant, the four men took two local residents hostage (in an apartment on Balcombe Street, Marylebone) and began a tense stand-off with the police. After six days, the four men surrendered, thus providing a major victory to the security forces. The men were charged with ten murders and twenty bombings and were jailed for life. During their trial, they claimed responsibility for the Guildford pub bombings and another incident in Woolwich, but these attacks were not included in the final list of charges.[33]

As government surveillance became more intense, the tactics of the Provisional IRA became more sophisticated. In the late 1970s they reorganized into 'cells' and placed small teams in England who, if caught, could not compromise the whole movement. Privately the British security forces recognized that it was dealing with a highly developed and dedicated organization.[34] Moreover, despite the Government's propaganda campaign, the organization still had sympathy and support outside Ireland, especially in the USA, which provided an estimated 75 per cent of the money used to provide arms, ammunition and explosives. In addition, between 1971 and 1974 the Provisional IRA had stolen an estimated 6,900 weapons and 1.2 million rounds of ammunition from American military bases.[35] In December, Harold Wilson made an unprecedented intervention when he attacked 'misguided Irish-American supporters' of the IRA, and suggested that American funds were largely responsible for the violence in Northern Ireland. He cited the Northern Ireland Aid Committee as the main fund-raising organization. He added, 'When they contribute their dollars for the old country, they are not help- ing their much-loved shamrock to flower. They are splashing blood on it.' The committee, which had its headquarters in the Bronx, New York, insisted that its fund-raising was on behalf of Catholic women and children.[36] A victory for the British government took place on

22 December 1975 when five Americans of Irish descent were indicted for attempting to ship weapons to the IRA.[37] Irish-American support continued, nevertheless. In his address to the two houses of Congress in Washington the following March, the Taoiseach, Liam Cosgrave, criticized the supply of money to Northern Ireland for arms. His intervention drew praise from Ian Paisley.[38]

Even as it seemed that the violence could not get worse, it did. Towards the end of 1975 two new groups emerged within the UVF: the Shankill Butchers and the Red Hand Commandos. The latter proved their deadliness on 19 December 1975 when they killed five Catholics, including one aged only fourteen, in two separate attacks. A feature of these and a number of other loyalist attacks was the suspicion of collusion by the security forces.[39] The year ended violently. On the last day of December three Protestant civilians were killed in a bomb attack carried out by the People's Republican Army, a cover name used by the Irish National Liberation Army, on the Central Bar, Gilford, County Down. This brought the total of those who had died in Northern Ireland during 1975 as a result of the conflict to 247, including 174 civilians.[40]

The year was significant for another reason. On 29 August 1975 Éamon de Valera had died, aged 92. His long political life had pre-dated the 1916 Rising and he had remained involved in politics until shortly before his death. He had founded the Fianna Fáil Party in 1926, and it had become the most successful party in the Republic. Increasingly, though, he had turned his back on militant republicanism. De Valera had served as both Taoiseach and President of Ireland, finally leaving office only in 1973. A nun who was nursing him reported that he whispered before he died, 'All my life I have done my best for Ireland; now I am ready to go.'[41] His death was mourned by Irish communities throughout the world, particularly in the United States where President Ford described de Valera as a 'symbol of Ireland'.[42] However, de Valera had failed in both of his 'cherished aims': to end the partition of Ireland and to restore the Irish language.[43] Moreover, during his terms in power, the economy had stagnated and mass emigration had continued. Like Daniel O'Connell, he had allied his vision of Irish nationalism with the Catholic Church, and by doing so had ignored the aspirations and anxieties of Irish Protestants. During his lifetime the divisions created by the partition in 1920 had become more entrenched. Nonetheless, de Valera's death marked the end of a political era.

In 1976 the death toll rose again, with 307 killed (220 of them civilians). It was to prove to be the second heaviest year for casualties in the Troubles.[44] The beginning of the year started as violently as the previous year had ended with horrendous reprisal murders. On 4 January six Catholics were shot dead in their homes; the following day, ten Protestants civilians were killed at Kingsmill and a member of the security forces was murdered in County Derry. Even by Northern Ireland standards, these murders were shocking and tougher action was called for, leading to the deployment of the Special Air Service in south Armagh, following a television announcement to this effect by Harold Wilson. In fact, the SAS had been operating covertly in Northern Ireland since 1973, when they had been asked to set up a new undercover unit for surveillance operations known as 14 Intelligence Company.[45] Wilson's actions placed the usually secret unit in the public eye and was indicative of a tougher approach to security. Shortly after their arrival, on 23 January, the IRA ceasefire was ended, although secret negotiations continued between the Provisional IRA and the British government.

In order to be seen doing something to fill the political vacuum, in January 1976 Harold Wilson pronounced that no British government would ever impose a united Ireland, indicating that his views had changed from a few years earlier. Privately he feared that a loyalist declaration of independence was imminent and the consequence would be surrendering the minority population, particularly the peaceable Catholic element, to anything that majority extremists might choose to inflict upon them.[46] To maintain the political momentum, Rees announced that the Convention would be reconvened at the beginning of February, for a period of four weeks. Robert Lowry, the Lord Chief Justice of Northern Ireland, was to be the Chairman. In this role Lowry went out of his way to work with the various factions, even sending a hand-written note to each of the 78 members. He also prepared a proposal for a voluntary coalition, as distinct from imposed power-sharing, an idea later taken up by William Craig.[47] Although the Convention limped along for a month, its demise was inevitable when the UUUC refused to agree to any SDLP involvement in any future Cabinet, which had been a stipulation by Rees. The government formally closed the proceedings of the Convention on 5 March 1976, thus bringing to an end the latest failed attempt at constitutional politics and power-sharing. Unofficially, negotiations were continuing between the government and Sinn Féin, although this was formally denied by Rees, who made a distinction between 'talks' and 'negotiations'. He was accused by Airey Neave of the Conservative Party and by unionists of giving 'political credibility' to Sinn Féin. Rees admitted that, in his opinion, political agreement alone would not end the conflict as 'The nature of the violence has changed. The ability of a very small number of people in the Province to cause trouble is much greater than I thought.'[48] Rees's pessimistic message held out little hope for an end to violence or direct rule in Northern Ireland. His fears were shared by the government in Dublin. At a meeting of high-ranking Irish officials in January, it had been concluded that the Convention would fail and that paramilitary organizations would take the place of politicians. It was also noted that Ian Paisley had become the dominant figure in the loyalist community.[49]

In June Ian Paisley revealed that the DUP had held secret talks with the SDLP. It was later announced by Paisley that Martin Smyth, Grand Master of the Orange Order since 1972, was doing a similar thing.[50] On 7 June, however, the United Ulster Unionist Council voted to oppose any talks between the Ulster Unionist Party and the SDLP. Faulkner's announcement of his resignation from politics on 18 August 1976 marked the end of an era; his own political journey had taken him from unionist supremacy, to liberal unionism, to power sharing, and finally to being out-of-power and out-of-favour. On 11 November the Ulster Loyalist Central Co-ordinating Committee issued a plan for setting up an Independent Northern Ireland. Consensus, however, could not even be reached within various political groupings: on 4 December 1976, for example, the SDLP debated a motion calling on Britain to declare its intention of withdrawing from Northern Ireland, but this was defeated by 158 votes to 111. The future of Northern Ireland appeared no clearer than in the years following the collapse of Sunningdale. Yet again, constitutional politics had lost their direction. Street politics, however, remained as brutal as ever.

In October 1976 Stephen McCann, a 21-year-old Catholic student, founder member of the Witness for Peace movement and author of the song 'What Price Peace?', was abducted and killed in Belfast by members of the Shankill Butchers. His head was severed and his body rearranged in such a way as to make his multiple wounds obvious.[51] In total, the Shankill Butchers were responsible for the torture, mutilation and murder of nineteen Catholics. A gruesome tribute to their activities was penned by Belfast-born poet Michael Longley. In 'The Butchers', he used Homer's *Odyssey* to provide a framework for the current situation. The gratuitous violence that Longley described historically – cutting off 'his nose and ears and cock and balls'[52] – had resonance with contemporary gratuitous violence. In both contexts, the mutilation was shocking. Longley later described the poem as 'a cleansing, a catharsis. I was purging feelings of distaste – distaste for Northern Ireland and its filthy sectarianism.'[53]

Violence was not confined to Northern Ireland and many of the killings in the Republic were just as sectarian. On 29 November 1975 a small loyalist bomb exploded in Dublin airport, killing one employee. On 19 December a car bomb was detonated without warning outside a pub in the centre of Dundalk, County Louth. Two men died and 21 people were injured. The Provisional IRA was blamed, although it subsequently appeared that the explosives used had been stolen from the IRA. On 7 March 1976 Patrick Mone, a 56-year-old farmer, was killed when a loyalist bomb exploded in County Monaghan. On Sunday 2 May 1976 Seamus Ludlow, a Catholic civilian from Dundalk, County Louth, was abducted and murdered. The IRA was initially blamed, but it later appeared that loyalists, probably the Red Hand Commandos in collusion with the UDR, were responsible.[54] These, and many other murders that took place in the Republic, were later shown to have been perpetrated by loyalists, assisted by members of the security forces.[55]

The Provisional IRA was also engaged in violent activities in the Republic and their campaign now included targeting politicians. On 15 July an explosion in the Special Criminal Court in Dublin allowed five republicans to escape from the basement in which they were being held. A high-profile murder took place only a week later, when, on 21 July 1976, the British Ambassador to Ireland, Christopher Ewart Biggs, was killed in a landmine attack on his official car in Sandyford, Dublin. His secretary, Judith Cook, was also killed in the explosion. Liam Cosgrave's government was shocked at this latest murder. The British government, in turn, was eager to exploit the Irish government's embarrassment.[56] The outcome was that even more repressive legislation was introduced in the Republic aimed at the IRA. The Dáil was recalled on 31 August, 'to consider emergency measures for the purposes of securing the public safety'. The explosions at the Special Criminal Court in Dublin and the murder of the British Ambassador and his Private Secretary were provided as justification for this intervention. When introducing the measure, the Taoiseach said that,

> arising out of the armed conflict now taking place in Northern Ireland, a national emergency exists affecting the vital interests of the State.
>
> I believe the terms of this motion clearly indicate the Government's view of the gravity of the situation which led me to request you to summon a special meeting of the House to consider emergency measures for the purpose of securing the public safety. The measures which we deem to be necessary to meet the situation comprise the motion I have just moved and legislative proposals contained in the Emergency Powers Bill, 1976 and the Criminal Law Bill, 1976.[57]

Cosgrave's prognosis was gloomy, declaring that there was 'no end in sight' while a 'horrifying series of counter-assassinations and counter-bombings resulted in the ghastly spiral of tit-for-tat killings'. The main power that was being sought was for an extension of the period of detention, to seven days, for persons suspected of connection with serious crimes, or suspected of being in possession of evidence or information regarding such offences. The Criminal Law Bill provided for a new offence of encouraging or persuading a person to join or assist in the activities of an unlawful organization. The bill was opposed by Fianna Fáil, led by Jack Lynch, who regarded it as a device for bolstering support for the coalition government and warned that it would worsen the situation. For some parliamentary critics, the bill was an over-reaction that would have a detrimental effect on inward investment and tourism.[58] Controversially, the Irish President referred the Emergency Powers Bill to the Supreme Court, where it was passed.[59] The bill was signed into legislation at midnight on 16 October 1976, but the new legislation did not stop IRA activities. A few hours later Michael Clerkin, a member of the Gardai who had been lured to an abandoned farmhouse near Portlaoise, County Laois, was killed by a booby-trap bomb; one of his colleagues was left both deaf and blind. The IRA claimed responsibility.[60] On the following day the Minister for Defence, Paddy Donegan, angered at the death of Garda Clerkin, called President Cearbhall Ó Dálaigh a 'thundering disgrace' due to his actions regarding the Emergency Powers Bill. This accusation led to the President tendering his resignation. Initially the Taoiseach refused to accept it, but Ó Dálaigh finally resigned on 22 October 1976, 'to protect the dignity and independence of the presidency as an institution'.[61] Clearly, the conflict was having an impact on even the highest levels of office in the Republic.

A consequence of the more draconian legislation was a hunger strike by republicans in Portlaoise Prison. It commenced on 1 March 1977, with twenty IRA prisoners refusing food. They wanted a public enquiry into the brutal way in which they were treated. They also demanded political status.[62] A hunger strike instigated by the INLA in the same prison two years earlier had been called off when government officials agreed to meet with the hunger strikers or their representatives, and a compromise had been reached.[63] The political atmosphere in 1977, however, was more uncompromising than it had been even two years earlier. Unlike in earlier hunger strikes, the prisoners were kept in isolation and denied visits by their families.[64] The treatment of the prisoners was criticized by the Bishop of Kildare and Leighlin, Patrick Lennon, whose diocese included Portlaoise. The Coalition government was also condemned by Bishop Daly of Derry for denying him permission to visit the prison – although, as he pointed out, he could freely visit those in the North.[65] The strike lasted for 47 days and ended through the intervention of Bishop James Kavanagh of Dublin. The strike had not achieved its aims,[66] but it had shown how far the political climate in Ireland had changed within a short space of time. It also demonstrated that increasingly repressive measures were not the solution to the armed struggle.

Borders

The ability of loyalist and republican paramilitaries to move freely across the border meant that patrolling it was a sensitive issue for both the British and Irish governments. In October 1975 two soldiers in the Irish Army, dressed in plain clothes, crossed into Northern Ireland on their way to the Crossmaglen area. They were apprehended by the security forces and found to have a Republic of Ireland Army .22 rifle in the boot of their car. No official protest was made to the Irish government on the grounds that 'The Royal Ulster

Constabulary questioned the man found in possession of the rifle and were satisfied with his explanation that he had forgotten to remove it from the boot of his car when he returned from a hunting expedition in the Republic on the previous day.'[67]

In March 1976 SAS soldiers crossed the border and abducted Seán McKenna, an IRA commander, from his home in Dundalk, before handing him over to a British Army patrol on the northern side of the border. This marked the beginning of a number of actions against the Provisional IRA that gave the unit the nickname of the Special Assassination Squad.[68] On 5 May 1976 eight members of the SAS were arrested in the Republic of Ireland. They were dressed in civilian clothes but were armed with machine guns, handguns, a pump-action shotgun and a dagger. The official explanation was that the soldiers had made a map-reading error and accidentally crossed the border. While in custody, the men were questioned about recent murders in the border areas. Privately the British government was exerting enormous pressure on the Irish government to drop the charges against the men, and was even considering stopping Irish immigration to Britain, and revoking social security and voting rights from the community that was already there. They also threatened to remove British Army patrols from along the border and warned of a loyalist backlash. These men were eventually each fined £100 in a Dublin court for carrying guns without a certificate.[69]

While war was continuing to be waged in Ireland, significant changes were taking place for imprisoned republicans. Internment had ended on 5 December 1975. Under its terms 1,981 people had been put behind bars without trial, of whom only 107 were loyalists. The treatment of political prisoners remained a central issue for republicans. In March 1975 Gerry Kelly and Hugh Feeney had been transferred to Long Kesh Prison and the Price sisters were transferred to Armagh Prison. Frank Stagg, however, had been forced to remain in an English jail. Each of these prisoners had been intermittently on hunger strikes and force-fed. Stagg commenced his third hunger strike on 14 December in protest at the government's refusal to transfer him to Northern Ireland: he died on 12 February 1976. Days before his death, at a rally in Belfast, the Vice-President of Sinn Féin, Máire Drumm, had warned:

Frank Stagg's death will be revenged as all our martyrs' deaths have been by the soldiers of *Oglaigh na hEireann*. If they send Frank Stagg home in a coffin I would expect the fighting men of Crossmaglen would send the SAS home in boxes. If Frank Stagg lives or dies the fight goes on. England is still the hangman of the world.[70]

News of his death resulted in rioting in Belfast and Derry.[71]

Stagg's body was returned to Ireland for burial in Ruben Church in County Mayo. Flouting Stagg's own wish, the Irish Special Branch prevented his remains from being buried in the Republican Plot, burying it ten metres away and covering the top with cement to prevent it from being moved. For six months there was a constant Special Branch presence in the cemetery. Neil Blaney, leader of Independent Fianna Fáil, accused the Irish Minister of Justice of using Stagg's burial as a 'provocation' to the IRA. The Minister refused to be drawn on this issue, or to disclose how much the policing operation had cost.[72] The IRA, however, got their revenge: in November a group of IRA men, accompanied by a priest, tunnelled down under the grave and removed the coffin. They reburied it in the Republican Plot, held a short religious service and then fired a volley of shots over the new burial site.[73]

A significant change in the status of paramilitary prisoners came following the ending of Special Category Status on 1 March 1976. After this date, male prisoners were sent to newly constructed buildings in Long Kesh known, because of their shape, as 'H Blocks'. Those convicted before this date remained in special compounds in Nissen huts, separated from the new intake. At the same time, the newly extended Long Kesh Prison was renamed the Maze, to denote a change of direction in dealing with security.[74] These actions formed a crucial part of the government's policy of 'Criminalization'. Ciarán Nugent was the first to be convicted under this new system on 14 September. He refused to wear a prison uniform and so was given a blanket.[75] A new form of protest had commenced.

Following the ending of Special Category Status other measures were introduced that suggested a new stringency in dealing with the conflict that put an emphasis on policing the problem, rather than finding a political solution to it. On 25 March Rees informed the House of Commons of new security measures that were being introduced.[76] In a reversal of the policy of the previous years, the RUC, helped by the Ulster Defence Regiment, was now to take primary responsibility for security in Northern Ireland. To fulfil this role, its numbers were to be increased, while the number of British troops was to be decreased. A few days after these announcements, the Prevention of Terrorism Act was reintroduced for a further year and its provisions were extended. On 1 May Kenneth Newman, an Englishman, replaced Jamie Flanagan as Chief Constable of the RUC, symbolizing the commencement of the new regime.

Despite the tightening up of security, violence intensified over the summer of 1976. The UVF declared a three-month ceasefire on 26 May, although it was not fully observed. Around the same time the United Unionist Action Council was formed, with its own para-military wing, the Ulster Service Corps. The latter was a vigilante group, which announced that it was going to organize patrols in counties Tyrone and Armagh to deal with the deteriorating security situation. Ian Paisley informed the House of Commons that he had taken part in some of the patrols.[77] The British government responded by sending 200 additional troops to Northern Ireland in early June.

In response to an increase in bombings and attacks on the security forces, in June and July further powers were given to the RUC, including the establishment of special investigation teams. When introducing these measures, Rees warned Parliament that violence was on the increase and they had to prepare for a 'long haul'.[78] Overall, this process of de-politicizing the conflict and giving the local security forces primacy over the British Army was referred to 'Ulsterization'. It aimed, among other things, to create a public perception that the conflict was not politically motivated, but criminal.[79] At the same time, the change of policy suggested that the various political initiatives had failed and more stringent security was the replacement.

On 10 August an incident in Belfast inadvertently resulted in the deaths of three children when the British Army shot dead an IRA member and the car that he was driving went out of control. Even in a society that was becoming inured to gratuitous violence, these deaths were shocking. (Their mother took her own life a few years later.) Within two days of the deaths, 6,000 people in the Andersontown area of Belfast had signed a petition calling for peace. Over the following weeks, a number of rallies organized by the children's aunt, Máiread Corrigan, and Betty Williams were held in Northern Ireland and London, calling for peace. By the end of the month up to 25,000 people were participating in the peace marches. Joan Baez attended a large rally in London and sang the international anthem for peace, 'We Shall Overcome'.[80] Initially they called themselves the Women's Peace Movement, but after the leaders were joined by the journalist Ciarán McKeown they became known increasingly as the Peace People.

From the outset the British media approved of the Peace People, even exaggerating numbers that attended the rallies in order to show the impact that the movement was having.[81] It was, however, disliked by republican and loyalist paramilitaries, the former regarding the movement as both pro-British and anti-republican. On 10 October 1977 it was announced that Máiread Corrigan and Betty Williams would receive the Nobel Peace Prize for their work. The Unionist-dominated Belfast City Corporation refused to hold a civic reception in honour of the prizewinners. The associated prize money of £80,000 was later to be the source of controversy within the Peace People; the decision to keep the money was criticized by even their supporters and put a strain on the relationship between the two women.[82] On 5 October 1978 the three leaders of the Peace People – Williams, Corrigan and McKeown – announced that they intended to step down from the organization. Internal squabbles and external criticisms had informed their decision. In the longer term, the movement appeared to have achieved little. One of its impressive achievements, however, was to provide a forum for Catholics and Protestants to come together and to seek a middle ground in the political spectrum.

A change of Prime Minister in Britain on 5 April 1976, with James Callaghan replacing Harold Wilson, did not lead to any immediate shift in policy. In September, however, the mild-mannered Rees was replaced as Secretary of State for Northern Ireland by the more determinedly gung-ho Roy Mason. In his first public appearance, he announced that he would try to improve the situation by reducing unemployment. More significantly, Mason viewed republican activities as simply a security problem and he turned away from attempting to find a 'political solution' to one based on observation of the law. Furthermore, rather than seeing the Provisional IRA as part of the solution, he characterized them as the problem – a problem that could be resolved by a resolute enforcement of the law. Within a few months in office he was stating that his actions 'were without question hurting the IRA'.[83] Like many British officials, he did not see loyalist violence as also being a significant part of the problem in Northern Ireland. Mason was loathed by nationalists for over-relying on a security clampdown and spurning political initiatives. Within a few months of coming to power, Mason oversaw the introduction of the Fair Employment Act, which brought into existence the Fair Employment Agency. Its powers were limited to religious and political discrimination in employment. The Race Relations Act of the same year extended to housing, education, goods and services. Unionists disliked it, believing it would encourage imagined grievances by Catholics. In fact, its power was limited and its chairman, Robert Cooper, a founding member of the Alliance Party, adopted a cautious approach, not wanting to coerce but to persuade people to change.[84] The objectivity of the FEA was questioned by some nationalists. They were also accused of changing reports in order to suggest a lessening in sectarian incidents, when in fact they were increasing.[85]

On 25 December 1976 the Provisional IRA declared a three-day ceasefire. It had been a violent year and a political solution appeared more elusive than ever. Moreover, bloodshed showed no signs of abating in 1977. On the first day of the New Year a fifteen-month-old baby was killed in a car bomb blast near Belfast, and on the same day a British soldier was killed, both by the Provisional IRA. A new element had entered the violence as the IRA increasingly targeted businessmen. This became evident on 2 February 1977, when Jeffrey Agate, Managing Director of the American Du Pont factory in Derry, was shot dead. Two more executives were killed over the next few weeks. The IRA justified their actions by saying 'those executed had played a prominent role in stabilising the British-orientated economy'.[86]

Divisions that had been simmering within various unionist and loyalist groups came to a head in the summer of 1977, when Ian Paisley threatened to call a general strike if Roy Mason did not take tougher action against the IRA. He was supported by the Ulster Workers' Council and the UDA, but condemned by the Vanguard Unionist Party, the Ulster Unionist Party and the Orange Order. Paisley responded by calling for more civil disobedience by Protestants if British policies did not change. In anticipation of the strike, Mason sent 1,200 additional troops to Northern Ireland and cancelled all police leave. The strike commenced on 3 May 1977. It had many of the features of the 1974 strike, including widespread intimidation that extended to a number of shootings of those who continued to work. Unlike the 1974 strike, however, it was opposed by many unionists. Significantly, workers in the Ballylumford Power Station did not support the strike. Privately the military were preparing to seize the power stations if it should prove necessary. The British government believed that Ian Paisley was responsible for the action, but were reluctant to arrest him.[87] The strike led to the demise of the UUUC, following accusations by James Molyneaux, leader of the Ulster Unionist Party, that some of its more militant members were planning to establish a provisional government in Northern Ireland. The UUUC called an end to the strike on 13 May; it had lasted for thirteen days. Both sides claimed a victory, although, compared to the 1974 strike, this one had less support and had been less disruptive. Three weeks later Mason announced that the RUC would be increased by 1,200 and the Ulster Defence Regiment would be increased to 2,500 full-time members. He also announced that there would be further undercover activity by troops. Mason's tough approach was confirmed when, on 12 September, he marked his first year in office with a speech in which he stated that 'the myth of British withdrawal is dead forever'.[88]

On 9 August 1977 the Queen began a two-day visit to Northern Ireland as part of her Jubilee celebrations. It was the first visit by the Queen for eleven years. It divided the community, with Union flags being displayed in Protestant areas only. Because of this, the Queen spent the night on the royal yacht, docked in Belfast Loch. Both the IRA and the SDLP protested, although in different ways – the IRA planted a number of bombs, the SDLP boycotted a reception. Security was tight with a specially strengthened contingent of 32,000 troops and police on duty, which made it the biggest royal security operation to date.[89] During her visit the Queen met Máiread Corrigan and Betty Williams for twenty minutes on the royal yacht.[90]

On 22 December 1977 the Provisional IRA announced its Christmas ceasefire. Little had changed in the year: violence continued and there was no political solution on the table. Mason's tough approach did not appear to be changing the political landscape in Northern Ireland. However, a positive sign, which Mason made much of, was that total deaths had fallen to 116 in 1977 and would drop to 88 by the end of 1978.

At the beginning of 1978 there were a number of calls for British withdrawal from Northern Ireland. Those making them included

Jack Lynch, who had been elected Taoiseach in June 1977, and Tomás Ó Fiaich, the Catholic Primate of Ireland. Ó'Fiaich's brand of nationalism upset many unionists, Protestants and British politicians, and led the *Daily Telegraph* to refer to him insultingly by the English form of his name 'Thomas Fee'.[91] Ian Paisley, less prosaically, referred to him as 'the IRA Bishop'. The SDLP debated British withdrawal but feared that there would be anarchy if it actually happened. This led John Hume to suggest, in February, a third option that he called an 'agreed Ireland', wherein the British government would work to reconcile both traditions. By the time of the SDLP's annual conference in November, though, British withdrawal was described as being 'desirable and inevitable'.[92] The British authorities were disappointed with this resolution, believing that it would make their task no easier.[93] When Hume replaced Gerry Fitt as leader of the party in 1979, he emphasized the need for a three-way solution, that is, improving relations between the two communities in Northern Ireland, relations between the North and South of Ireland, and between Britain and Ireland. This approach was to form the basis of the party's policies for the succeeding decades.[94]

Reconfigurations were taking place within unionism. The Vanguard Party dissolved on 25 February 1978 and many of its members, including William Craig, joined the Ulster Unionist Party. The UUP continued to be the largest unionist party. It was led by Harry West, who had repeatedly refused to hold talks with Ian Paisley of the DUP.[95] Mason was afraid that if Jack Lynch's government made too many demands for a united Ireland, the outcome would be to push West and Paisley together. West had already broken off talks with the British government, citing Lynch's statements on unity as the reason.[96]

The more nationalist statements of the Fianna Fáil government, combined with continuing IRA violence, were also straining relations between the Irish and British governments. This became evident following the bombing of the La Mon restaurant, near Belfast, on 17 February 1978, when twelve people, all Protestant civilians, were killed and 23 were badly injured. Many of the victims were members of the Irish Collie Club and the Northern Ireland Junior Motor Cycle Club. Mason described the bombing as 'An act of criminal irresponsibility' carried out by 'remnants of IRA gangs'. Many loyalists blamed Mason's 'complacent' attitude to security, which in their view had allowed the attack to take place.[97] Mason, in turn, was angry with what he regarded as the lax attitude of the Dublin government; he informed James Callaghan that 'the cross-border movement of terrorists and supplies continue to present special problems'.[98]

A further problem for Mason was that of republican prisoners who were continuing to seek political status. These demands were supported by the SDLP. Throughout 1978 there were indications that the prisoners were stepping up their protest. Albert Miles, the deputy governor at the Maze Prison, recorded on 1 April that, 'The increase in protests is seen as a deliberate attempt to embarrass the prison service and to harass prison staff.' Following complaints by a number of Catholic clergymen, a British official responded, 'There are going to be no concessions on the question of special treatment for prisoners, no matter how such treatment may be described'. On 1 August 1978 Tomás Ó Fiaich, who had visited Republican prisoners in the Maze Prison on 30 July 1978, issued a statement saying that the prisoners engaged in the 'blanket protest' were living in 'inhuman' conditions and that prison conditions reminded him of a Calcutta slum. He warned the government that 'The problem of these prisoners is only sowing the seeds of future conflict.'[99] Although Mason made it clear that the government was determined to stand firm, private memos indicated that they were worried about the international impact of the protest and the value it was having for the IRA in terms of propaganda. In October Mason was briefed that 'Humanitarian concern makes the present regime vulnerable, especially if something goes suddenly wrong, and human concern can turn into political pressure, especially if it emerges that we may be vulnerable at the European Court.'[100] Albert Miles was shot dead in November. Both sides were as entrenched as ever as the year drew to a close.

In early November 1978 a secret British Army intelligence document, 'Northern Ireland: Future Terrorist Trends', was uncovered by the *New Statesman* magazine. Tellingly, the rest of the British media ignored it. The document warned that the campaign of violence was likely to continue while Britain remained in Ireland and that there was no prospect of political change for five years. At the same time, it advised that the ability, expertise and professionalism of the Provisional IRA were increasing and that the adoption of the new cell structure had made them less vulnerable to infiltration. It cautioned:

The Provisional IRA (PIRA) has the dedication and the sinews of war to raise violence intermittently to at least the level of early 1978, certainly for the foreseeable future . . . Our evidence of the rank and file terrorists does not support the view that they are merely mindless hooligans drawn from the unemployed and unemployable. PIRA now trains and uses its members with some care. The Active Service Units (ASUS) are for the most part manned by terrorists tempered by up to ten years of operational experience.[101]

Clearly the IRA could be contained, but not defeated. At the end of 1978 the IRA leadership secretly proposed a ceasefire and peace talks to the British government. They sent a message to the Prime Minister saying that it was 'time to talk and end the present violence'. The British refused the offer.[102] James Callaghan and Roy Mason had decided, following the La Mon bombing in February, not to negotiate any more. The Provisional IRA settled into a war of attrition referred to as 'the long war'. In December, a week before Christmas, bombs exploded in Bristol, Coventry, Liverpool, Manchester and Southampton.

The political impasse that had been a feature of Northern Ireland politics in 1978 continued into the next year. A major change occurred within British politics, however, that was to have significant repercussions in Ireland. On 28 March 1979 the Labour government lost a vote of no confidence by 311 votes to 310. The votes of the Northern Ireland MPs were decisive in bringing down Labour, with eight Unionists voting against them. A general election held on 3 May 1979 returned a Conservative government with Margaret Thatcher as Prime Minister. Within Northern Ireland, the Democratic Unionist Party, led by Ian Paisley, gained two seats from the Ulster Unionist Party.

The rise of Ian Paisley as the leading spokesperson for unionism/loyalism was confirmed by the results of the elections to the European Parliament on 7 June 1979. Paisley topped the poll with more than 29 per cent of the first preference votes and was elected on the first count. John Hume, deputy leader of the Social Democratic and Labour Party, received 24.6 per cent of the vote and narrowly missed the quota, but was elected on the third count. John Taylor of the Ulster Unionist Party received 11.9 per cent of the first preference votes and was elected on the sixth count. It was a stunning triumph for Paisley, who would continue to top these polls until 2004.[103] Paisley's success showed that he was a major force to be reckoned with in unionist politics. His rabble-rousing style, however, was evident even on the international stage. On his first day in the Parliament he attempted to interrupt the President of the European Council, Jack Lynch, who was also Taoiseach, but he was shouted down by fellow MEPs.[104]

The Conservative Party's manifesto had stated in relation to Northern Ireland that:

> We shall maintain the Union of Great Britain and Northern Ireland in accordance with the wish of the majority in the Province. Its future still depends on the defeat of terrorism and the restoration of law and order. We shall continue with the help of the courage, resolution and restraint of the Security Forces to give it the highest priority. There will be no amnesty for convicted terrorists.
>
> In the absence of devolved government, we will seek to establish one or more elected regional councils with a wide range of powers over local services. We recognise that Northern Ireland's industry will continue to require government support.[105]

On 30 March 1979, just a few weeks before the election, the INLA killed Airey Neave, the Conservative Party Shadow Spokesperson on Northern Ireland, with a booby-trap bomb attached to his car in the House of Commons underground car park. It was one of the most audacious attacks perpetrated by republicans in Britain. Neave's uncompromising approach to Northern Irish politics meant that he had also been disliked by the Dublin government and the SDLP. He blamed the former's lack of decisive action for a situation in which there were 'far too many people skulking in the Republic who are wanted by the RUC'.[106] Neave had been a close friend and campaign manager of Thatcher's. He was also thought to have been one of the masterminds behind the campaign of dirty tricks and black propaganda.[107] His death did not deter the new government from following Neave's hard-line approach to Northern Ireland, which placed increasing emphasis on military rather than political interventions.

Humphrey Atkins was appointed as Secretary of State for Northern Ireland. One of the first questions he was asked in the

House of Commons related to what he was going to do to inform international opinion about current events in Northern Ireland. To a large extent this remark was motivated by comments made by the Irish-American politician Thomas (Tip) O'Neill, then Speaker of the House of Representatives, criticizing the lack of political initiative in Northern Ireland. He was supported by Senator Edward Kennedy, Senator Daniel Moynihan and Hugh Carey, then Governor of New York, who were known collectively as the 'Four Horsemen'.[108] While visiting Ireland in April, O'Neill had accused the British government of using Northern Ireland as a 'political football' and that the new government should pursue a major political initiative without delay.[109] Despite reassuring the House of Commons that he would be using his 'best endeavours' to make political progress and to inform international opinion, only a month later Atkins informed them that, following criticisms of the RUC in a New York newspaper and by Speaker O'Neill, the British Ambassador in Washington had expressed the British government's 'surprise and regret'.[110] Regardless of the efforts of various Secretaries of State, it seemed that the IRA was winning the propaganda war outside Britain and Ireland. Events later in the year, however, resulted in widespread condemnation.

On 27 August 1979 the Queen's cousin Earl Mountbatten, aged 79, was killed by a booby-trap bomb left by the IRA on a boat near Sligo in the Republic of Ireland, where he was holidaying. Three other people were killed in the explosion: Lady Brabourne, aged 82; Nicholas Knatchbull, aged fourteen, who was Mountbatten's grandson; and Paul Maxwell, aged fifteen, who was a crew member on the boat. Both the INLA and the IRA initially claimed responsibility.[111] Shortly afterwards, the IRA issued a statement claiming, 'This operation is one of the discriminate ways we can bring to the attention of the English people the continuing occupation of our country.'[112] Few agreed that Mountbatten was a 'discriminate' target, although it appeared he had been an easy one, taking few security precautions: when asked shortly before he died if he feared the IRA, his response had been, 'What would they want with an old man like me?'[113] There was international public outrage at these murders. In India, where Mountbatten had helped to bring about independence in 1947, a week of mourning was declared.[114] Mountbatten was given a ceremonial funeral in Westminster Abbey. Both the President of Ireland, Patrick Hillery, and the Taoiseach, Jack Lynch, attended a memorial service for Lord Mountbatten in St Patrick's Cathedral in Dublin. The attack was believed to have hardened the hearts of many British people against the IRA and to have confirmed the hard-line stance taken against them by Margaret Thatcher's government.[115]

Only hours later, eighteen British soldiers were killed in an IRA attack at Narrow Water, near Warrenpoint, County Down. It was the highest death toll suffered by the British Army in a single incident since it had arrived in Northern Ireland. The attack began when the IRA exploded a 500 pound bomb as an army convoy was passing. Six members of the Parachute Regiment were killed in this first bomb. As other troops moved into the area a second bomb was detonated killing ten more members of the Parachute Regiment and two of the Queen's Own Highlanders. A gun battle then broke out between the IRA, from positions in the Irish Republic, and British soldiers in Northern Ireland. A civilian was killed on the Republic side of the border by soldiers firing from the north. The British soldiers were under strict orders not to pursue their attackers into the Republic.[116] The death toll on this single day was widely condemned, but it sent a message to the new government about the capacity and determination of the IRA.

In September 1979 Pope John Paul II visited Ireland, the first time that a reigning pope had done so. Following his arrival, he delivered an open-air sermon to more than one-and-quarter million people – nearly a third of Ireland's entire population – in Phoenix Park, Dublin. He had originally intended to visit Armagh, but it was decided, after the deaths of Mountbatten, the others on his boat and the eighteen British soldiers, that he should not go to Northern Ireland for security reasons. Consequently he only travelled as far north as Drogheda, where he spoke to an estimated 250,000 to 300,000 people. There, his message of peace was clear:

On my knees I beg you to turn away from the paths of violence and return to the ways of peace. To Catholics, to Protestants, my message is peace and love. May no Irish Protestant think the Pope is an enemy, a danger or a threat . . . I appeal to young people who may have become caught up in organizations engaged in violence. I say to you, with all the love I have for you, with all the trust I have in young

people: do not listen to voices which speak the language of
hatred, revenge, retaliation.[117]

The most important event that evening was his meeting with representatives of the non-Catholic churches at the Dominican convent
in Cabra.

Pope John Paul then hosted an ecumenical meeting in Dublin
where he welcomed clergymen from the Church of Ireland, the
Presbyterian, Lutheran, Methodist and Moravian churches, the
Society of Friends and the Chief Rabbi. He had planned to address
them while standing, but he commenced by telling them that he
was tired and would have to sit down. The Pope's ecumenical message did not convince everybody: the Orange Order sent the Pope
a letter criticizing his visit on political and theological grounds.[118]
The Pope also addressed an audience in Galway of approximately
200,000 people, most of whom were young, drawing from the Papal
visitor the phrase, 'Young People of Ireland, I love you.' But his message to them was both serious and conservative, asking that they:

> Do not close your eyes to the moral sickness that stalks your
> society today and from which your youth alone will not
> protect you. How many young people have already warped
> their consciences and have substituted the true joy of life
> with drugs, sex, alcohol, vandalism and the empty pursuit
> of mere material possessions?[119]

Despite his conservative messages the Pope's visit had united members of the Catholic Church in Ireland, but it had done little to
reassure non-Catholics of their place in a united Ireland.

Economy

The British and Irish economies in the 1970s were characterized by
high inflation and large-scale unemployment. In 1975, out of a population of only just over three million, some 90,000 people in the
Republic were unemployed. There was also an increase in industrial
unrest: 1979 proved to be the worst year ever for industrial disputes,
which cost the economy more than 1,460,000 working days. In
Northern Ireland during this decade unemployment amongst males
rose above 30 per cent. One solution to the poverty and political

turmoil was emigration, which had been a feature of Irish life since the nineteenth century, peaking during the Famine period of the late 1840s, and again (in the Republic) after the Second World War. Seán Lemass's attempts at fostering internal investment and attracting foreign investment, however, meant that the economy in the Republic witnessed the start of a slow economic recovery that was to bear fruit in the 1990s. Significantly, for the first time in decades, the 1970s saw a net inflow of immigrants to the Republic, most of whom were returning Irish.[120] This situation was short-lived, with the economic downswing in the 1980s creating a new generation of emigrants, a large number of whom were highly educated. In contrast, the population of Northern Ireland had been increasing since the creation of the state. However, it suffered a large outflow of its people in the early 1970s as a consequence of the onset of the violence. This was combined with a fall-off in birth rates.[121] As a result, Northern Ireland experienced little or no growth in population during this decade.[122]

Against the backdrop of violence and political impasse, attempts were made to revive the flagging Northern economy. Attracting in-ward investment was made more difficult by the Provisional IRA's targeting of businessmen and businesses. The United States was to play an important role in economic regeneration. The official policy of President Carter's government on Northern Ireland was cautious, stating that a resolution had to be reached internally but that the United States would be willing to offer limited help, within 'the non-involvement framework'.[123] At the end of August 1977 President Carter gave a speech on Northern Ireland that was worded in such a way as to avoid controversy or appear to be favouring either side. He said that if a peace settlement should occur, the American government would assist in creating jobs in the region. He also called on Americans not to provide financial and other support for groups using violence in Northern Ireland. Carter's intervention had the support of leading Irish-American politicians including Ted Kennedy, Tip O'Neill and Daniel Moynihan. The *New York Times* described Carter's speech as being phrased in 'carefully inexplicit terms' and contrasted his reticence on this occasion with the fact that on St Patrick's Day in 1976 he had worn a pin saying 'Get Britain out of Ireland'.[124]

Within Northern Ireland, there appeared no end in sight to the political stalemate and the violence. In 1978 Roy Mason declared that, 'I shall continue to give at least as much attention to economic and social matters as to politics and security. The need is very great: unemployment went over 13 per cent in the July and August figures.' He told the Prime Minister that this approach would require money, warning that 'If direct rule is not seen to be working, we shall be in trouble'. At this point, Mason had already obtained agreement from his government to provide a state subsidy for a luxury sports car company in Belfast.[125]

Mason announced to a packed press conference in Belfast on 2 August 1978 that a sports car factory to create 2,000 new jobs was to be built in West Belfast. The man who was to make this happen was an elegant American, John DeLorean. The governments of Puerto Rico and Spain had wanted DeLorean to base his factory in their countries, as had Detroit (although the Irish Republic had rejected DeLorean's proposal). DeLorean built the new factory in record time on a greenfield site that straddled both communities. At its peak it would employ 2,500 people, taken equally from the (Catholic) Twinbrook estate and (Protestant) Dunmurry. Because it brought both sides together, it was regarded as a flagship project for the government, but it proved to be a costly one. Although Mason had described the new factory as a 'great breakthrough' in securing foreign investment in Northern Ireland, in reality it required an initial British investment of £54 million out of a total of £65 million. A further £10 million was given when this ran out. By the early 1980s it was obvious that the DeLorean project was a chimera. The new Conservative Prime Minister, Margaret Thatcher, was able to cite it as an example of the financial profligacy of the previous Labour government.[126]

Both the United Kingdom and the Irish Republic had been admitted to the European Economic Community in 1973. The Republic's admission allowed opportunities for both economic development and for involvement in international politics. The immediate beneficiaries of the union were Irish farmers, who were no longer tied to the low-priced British market. By 1978 there had been an increase of 45 per cent in real prices received by them.[127] A further, unlooked-for consequence was that membership of the EEC brought the economies of the North and the South closer together, with a corresponding move away from dependency on Britain.[128] There were also diplomatic benefits, especially for the Republic. Ireland held the Presidency in 1975 and 1979 and both times it was judged to be successful.[129] The Irish Republic was showing that, despite its size and geographical position, it was prepared to play its part as a good citizen of Europe.

Censorship

The willingness of the government in the Republic to use censorship in order to control the reporting of the conflict had become evident in 1972 when a Fianna Fáil government sacked the RTÉ Authority after the station broadcast a report of an interview with the IRA Chief of Staff, Seán Mac Stiofáin. The journalist, Kevin O'Kelly, was jailed in Mountjoy Prison for refusing to name the voice on the taped interview.[130] The approach of the Coalition government after 1975 was even more stringent. This was not surprising given that the Minister for Posts and Telegraphs, Conor Cruise O'Brien, was virulently anti-republican. In the previous decade his politics had undergone a dramatic change. Not only had he moved from the left to the right, but he had repositioned himself dramatically from opposing the muzzling of RTÉ in 1972, when in Opposition, to, when a Minister, helping to 'copper fasten and perfect it'.[131] As early as 1973, O'Brien accused RTÉ of allowing a 'spiritual occupation' by the IRA. Journalists who did not share his perspective were effectively demoted. Many journalists, however, did share it. Within RTÉ, helped by the creation of a number of unofficial 'watchdog groups', self-censorship and anti-republican sentiment became widespread. It was promoted by members of the Workers' Party, who themselves had evolved out of Official Sinn Fein – and who were possibly the most virulent opponents of Provisional Sinn Fein. One of the leading members of this group, RTÉ producer Eoghan Harris, disparagingly referred to anyone whom he considered to be soft on the republican struggle as a 'hush puppy'. [132]

In 1976 the National Union of Journalists in Ireland admitted that the government's approach to security was not being questioned by RTÉ. The main national newspapers were similarly cautious and O'Brien wanted to prosecute the minority of reporters and editors, such as Tim Pat Coogan, who did not conform.[133] As a consequence, news coverage was uneven and investigative journalism was restricted. Allegations against the British involvement in miscarriages of justice, such as that of the Birmingham Six, were largely ignored. Security issues were reported in a partial way. In relation to the activities of Sinn Féin, correspondents stated that 'ministerial restrictions' affected coverage. A system of self-censorship was securely in place at the conclusion of O'Brien's tenure as minister. Even after 1977, when the Coalition government was replaced by Fianna Fáil and O'Brien lost his parliamentary seat, the system that he had created remained in place.[134] The 1971 and 1977 bans were not removed until 1993. As a consequence of this censorship – both official and unofficial – open debate was closed down and the role of RTÉ in providing a forum for explaining what was going on in the North was removed. Furthermore, the long-term consequences of censorship of militant perspectives were that by the time of the Peace Process, people in the Republic had 'huge gaps in their understanding and unrealistic expectations'.[135]

The British government did not exert the same legislative control over broadcasting the Troubles as the Irish government. By the mid-1970s, however, the British media had come to regard the problems of Northern Ireland as a forbidden area. One historian of the BBC found that the unspoken censorship had become so powerful that when writing up his findings 'the suppression effect had led me to under-utilize material gathered in my earliest field notes'.[136] Additionally, a number of researchers, both in the media and academia, not only pre-empted the British state by a number of years in their willingness to self-censor, but adopted the attitudes of the state in determining the 'legitimate voices' to be interviewed, often excluding Sinn Féin on the grounds that they were terrorists.[137] Whatever the reason, such attitudes reinforced the British government's policy of criminalization.

The day-to-day reporting of events in Northern Ireland was, according to Father Raymond Murray, guilty of 'silence and omission'. He admitted that when the British and Irish did take an interest in the violation of human rights in the province, it was extremely useful, but overall he believed 'the media have failed us utterly over ten years'.[138] The journalist Peter Taylor, when explaining some of the problems that were 'inherent' when reporting Northern Ireland, stated that: 'No other domestic or foreign political issue is beset with the pressures that journalists face when they attempt to report, analyse and place in perspective the most pressing political issue on their doorstep.'[139] Paul Madden identified at least 28 dramas and documentaries, produced between 1970 and 1978 and dealing with Northern Ireland, that had been 'banned, censored or delayed'.[140]

Two programmes concerning the systematic abuse of detainees in Northern Ireland demonstrated how powerful investigative reporting could be. In 1976 paramilitary prisoners alleged they had been abused while in custody in order for confessions to be obtained from them. These claims were supported by a number of doctors. A leading Belfast defence lawyer, P. J. McGrory, speaking on behalf of a large number of solicitors, told Roy Mason that the legal profession 'shared the conviction that ill-treatment of suspects by police officers with the object of obtaining confessions is now common practice'.[141] The government and the public did not take these accusations seriously until, on 2 March 1977, the BBC 'Tonight' programme looked at interrogation techniques employed at the Castlereagh Police Holding Centre in Belfast. Later in the year Thames Television broadcast 'Inhuman and Degrading Treatment?', which featured ten cases – eight Roman Catholics and two Protestants – of alleged maltreatment at Castlereagh between February and October 1977. Initially the RUC had refused to cooperate, and so the programme was going to be dropped on the grounds of lack of balance in reporting. This was overcome when the Chief Constable agreed to make a statement to camera.[142]

Both programmes were critical of the methods used in Castlereagh. One of the doctors who participated in the television programmes was subsequently the subject of a smear campaign reported in the conservative *Daily Telegraph*.[143] Nonetheless, the public outcry that followed these programmes led Amnesty International to carry out its own investigation on police interrogation methods.[144] The Amnesty report, published on 13 June 1978, upheld the claim of the television programmes that people held in Castlereagh had been ill-treated. The RUC Chief Constable, Kenneth Newman, rejected its findings but the Home Secretary, Roy Mason, was forced into promising an enquiry, to be chaired by an English judge, Harry Bennett.[145] A programme based on the findings by Amnesty, due to be broadcast in June 1978, was banned by the Independent Broadcasting Authority.[146] The Bennett Report was released on 16 March 1979 and confirmed the evidence, presented in the television programmes and by Amnesty, that the injuries sustained while in custody were not self-inflicted. The report made a number of suggestions, of which the government undertook to implement the installation of closed-circuit television cameras in interview rooms, and the right of those being detained to have access to their solicitor after 48 hours in custody. As some lawyers pointed out, having access to a legal representative only after two days in custody was often too late to ensure that due processes had been followed and confessions had not been coerced.[147] Some of the other recommendations were later implemented when the Conservative Party came to power in May 1979. These changes, however, only came about following multiple complaints by professionals, media exposés, public controversy, unofficial enquiry and a reluctantly appointed official enquiry. The two British-produced television programmes had been an important catalyst in this process.

Brutality against republican prisoners was not confined to the North, but, largely as a result of censorship of the media and the anti-republican spirit fostered by the Coalition government, it was less discussed in the Republic. A group within *An Garda Síochána*, known as the 'Heavy Gang', systematically brutalized detainees. A number of confessions obtained under these circumstances subsequently collapsed in court.[148] Although the Coalition government and its successor, Fianna Fáil, were shown an unpublished Amnesty International report of 1977 outlining cases of brutality, they chose not to act.[149] The election of a Conservative government in Britain in 1979 marked the beginning of a more fraught relationship between the British media and the government. Following a controversial 'Panorama' documentary in November 1979, which had shown the IRA enforcing roadblocks in Northern Ireland, and which Margaret Thatcher believed the BBC had set up, she announced, 'My Right Honourable Friend the Home Secretary (Whitelaw) believes it is time the BBC put its house in order.'[150]

Beyond television, Irish writers were also coming to terms with the continuation of violence. The Arts Council of Northern Ireland had been formed in 1962, replacing the Committee for the Encouragement of Music and the Arts. Artists responded in different ways. Writers such as Sam Hanna Bell, known for his 1951 novel *December Bride*, wanted to stimulate 'cultural renewal'.[151] The poet Derek Mahon, in his anthology *The Snow Party*, published in 1975, followed the themes of his earlier work, exploring a sense of displacement in Northern Ireland. He was writing as an outsider and an observer to what was going on, while denouncing the elite who distanced themselves from the violence.[152] In 1979 Mahon became a real outsider, leaving Northern Ireland and vowing never to live there again.[153]

A poet who was attracting international attention was Seamus Heaney. When his anthology *North* was published in June 1975, Heaney declared that, up to this point, he had not been tough enough politically. He admitted to a 'moral confusion' about what he should be saying.[154] His answer seemed to be to search for a pre-colonial, pre-sectarian island of Ireland.[155] *North* had its critics, especially among those who were avowedly anti-republican, including the literary critic Edna Longley, who had advocated a separation between poetry and politics. She disapproved of Heaney's 'liberal lamentation' and suggested that his move to the Republic had made him more publicly Catholic.[156] An even more fierce criticism of the collection was provided by Cairán Carson, who suggested that Heaney 'seems to have moved – unwilling perhaps – from being a writer with the gift of precision, to become the laureate of violence – a mythmaker, an anthropologist of ritual killing, an apologist for "the situation", in the last resort, a mystifier'.[157] Heaney, however, was caught in the political no-man's-land of being considered either too political or not political enough.[158] Moreover, being political had its dangers. The poet Michael Longley received so many death threats in the 1970s that he considered leaving Belfast.[159] For some, he represented a voice of reason and moderation; to others, he was a traitor.

Much of the writing was critical of the violence, especially of the role of the IRA in perpetuating the bloodshed. Brian Friel's play *Volunteers* (1975) depicted Irish republicans as being lost in an unchanged, and therefore unrealistic, view of the nationalist struggle. Both Edna Longley and Conor Cruise O'Brien were persistent critics of artists who used their medium to convey a political message. Significantly, though both were highly critical of writings sympathetic to the nationalist struggle, they held unionism up to less cultural scrutiny. In 1975 O'Brien published 'An Unhealthy Intersection' in the *New Review*, in which he talked about the junctions between literature and politics, which he believed should be regarded with suspicion as it was 'infused with romanticism, which in politics tend in the direction of fascism'.[160] An even starker warning was contained in an *Irish Times* article written by O'Brien entitled 'Politics and the Poet'. Quoting from Yeats – 'Did that play of mine send out certain men the English shot?' – O'Brien responded, 'The probable answer is, Yes, it did.'[161] Later that year, in his capacity as a minister in the Coalition government, O'Brien banned the IRA from the Irish airwaves.

In 1975 the Druid Theatre Company was founded in Galway by Garry Hynes, Mick Lally and Marie Mullen. It was the first professional theatre company in the Republic of Ireland outside Dublin. Other changes were taking place in the Republic as the fruits of Charles Haughey's 1969 legislation exempting artists from paying taxation became evident. By the beginning of 1975, the Republic had been described as a tax haven for artists. Since the introduction of the law, 661 people had claimed cultural status, of which 482 had been accepted. This number included the English playwright John Arden, the playwrights Hugh Leonard, who had returned from Britain, and Brian Friel, who had moved from Derry to County Donegal, and the New York-born author J. P. Donleavy.[162] The seeds were being planted for a cultural renaissance that saw fruition in the 1990s. By coincidence, Charles Haughey, the architect of this revival, was elected Taoiseach by Dáil Éireann on 11 December 1979 following the resignation of Jack Lynch. As 1980 approached, and while Northern Ireland remained without its own parliament, Charles Haughey and Margaret Thatcher, two new leaders both known for their conviction politics, were now responsible for trying to find a solution to more than a decade of violence and mayhem.

SIX

Hunger

The first day of 1980 commenced with customary violence in Northern Ireland. A sixteen-year-old girl was shot dead at a British Army checkpoint in Belfast while joyriding. On the same day, two undercover members of the British Army were mistakenly shot by fellow soldiers. The pattern of violence was changing, however, with members of the police and prison security replacing the British Army as a key focus of republican violence. Between January and October 1980, of the 61 people who died as a result of the conflict, only seven were British Army regulars, while fifteen were members of the RUC or UDR.[1] To a large extent this was due to the policy of 'Ulsterization', which had foregrounded the role played by local security forces. As a consequence, the number of British troops was reduced to 12,000, the lowest in a decade.

Killings and bombings continued throughout the year, but a particularly poignant death occurred on 21 January when Anne Maguire was found dead in what was believed to be a case of suicide. Three of her children had been killed by a runaway car in 1976. She had three surviving children.[2] At this stage the Peace Movement, which had been founded in response to the death of her children, was foundering. In February, Betty Williams became the first of its leaders to resign and immediately left Ireland, never to return. The movement had lost its direction and was riven by internal squabbles.[3] The failures of the Peace Movement represented a microcosm of the difficulties in ending the violence in Northern Ireland.

Against the continuing background of carnage and disarray, Humphrey Atkins, the Conservative Secretary of State, made an attempt to find a constitutional solution. In January he convened a conference at Stormont involving the Democratic Unionist Party (DUP), the Social Democratic and Labour Party (SDLP) and the

Alliance Party. The Ulster Unionist Party (UUP) refused to participate. A parallel conference was also held, the main purpose of which
was to allow the SDLP to explore the 'Irish dimension', a topic that
was excluded from discussion in the main conference. The DUP
refused to take part in the second conference. Like other Secretaries
of State, Atkins had failed to breach the political divisions. Although
the talks continued until 24 March, no agreement was reached.
Within the House of Commons, however, the most in-depth and
persistent questions concerning the conference related to the cost of
the phone and bar bills during the talks.[4]

On 16 February, while the talks were continuing, Charles
Haughey, the Taoiseach, called for a joint initiative on behalf of the
British and Irish governments to try to find a political solution to
the conflict in Northern Ireland. Despite holding such high office,
Haughey was a divisive figure in Irish politics and even within his
own Fianna Fáil Party. He was the first Taoiseach to be a millionaire
and his great, and largely unaccounted for, wealth, as well as his
flamboyant lifestyle, made him an easy target for parody and envy.
According to the historian Joseph Lee, Haughey 'played the green
card with skill', balancing the conflicting demands of various nationalist groups.[5] His part in the 1970 Arms Trial, when he was accused of assisting the illegal import of guns for the IRA, had given
him republican credentials that he never lived up to. In 1961, as Minister for Justice, he had helped to defeat the IRA by reintroducing the
Special Criminal Court.[6] His own father had been in the IRA in
Derry, but on being appointed Taoiseach one of his first acts was to
condemn republican paramilitaries. While Haughey's relationship
with militant republicanism was ambivalent, his relationship with
unionists was clearer: they did not trust him. Following fresh allegations in *Magill Magazine* in 1980, his political opponent, Garret
Fitzgerald, was keen to point out that Haughey's connection with
illegal arms importation meant he:

> still has an evident and profound effect on the Government's
> Northern policy, for it blocks off the option of a political
> opening towards the Northern majority. The Taoiseach is
> thus forced, because of the way he knows he is regarded by
> the Northern majority following the events of 1970, to pur-
> sue a policy based exclusively on dependence upon British
> goodwill.[7]

In February 1980, during the Fianna Fáil *Ard Fheis*, Haughey described Northern Ireland as 'a failed political entity'. Unionists were furious and never forgave him.[8] Despite his making intermittent conciliatory overtures to Northern unionists, his method of playing the Orange card was to both ignore and underestimate the strength of their dislike. When Haughey visited Belfast for what proved to be the final time in 1990, thousands of loyalist protesters fought street battles with the RUC.[9]

Haughey sought to resolve the problems in Northern Ireland through a joint initiative by the Irish and British governments. In May 1980 the Taoiseach travelled to London to meet with Margaret Thatcher. The day before the meeting, in response to a question by James Molyneaux of the Ulster Unionist Party, who challenged her on 'discussing the internal constitutional affairs of the United Kingdom with external representatives of any Government or politicians', the British Prime Minister had stated, 'The future of the constitutional affairs of Northern Ireland is a matter for the people of Northern Ireland, this Government and this Parliament, and no one else.'[10] Her response did not augur well for the meeting. Yet, Haughey appeared to charm Thatcher, possibly helped by his gift of an antique Irish silver teapot.[11] The day after their meeting a statement was issued that spoke of the 'unique relationship' between the two countries. The leaders had agreed to 'new and closer political co-operation between their Governments and to hold regular meetings to review progress'.[12] Shortly afterwards, Haughey appeared on the British current affairs programme 'Panorama', and appealed for Britain to withdraw the constitutional guarantee to the unionists, which he described as 'the stumbling block' to progress. He suggested a federal solution as a possible alternative.[13]

The British government was involved in a number of unsuccessful attempts to hand some power back to the elected representatives in Northern Ireland. In July 1980 'The Government of Northern Ireland: Proposals for Further Discussion' was published, suggesting two possible options as potential solutions to the conflict. This was a follow-up to the Conference of Northern Ireland earlier in the year, which the Ulster Unionist Party had refused to attend.[14] But unionists continued to oppose power-sharing and nationalists refused a return to majority rule, so again, constitutional politics were at an impasse and politicians in Northern Ireland remained as polarized as ever.

In December 1980 Haughey hosted a summit meeting with Margaret Thatcher in Dublin Castle. It was the first time that a British Prime Minister had visited Dublin since partition in 1921, and took place when hunger strikes were being held in both the Maze and Armagh prisons over the demand for political status. Thatcher was accompanied by the Foreign Secretary, Lord Carrington, and by Humphrey Atkins, the Secretary of State. Haughey described the meeting as a 'historic breakthrough' and, he informed the Dáil, 'The British delegation was, in terms of its composition, the most important to visit this country since the foundation of this State, or indeed for a long time before then'.[15] In a press interview, however, Thatcher played down its significance, pointing out that, 'I took with me a customary bilateral team of the kind which I would take to France or to Germany or anywhere else in the Community'.[16] On a personal level, the meeting was a considerable success and Thatcher again appeared charmed by the Irish Taoiseach. Following the meeting the phrase 'totality of relationships' was frequently used, suggesting British acceptance of the role of Ireland in the future of Northern Ireland. Thatcher reported she and Haughey had had a tête-à-tête for over an hour and they had agreed 'very strongly' on a number of issues: 'that violence is no way forward. That we must have maximum cooperation on security. That there is no point in a hunger strike and that we both hope that it will end very quickly.'[17] The joint communiqué was no sooner agreed than Haughey overplayed his hand by publicly saying there would be assemblies in Dublin and Belfast and by implying that it provided a step in the direction of Irish unity. Thatcher was furious with this interpretation and Haughey was forced to back down.[18] The relationship that he had established with Thatcher was irreparably damaged. Although little was achieved as a result of the joint meetings in 1980, the 1985 Anglo-Irish Agreement signed by Garret FitzGerald and Margaret Thatcher (which Haughey opposed) contained many of the elements of the 1980 settlement. Haughey's initiative, therefore, had laid some of the groundwork for a peace settlement – although it took many more years, and deaths, to achieve it.

When he came to power in 1979 the Taoiseach promised that he would tighten security, particularly in the border regions. While Haughey was involved in talks with the British government, the IRA's activities were increasingly focused on attacking police officers in Northern Ireland and on bank raids. In 1978 and 1979 £400 million had been stolen by armed men and the annual cost of security had risen to £200 million. Higher costs were inevitable as in 1979 it was decided to increase the size of the Irish Army and of the *Garda Síochána*, the latter by 500. Pay and conditions were also to be improved. This heavy burden on Irish taxpayers at a time of high unemployment led Deputy Paddy Harte of Fine Gael to suggest that, 'We should spell out clearly to the men of violence that the amount of money they are forcing the taxpayers to pay to contain the violence which they are generating could be spent on providing houses and better social security entitlements, all the things which are very necessary.'[19] Largely due to the continuation of bank robberies, the Republic further strengthened its surveillance of the border region. In early September 1980 Haughey's government announced that they would spend approximately £240 million to deploy more helicopters and spotter aircraft. The money would also be used to equip special detective teams with Israeli UZI submachine guns, to utilize unmarked police cars and to pay money for inside tip-offs.[20]

A salacious and unresolved scandal came to light on 3 April 1980 when three staff members of the Kincora Boys' Home in Belfast were charged with acts of gross indecency. They were all convicted the following year. The home was run by William McGrath, a member of the Orange Order and of Ian Paisley's Free Presbyterian Church. He was also involved with the paramilitary organization Tara.[21] This scandal was made public as a result of an article in the *Irish Independent*, which suggested that the boys' home had been operating as a gay brothel for leading loyalists and civil servants. It was later revealed that the British Army had informed the RUC about what was going on prior to the publication of the article, but they had not acted on this information.[22] Moreover, a file on the homosexual activities, which were still a criminal offence in Northern Ireland, had been compiled by a retiring police officer as early as 1971 and been given to a senior member of staff, who had chosen not to act on it.[23] The attention in the media resulted in a private enquiry being set up by the Secretary of State in 1982, but it was abandoned when many of its members suddenly resigned. A second enquiry was headed by a chief constable, George Terry, and a judge, William Hughes. The subsequent inquiry (referred to as both the Hughes Inquiry and the Terry Inquiry) was completed in 1985, but it was not published on the grounds that there was no case to answer. The report had also stated that there was no case of cover-up, although there were 'organisational weaknesses in the child-care system and those errors had been made'.[24] Despite rumours of prominent loyalists also abusing the boys, there were no further convictions. Justice Hughes subsequently claimed that not all of the relevant papers had been made available to him.[25]

Following the violent deaths of five of the key witnesses and the award of large out-of-court settlements to certain former residents of the Kincora Boys' Home in 1988, a number of Labour MPs, led by Ken Livingstone, raised the matter in the British Parliament.[26] Colin Wallace, who had been involved in 'Psy Ops', or dirty tricks, on behalf of the British Army in Northern Ireland, later claimed that, although they had known what was going on in Kincora since the early 1970s, some members of the British government wanted to use the information to provide leverage for blackmailing leading unionists.[27] A leading civil servant, Sir Michael Quinlan, asked if there could be a public investigation on Kincora, but this was refused.[28] In 1991 Ken Livingstone asked Brian Mawhinney, then the Secretary of State for Northern Ireland, if he would allow the Hughes report to be published, but he refused.[29] Overall, this murky affair provided a particularly unpalatable example of a dirty war in which innocent young boys were the unwitting victims.

Hunger Strikes

In 1980 and 1981 constitutional politics in Ireland were overshadowed by the hunger strikes. When reporting to the Dáil on his meeting with Margaret Thatcher in May 1980, Haughey had stated, 'The Irish Government's deep concern and anxiety about the H-Block situation figured prominently in our discussion.'[30] The role of the prisoners and of paramilitary prisoners was to dominate much of political discourse in the subsequent years. Since the withdrawal of Special Category Status in 1976, a number of republican prisoners in both Long Kesh and Armagh women's prison had been involved in a dirty protest, also called the 'no wash' protest. The prison authorities proved to be increasingly intolerant of the protest and in February 1980 had removed toilet facilities from the women in Armagh.[31] On 26 March 1980 the British government announced that from 1 April there would be no entitlement to Special Category Status for members of paramilitary organizations regardless of when the crimes had been committed. This change of policy suggested that the government was trying to provoke a confrontation with the prisoners.

The conditions within Long Kesh, which had been officially renamed Her Majesty's Prison (HMP) Maze, had been of concern to members of the Catholic Church hierarchy. In 1978 Tomás Ó Fiaich, the Catholic Primate of Ireland and a constant critic of IRA violence, had compared conditions within it to the slums of Calcutta. The response of the Northern Ireland Office to his harrowing description was that: 'These criminals are totally responsible for the situation in which they find themselves. It is they who have been smearing excreta on the walls and pouring urine through the cell doors. It is they who by their actions are denying themselves the excellent modern facilities of the prison.'[32] On 5 March 1980 Ó Fiaich, together with Edward Daly, the Bishop of Derry, met with Humphrey Atkins to express their concerns about conditions in the prison. By October Ó Fiaich had met with Atkins on five occasions, but the meetings achieved nothing. The British government was able to convince the European Commission on Human Rights, who published their report in June 1980, that the prison conditions had been self-inflicted.[33]

On 27 October 1980 seven republican prisoners began a hunger strike to protest the withdrawal of Special Category Status. Their aims were condensed into five demands: freedom of association with fellow prisoners; the right to wear their own clothes at all times; freedom from prison work; the right to normal visits and recreational facilities; and the full restoration of remission rights. The hunger strikers were Tom McFeeley, Brendan Hughes, Raymond McCartney, Leo Green, John Nixon, Tommy McKearney and Sean McKenna. Hughes had been the Commanding Officer (OC) for the prisoners, but when he commenced the strike he was replaced by 26-year-old Bobby Sands, who had been sentenced to fourteen years imprisonment for possession of a gun.[34] The hunger strike had been used as a tool to win Special Category Status in 1972, and republican prisoners hoped that in 1980 it would prove similarly effective. Consequently, 'Rather than some obsessive death fast, the 1980 strike was an attempt, albeit a drastic and dangerous one, practically to achieve what republicans considered to be their due treatment in jails.'[35]

On 20 November the Prime Minister informed the House of Commons that 'The Government will never concede political status to the hunger strikers, or to any others convicted of criminal offences in the Province.'[36] It was a point she was to make many times in public. Kevin McNamara, a Labour MP, reminded her that in Northern Ireland people were not convicted 'before a judge, with a jury, and with properly corroborated evidence' and recommended that these rights be restored. He received support from an unusual source, Merlyn Rees, a former Secretary of State for Northern Ireland who had been responsible for ending Special Category Status. Rees suggested that the Emergency Provisions Legislation should be re-examined, taking into account the concerns raised by McNamara. These suggestions were summarily dismissed by Thatcher.[37]

On 1 December three women in Armagh Prison – Máiréad Farrell, Máiréad Nugent and Mary Doyle – joined the strike, despite appeals from the republican leadership not to do so. Their joint statement said, 'We are prepared to fast to the death, if necessary, but our love for justice and our country will live forever.'[38] Since 1976 the women, led by Farrell, had protested against the withdrawal of political status by refusing to do prison work. As punishment they were locked up for up to 23 hours a day and denied food parcels, newspapers, cigarettes and the same rights to visits and letters as other prisoners. Earlier in 1980 they had been denied access to washing and toilet facilities. The women made it clear that they were not going on hunger strike as an act of solidarity, but in order to win political status in their own right.[39]

Twenty-three male prisoners joined the strike on 15 December, and a further seven on the following day. There had been some indications that the government was seeking a solution to the situation, with both Thatcher and Atkins making some moves towards general prison reform. The Prime Minister had even suggested that 'it is a question of getting what is already available home [sic] to those prisoners who are on hunger strike, because, really, most of the things, the ordinary things on humanitarian grounds which they had been asking for, are already available to all prisoners under ordinary prison rules.'[40] In a radio interview on the same day, after reiterating that political status would not be granted, Thatcher went on to say that, even before the hunger strikes, she and Atkins had been considering 'whether prisoners in Northern Ireland should be allowed to wear civilian clothing, issued by the Governor of the prison'.[41] On 18 December the Northern Ireland Office released a document that met some of the five demands. On the same day, Sean McKenna was so ill he had to be moved to the Royal Victoria Hospital. Brendan Hughes, who had been on hunger strike with the other six original protesters for 53 days, decided to call off the protest without consulting Bobby Sands. Some of the hunger strikers later claimed that they believed at this point that all of their demands had been met.[42] The three women were more sceptical about a settlement having been reached and continued to fast for a further day.[43]

Following the ending of the first hunger strike, the prisoners believed that they would be able to wear their own clothes. In fact, what the government had in mind was 'civilian-type clothing', a uniform of a different sort. On 10 January 1981 the republican newspaper *An Phoblacht* reported that British intransigence and inactivity was causing unrest among the prisoners, hoping 'to capitalise on any confusion in the present situation, and to demoralise the prisoners by denying them the settlement that their hunger strike had won'.[44] The paper warned that the prisoners would not be acquiescent.

On 1 March 1981 a second hunger strike commenced with Bobby Sands, a Provisional IRA prisoner, refusing food. The dirty protest was called off in both the Maze and Armagh prisons on the following day. Unlike in the previous year, prisoners who joined the strike were to do so one at a time and at staggered intervals. Members of both the IRA and the INLA were to be involved.[45] Síle Darragh, the OC in Armagh Prison, asked that the women also join this hunger strike, but permission was denied by the leadership of the IRA.[46] During the first seventeen days of his hunger strike, Sands kept a diary. On the first day he wrote:

> My heart is very sore because I know that I have broken my poor mother's heart, and my home is struck with unbearable anxiety. But I have considered all the arguments and tried every means to avoid what has become the unavoidable: it has been forced upon me and my comrades by four-and-a-half years of stark inhumanity.
>
> I am a political prisoner. I am a political prisoner because I am a casualty of a perennial war that is being fought between the oppressed Irish people and an alien, oppressive, unwanted regime that refuses to withdraw from our land.
>
> I believe and stand by the God-given right of the Irish nation to sovereign independence, and the right of any

Irishman or woman to assert this right in armed revolution. That is why I am incarcerated, naked and tortured.[47]

Sands knew there was a strong possibility that he would die. Danny Morrison, who was an envoy between the Sinn Féin leadership and the prisoners in 1981, concurred: 'I remember saying to Bobby, Thatcher will not back down. I came away knowing that his mind was set, too, though. He knew what he had to do and how it would end.'[48]

From the outset Sands's actions attracted international support. An unexpected twist came when Frank Maguire, MP for Fermanagh and South Tyrone, died on 5 March. It was decided that Sands should stand as a candidate: when the SDLP agreed not to put forward a candidate, the competition was between a republican and a unionist, Harry West. Sands won the election on 10 April by more than 1,000 votes. His win was a stunning victory for the IRA and a massive public defeat for the British government. Approximately 30,000 people voted for Sands, demonstrating that even people who did not support the republican cause did not want him or the other prisoners to die in this way.

Following Sands's election, the question arose: could Margaret Thatcher allow a fellow MP to starve to death?[49] It was quickly answered. Sands died on 5 May, after 66 days on hunger strike. He was aged 27. A week before his death, the Pope's envoy had visited him twice and tried to persuade him to end the strike.[50] The announcement of Sands's death prompted extensive rioting, which extended to the Republic. There were twenty deaths in the three weeks following his death. Sands was to be buried in the Republican Plot in Milltown Cemetery in Belfast. On the eve of his funeral, the British government sent 600 extra troops to the North. More than 100,000 people attended, in silence. There was immense international interest also, though opinion was divided, a situation summed up by Tom Hritz in the *Pittsburgh Post*:

What is Bobby Sands? A saint or a sinner? A hero or a coward? A soldier or a thug? There was a time when Tom Hritz could have answered that question very simply: sinner, coward and thug – no question about it. Now he has no easy answers. Only tough questions.[51]

In the House of Commons, Thatcher did not observe parliamentary protocol by expressing sympathy with the death of a fellow member. Three days after his death, when speaking to the Scottish Conservative Party, she spoke of the increase in IRA violence:

> One of their members has chosen to kill himself – a needless and futile waste of his life. I say 'futile', Mr President, because the political status sought by the hunger strikers will not be granted. The Government's position is clear. Crime is always crime, whatever the motive. Murder is never anything other than murder.[52]

The day after Sands died, four prominent Irish American politicians, Senators Kennedy and Moynihan, Congressman O'Neill and Governor Carey, wrote to Thatcher condemning violence but saying that the British government's 'posture of inflexibility' would only exacerbate it. Thatcher denied that this was the case, arguing that the British government had demonstrated 'great flexibility' in dealing with the prisoners. On the issue of special status, she responded:

> Political status would mean that the prisoners, not the prison authorities, would determine what the day to day regime within the prison should be. On this the government will not compromise. It is not prepared, through the granting of political status, to legitimise criminal acts undertaken in pursuit of political ends. It is not prepared to surrender control of the prisons. It is not prepared to be coerced by protest action, in whatever form, into changes for which there is no justification on humanitarian grounds. We know from experience that to do so would not bring the protests to an end. On the contrary, yielding to coercion would provoke further coercion, and would encourage more young people to follow the path of violence.[53]

Frankie Hughes died on hunger strike on 12 May. A few days later, Sinn Féin announced that a republican prisoner would be joining the protest every week. When Neil Blaney asked the Dáil to express sympathy with the bereaved families of Bobby Sands and Frankie Hughes, he was ruled to be out of order by the Speaker.[54]

On 21 May two more hunger strikers died – Raymond McCreesh and Patsy O'Hara – leading Tomás Ó Fiaich to criticize the British government's handling of the situation. If the prisoners hoped to force any backdown by the British government, Thatcher made it clear that they were mistaken. In a television interview in Belfast on 28 May, she referred to the hunger strike as the IRA's 'last card' and stated, 'You can't compromise with violence, ever. You have to beat it.' When asked about political status, she responded:

That they can never have. Murder is murder – whatever the motive. There can be no compromise for that and if there were I should be putting the lives of hundreds and thousands of men, women and children at stake. It is for them to end it. It is they who are being inflexible, intransigent, coldly, brutally cynical in the way they are carrying it out.[55]

Sinn Féin's move into electoral politics was confirmed in the general election in the Republic on 11 June, when a number of seats, as far south as County Cork, were contested by Anti-H Block candidates. Kieran Doherty, who was on hunger strike, won the seat for the Cavan-Monaghan constituency. Paddy Agnew, an H-Block prisoner who was not on hunger strike, topped the poll. Overall the election was a defeat for Haughey's Fianna Fáil Party, which lost important votes to H-Block candidates. A Fine Gael-Labour Party coalition was returned, with Garret Fitzgerald as Taoiseach. Now in opposition, Haughey made his strongest statement ever in condemning the British government.[56] The election revealed how much support the hunger strike had in the Republic, despite media restrictions placed on the campaign. The British government was clearly also concerned about the electoral support for the H-Block candidates. The day after the Irish election legislation was passed banning prisoners in any part of the United Kingdom from standing for Parliament.[57] As Sinn Féin realized, and as the Irish and British governments feared, the hunger strike had ignited nationalist feelings in Ireland in a way that nothing had since 1916.[58]

Humphrey Atkins issued a statement on 30 June affirming that Special Category Status would not be reintroduced and that the government would retain control of the prisons.[59] Privately, though, negotiations were taking place between the government and the IRA. Almost three decades later, it was revealed that on 5 July

Thatcher had agreed to a secret offer being made to the strikers that met many of their key demands. The leadership of the IRA/Sinn Féin, however, rejected the offer. Afterwards the British government denied that any such proposition had been made.[60]

On 8 July, a fifth hunger striker died. The new Taoiseach, Garret Fitzgerald, made a statement to the Dáil:

> Mr Joe McDonnell who was on hunger strike in the Maze prison died shortly after five o'clock this morning. Our deepest sympathy goes out to his widow whom I met last Friday, and to his family and friends as it must go out to the family and friends of every victim of the continuing violence in Northern Ireland.[61]

Charles Haughey, now leader of the Opposition, responded that,

> a solution could have been found and should have been found. I would urge even now that the situation be not allowed to continue any further and that whatever is necessarily involved in finding a solution should be undertaken . . . nothing should be allowed to stand in the way of a solution.[62]

In early August 1981 a new statement was smuggled out of the Maze seeking a settlement with the British government. A republican spokesman described it as a 'practical reinterpretation of the five demands'. The British government disagreed. Atkins responded, 'To my profound regret I can see nothing in this latest document which represents any substantial change.' He also reiterated that the government would not reintroduce Special Category Status or anything similar to it.[63] At this stage, eight hunger strikers had died and Thomas McElwee, a 23-year-old member of the Provisional IRA, was reported as being very ill. On the same day, Sir Leonard Figg, the British Ambassador in Dublin, officially rejected a proposal made by the Irish government that the demands should be granted to non-protesting prisoners.[64] The day after the prisoners' statement was issued, McElwee died. His death was followed by street rioting, during which two civilians were killed.[65]

Kieran Doherty TD died on 2 August. In keeping with parliamentary protocol, Garret Fitzgerald made a statement to the Dáil asking the Speaker to 'convey to the parents and the family of the late Deputy the sympathy of the House in their loss, which has added to the burden of sorrow that violence has brought to so many people in Northern Ireland'. His actions were endorsed by Haughey.[66] On 13 September Jim Prior replaced Atkins as Secretary of State for Northern Ireland. It was widely known that Thatcher and Prior did not get on. A few days later, he visited the Maze and met with the strikers.

As more men died, there was a widening divide between the IRA leadership and the families of the strikers, who wanted a resolution to be reached. Fearing that the deaths would be allowed to continue, each having a diminishing impact on public opinion, some families agreed to medical intervention.[67] On 30 September a statement was issued saying the hunger strike was effectively over; it came fully to an end on 3 October. Ten young men had died slow, painful deaths. Some of those who were on hunger strike when the protest came to an end felt guilty and disappointed that they had survived. Moreover, they feared that ending it would 'demoralise and undermine the whole struggle'.[68] A few days after the strike ended, Jim Prior, the new Secretary of State, made significant concessions to the prisoners, including the right of all prisoners to wear their own clothes, the restoration of lost remission and greater freedom of association. The ending of prison work was conceded some time later. A historian of the hunger strike, David Beresford, believed that if the right to wear civilian clothes had been conceded by Humphrey Atkins in the previous year, it was unlikely that the second and deadly hunger strike would have taken place.[69]

Like Bloody Sunday, the hunger strike was a watershed in the Troubles. Its impact extended far beyond Northern Ireland and it polarized public opinion internationally, just as it did within Ireland. Even those who deplored IRA violence admired the courage and conviction of those on strike and denounced the apparent inflexibility and indifference of Margaret Thatcher. During the protest, a survey of 73 newspapers around the world carried out by the BBC suggested that world opinion was sympathetic to the republican cause.[70] The elections of Sands and Doherty paved the way for a new approach by republicans, summed up in the phrase 'the Armalite and ballot box strategy'. In the longer term, 'the strategy of pursuing parallel military and electoral ends has paid major political dividends for Irish Republicans'.[71]

In the following decades the question was asked: did some of the hunger strikers die for no reason?[72] Initially it was the prisoners themselves who wanted a hunger strike. One British civil servant believed that the leaders of the IRA would have been happy with a continuation of the dirty protest, as it was 'fairly easy to represent it as if it were the fault of the British authorities and to arouse very understandable sympathy about the conditions in which these prisoners were being expected to live'.[73] Gerry Adams, then Vice-President of Sinn Féin, confirmed that he had not initially supported the prisoners' actions, 'because I thought that people were going to die. And also, to be quite tactical about it, because we couldn't afford another huge prison crisis which then ended the same way as the first one.'[74] As the strike progressed and more prisoners died, however, impetus to continue also came from the Sinn Féin leadership outside the prison.

In 2005 Richard O'Rawe, the publicity officer for the hunger strikers within the Maze Prison at the time, wrote that only hours before Joe McDonnell died, on 8 July, a deal was rejected by the IRA leadership outside of the prison. He accused them of wanting to exploit the political and propaganda gains that they were winning.[75] In 2009 the *Sunday Times*, which had successfully appealed for the release of certain of Margaret Thatcher's papers under the Freedom of Information Act, made similar claims. The documents confirmed that in early July Thatcher had authorized secret negotiations with the IRA and, in a reversal of her previous stance, said she was willing to meet many of the key demands. The IRA turned down the offer. Atkins assumed that it was the tone, rather than the content of the offer, that they did not like and a second offer was prepared.[76] It was rejected as well. The INLA, who also had men on hunger strike, stated that they were not made aware of this offer. The article in the *Sunday Times* suggested that five or six prisoners may have died simply to advance the politics of Sinn Féin and to ensure that Owen Carron won the parliamentary seat left empty as a result of Sands's death. It indicated that Gerry Adams, then Vice-President of Sinn Féin, was complicit in this decision.[77] Shortly afterwards, Garret Fizgerald, the former Taoiseach, suggested that, 'if the IRA had allowed them, the 1981 hunger strikers would have accepted either of two deals on offer to them in the days and hours before Joe McDonnell became the fifth man to die'.[78]

Both Danny Morrison and Brendan MacFarlane, who were the main conduits for information, denied that the deal being offered was as straightforward as suggested.[79] Additionally, MacFarlane pointed out that the government had refused to talk directly to the hunger strikers.[80] Moreover, at the end of July representatives from Sinn Féin and the Irish Republic Socialist Party had suggested that the hunger strike should be suspended for three months, but the prisoners rejected this. This proposal was made three weeks before the Fermanagh/South Tyrone election on 20 August. What these allegations and counter-allegations demonstrate is that almost 30 years after the ten men died, their deaths remained controversial and some of the old ideological battles were still being played out.

Regardless of the controversy, an ongoing fascination with what happened during the 1981 hunger strike has been demonstrated by a number of films on this topic, including *Some Mother's Son* (1996), *H3* (2001) and the Italian *The Silence of the Skylark* (2005), which was a reference to Sands's love of birds. In 2008 the hard-hitting film *Hunger*, based on the final days of Bobby Sands, won the prestigious *Camera d'Or* award at Cannes. In February 2009 it swept the board at the Irish Film and Television Awards, winning six awards. Earlier in the month, the actor playing Sands, Michael Fassbender, had won the British actor of the year award at the London Critics' Circle Awards.[81] For many, the 1981 hunger strike has been remembered simply through the character of Bobby Sands, who, with his open, fresh-faced smile, was juxtaposed against a determinedly granite image of the 'Iron Maiden', Margaret Thatcher. Sands became the poster boy of the hunger strike, providing an iconic and enduring image of the struggle. Moreover, despite having left school at fifteen, he was a prolific writer of prose and poetry, and so left a considerable written legacy. Sands's name lives on in a number of streets and monuments named after him, as far away as France, Iran, Cuba, Australia and the USA.[82]

For loyalists and their supporters, Sands remained a figure of hate and derision: the lyrics sung by fans of Rangers Football Club to the tune of 'She's Coming Round the Mountain', for example, taunts him with the offer of food:

Could you go a chicken supper, Bobby Sands?
Could you go a chicken supper, Bobby Sands?
Could you go a chicken supper, you dirty Fenian f——r
Could you go a chicken supper, Bobby Sands?[83]

The republican hunger strikes overshadowed the activities of some loyalist prisoners. On 10 December 1980 six members of the Ulster Defence Association had refused food, demanding segregation from republican prisoners. The protest was called off after six days, when the republican strike ended, but continued in other ways, including a no-wash campaign. In 1983 loyalists were segregated in the Maze. Two years later loyalist prisoners in Magilligan Prison went on hunger strike, seeking segregation there. None of the participants fasted for long enough to inflict any long-term medical injury on themselves.[84]

Despite the concessions made in October 1981, life in prison following the hunger strike was made more difficult for the women in Armagh, possibly as punishment for their participation. Since 1972 women prisoners had been subject to strip-searches, but after 1982 a policy of regular random strip searching was instituted. The number of searches was again increased in March 1983 and was particularly concentrated on non-sentenced prisoners. In 1986 the women were moved from Armagh, an old Victorian prison, to a newly built high-security prison at Maghaberry. Despite protests from feminist and human rights groups, the random searches continued. Nothing was found, but these searches always increased during times of heightened political tension, and were clearly used as a technique to intimidate, humiliate and control the women prisoners.[85]

Death and Destruction

Sectarian attacks, bombings and tit-for-tat violence were a feature of the 1980s, just as they had been of the 1970s. Between 1970 and 1981, more than 42,000 rubber, and later, plastic bullets had been used by the security forces. In 1981, the year of the main hunger strike, almost 30,000 were fired, resulting in seven deaths, three of whom were children.[86] On 13 May 1982 the European Parliament called on member states not to use plastic bullets. The Northern Irish Catholic Church and the British Labour Party also asked that their use be halted. These recommendations were ignored.[87] In July 1982 the Provisional IRA exploded bombs in London that caused the deaths of eleven soldiers and multiple injuries to both soldiers and civilians. These atrocities occurred at Hyde Park and Regent's Park in London. In the second incident seven army bandsmen were killed as they were playing a concert – at the time of the explosion, a medley from the musical *Oliver!* Public opinion in Britain and throughout the world was outraged. The attack on ceremonial guardsmen was regarded as particularly awful. Charles Haughey, the Taoiseach, was harsh in his criticism, saying, 'those responsible for these inhuman crimes do irreparable damage to the good name of Ireland and to the cause of Irish unity'. James Prior repeated a call to Irish Americans to stop supporting the IRA.[88]

An INLA bomb that exploded on 6 December 1982 during a disco at the Droppin' Well Pub in Ballykelly, County Derry, killing seventeen people and seriously injuring 30, resulted in widespread condemnation. The dead included eleven British soldiers and six civilians. Margaret Thatcher informed the House of Commons that: 'This is one of the most horrifying crimes in Ulster's tragic history. The slaughter of innocent people is the product of evil and depraved minds, and the act of callous and brutal men. No words can express our absolute revulsion and complete condemnation.'[89] During the same session, calls were made to condemn the Labour MP Ken Livingstone, who had invited some of the leaders of the Provisional IRA to Britain. Thatcher responded that 'Members were astounded that the invitation . . . was ever issued. I believe that the nation would now find it intolerable if it were not withdrawn.'[90] The invitation was not withdrawn but Gerry Adams and Danny Morrison were denied entry under the Prevention of Terrorism Act.[91]

England, especially London, continued to be a target for the IRA. A bomb exploded outside Harrods department store just before Christmas 1983. Although a warning had been given, it was judged by the security forces to have been inadequate. The IRA admitted responsibility but said that the bombing was unauthorized and they apologized for the civilian deaths. The Home Secretary, Leon Brittan, told the House of Commons, 'I find the disclaimer of responsibility utterly contemptible.' The Labour MP Gerald Kaufman concurred:

> We in the House of Commons, and the British people whom we represent, are united in our utter and implacable determination to stand firm against the evil men who perpetrated this deed, and who now characteristically and contemptibly seek to creep away from the consequences of their inhumanity. The British Parliament will make no concessions to the bullet and the bomb.[92]

One of the most audacious attacks by the IRA, which took it to the heart of British politics, was the bombing of the Grand Hotel, Brighton, during the Conservative Party Conference in October 1984. Five people were killed and many others seriously injured. Thatcher and her husband, Denis, only narrowly escaped injury. In its wake, the IRA issued a statement warning the Prime Minister, 'Today we were unlucky, but remember, we only have to be lucky once; you will have to be lucky always. Give Ireland peace and there will be no war.'[93] At Thatcher's insistence, the conference opened at 9.30 am that day, as had been scheduled. She informed the delegates, 'This attack has failed. All attempts to destroy democracy by terrorism will fail.'[94]

Two new tools were increasingly used by the security forces in the fight against the IRA and the INLA: the use of informers – referred to as 'supergrasses' – and a 'shoot-to-kill' policy. The success of the former was boasted about by the security forces; while they denied the use of the latter. On the evidence of supergrasses, people could be convicted of serious crimes, based on uncorroborated evidence and in a trial before a single judge and no jury – the Diplock system. The first supergrass trial took place on 11 April 1983 in Belfast. Fourteen members of the Ulster Volunteer Force were jailed for a total of 200 years, largely on the evidence of one man, Joseph Bennett. In August, 22 members of the IRA were imprisoned for a total of more than 4,000 years, largely on the sole evidence of Christopher Black. In total, evidence provided by these two men would lead to the conviction of 300 people. The supergrasses were granted immunity from prosecution for their testimony. Approximately 30 former activists turned informer during this period. In 1986, eighteen of those convicted on Black's evidence had their conviction overturned.[95] In the short term, the evidence given by informers and the subsequent arrests undoubtedly had an impact on the republican movement. By 1984 Northern Ireland had the largest prison population in Europe – 164 per 1,000 compared with 35 per 1,000 in the Republic – and the vast majority were young, male and Catholic.[96]

Both major parties in the Republic were critical of the supergrass system, although their responses differed. In a debate in the Dáil, Dr Rory O'Hanlon of the opposition Fianna Fáil Party described the system as 'totally alien to both Irish and British Court practice and contrary to the principles in accordance with which justice is administered throughout the democratic world'. He pointed out that those on remand could be held for up to 21 months, which he described as a different form of internment. Moreover, he believed that the RUC were compelling informers to give false information on people whom the police wanted to arrest. Overall, O'Hanlon described it as 'a ludicrous situation'.[97] Peter Barry, the Irish Minister for Foreign Affairs, responded that: 'It is very important, in Anglo-Irish relations and in our relations with the two sides of the community in Northern Ireland, that the Irish Government and Dáil Éireann be seen to take a measured and responsible view of this problem.'[98] He refused to condemn the system outright, only suggesting it should be used sparingly and with due caution.[99] The use of supergrasses was condemned in a report by Lord Gifford, a Labour peer who had been commissioned by a British civil liberties group to investigate their use. In 1984 he published a book that was highly critical of the system.[100] Nonetheless, supergrasses continued to be used, suggesting that in Northern Ireland the process of justice had again been subverted for political ends.

While the ranks of the IRA were being depleted by the supergrass trials, a psychological victory came on 25 September 1983 when 38 Irish prisoners escaped from the Maze. One prison officer was killed in the breakout. It triggered one of the largest British manhunts ever, with the Dublin government increasing surveillance on the border areas. Although nineteen men were recaptured, the IRA was jubilant and referred to it as 'the great escape'. Prior to the successful jailbreak, the Maze had been regarded as a fortress, and an angry Margaret Thatcher promised a 'very deep enquiry'. Ian Paisley called for the immediate resignation of the British Under-Secretary, while Prior promised to resign if he was found to be at fault.[101] When the report was released in January 1984, it revealed instances of corrupt practices, lax security and procedures not followed. Staff had become 'complacent' and 'lazy', and the Governor had not been up to the task of managing 'the most difficult and important prison in the United Kingdom'.[102] The resignation of the Governor allowed for a new regime to be introduced.

From the end of 1982 there were a number of incidents when republicans, usually unarmed, were killed by a covert security operation. The continued allegations of a shoot-to-kill policy were confirmed when an RUC officer involved in one of these incidents admitted that he had been told to lie in his statement. The public outcry resulted in the appointment in 1984 of the Deputy Chief

Constable of Greater Manchester, John Stalker, to investigate the shooting by police of six men – five of them republican suspects. Stalker tried to obtain access to a secret MI5 tape recording of one of the shootings. In June 1986, when Stalker was about to make his final report, recommending the prosecution of a number of officers, he was summarily removed from the inquiry and suspended for allegedly consorting with criminals. He was subsequently cleared of these allegations, but he was not returned to the inquiry. It was taken over by Colin Sampson, but its findings were never made public. It was later alleged by Stalker that Sir John Hermon had tossed the report across the room in fury and, for five months, Hermon had refused to allow him to send it to the Director of Public Prosecutions. Stalker suspected that responsibility for the cover-up ultimately lay with higher authorities in Britain.[103]

A number of other shoot-to-kill incidents occurred, including a blatant example involving the killing of eight IRA members who were ambushed by the Army and the SAS when they were attacking an RUC station in May 1987 in Loughgall. In 2001 the European Court of Human Rights ruled that their rights had been violated as no proper investigation had ever been held. The court awarded each of the victims' families £10,000 in compensation – the first time it had given compensation in such a case. The ruling was criticized by David Trimble of the Ulster Unionist Party, who described it as 'astonishing and perverse'.[104] An even more controversial incident in March 1988 involved the shooting by the SAS in Gibraltar of three IRA members, one of whom was Máiréad Farrell. It soon became apparent that the three dead were unarmed, leaving some human rights groups to criticize the use of excessive force against the IRA. In the British House of Commons, Conservative MP Ian Gow raised the issue to disparage a letter by Amnesty International 'apparently on behalf of three terrorists – mercifully now dead'.[105] When questioned during a visit to Australia about Amnesty's criticisms, Thatcher denied having seen them and suggested that the reporter should not give the IRA publicity by asking such questions.[106] At the Conservative Party Conference later in the year, Thatcher was applauded when she praised those who were trying to defeat the IRA, 'for facing danger while keeping within the rule of law – unlike the terrorist who skulks in the shadows and shoots to kill'.[107] In September 1995 the European Court of Human Rights judged the British government to have failed 'to uphold the standard expected of a democratic government'. The Deputy Prime Minister, Michael Heseltine, rejected the findings and stated that the British forces would do the same again. He also warned that the judgement would encourage a 'terrorist mentality'.[108]

The shootings in Gibraltar were to have violent, unforeseen consequences. Daniel McCann, Sean Savage and Máiréad Farrell were buried in the Republican Plot in Milltown Cemetery in West Belfast on 16 March. An estimated 10,000 people attended. Michael Stone, a loyalist, attacked the funeral cortège by shooting and throwing grenades randomly, killing three and wounding many more. His attack was watched on television screens throughout the world. Unusually, Tom King, the Northern Ireland Secretary, and Gerry Adams responded in the same way, both calling for calm. Adams, however, accused the RUC of collusion in the attack.[109] He had wondered why there were so few members of the security forces in evidence on the day, and believed it had been to facilitate Stone's assault.[110] Stone was generally regarded as a maverick on the fringes of various loyalist groups, but who had acted alone on this occasion. He was subsequently shown to have had connections to a secret unit of British Military Intelligence.[111]

More violence occurred three days later at the funeral of Kevin Brady, one of Stone's victims. Two British soldiers armed with Browning automatic pistols drove into the funeral procession. One of them, Corporal Derek Wood, fired a gun into the air. The mourners feared they were being attacked, as had been the case only a few days earlier. The soldiers were dragged from the car, brutally beaten, stripped and later shot. Graphic footage of the beatings and the shootings brought the violence of Northern Ireland life into people's sitting rooms. The Army claimed that the men were technicians, doing routine work in West Belfast; nationalists believed that they had been engaged on some undercover work.[112] Three men received life sentences for the murders in 1992. The argument that they were acting in self-defence, in light of events earlier in the week, was ignored.[113] The shooting of the three unarmed IRA members in Gibraltar had resulted in five more deaths.

Post Hunger Strike Politics

The cycle of violence, and the ever-more repressive measures taken by the government, made finding a political solution more difficult but also more imperative. Increasingly, attempts were made to find a constitutional settlement to the situation in Northern Ireland that involved the participation of the Dublin government. Cooperation between the Irish and British governments, initiated by Charles Haughey, was an unwelcome development to many unionists. Following the summit meeting at the end of 1980, Thatcher was called to task by unionist politicians and she had a meeting with Ian Paisley and Peter Robinson on 17 December to reassure them of her intentions.[114] Paisley clearly was not reassured and in February 1981 he devised the 'Carson trail', in order to protest against on-going negotiations between the two governments. In so naming it, he was deliberately portraying himself as the successor to Edward Carson, who had successfully resisted Home Rule after 1912. To leave the British government in no doubt about his intentions, he also marched 500 men up a hill in Antrim, each brandishing firearm certificates.[115] On 12 February he was suspended from the House of Commons for repeatedly calling Humphrey Atkins a liar. A few months later, he repeated his behaviour with the same outcome.[116] During a two-day visit by Thatcher to Northern Ireland in March, in an effort to assuage unionist fears, Paisley led a convoy of cars that attempted to break through the security cordon at Hillsborough Castle, where she was staying. When this was unsuccessful, they travelled to a local Free Presbyterian church and 'sang two hymns and Mr Paisley read from the Bible and prayed for "guidance in the valley of darkness"'.[117] He then embarked on a war of words with the Prime Minister, accusing Thatcher of 'lying through her teeth', to which she responded by calling him a 'desperate man' and describing his protest as ridiculous.[118]

That unionists in Northern Ireland did not regard Paisley as ridiculous was evident from the large attendances at the rallies he held throughout the province. Some were held in the evening and replicated the display of gun licences. Moreover, the growth in nationalist feeling as a result of the hunger strikes reawakened the fears of militant unionists, a fact exploited by Paisley. In March 1981 he launched his own paramilitary group, the 'Third Force', which grew to 5,500 members. Members of this shadowy militia wore armbands bearing a slogan from the Carson era, 'For God and Ulster'. When James Prior, the new Secretary of State, publicly criticized 'private armies', Paisley dismissed him as 'nothing better than a squatter'. Following the murder of the Reverend Robert Bradford by the IRA in November, Paisley warned, 'My men are ready to be recruited under the crown to destroy the vermin of the I.R.A. But if the crown refuses to recruit them, then we will destroy the I.R.A. ourselves.'[119]

On 23 November he held a day of action, urging all Protestant businesses to close. Thousands obeyed. Paisley's actions in 1981, which demonstrated as much vitriol against the British government as they did against the IRA, led some British politicians to believe that he was positioning himself as the first president of an independent Northern Ireland.[120] Certainly, he was proving to be the leader of unionist discontent. Moreover, his notoriety was spreading. The week before Christmas, the US State Department decided to revoke his visa. A spokesman on Paisley's behalf described it as a 'denial of free speech' and accused the US government of hypocrisy because they allowed IRA sympathizers to come and go without hindrance.[121] Paisley was now a figure of controversy on the world stage.

One of the legacies of the hunger strikes was the rise of Sinn Féin, which had demonstrated its potential as a force in electoral politics. This development worried both the Irish and British governments and prompted them to seek new political solutions.[122] On 6 November 1981, following a summit at Downing Street, Margaret Thatcher and Garret Fitzgerald decided to establish the Anglo-Irish Inter-Governmental Council. One of its aims was to give 'institutional expression' to the relationship between Britain and the Republic.[123] Tax increases proposed by Fitzgerald's Coalition government led to its downfall in February 1982. A minority Fianna Fáil government, led by Charles Haughey, replaced it.

In early 1982 the British government created a new assembly in Northern Ireland. It had no substantive powers but it was to contribute to the process of 'rolling devolution'. Seventy per cent agreement was required before any powers were devolved. Its support was limited to the Democratic Unionist Party and the Alliance Party, the former believing that if it were successful, it would allow them to regain control of the government of Northern Ireland.[124] The SDLP opposed it on the grounds that insufficient recognition was given to the Irish dimension.[125] However, they did take part in the elections in October 1982, as did Sinn Féin, who won more than 10 per cent of the first preference vote. Both nationalist parties refused to take their seats. The election marked the entrance of Sinn Féin into electoral politics in Northern Ireland, an occurrence that alarmed both the British government and the SDLP. The Assembly was officially dissolved in June 1986, but its ineffectiveness was apparent from the outset.

The Dublin government, led by Garret Fitzgerald since the end of 1982, continued to try to find a constitutional solution to the problems of Northern Ireland. An initiative resulting from the cooperation between the Dublin government and the SDLP was the New Ireland Forum of 1983 and 1984, which suggested that a united Ireland was the preferred option for the future. Many of its terms of reference had been drawn up when Haughey was in power, but he rejected it, as did many unionists.[126] The UUP, the DUP and the Alliance Party all refused to take part in the Forum. One of its proposals was joint rule over Northern Ireland by both governments, which Thatcher rejected. Nevertheless, the Forum provided a mechanism for 'intense negotiations' between the two governments.[127] For its supporters also, it was a way of neutralizing the electoral rise of Sinn Féin. In the British General Election in June 1983, Gerry Adams had won a seat, taking it from the SDLP, which also won only one seat. In December 1982 Adams and Morrison had been banned from entering Britain under the Prevention of Terrorism Act. This ban was now lifted although, in keeping with the abstentionist policy of Sinn Féin, Adams refused to sit in the British Parliament. At the end of 1984 Thatcher blamed the lack of progress over constitutional politics on 'terrorism, intimidation [that] stops the very reconciliation that we would wish to see, that we work for, and I believe that the majority of people there want to see'.[128]

Despite opposition from within Ireland, an outcome of the New Ireland Forum was the signing of the Hillsborough, or Anglo-Irish, Agreement in November 1985. The agreement recognized British sovereignty over Northern Ireland but, in return for agreeing to increased security arrangements for Northern Ireland, the Irish government was to have more say in the future of the province through an intergovernmental conference. It also recognized the existence of two cultures in the North, and the need to reconcile them.[129] Unionists, however, had not been formally consulted in the reaching of this agreement. The Agreement was welcomed by moderate voices in Britain and Ireland, but deplored by republicans and loyalists alike, the latter being vehemently opposed to giving Dublin any influence over the affairs of Northern Ireland. Each of the fifteen

Unionist MPs resigned, accusing the Prime Minister of 'treachery' (as stated by Enoch Powell) and insisting there be a referendum on the Agreement in Northern Ireland. A one-day strike was organized in protest. The MP Ian Gow, formerly one of Thatcher's closest allies, resigned in protest, informing her that this change of policy would 'prolong and not diminish the agony of Ulster'.[130] Gow subsequently established an anti-Agreement group. He was murdered by the Provisional IRA in 1990. His obituary in the *Daily Telegraph* read, 'His view on Ulster was straightforward: the terrorists must not win.' A Memorial Fund was set up in his honour to finance 'good causes' in Northern Ireland.[131]

Despite the apparent lack of progress made in the early 1980s, structures were put in place, language was agreed on, and agreements were reached that showed a tacit recognition by Britain of the Republic's role in the future of Northern Ireland – what Haughey had referred to in 1980 as 'the totality of relationships within these islands'.[132] Meanwhile, one of the aims of the Anglo-Irish Agreement was to establish a strong London-Dublin partnership that could undermine Sinn Féin's support in Ireland by resolving nationalist grievances through constitutional rather than violent means. The failure to consult unionists, however, gave them a profound mistrust of the British government and, in the years after 1985, the abolition of the Agreement became 'a key objective of unionist policy'.[133]

The increasing cooperation between the Dublin and London governments after 1985, especially on matters relating to security, failed to diminish the violence. In November 1987 a bomb exploded in Enniskillen town centre in County Fermanagh during a Remembrance Day Service. Eleven people – all civilians – were killed, and more than 60 injured. A remarkable feature of the suffering was the message of peace that came from it. In the forefront was Gordon Wilson, whose daughter had been killed in the explosion, while he had been injured. Although he felt those responsible should be punished, Wilson said that he forgave them. He also pleaded that no other group should seek revenge for the bombing.[134] This spirit of humanity was echoed by the SDLP MP, Seamus Mallon, who asked the Prime Minister not to use the suffering in Enniskillen for political ends, as 'the job of politics in the north of Ireland now is to translate the humanity, compassion and forgiveness of the relatives of people who have suffered in Enniskillen into politics in the north of Ireland for the betterment of all the people there'.[135]

The international outcry and condemnation of the IRA was unprecedented. Some of the leadership of the IRA and Sinn Féin denied that they had authorized the bombing, but the Fermanagh Brigade of the IRA was disbanded. Gerry Adams privately suggested that they should commence a ceasefire in order to mitigate some of the political damage they had done.[136] Ten years later, Adams apologized publicly for what he described as a 'huge tragedy'. In the short term, the Enniskillen bombing damaged Sinn Féin: in the council elections of 1989, the number of seats held by the party halved from eight to four.[137]

The Enniskillen bombing proved to be an important step in moving Sinn Féin to seek a constitutional alternative to the violence. In early 1988 they held secret meetings with John Hume of the SDLP, both agreeing that the Irish people had a right to self-determination. This round of intense negotiations came to an end on 5 September.[138] The fact that Sinn Féin was involved in secret peace talks was not obvious from the activities of its military wing. In 1988 the IRA stepped up its campaign against British soldiers, not only in Northern Ireland and Britain, but elsewhere in Europe. In May 1988 three British servicemen were killed by the IRA in the Netherlands. In June six soldiers, who had just finished running in a local marathon, were killed in Lisburn, near Belfast, when a bomb attached to the bottom of their van exploded. Early in August a soldier died in a bomb blast at a London barracks, despite tight security, and another British soldier was shot dead in his car in Belgium. Eight soldiers were killed on 21 August while travelling in an unmarked bus near Ballygawley in County Tyrone. The dead were all aged between eighteen and 21 years. Nineteen others were injured. These successful attacks led to some speculation that the IRA could have an agent in the high ranks of the British Army. Thatcher's government came under pressure from unionists to reinstate internment.[139] Haughey declared the Ballygawley killings to be 'an atrocity', but it clearly put strain on his relationship with Britain. Thatcher made a surprise one-day visit to the province in September to discuss security in the light of the upsurge in violence. When visiting a local industry she said, 'If only we could get rid of terrorists, which we must do, there is a prosperous and secure future for the people of Northern Ireland.'[140]

Economic and Social Stagnation

Both Northern Ireland and the Republic suffered economic problems in the 1980s. Although some of the difficulties, such as inflation
and increased oil prices, were global, Ireland suffered particularly
badly. The economic situation in the Republic was not helped by
political instability and constant changes in government, with power
oscillating between Charles Haughey of Fianna Fáil and Garret
Fitzgerald of Fine Gael. A respite from the internal problems of the
Republic was provided in the summer of 1984 when President
Ronald Reagan visited Ireland. Like John F. Kennedy before him, he
came proudly displaying his Irish heritage: his family was alleged to
have come from the small town of Ballyporeen in County Tipperary. Also, like Kennedy, Reagan was allowed to address a joint session of the Irish Parliament, thus becoming only the second foreign
guest to be allowed to do so.[141] Unlike that of Kennedy, however,
Reagan's visit was controversial, largely due to the unpopularity of
US foreign policy. Not all objected, however, and a pub in Ballyporeen was renamed The Ronald Reagan Lounge.[142]

Haughey's skills at accumulating personal wealth were not
transposed to the economy. His party's ill-judged budget of 1977,
based on borrowing, increased public spending and tax cuts, exacerbated the problem.[143] In 1980, in a famous TV address, Haughey
declared: 'We are living way beyond our means – and borrowing at
a rate which just cannot continue'. Despite his words, higher government spending followed, in a desperate bid to retain power in
the 1981 election. As a consequence, between 1980 and 1982 the
national debt doubled, yet rising budget deficits were dealt with by
even higher borrowings.[144] It was not until the spring of 1983 that
inflation subsided and there were faint hopes that the worst of the
recession was over, although the new Taoiseach warned the public
of the dangers of 'false dawns'.[145] In fact, much of the 1980s was
marked by high unemployment and large-scale emigration. By the
middle of the decade Ireland had reaped the initial benefits of
belonging to the European Economic Community. Membership
had attracted subsidies to build better infrastructure. Years of pro-
tectionism and fiscal mismanagement, however, meant that the
Republic did not have enough competitive products to sell within
the Community.[146] High unemployment aroused the conscience of
Irish musicians who, in May 1986, held a fourteen-hour benefit

concert in Dublin known as 'Self-Help'. Bono, the lead singer of the successful group U2, preceded his performance by proclaiming, 'This is a song about pride – don't let them take it away!' Job pledges and donations were made on the day, but the structural problems were too deep to be solved in this way.[147]

The economic downswing in the 1980s created a new generation of emigrants, although, unlike earlier generations, a large number of them were highly educated and highly skilled. In the United States – still a favoured destination for Irish migrants, both legal and illegal – they were referred to as 'the new wave'.[148] Within Ireland, this 'brain drain' caused some concerns: in 1980, only 8 per cent of college graduates were leaving Ireland; by the end of the decade, this had risen to 30 per cent. Moreover, half of all engineering and 70 per cent of architecture students emigrated within six months of graduation.[149] Critics of the brain drain accused the government of educating its young simply to export them. By the end of the 1980s there was pessimism that 'as a small-scale, geographically peripheral, unindustrialized and ex-colonial economy, Ireland cannot provide sufficient challenging jobs for its graduate population, which is itself increasing'.[150] More worryingly, it appeared that the Irish economy would become bankrupt unless fiscal austerity could be agreed on and implemented.[151] This dramatic change in approach was to contribute to the economic phenomenon of the 1990s known as the 'Celtic Tiger'.

The Northern Ireland economy also fared badly in the 1980s. Between 1980 and 1983, unemployment rose from 10 per cent to 17 per cent despite an extra public spending package of £48 million provided by the British government in August 1980.[152] The decade started with a series of closures and lay-offs. In June 1980 the Grundig Company announced that its factory in Belfast would close with the loss of 1,000 jobs. A Grundig manager, Thomas Niedermayer, had been kidnapped and killed, possibly by accident, by the IRA in 1973.[153] His remains were not found until 1980.[154] In September 1980 the Du Pont factory closed in Derry. The following year, both Courtaulds and ICI closed their factories in County Antrim, blaming cheap international competition.[155] In 1982 the British government announced that it would be giving no further economic support to the financial white elephant, the DeLorean Company. Without subventions, it clearly could not survive. The plant closed later that year with the loss of 2,500 jobs. DeLorean railed against the Conservative government, saying, 'The UK government closed [the plants] because the Catholic employees were said to be turning to the IRA.'[156] Closures and staff lay-offs followed at Harland and Wolff, British Enkalon, Michelin and Goodyear. Unemployment grew but so did emigration; without that safety valve, unemployment may have been twice as high.[157] In addition to the closures, the IRA's campaign to disrupt business and investment in Ireland also contributed to the economic uncertainty. In the 1980s the republicans kidnapped a number of high-profile businessmen. Shergar, then the world's most valuable racehorse, was kidnapped in 1983; the horse's remains were never found.[158] Whatever the reasons for the poor economic performance, on all indicators of development, Northern Ireland not only showed itself to be the poorest region in the United Kingdom in the early 1980s, but also one of the poorest areas within the European Community.[159]

The economic torpor was mirrored by social inertia on both sides of the border. Within both the Republic and Northern Ireland, social and religious conservatism were a feature of the 1980s. There were some attempts to modernize the Republic, with women's groups often being in the forefront of the demand for change. There were also attempts to entrench its conservatism in law. On 7 September 1983 a referendum was held on whether to include an amendment to the Irish Constitution banning abortion. Although abortion had been illegal since 1861, some self-termed 'pro-life' groups, led by the Society for the Protection of the Unborn Child, wanted it to be prohibited by the Constitution. They were vigorously opposed by others, including the Women's Right to Choose Group, which had been founded in 1980. Despite an estimated 4,000 Irish girls and women going to Britain every year for an abortion, there had been no real demand in Catholic Ireland for the law to change.[160] Nonetheless, the debate leading up to the referendum proved to be highly emotive. When the counting was completed, 66.9 per cent had voted in favour of the 'pro-life' amendment. In 1986 Justice Hamilton ruled that the provision of information on how to obtain an abortion abroad would be in breach of the Constitution, since it undermined the right to life of the unborn. Some students' unions were later to challenge this decision by distributing relevant literature.[161] Unionists in Northern Ireland could point to the outcome of the abortion referendum as a demonstration of the ongoing hold of the Catholic Church in the Republic. Since the

Stormont government had chosen not to adopt the 1967 Act that made abortion legal in England and Wales, abortion was not available in Northern Ireland. Instead, an estimated 1,500 women travelled to Britain each year seeking an abortion. Moreover, opposition to any change in Northern Ireland came not only from the Catholic Church, but also from Protestant and evangelical groups, including Ian Paisley's Free Presbyterian Church.[162]

Divorce had been prohibited in the South in 1925, when the new Irish state was in its infancy. By passing this law, the state had given an early indication that on social issues it was taking a different stand from the six counties in the North.[163] A referendum on divorce held in the Republic in June 1986 was bitterly contested. Although the Catholic Church hierarchy was opposed to divorce, overall they took a moderate stance. A more powerful argument against it proved to be issues relating to land and inheritance laws. Anti-divorce activists also argued that the livelihoods of women and children would be put at risk if divorce was permitted.[164] The referendum was lost by 63 to 37 per cent. By the 1990s the only western countries to constitutionally ban divorces were Chile, Malta and Ireland.[165] In both debates on abortion and divorce, 'the forces of moral conservatism had showed themselves to be far better skilled in modern pressure groups techniques than those who sought to modernize Irish society'.[166] Furthermore, despite the results of the referenda, the accompanying debates had demonstrated that many Irish people wanted a more secular society.

Homosexuality was an issue over which both the Republic and Northern Ireland took a conservative approach in the 1980s, at times giving legitimacy to the actions of homophobic groups. Within the Republic, homosexuality and sodomy were illegal and could be punished by imprisonment. Attacks on homosexuals were rarely punished: as late as 1982, for example, when Declan Flynn was murdered by a homophobic gang in Dublin, his assailants, although tried and found guilty, were given suspended sentences.[167] David Norris, a lecturer at Trinity College and a founder of the Irish Gay Rights Movement in 1974, challenged the laws that criminalized sodomy in the early 1980s. After hearing Norris's case, Justice McWilliams of Ireland's High Court ruled that sodomy should remain illegal, because, 'Nature dictates that the purpose of reproduction is procreation.' Norris's lawyers appealed to the Supreme Court, but their efforts to decriminalize sodomy were not to be rewarded: on 22

April 1983, by a 3–2 decision, the Court upheld the constitutionality of Ireland's anti-sodomy laws.[168] Norris's response was to take his case to the European Court of Human Rights.[169] Mary Robinson was his lawyer. They finally won the case in 1993.

In Northern Ireland the 1967 legislation on homosexuality, as with abortion, had not been adopted by the Stormont government. In October 1981 the European Court ruled that the British government was discriminating against homosexuals by treating homosexuality as a crime in Northern Ireland. A few months later, in February 1982, the British government announced that it would amend laws in Northern Ireland relating to homosexual acts to bring them into line with Britain.[170] Ian Paisley responded by reviving his 'Save Ulster from Sodomy' movement, which he had founded in 1977. In 1982, when the first Gay Rights Conference was held in Queen's University Students Union, members of the DUP and Free Presbyterian Church protested against it, brandishing 'Save Ulster from Sodomy' placards. The next day, delegates to the National Union of Students conference had printed tee-shirts with the slogan 'Save Sodomy from Ulster'.[171] Homosexuality was to remain anathema for many members of the DUP – and to some members of the Paisley family: as late as 2007 Ian Paisley Jr, in an interview in *Hot Press* magazine, made homophobic comments that were widely criticized in all parts of Ireland.[172]

Adherence to traditional Catholic teachings remained high in the 1970s with more than 90 per cent of Catholics attending Mass at least once a week. By the end of the 1990s, it had dropped to the low 60s. The process of disengagement had commenced in the 1980s.[173] However, divorce, contraception and abortion remained illegal. The dissatisfaction of sections of Irish youth with the Republic's traditionalist approach was expressed by the Boomtown Rats, a Dublin Irish punk/new wave pop group, whose 'Banana Republic' (1980) included the accusation that the Republic was controlled by police and priests, and that this had contributed to the country becoming a 'Septic Isle'.[174]

A few years later their lead singer, Bob Geldof, was to achieve fame and global praise for putting together an international music concert to raise funds for famine in Ethiopia. The concerts and the subsequent single – 'Do They Know It's Christmas?' – were an overwhelming success, bringing together the leading British, Irish and American musicians of the day. In total, Live Aid and associated events raised £150 million for famine relief.[175] Geldof also politicized the issue when he publicly berated Margaret Thatcher for her policies on this issue. In recognition of his charity work, Geldof received a nomination for the Nobel Peace Prize and an honorary British knighthood in 1986.[176] The rebel Irish rocker was thus being distinguished by the most conservative of British institutions.

Underlying what appeared to be a stagnant decade economically and socially, changes were taking place that transformed various aspects of Irish society and challenged its traditional patriarchy. Between 1971 and 1987 the number of women in the Southern workforce grew by more than 40 per cent. During the same years, the number of married women in paid employment outside the home grew by 500 per cent.[177] Yet, despite the existence of the 1974 Anti-Discrimination (Pay) Act, by 1992 earnings by Irish women remained at only 70 per cent of that of men.[178] Nonetheless, breaking free from the constraints of the home and of economic dependence transformed the expectations of women and this was an important factor in the changes that took place in the Irish Republic in the 1990s.

Regardless of the political and economic backdrop, the 1980s proved to be a culturally rich decade. In the Republic poets such as Eavan Boland, Thomas Kinsella and Brendan Kennelly, playwrights Bernard Farrell and Tom Murphy, writers John McGahern, John Banville and Jennifer Johnson, as well as the emerging novelist Patrick McCabe, all enjoyed critical approbation. At the end of the decade, also, Marina Carr was being noted as a remarkable new playwright and Jim Sheridan was hailed as a film director with enormous potential. International fame, acclaim and commercial success were achieved by a number of Irish artists, including the novelist Maeve Binchy, the rock group U2, and the film director Neil Jordan. Furthermore, artists in the Republic were helped by the founding of *Aosdána* in 1980, which was a self-electing group of artists who had a basic income guaranteed by the state. It had been an initiative of Charles Haughey, who throughout his long political career had shown an abiding interest in promoting Irish culture. The political turbulence of the 1980s, however, found little outlet in the writings of these artists. According to the cultural critic Declan Kiberd, the traumatic events of the 1980s passed 'without finding their laureate'.[179]

Northern Ireland in the 1980s was inevitably dominated by the ongoing violence, but as had been evident in the previous decade, the conflict did not stifle the cultural vibrancy of the province. Seamus Heaney continued to find new audiences outside Ireland, to such an extent that in 1982 he was included in the *Penguin Book of Contemporary British Poetry*. He objected in verse, pointing out that his passport was green, that is, Irish. Even more pointedly, he added that he had no desire to toast the Queen.[180] He later revealed that he had objected to being labelled British and had used his poetry to make a political statement, because he felt 'honour-bound to break silence about the whole British/Irish thing'.[181]

Other writers such as Paul Muldoon, John Montague, Michael Longley, William Trevor, Seamus Deane and Brian Moore also enjoyed success outside the island of Ireland. They were joined by a new generation of writers who brought Protestant and female voices into the cultural mix. The most successful of the new generation were the poets and literary critics Tom Paulin and Seamus Deane, the poet Eilish Martin, the writers Bernard MacLaverty and Anne Devlin, and the poet Medbh McGuckian, who in 1986 became the first woman writer-in-residence at Queen's University. Her collections of poetry also won literary awards in both Britain and Ireland.[182]

In theatre, the Donegal-born Frank McGuinness consolidated his reputation with his 1985 play, *Observe the Sons of Ulster Marching Towards the Somme*. According to the critic Michael Parker, 'his drama serves as a timely reminder of how unionist imaginations in the present are haunted by the sacrifices of past generations, and how cultural growth and maturation are possible only when those who make up the people on the island come to terms with the heterogeneity within their ranks'.[183] The end of the decade witnessed the emergence of a brilliant new playwright, Gary Mitchell, whose loyalist background gave him the credentials to write with authority about his community, but by doing so he alienated some of them to such an extent that he was driven from his home by loyalist paramilitaries in 2005.[184] Attempts to find a middle ground in Northern politics continued, although the hunger strike of 1981 threw a long shadow over the nationalist community. Nevertheless, in *Billy – Three Plays for Television* (1982–7) and *Lost Belongings* (1987) the writers Graham Reid and Stewart Parker used the medium of television to explore life in working-class loyalist communities and the difficulties of breaking out of that milieu.[185]

An exciting development for Northern Irish theatre occurred in 1980 when the much-lauded playwright Brian Friel, together with a young actor, Stephen Rea, helped to found the Field Day Theatre Company to provide a forum for Northern plays. By doing so, they were eligible to access money from the Northern Ireland Arts Council and others. The company's first production, the world premiere of Brian Friel's *Translations*, was presented at the Guildhall in Derry on 23 September 1980. The actors were primarily from the North, and included not only Rea, but also Liam Neeson, a young actor from Ballymena, County Antrim. It opened to instant acclaim.[186]

Uncertainty about how to address the conflict remained evident in all aspects of Irish culture in the 1980s. Field Day helped to change the cultural landscape in Northern Ireland, however, by engaging with political issues in the heart of the arena in which they were being played out.[187] In regard to *Translations*, Friel said that he wanted to write a play 'about the death of the Irish language and the acquisition of English, and the profound effects that that change-over would have on a people'.[188] No Irish was spoken in the play. The opening of *Translations* and the creation of Field Day marked a small but significant cultural shift from Dublin as the cultural centre of Ireland. During its existence the company produced ten new plays by some of Ireland's leading writers, as well as the celebrated *Field Day Anthology of New Irish Writing* and the *Field Day Pamphlets* series. When asked about the relationship between Field Day and Irish nationalism, Friel explained, 'I think it should lead to a cultural state, not a political state. And I think out of that cultural state, a possibility of a political state follows. That is always the sequence.'[189] The political nature of Friel's plays engaged literary critics over the succeeding decades. While early critics tended to view him as espousing 'a relatively unproblematicized Irish nationalism', by the early twenty-first century his work was being re-examined within the framework of post-nationalist discourses and subaltern studies. His frustrations with Irish nationalism and with the unionist and nationalist position were revealed to be more complex than had sometimes been suggested.[190] According to one recent analysis: 'Brian Friel wrote post-colonial drama before the term was coined or theoreticians and critics discovered its potential'.[191]

Despite the opening of Field Day, theatre in Ireland remained a middle-class vehicle and those involved with it tended to have little direct involvement with the violence being played out each day on the streets of Northern Ireland. A very different approach was taken in 1983 when republican prisoners in H-Block decided to perform their own plays. The purpose was both educational and morale-boosting, and it was regarded as a way of encouraging political debate, especially among non-republican prisoners.[192] Little has survived of these attempts to challenge literary and theatrical conventions, and to give a literary voice to those who had been denied one by the governments of both Britain and Ireland.

Censorship continued to be used throughout the 1980s as a way of stifling not only republican voices, but also those who expressed any sympathy with the course they were promoting. In 1981 the BBC banned 'Invisible Sun', a single by the band the Police, the lyrics of which referred to the 'barrel of an Armalite' and 'keeping out of trouble like the soldiers say'. It continued 'And they're only going to change this place by killing everybody in the human race'.[193] A more hard-edged criticism of Thatcher's policies in Ireland was made by the Pogues in 1987, with the single 'Streets of Sorrow/Birmingham Six'. The BBC banned it, and a live performance on 'Friday Night Live' was abruptly interrupted by adverts.[194]

British television broadcasting was also closely monitored, although the pattern of self-censorship continued. ITV was put under enormous official pressure not to broadcast Death on the Rock, a British TV documentary made by Thames Television investigating the circumstances surrounding the killing of three unarmed IRA members in 1988 (see above). Following its showing, the government set up an inquiry, which concluded that the programme was generally accurate. Thatcher rejected its findings and Thames Television did not get its franchise renewed.[195] Moreover, the government punished what it described as 'irresponsible journalism' with the passing of broadcasting restrictions in October 1988, which prohibited the words spoken by anybody who supported (in the broadest sense) a proscribed organization.[196] Some broadcasters responded by using the voice of actors or sub-titles. The response to Death on the Rock showed that when it came to reporting Northern Ireland, the government was willing to stifle both information and public debate.

Following the broadcast of Death on the Rock, a ban that was similar to, though less rigorous than, that in place in Ireland was introduced in October 1988 by Douglas Hurd, the Home Secretary, and remained in force for six years. Although eleven organizations were included in the ban (later increased to thirteen), it was sometimes referred to as 'the Sinn Féin ban', suggesting the group at which it was largely targeted. More bizarrely, groups such as *Cumann na Bann* (a largely defunct women's group founded in 1900) were included in the veto. Inevitably, British liberals disliked the ban and it was mocked by countries such as the Soviet Union, who used it to show the hollowness of British democracy.[197] The ban followed a period of escalating violence that commenced with the shootings in Gibraltar, and led to the indiscriminate murder of three people attending their funerals, and the killing of two out-of-uniform British soldiers during the follow-up funeral. Its timing also meant that it would damage Sinn Féin's chances of continuing electoral success using a strategy towards which it had been moving since the death of the ten hunger strikers and Bobby Sands's electoral success in 1981. A decade that had commenced with hunger strikes was coming to a close with continuing violence, repression, misinformation and intransigence. Political divisions appeared to be as wide as ever, with little prospect of peace on the horizon.

SEVEN

Overtures

The year 1989 marked the twentieth anniversary of British troops being deployed to Northern Ireland, initially to protect the Catholic population. The murders, bombings and destruction, which had been a feature of local life since that time, continued. The IRA marked the anniversary by intensifying its campaign against the armed forces both in Northern Ireland and in England. Some attacks were particularly lethal and shocking. On 22 September 1989 a bomb exploded in the barracks at Deal, Kent, which housed the Royal Marines School of Music. The explosion destroyed the recreation centre, killing ten musicians in the staff band and injuring twenty-two, one of whom died later. Most of the victims were teenagers.[1] When visiting the injured in hospital, Margaret Thatcher exhorted journalists who questioned her about security arrangements:

> Do not let that deflect you from whose fault it was. It was the fault of the monsters who did common murder. That is whose fault it was and no-one – but no-one – who is against violence or murder should harbour them, give them safe haven – they should come forward and give any information they have.[2]

In the same year, the so-called 'Guildford Four' were released on 19 October. They had been imprisoned in 1975 for bombings in Guildford, Surrey, and had spent fifteen years in jail for a crime they had not committed. Their imprisonment was described as the biggest miscarriage of justice to have taken place in Britain. The investigation leading to their release had also thrown doubt on the integrity of the British police.[3] The case was a grim reminder that British justice was not always just.

Various political initiatives had been tried and failed. Hopes for peace remained as elusive as ever. Northern Ireland was still governed by Direct Rule, and Margaret Thatcher, British Prime Minister since 1979, was still in office. Over the preceding decade, the government of the Republic had alternated between Charles Haughey of Fianna Fáil and Garret Fitzgerald of Fine Gael, sometimes in quick succession. A Republican, George H. W. Bush, was President of the United States and both he and his predecessor, Ronald Reagan, had shown relatively little interest in the affairs of Northern Ireland or wished to risk offending their ally Thatcher by endorsing the support for nationalists shown by some Irish Americans.[4]

For years, the legal process in Ireland had been subverted to the political exigencies of successive British governments. Thus paramilitaries, especially republican paramilitaries, had been denied access to the normal channels of justice. Increasingly, solicitors who acted on behalf of republican prisoners were themselves regarded as criminals. In January 1989 a Home Office Minister, Douglas Hogg, caused uproar when he said that some solicitors in Northern Ireland were 'unduly sympathetic to the IRA'.[5] Hogg refused to expand on this statement or to back down, simply saying that he had been given this information by 'people who are dealing with these matters'.[6] On 12 February two masked men broke into the Belfast home of the solicitor Pat Finucane and shot him dead, injuring his wife in the process. His three children also witnessed the murder. The following day, the Ulster Freedom Fighters (UFF) claimed responsibility. Before his death, Finucane had represented a number of members of the IRA and the INLA, including Bobby Sands.[7] Some of his siblings were closely involved with the IRA. Finucane, however, was a successful criminal lawyer who had acted on behalf of republican clients.[8] Prior to his death, Finucane claimed that he had received a number of death threats, the majority of which had been made by officers in the RUC.[9] Giving credibility to Hogg's claims, and consolidating his unpopularity with nationalists, John Hermon, Chief Constable of the RUC from 1980 to 1989, insisted that 'Pat Finucane was associated with the IRA and he used his position as a lawyer to act as a contact between suspects in custody and republicans on the outside.'[10]

Finucane's death was initially thought to be at the hands of two members of the UDA, acting in collusion with the security forces. It was later alleged that Finucane had been murdered by a loyalist death squad deployed by a British Military Intelligence Unit and headed by a female officer. Their targets were republicans and nationalists.[11] 'The Dirty War', an edition of BBC TV's investigative 'Panorama' series, made fresh claims in 1992 about the role of Brian Nelson, a British Army Intelligence agent, and about various loyalist bombings and murders, including that of Finucane.[12] Claims of an 'inner circle', comprised of members of the RUC and UDR, acting in collusion, were made in a British Channel Four programme, *The Committee*, shown in October 1991. The RUC Chief Constable, Sir Hugh Annesley, claimed that the programme-makers had been duped by someone with a grudge against the RUC. Nonetheless, they were fined £75,000 in the High Court for refusing to name their sources – who actually numbered more than 100.[13] If the fine was meant to deter the media from investigating this topic, it failed. In 1992 two 'Panorama' programmes alleged that collusion had led to the death of up to 80 Catholics, including Pat Finucane, and other sections of the British and Irish media took the claims seriously. The *Irish Times* believed that the programmes '*prima facie* amount to a serious indictment of the British government's security machine, through much of the 1990s and possibly earlier'.[14] The *Irish News* claimed that the investigation 'represented a massive contribution towards the search for the truth'.[15] And the *Mirror* declared:

> The brutal imagery of Pat Finucane's murder on Panorama last night was a chilling reminder of a sick past. Allegations of state involvement in murder are shocking. The truth must be known about what happened to Pat Finucane. Until it is, many people will find it impossible to place their faith in the forces of law and order.[16]

Nor was outrage confined to Britain and Ireland. The *New York Times* pronounced that:

> Last week the BBC aired an interview with Ken Barrett, the confessed gunman in the killing, who said unambiguously that the death squad to which he belonged had shot Mr Finucane at the direction of Northern Ireland police and British Army officers. Britain has long resisted pressure for an independent public investigation into the murder of Mr

Finucane and others in which official collusion is suspected.
It is now imperative for London to acknowledge that only
a full and public airing can do justice in these cases.[17]

Belatedly, it seemed, the mainstream media were taking claims of
collusion seriously.

Collusion was confirmed by the Stevens Inquiry (in fact, three
inquiries), which reported in 2003. It had been established in response
to sustained claims of collusion by the British Irish Rights Watch, a
group established in 1990 to monitor the human rights dimension of
the conflict.[18] The Stevens Inquiry verified the existence of British
Army agents, referred to as 'Covert Human Intelligence Sources',
and even named a number of those who had been involved in various cases of collusion. By the time Stevens reported, a covert agent
known as 'Stakeknife' had been uncovered. Freddie Scappaticci, a
republican from Belfast, had become a British agent operating at the
highest security levels of the IRA. His presence had greatly damaged
the organization.[19] The revelations concerning him and his activities confirmed that a covert war had been going on for years.

The Inquiry was hampered from the outset. John Stevens, Commissioner of the Metropolitan Police Service, admitted that:

> Throughout my three Enquiries I recognized that I was
> being obstructed. This obstruction was cultural in its nature
> and widespread within parts of the Army and the RUC. I am
> confident that through the investigative efforts of my
> Enquiry team, I have managed to overcome it and achieve
> the overall objectives of my Enquiry [sic].

Nevertheless, crucial evidence was withheld or destroyed, information was leaked, and the Incident Room was destroyed by fire –
apparently arson – all suggesting the extent of information that
needed to be kept hidden. Regardless of these impediments, Stevens
reported that:

> I have uncovered enough evidence to lead me to believe that
> the murders of Patrick Finucane and Brian Adam Lambert
> could have been prevented. I also believe that the RUC
> investigation of Patrick Finucane's murder should have
> resulted in the early arrest and detection of his killers.[20]

Although numerous convictions followed, nobody was prosecuted for the murder of Pat Finucane. The Finucane family had not
cooperated with Stevens as they wanted a full public and independent inquiry. They were supported by Labour MP Kevin McNamara,
who had called for a debate on the report in the House of Commons. He was critical of the response of his own party, pointing out
that it should have been the Secretary of State, Paul Murphy, who
called for the debate. McNamara's message was unequivocal and
highly critical:

> I believe that the findings of Sir John Stevens – even in the
> form of an interim overview – represent the most damning
> indictment of the security services and by implication Gov-
> ernment practice I can recall . . .
>
> I believe the public has been kept in the dark for too long.
> I believe the Government has colluded in unlawful activi-
> ties of its agents.
>
> I believe those that are guilty must be called to account –
> however high up. Where there is sufficient evidence, they
> must be prosecuted and punished.
>
> It is clear that existing mechanisms for oversight and
> scrutiny of the intelligence services have failed. A commit-
> tee that is appointed by the Prime Minister, meets in secret
> and has its reports vetted in advance of publication cannot
> provide the accountability we are entitled to demand . . .
>
> The charges made by Sir John Stevens are the most seri-
> ous to be faced by any Government in Britain. They go to
> the very heart of our democracy. Our commitment to
> human rights, to the rule of law and to justice in Northern
> Ireland will count for nothing if we cannot address these
> matters openly and honestly.[21]

Failure to prosecute resulted in Geraldine Finucane, Pat Finucane's
widow, initiating her own actions, including seeking damages from
the Ministry of Defence.[22] For twenty years, Finucane's death
would be a source of anguish to his family, of anger and frustration
to nationalists, and a subject of evasion and obfuscation by the
security forces and government officials. It was not until 2005 that a
further inquiry, albeit of limited scope, was announced. This
followed years of pressure from his family, the SDLP and Sinn Féin

and, intermittently, the Irish government and a number of Labour and American politicians.[23] They continued to demand an independent inquiry. In 2007 it was announced that no member of the security forces would be charged with the murder. The BBC also recognized the existence of a 'hidden war' and suggested that Finucane's controversial killing lay at the heart of it.[24] In a society where injustice had become commonplace, Finucane's death and its aftermath were glaring indictments of the shortcomings of a society in which justice and the due legal process had become a chimera.

Local government elections were held on 17 May 1989. Although the dominant political parties continued to be the Ulster Unionist Party and the SDLP, the Democratic Unionist Party won almost 18 per cent of the vote, and Sinn Féin won over 11 per cent. Sinn Féin achieved this result despite the continuing media bans by the governments of the Republic and Britain. However, the IRA's bombing campaign in the previous year, notably in Enniskillen on Remembrance Day, had lost them support that would take years to regain. Nonetheless, the British government's concern about the electoral rise of Sinn Féin was evident in the introduction earlier in the year of an Act that compelled candidates to sign a form saying that they had not engaged in, nor did they endorse, acts of violence.[25] The electoral process differed in other ways from that in the rest of the United Kingdom, with strict rules governing the production of identification by voters.[26]

In the European elections in June 1989, the DUP proved to be the most popular party, winning almost 30 per cent of the vote. The result was an indication of the changing balance of power between the two main unionist parties. The SDLP won the second largest numbers of votes – over 25 per cent – with Sinn Féin winning less than 10 per cent.[27] In the Republic, Fianna Fáil gained over 30 per cent of first preference votes, with Fine Gael gaining less than 22 per cent.[28] A European-wide survey on the four main issues that affected voters' choices revealed that in the Republic they were: 1. Emigration; 2. Fiscal crisis; 3. Northern Ireland; 4. Reduction of direct taxation. In Northern Ireland they were listed as: 1. Community relations; 2. Affordable housing and homelessness; 3. Falling standards in health service; 4. Cutbacks in schools and universities.[29] The survey suggested that the problems of the North were of less importance than economic ones to people in the Republic.

There was a General Election in the Republic in June 1989. The Dáil had been dissolved in May, following the defeat of the minority Fianna Fáil government on a private member's bill. The fact that calling a General Election was not essential at that time led to rumours that Haughey wanted to increase his party's majority. The June election returned Fianna Fáil to power in coalition with the Progressive Democrat Party. The Progressive Democrats had been formed from a rancorous split within Fianna Fáil in 1985, one of the major divisions relating to Haughey's style of leadership. The alliance marked a remarkable compromise in that the PDs were willing to accept Haughey as the new Taoiseach and Fianna Fáil had never before been part of a Coalition government.[30]

As the voting patterns had shown, Northern Ireland and the economy continued to be the major problems facing both the Irish and the British governments. The Anglo-Irish Agreement had provided for the two governments to meet regularly to discuss Northern Ireland. The continuing refusal of the unionists to participate in talks that included an 'Irish dimension' limited an opportunity for real progress. A number of issues also continued to be contentious, with little middle ground. Accusations of collusion between the security forces and loyalist groups were given substance when, in September 1989, the UFF claimed that it had been given secret files on members of the IRA. Nationalists called for the disbanding of the Ulster Defence Regiment. At this stage, seventeen members of the UDR had been found guilty of murder, their victims Catholics whom they suspected of having republican links. Charles Haughey entered the debate when he announced that in the October meeting of the Anglo-Irish Conference he was going to raise the issue of the future of the regiment. Ian Paisley, leader of the DUP, informed the British House of Commons that:

> A concentrated and concerted effort is being made by the IRA, the Dublin Government, the Social Democratic and Labour Party and a certain unextraditable Roman Catholic priest utterly to discredit the Ulster Defence Regiment which has lost 180 members by the murderous actions of Republican terrorists in Northern Ireland . . . members of the Ulster Defence Regiment have been treated as terrorists.[31]

Thatcher continued to publicly praise members of the UDR as 'brave, brave, brave men' and the Minister for Defence informed his fellow MPs that they should not 'allow the actions of a few to tarnish the reputation of the overwhelming majority of the UDR, who carry out their duties professionally, loyally and impartially'.[32] As the murder of Pat Finucane had demonstrated, accusations of collusion remained unresolved and continued to fester.

The constitutional future of Northern Ireland had reached an impasse. In November 1989 the Dáil held a two-day debate on Anglo-Irish relations. There was some disappointment with the lack of progress made as a result of the Anglo-Irish Agreement, especially in regard to economic, social and cultural initiatives. In regard to political issues, the general consensus was that progress over the preceding years had been 'erratic'.[33] Unlike many of the debates of the preceding years, there was more emphasis on breaking down cultural barriers and engaging in dialogue with the Protestant community. A further shift had taken place whereby the IRA, and not unionists, were viewed by many as the biggest barrier to progress, even by members of Fianna Fáil. The Minister for Energy averred:

> The greatest single problem to be solved on the island of Ireland today is the 20 year campaign of murder, intimidation and violence in Northern Ireland. In recent years around the world we have seen a cessation of some of the bloodiest wars since the end of the Second World War – the awful Iran/Iraq conflict has ceased and the Russians have pulled their troops out of Afghanistan. Despite recent setbacks, strenuous efforts have been made to bring peace to Central America.
>
> Elsewhere, the Berlin Wall is crumbling; the Iron Curtain is melting and in South Africa, the white régime is finally beginning to dismantle apartheid and to set the imprisoned black African leaders free.
>
> But, in Northern Ireland, death still lurks in the hedgerows, in culverts and in back alleys, as the Provisional IRA carry on their self-declared and self-mandated murder campaign of ordinary people. Their whole campaign has become not merely the antithesis of democracy, but is even a perversion of language as they talk of liberation and peace with justice.[34]

During the debate one Deputy suggested that the only way out of the impasse was 'through dialogue'.[35] Nobody, however, seemed to be suggesting that this should be extended to republicans. The latter point was evident following an invitation made to Gerry Adams, the leader of Sinn Féin, to speak at a fringe meeting on Northern Ireland during the Labour Party Conference. The invitation was disliked by the Labour Party leadership and it caused fury within the Conservative Party. Neil Kinnock, the leader of the Labour Party, wrote to the Minister of Defence saying:

> neither I nor my colleagues who form the great majority of the Labour Party give any quarter to Sinn Féin, whatever form it takes, and that I believe that those who applaud Gerry Adams and his associates are profoundly wrong and that I have told them so in very direct terms . . . You are also aware that I have no power to prevent people who have committed no known offence being in Brighton or speaking to a public meeting. Neither, in a free country, have you.[36]

Allowing Adams to speak was also opposed by the nationalist newspaper, the *Irish News*, which asserted:

> We have regrettably too many who adopt an ambiguous and inherently dishonest attitude. Gerry Adams and other Sinn Féin spokespeople unapologetically proclaim support for cold-blooded murder that leaves a pathetic and all-too-often overlooked tragic multitude of widows, widowers, orphans and friends. To admit Gerry Adams and colleagues to the public halls of civilized democratic debate is increasingly and properly perceived as deeply offensive and repugnant to Christian and humanitarian standards.[37]

Worse was to come. At the beginning of November, Peter Brooke, the new Secretary of State for Northern Ireland, gave an interview in which he made two highly controversial statements: firstly, that the IRA could not be militarily defeated; and secondly, that he would not rule out talking with Sinn Féin as a way of bringing an end to the violence. When asked if he would ever consider speaking to Gerry Adams, he responded, 'Let me remind you of the move towards independence in Cyprus and that a British minister stood up in the House of Commons and used the word "never" . . . within two years, there had been a retreat from that word.'[38] Condemnation was swift and uncompromising. Ian Paisley described Brooke's remarks as 'treachery'.[39] Margaret Thatcher, when questioned, reiterated her usual message, 'the IRA cannot win, will not be allowed to win. Cannot win – and that is right.'[40] In the British press, Brooke was lambasted and given the sobriquet 'babbling Brooke'.[41] Criticism was not confined to Britain and Ireland. An article in the *Boston Globe* was titled, 'Is Peter Brooke the right man for Northern Ireland?', and suggested that he was 'still feeling his way around the political mine field that is the North of Ireland'.[42] When, under pressure, Brooke withdrew his comments, the headline in one Irish newspaper read, 'IRA will never win says harassed Brooke'.[43] His earlier words were prophetic, however, and many of the criticisms levelled at him proved to be both hypocritical and short-sighted.

By the end of 1989 little progress appeared to have been made in finding a political solution or even a compromise within Northern Ireland, with unionists refusing to participate in talks and republicans being denied an opportunity to talk. But pressure to communicate was increasing. In July 1990 Nelson Mandela, recently released prisoner and President of the African National Congress, visited Dublin. He urged the British government to talk to the IRA, pointing out 'People are slaughtering one another when they could sit down and address the problems in a peaceful manner.'[44] Mandela's message of peace and reconciliation was poorly received in Britain. Neil Kinnock called the remarks 'extremely ill-advised'; Tory MP Teddy Taylor said the comments made it 'difficult for anyone with sympathy for the ANC and Mandela to take him seriously'.[45] The following year, during a visit to Dublin, Archbishop Desmond Tutu created a storm of outrage by saying that, if political talks were to be meaningful, they had to be inclusive. He specifically referred to Sinn Féin in this context.[46] The message from the British government was unequivocal; they would not engage in talks with the IRA.

Déjà Vu

The 1990s commenced with few overt signs for optimism. Despite a number of attempts by Peter Brooke to involve unionists in political initiatives, they refused to participate unless the Anglo-Irish Agreement was suspended.[47] Increasingly, unionists were objecting to articles 2 and 3 of the 1937 Irish Constitution, which laid claims to the 'national territory' of Ireland, saying that these irredentist claims to a united Ireland were an impediment to any talks that included the Republic.[48] These objections were not new and were to re-emerge a few years later. A statement by Brooke on 9 November 1990, claiming that Britain had no 'selfish strategic or economic interest in Northern Ireland: our role is to help, enable, encourage' and accept its unification if achieved by consent, was to prove to be an important milestone in constitutional politics. Amongst other things, it facilitated further talks between the SDLP and Sinn Féin, by clarifying Britain's role if a pan-nationalist movement was ever successful. But while the statement might have heartened national-ists, it sent a chilling message to unionists.[49]

Nonetheless, in spring 1991, Brooke was able to persuade the Anglo-Irish Intergovernmental Conference to suspend further meet-ings, as a way of enticing unionists back to the table. The unionists, aware that since the signing of the Anglo-Irish Agreement they had become marginalized from political debate, were anxious to re-engage. As James Molyneaux explained, it was now time to act as 'insiders rather than outsiders in the British political system'.[50] The desire of loyalists to resume the political process was demonstrated when the Combined Loyalist Military Command, acting on behalf of the Ulster Volunteer Force, the Ulster Freedom Fighters and the Red Hand Commandos, announced a ceasefire beginning on 30 April 1991. The announcement carried a warning: if the IRA stepped up its activities during this period, the loyalists would take retaliatory action. The ceasefire took many people by surprise. According to the historian of the UDA, Ian Wood, 'The ceasefire was a politically sophisticated move, intended to wrong foot the IRA and to modify paramilitary loyalism's uncompromising image.'[51] The ceasefire was called off on 4 July, when the talks appeared to be foundering. It had lasted for ten weeks, with only one killing – apparently unautho-rized by the leadership – during that period.[52] More worryingly, in the wake of the ceasefire, loyalist attacks intensified. Yet it was not until 10 August 1992 that the UDA was belatedly proscribed, or so it appeared to nationalists. The group responded by stepping up its activities on an ever-more indiscriminate basis, as the murder on 27 September of Gerard O'Hara, an eighteen-year-old Catholic schoolboy, demonstrated. He was shot seventeen times in front of his mother, who begged that she be shot instead. One of the men who carried out the murder later described O'Hara as: 'a fair target . . . he'd have been a Provo [member of the Provisional IRA] too if he had lived long enough. It was an act of war. I had no remorse over it, none.'[53] A fact overlooked by the media in both Ireland and Britain, and ignored by the mainstream politicians, was that in 1992 loyalists killed more people than republican paramilitaries – 39 compared with 36. This statistic represented a major shift in the armed conflict. The fact that loyalist activity in this year was not an aberration was confirmed by a statement issued by the UDA on the last day of 1992 warning that it was going to escalate its campaign to 'a ferocity never imagined'.[54]

The talks, convened by Peter Brooke and his successor Patrick Mayhew, commenced on 17 June. They involved the UUP, the DUP, the SDLP and the Alliance Party. From the start, they proved to be bad-tempered and fractious, with disagreements even over the venue. By the end of summer, the talks had broken down with no consensus being achieved. They were resumed in September, but the parties continued to be divided, not helped by a series of leaks to newspapers. The DUP remained on the fringes of the meetings and refused to be part of a delegation that travelled to Dublin. The fact that the leading unionist party was willing to travel to Dublin and engage in talks with mainstream Irish nationalist parties indicated a significant shift towards a more liberal and pragmatic position. They were willing to accept an Irish dimension and power-sharing.[55] More militant unionists, however, as represented by the DUP together with a disgruntled faction within the UUP, were unhappy with these symbolic compromises. The talks finally collapsed in November 1992. Sinn Féin had not been allowed to take part in the Brooke/Mayhew talks. At the end of the year, in a speech given at the University of Ulster, Mayhew said that Sinn Féin could be involved in future talks if the IRA ended its violent campaign.[56] On Christmas Eve the IRA called a three-day ceasefire.

Miscarriages of justice continued to be exposed, and allegations of instances of shoot-to-kill and collusion between loyalist paramilitaries and the security forces continued. In February 1990 the case of the 'Winchester Three', IRA members who had allegedly been plotting to kill Tom King, was overturned by the Court of Appeal on the grounds of prejudicial pre-trial publicity.[57] In March

1991 the 'Birmingham Six', who had been imprisoned for the bombing of two pubs in 1974, with massive loss of life, were freed. The police were found to have forged confessions and other evidence. Their release was reported throughout the world and clearly dented the reputation of the British legal system.[58] In June 1991 the conviction of a family known as the 'Maguire Seven' was quashed by the High Court in London. They had been convicted in 1976 of running an IRA bomb factory, based on faulty and sloppy forensic evidence.[59] Such miscarriages of justice gave some credibility to the IRA's accusations that the British state was more concerned with damaging the IRA than with finding a solution to the conflict.

A 'Panorama' programme broadcast in February 1990, 'Ulster's Regiments – a Question of Loyalty?', examined leaks from the UDR to Protestant paramilitary groups.[60] It renewed debates about whether the UDR should disband. Less media coverage, however, was given to an apparent miscarriage of justice involving four members of the UDR, referred to as the 'Armagh Four'. In 1986 they had been convicted of killing a Catholic, despite protesting their innocence. Six years later, when Brooke granted an appeal, three of the men were acquitted.[61] Ian Paisley Jr used their case to highlight the fact that the Northern Ireland legal system was impartial.[62] Such cases, however, were unusual. The relative lack of coverage given to these men, especially when contrasted to the publicity given to the 'Guildford Four', was regarded by some unionists as proof that they had lost the propaganda war. The image of the unionist community portrayed by the media – both in Britain and further afield – was overwhelmingly negative: people who were intransigent and inflexible and ultimately barriers to peace and progress.[63]

The violence continued. The sense of déjà vu was captured by the historian J. Bower Bell:

> It all blurred. There were rush hour bombs in Belfast, the security forces accused of excess violence, and more funerals, further protests, and the army still at the end of the lane. And that army along with the police was always stretched by the constant, unremitting IRA incidents too small to reach the media, too dangerous to ignore; single shots, minor sabotage, arson, trap bombs, false reports, and ineffectual explosions.[64]

Some incidents, however, were deemed more shocking than others. These included the murder by the IRA in May 1990 of two Australian tourists in the Netherlands, apparently mistaken for off-duty soldiers. At the trial of the three IRA suspects, it was claimed that they were members of a republican cell that had been established early in 1990.[65] On 30 July British MP Ian Gow, an implacable enemy of republicanism, was killed by the IRA. He had been a close friend and adviser to Margaret Thatcher, although they had disagreed over the Anglo-Irish Agreement. When asked for her reaction to the news, the Prime Minister responded:

> Ian would be the first to say, like Airey, that terrorists must *never* win, and if he could speak to me now he would say: '*You fight* that battle against them, you bring them to justice to see that they're properly condemned and found guilty for what they have done'. And that's how we shall carry on.[66]

Later in the year the IRA devised a new tactic: using men they considered as collaborators as human proxy bombs. It generally involved tying somebody to a car laden with bombs and forcing them to drive to the military target. Five soldiers were killed in this way in an attack on the Coshquin checkpoint near Derry, while the human 'proxy bomb', Patsy Gillespie, was blown up and his body was never recovered.[67]

On 7 February 1991 there was a mortar attack on 10 Downing Street. Four people were injured. The new Prime Minister, John Major, described it as 'a deliberate attempt both to kill the Cabinet and do damage to the democratic system of government'.[68] Like the earlier Brighton bomb, it signalled the IRA's willingness to take its campaign to the heart of the British establishment. As the IRA realized, bombs in England attracted far more publicity and outrage than bombs in Northern Ireland.

Violence continued in 1992. In January a bus carrying civilian workers from a military base was blown up at Teebane, County Armagh: eight Protestant men were killed and six were severely injured. Later that day, Peter Brooke appeared on the popular RTÉ entertainment programme 'The Late Late Show' and was persuaded to sing 'My Darling Clementine' by the show's host, Gay Byrne.[69] It was insensitive, and unionists were incandescent – seizing political capital from a spontaneous gesture. Brooke, who had shown both imagination and commitment when dealing with the problems of Northern Ireland, was forced to offer his resignation. The cycle of tit-for-tat killings persisted. Five Catholics were shot dead by a loyalist gunman in a betting shop in the Ormeau Road in Belfast two weeks after Teebane.[70] During the annual marches in July, Orangemen 'ostentatiously' held up five fingers when they passed the betting shop. Their conduct was condemned by the new Secretary of State, Sir Patrick Mayhew, who said it 'would have disgraced a tribe of cannibals let alone Protestants marching under the flag of the United Kingdom'.[71] Three Catholics were killed in a similar incident in a betting shop later in the year.[72]

London continued to be a target for IRA bombs, some more deadly than others. In April, two lorries containing home-made bombs destroyed the Baltic Exchange, which was the commercial centre of world shipping. Three people were killed, including a fifteen-year-old girl. The cost to the taxpayer for this destruction was £800 million, a grim reminder of how much damage and disruption the IRA could cause with relatively few resources.[73] Loyalists accused the IRA of attacking London as a way of gaining political leverage; Britain's commercial centre would be wrecked unless concessions were made.[74]

An incident that shocked the world took place on 20 March 1993, when the IRA planted two bombs in the centre of Warrington in the north of England. A warning had been given but it was inadequate. More than 50 people were injured, and two young boys died: Jonathan Ball, aged three, and a few days later Timothy Parry, aged twelve, most of whose face had been blown away in the second bomb blast. The IRA issued a statement saying that they 'profoundly' regretted the two deaths and the injuries. Loyalist paramilitaries responded by killing six Catholics in Northern Ireland, bringing the number they had killed that year to 25. Anger against the IRA within Britain and the Republic reached new heights. In Dublin, where many people had become desensitized or indifferent to the conflict, a Book of Condolences was opened and 20,000 people took to the streets to protest.[75] In a statement to the Dáil, the Taoiseach said:

> This bombing, whose victims were the young and defenceless, is the latest outrage in the long series of cruel and cowardly acts perpetrated by the Provisional IRA in Northern Ireland and further afield. Their expressions of regret at

Saturday's bombing are rightly viewed with contempt and incredulity by all reasonable people in Ireland, North and South, and in Britain.

The IRA's campaign of violence has served not only to increase human suffering, but has deepened divisions within Ireland. It is long past time for it to be brought to an end.[76]

The bombing was condemned in the United States as well. Referring to a recently released film about the IRA, the *New York Times* asserted:

The killers showed more practiced cunning that their clumsier counterparts in the acclaimed film 'The Crying Game' . . . That these killers call themselves loyalists or republicans trashes decency and meaning. It takes no courage to murder children and injure 50 people in a crowded shopping centre. It is no less repellent for Protestant gunmen to play God by slaughtering still more civilians. One may justly conclude that the killing has become an end in itself, a game in which politics gives a specious licence to those who find fulfillment in spilling blood.[77]

Despite a massive police hunt and notwithstanding the international outrage, the Warrington bombers were not caught. The families used the publicity to establish a Peace Centre where young people could learn about reconciliation and conflict resolution.[78] In 2007 Gerry Adams met the parents of Timothy Parry and apologized to them for their son's death and that of other 'non-combatants'. Colin Parry admitted that meeting Adams face-to-face was difficult, but 'easier than holding my son dying'.[79]

A change had come about, though, that received little public attention. In 1985 loyalist paramilitaries had killed only two people. The next year it was sixteen, then seventeen, building in 1993 to 47 victims.[80] Loyalists were responsible for a total of 124 deaths between 1991 and 1994, which represented 56 per cent of the total.[81] They had overtaken the IRA in terms of acts of murder. Yet the attention of the security forces and of the media remained almost exclusively focused on the republican groups. Just as worryingly, a phone poll taken by the *Belfast Newsletter* in 1993 revealed that 42 per cent of callers supported the latest phase of loyalist violence; 82 per cent believed that loyalist violence would cease when the IRA called a ceasefire.[82] It seemed that street politics were continuing to set the agenda in Northern Ireland.

Further atrocities followed. On 23 October 1993 an IRA bomb exploded prematurely in the Protestant Shankill district of Belfast, killing one of the bombers and nine civilians. Fifty-seven people were injured. The IRA was condemned but some of the most scathing criticism was reserved for John Hume, who had been involved in talks with Gerry Adams in the preceding months. The long-term consequences were dismal, one newspaper warning that the bombing:

> has all but guaranteed that more will die in retaliation.
>
> It has significantly decreased the chances of success of the peace initiative launched by John Hume of the SDLP and Sinn Féin's Gerry Adams; it has raised the question of how much control and influence Mr Adams has over the military members of his movement.[83]

More violence did ensue. In the week following the Shankill bombing, twelve Catholics were killed by loyalist paramilitaries.[84] This included the murder of six Catholic civilians and one Protestant in the Rising Sun Bar in Greysteel, County Derry. The murderers preceded their shooting by shouting 'trick or treat' – a reference to the fact that it was Halloween. It was later claimed that one of the gunmen was a police agent and the RUC had hidden important evidence to protect him, a claim not investigated until 2006.[85] A week after the Greysteel murders, thousands of people attended a peace walk and prayer meeting in the village. Peace rallies were held in the Republic.[86] The carnage, however, did not end.

In the early months of 1994, as a result of the Downing Street Declaration and ongoing talks between John Hume and Gerry Adams, there was speculation that a ceasefire was imminent. In the interim, violence and death continued. In Northern Ireland the various loyalist paramilitary groups intensified their campaign, even though they knew that an IRA ceasefire was expected.[87] Figures released by the Northern Ireland Office in June 1994 confirmed that loyalist groups had overtaken the IRA as the principal takers of life in the province.[88] The IRA remained active too: Heathrow Airport, London, was subject to several mortar attacks and a number of leading loyalists were also killed by the IRA, making retaliation inevitable.

Some loyalists regarded this as a tactic by the republicans to provoke further violence by their adversaries and thus ensure that if an IRA ceasefire was announced, the UDA could be cast as the peacebreakers.[89] Whatever the reason, lives continued to be lost.

One of the more deadly incidents occurred on 18 June 1994, when the UVF killed six Catholic men and wounded five others in a gun attack on a bar in Loughlinisland, County Down. The people in the bar were watching a televised World Cup football match of Ireland versus Italy when the gunmen entered. One of those killed was aged 87. According to a BBC report, the gunmen ran laughing to their getaway car.[90] The UDA later claimed that the IRA had held a meeting at the pub, but this claim was unfounded. The attack was widely condemned. Patrick Mayhew, then Secretary of State for Northern Ireland, referred to it as 'an inhuman act of savagery and injustice. The moral squalor of those who carried it out is beyond description.' Until that point, the community in the small town had little direct experience of the violence. What did emerge was that: 'The owner of the bar, Hugh O'Toole, had left with a group of his regular customers some hours earlier to help to repair an orphanage in Romania. Both Catholics and Protestants were in the party.'[91] It was subsequently revealed that the RUC had destroyed vital evidence, including the getaway car, leading the families to suspect collusion.[92] The IRA responded to the Loughlinisland deaths by firing rockets during a UVF funeral. The cycle of violence was continuing and some commentators feared even more extreme loyalist violence would ensue.[93] There appeared to be no end to the depravity and carnage. On 31 August 1994, however, at the end of another summer of reprisal killings and gratuitous bloodshed, the IRA declared a cessation of its military activities.

Changes

The political situation in the North frequently overshadowed changes that were taking place in other areas of Irish society. Throughout much of the 1980s the economies of the North and South had been languishing, suffering from high unemployment and high inflation, which had contributed to high levels of emigration. The poverty of inner-city Dublin was captured in a series of books by a local schoolteacher, Roddy Doyle. The 'Barrytown Trilogy', comprised of *The Commitments* (1987), *The Snapper* (1990) and *The Van* (1991), portrayed life on a fictional working-class estate in Dublin, similar to the area where Doyle taught in real life. Despite some profanity and unpalatable social issues, including unwanted pregnancies, wife beatings and unemployment, the writing was humorous, and the trilogy achieved both critical and commercial acclaim on both sides of the Atlantic: *The Van* was shortlisted for the 1991 Booker Prize. For readers outside Ireland it provided a counterpoint to an Ireland of shamrocks and leprechauns, or of stunning green countryside. One American critic pondered:

> Relentless poverty. Foul mouthed Irish. Little hope for the future. Reproducing like rabbits because they are old-school Irish Catholics and there is fook [sic] all else to do . . . In the USA, this kind of poverty sends people over the edge. Street gangs, wars between drug lords, drive-by shootings, jails bulging at the seams. But in Doyle's Barrytown, Irish poverty has a gentler, kinder side.
>
> Doyle writes a world where there are no drugs, families and communities stay together to support each other, and nearly no one goes to jail or gets shot . . . And Barrytown's poor remain proud, even powerful.[94]

Each of the three books was filmed. The most successful was *The Commitments*, directed by Alan Parker and released in 1991. It revolved around the formation of a soul band in North Dublin, a theme that allowed for an engaging soundtrack. The film, like the book, explored some of the tensions in Irish society and firmly anchored them in 'its working class milieu . . . captured largely in the characterization, dialogue and setting'.[95]

The poverty, unemployment and urban squalor that Doyle had captured so finely in his books disappeared under the patina of the 1990s economic miracle, widely referred to as the 'Celtic Tiger'. Charles Haughey, when Taoiseach in the early 1980s, had been associated with high government spending and poor economic management. During his fourth and final period in office (1989–92), working with Ray MacSharry as Finance Minister, he implemented a policy of fiscal rectitude achieved through spending cuts. As a result, by the mid-1990s the Irish economy had undergone a major transformation. Haughey was helped by an improving global economy and a compliant Opposition. Since 1987 Fine Gael, led by Alan

Dukes, had supported Haughey's economic policies. This departure, known as the Tallaght Strategy, suggested that, unusually in Irish politics, both parties were willing to work together in the national interest.[96] Dukes's service had led to a proposal by his colleague John Bruton that he, rather than Haughey, be appointed Taoiseach following the 1989 election. Bruton's justification was that:

> In the last two and a half years in this House Deputy Dukes has shown a willingness to respond in an open-minded way to the deep economic and social problems facing this country.
>
> In allowing the previous Government to pursue their economic policies without obstructive opposition, he made a completely new departure in Irish politics. In this, he showed he was the politician in Ireland most able to reach across the political divide and bring an atmosphere of reality and practical patriotism to Irish political life.[97]

An initiative in which Haughey took a personal interest was the International Financial Services Centre. The idea had been rejected by the previous coalition government. Haughey, working closely with three civil servants, built the centre to be a platform for international excellence that went on to employ more than 18,000 people. This low-tax centre attracted many foreign institutions.[98] On a personal level, Haughey's autocratic style of government – leading to his nickname, 'the Boss' – and his massive personal fortune continued to make him an object of parody and suspicion by some sections of the press. However, his fourth term in office proved to be Haughey's longest and most successful. It included the Presidency of the European Union in 1990, where he proved to be adept at international power-broking, and when:

> Abandoning his previous scepticism about the effects of European integration on Irish neutrality, he now emerged as a full-blooded advocate of political union on the road to Maastricht. He struck up a singularly good rapport with the French President François Mitterrand, whom he liked to regard as a kindred spirit. Chancellor Helmut Kohl was grateful for his prompt support for German unification. Ireland was to be rewarded with the generous allocations of

structural funds that fuelled the unprecedented economic boom of the 1990s.[99]

Building relationships within Ireland proved to be more difficult. On 11 April 1990 Haughey made the first official visit to Northern Ireland by a Taoiseach since that by Seán Lemass in 1965. When he addressed a conference in the Europa Hotel in Belfast, organized by the Institute of Directors, 400 loyalists staged a protest against the visit. Some of them, including the future leader of the party, David Trimble, gathered on the rooftop of the UUP headquarters nearby.[100] Protestors said that, while they did not object to more cross-border trade, they viewed the latest initiative as 'creeping economic unification' that would provide 'the back door to Dublin rule'.[101]

Haughey's long and, at times, controversial political career ended ignobly. He was forced to resign in February 1992 following allegations that he had known that the phones of a number of political journalists had been tapped. In characteristically defiant style, in his final speech to the Dáil, he quoted from *Othello*, 'I have done the State some service, and they know it, no more of that,'[102] Suspicions about Haughey's unaccounted-for wealth were confirmed by a number of tribunals in the 1990s, proving that he had accepted large payments from wealthy businessmen. Sebastian Barry's drama *Hinterland*, loosely based on Haughey's life, opened at the Abbey Theatre, Dublin, in 2002 and caused uproar: 'Haughey dispatched a member of his legal team to the Abbey, and there were reports that his family was seeking an injunction against the production'.[103] When the play moved to London, there was some interest, owing to the controversy surrounding it, but it was generally deemed to be dull. The *Daily Telegraph* critic opined, 'Whatever Haughey's failings, he surely didn't deserve quite so windy and indigestible a play as this.'[104] When Haughey died in 2006, the consensus was that his genuine skills and abilities had been damaged by his frequent poor judgement, his personal greed and his arrogance.[105] Nonetheless, his contributions to the peace process and to Ireland's economic regeneration were considerable.

Economic regeneration in the North proved to be more difficult to achieve, hampered by the ongoing conflict. In recognition of this, a number of initiatives were undertaken to channel money to the province. The Irish and British governments had attempted to ease the situation by establishing the International Fund for Ireland (IFI) in 1986, in order 'to promote economic and social advance and to encourage contact, dialogue and reconciliation between nationalists and unionists throughout Ireland'.[106] Financial contributions came from the United States of America, the European Union, Canada, Australia and New Zealand. The US was the largest donor, and by 1993 had contributed $210 million. In 1988 it was decided to channel a large portion of the Fund's finances to towns that were designated as 'disadvantaged'. Most of these were situated in Northern Ireland or in the six adjoining border counties.[107] The activities of the IFI were not liked by some unionists. Ian Paisley described the grants as 'blood money' and 'thirty pieces of silver'. He was particularly infuriated when, in 1990, the Apprentice Boys of Derry were successful in getting funding to cover the costs of a heritage centre. He regarded the offer of financial assistance as 'bribery' to the Protestant people, to make the Anglo-Irish Agreement more palatable.[108]

The Northern economy benefited from money given by the European Council. It was agreed that from 2000 the province would receive support from the Structural Funds, as an 'Objective 1, in Transition Region'.[109] Nonetheless, the Northern economy remained in the doldrums. South Antrim had the second highest unemployment rate in the United Kingdom.[110] Richard Needham, the Minister for Economic Development, blamed the lack of progress on the IRA bombing campaign, which was increasingly focused on destroying the infrastructure and commerce, and which had hindered inward investment.[111] The IRA ceasefire in 1994 provided an immediate boost to investment in the province.

The contribution of women to the political process has often been overlooked in both the North and South of Ireland.[112] The status of women received an unexpected boost when, in December 1990, Mary Robinson, supported by the Labour Party, was elected President in the Republic. She was the first woman to hold this position. Robinson was known to be a feminist and civil rights activist, tolerant on many social issues ranging from contraceptives to homosexuality, and her election was viewed as symptomatic of a change towards a more liberal society. She brought a new energy, visibility and compassion to the position. She also gave relevance to what had previously been a largely ceremonial role. One of the first things Robinson did was place a candle in the window of her official home, *Áras an Uachtaráin*, for the diaspora, which had increased and multiplied through the preceding decade.[113] She also used her office to reach out to gays and lesbians, the unemployed and the travelling community.

Politically, President Robinson proved to be both ground-breaking and controversial in her approach. In 1993 she became the first Irish President to meet the Queen. She was the first head of state to visit Somalia, when it was suffering from famine. While Robinson was much admired on the international stage, Northern unionists disliked her. In January 1991 a proposal that she pay an official visit to Belfast was rejected by unionist councillors on Belfast City Council.[114] In June 1993 she paid an unofficial visit to community groups in Belfast, despite both the British government and the NIO advising against it. During the visit Robinson met Gerry Adams, then President of Sinn Féin, and shook his hand. Unionists were furious. Ian Paisley delivered a letter by hand to John Major and raged that:

> Attempts have been made to put Mary Robinson, the president of the Irish Republic, on a par in Ulster with Her Majesty the Queen. The said lady was happy to shake Gerry Adams's bloody hand on her visit to Belfast. Portraits of our Queen are, however, banned from workplaces under legislation flowing from the Anglo-Irish dictat. The people of Ulster will never lie down and capitulate to your Dublin plans.[115]

Being a successful woman in politics brought criticisms that were rarely directed at men. Pádraig Flynn, a Fianna Fáil politician, attacked her private and family life saying that President Robinson:

> has to have new clothes and her new look and her new hairdo, and she has the new interest in family, being a mother and all that kind of thing. But none of us who knew Mary Robinson very well in previous incarnations ever heard her claiming to be a great wife and mother.[116]

Before becoming President, Mary Robinson had used her considerable legal skills to champion the right to choose with regard to contraception, divorce and homosexuality. In the early 1990s these issues remained contested battlegrounds in the fight for sexual freedom and women's rights, and for defining the role of the Catholic Church in society. Abortion proved to be particularly problematic and contentious. The issue was brought into the public arena by a number of cases that showed that simply banning abortion was more complex than earlier debates had tried to suggest. In 1992, in what became known as the 'X' case, the Irish High Court placed an injunction on a fourteen-year-old girl to prevent her travelling to England to get an abortion. Following an appeal – and massive public protests – the decision was overturned. The Supreme Court ruled, by a majority of two to one, that there was a serious threat to the life, as opposed to the health of the girl, since she had threatened suicide. This provided the grounds for lifting the injunction.[117] The case occurred a few months before a referendum on the Maastricht Treaty, which created the more unified European Union. Haughey acted to ensure that this and all other treaties deriving from the European Union would not interfere with Ireland's internal laws on abortion.[118]

Anti-abortion groups opposed the ruling in the 'X' case. In order to protect the 1983 amendment to the constitution, they called for another referendum, which was held in November 1992. Three amendments were proposed: that the possibility of suicide was not a sufficient threat to justify an abortion – the proposal was rejected; that the prohibition of abortion would not limit freedom of travel from Ireland to other countries where a person might legally obtain an abortion – the proposal was approved; that Irish citizens have the freedom to pursue and learn about abortion services in other countries – the proposal was approved. As a result, an amendment was made to the Constitution that read:

> The State acknowledges the right to life of the unborn and, with due regard to the equal right to life of the mother, guarantees in its laws to respect, and, as far as practicable, by its laws to defend and vindicate that right.
>
> This subsection shall not limit freedom to travel between the State and another state.
>
> This subsection shall not limit freedom to obtain or make available, in the State, subject to such conditions as may be laid down by law, information relating to services lawfully available in another state.[119]

Despite the referendum, the abortion laws in the Republic remained both confusing and restrictive. This became evident in 1997 when a further case exposed the inconsistencies of legal judgements. This involved a thirteen-year-old girl from the travelling community who had been raped by an adult neighbour. Because of her parents' circumstances, she was taken into care. The girl wanted an abortion; her parents opposed it. The District Judge ruled that she could go to another jurisdiction to seek a termination.[120] The Irish legal system was giving sanction to something that the referendum a few years earlier had sought to forbid, and which had been forbidden in the 'X' case. The Archbishop of Dublin, Desmond Connell, attacked the court decision and said that the Church would consider paying for an appeal.[121] A week later, a poll in the *Irish Times* showed that 77 per cent of participants believed that abortion should be permitted in the state in limited circumstances; only 18 per cent believed that it should not be permitted in any circumstances.[122] For most of the 1990s, however, the Republic's abortion laws remained the most repressive in Europe, with legislation lagging behind the demand for change. Politicians cynically referred to it as 'an Irish solution to an Irish problem', but the ban on abortion meant that up to 7,000 Irish women travelled to Britain each year to seek a termination.[123] In the early 1990s, as in the 1960s, Ireland, both North and South, remained socially conservative on a number of issues. By the middle of the decade, however, a number of significant changes challenged the political, religious, economic and cultural profile of Ireland, as peace and prosperity came to the island at last.

EIGHT

Ceasefire

The violence that had been a feature of the early 1990s often over-shadowed the constitutional attempts that were being made to bring about peace. Despite the apparent political stalemate, throughout the 1980s there were attempts to find a way out of the seemingly intractable cycle of bloodshed and retribution. Moreover, regardless of the continuation of the armed struggle, Sinn Féin, in particular, was developing a philosophy that was both more sophisticated and more conciliatory – although their adversaries chose not to recognize these advances.

This change in direction, and the 'stepping stones' that were put in place to achieve it, appear to have been part of a longer-term strategy, largely masterminded by Gerry Adams. A crucial part of this process was the 1986 Sinn Féin *Ard Fheis*, when Adams used his Presidential Address to argue for political change, including Sinn Féin registering as a political party in the Republic in order to contest future elections. Effectively, this would mean giving recognition to the state for the first time in the party's history.[1] Any fears that this new strategy would mean an end to the armed struggle was neutralized by leaks in the period before the conference about a massive shipment of arms from Libya.[2] Adams won the vote, although some suspected that this unusually well-attended conference had been deliberately packed with his sympathizers.[3]

In addition to the move towards electoral politics, a new approach was being developed to recast both the language and the source of the conflict. These changes were encapsulated in the document *Scenario for Peace*, first published in 1987 but relaunched in 1989. It opened by saying:

This document is presented by Sinn Féin for discussion and as an answer to those who claim that there is no alternative to the continuation of British rule. It does not represent the definitive republican position, nor is it exclusive of other proposals dealing with alternative scenarios for a British withdrawal from Ireland.[4]

The focus of the remainder of the document was on justice, and the right of Irish people to self-determination, while pointing to:

The perennial cycle of oppression/domination/resistance/oppression has been a constant feature of the British government's involvement in Ireland and the Irish people's rejection of that government's usurpation of the right to exercise control over their political, social, economic and cultural destiny.[5]

Part of Sinn Féin's political re-direction involved talking with other parties in order to achieve consensus; other parties, however, were not willing to admit that they were talking to Sinn Féin – at least in public.

Although the secret talks between Gerry Adams and John Hume of the SDLP had officially ended in September 1988, unofficially talks continued, both directly and indirectly. Father Alec Reid, a Redemptorist priest from Tipperary and based in Belfast, frequently worked as Adams's intermediary and thus played a crucial role as a peace-broker. Although the public were not aware of these talks, Hume kept both the British and Irish governments informed about them. Haughey approved of these negotiations although, like Hume, he emphasized that the continuation of violence was weakening the nationalist movement.[6] Towards the end of 1988 a meeting took place in Germany between the DUP (represented by Peter Robinson), the UUP (Jack Allen), the SDLP (Austin Currie) and the Alliance Party (Gordon Mawhinney). The aim was to attempt to launch peace talks again. Alec Reid was also present, although in an unofficial capacity. Although his presence was known in advance, 'it kept the unionists in terror of discovery for months afterwards. At that time, talking to Sinn Féin was possibly the most unforgivable sin in the book, and even being in the same room as a surrogate figure like Reid would have caused an outcry.'[7]

Despite public indignation at Peter Brooke's suggestion in 1989 that he would talk to Sinn Féin, some civil servants in the Northern Ireland Office had been communicating secretly with Sinn Féin throughout the late 1980s, mainly through the medium of Father Reid. Since 1987 Adams, through Reid, had been involved in negotiations with Tom King, then the Northern Ireland Secretary. MI5 had been involved on behalf of the government, but most of the civil servants in the NIO, and even Peter Brooke, were kept in the dark about the full extent of the negotiations.[8] Clearly authorization had been made at a very senior level. Publicly, official government policy continued to be to ignore and isolate Sinn Féin; privately, talks were taking place of which even the Secretary of State had not been made fully aware. Secret talks, which included the offer of a cease-fire, had also been carried out with Charles Haughey, again using Reid as the peace-broker. Haughey permitted his own political adviser, Martin Mansergh, to meet with Sinn Féin.[9] Not only were high-ranking officials in the British and Irish governments kept in the dark about many of these discussions, Adams also kept them secret from even the Army Council of the IRA.[10]

In 1990 Adams and other leading republicans commenced meetings with leading Protestant clergymen. Fr Reid, together with a fellow Redemptorist priest, Fr Gerry Reynolds, acted as the facilitators.[11] This was part of an initiative to understand the rights of Protestants and unionists – an approach that had often been missing in the nationalist struggle.[12] The secrecy was essential because many Protestants disapproved of any dialogue with republicans. A Presbyterian minister involved in the talks, Rev. Ken Newell, later admitted that as early as 1992 he had become convinced that Adams and his colleagues were serious about wanting peace.[13] When news of these ecumenical talks became public, Newell and his colleagues were severely criticized, especially by Ian Paisley. In 2005, however, Newell was awarded an OBE for his work in trying to bridge the sectarian divide.[14]

On 22 November 1990 Margaret Thatcher resigned as leader of the Conservative Party and as British Prime Minister. Effectively, she had been ousted from power by her own party. She was replaced by John Major, an unknown quantity in mainstream politics. Brooke remained as Northern Ireland Secretary until April. Faced with an increase in attacks and killings, one of the first things that Major did was to send an additional 300 (later increased to 600) regular soldiers to Northern Ireland and to call up 1,400 UDR reservists.[15] This brought the number of soldiers in the province to over 11,000. An early indication that possibly things were changing came on 23 December, when the IRA declared a three-day ceasefire. It was the first time they had done so for fifteen years. It seemed that Gerry Adams was giving a signal to the British government; for some in the IRA the purpose of the message was unclear as they remained in the dark about the secret negotiations taking place in their name.[16]

Thatcher's demise, in many ways, marked the end of an era, including in Northern Ireland politics. The end of another era in Anglo-Irish politics came when, in February 1992, Charles Haughey was replaced by Albert Reynolds as both leader of Fianna Fail and as Taoiseach. Haughey's final months in power had been beset by scandals and political misjudgements. By refusing to appoint Haughey supporters to his first cabinet, Reynolds was signalling a new beginning in Irish politics.[17] He also re-energized policies on Northern Ireland. He privately encouraged John Hume to continue to talk to Sinn Féin. His reasons, he explained were:

> For over 20 years, successive Governments largely succeeded in protecting the stability of this State from attack, but the price of keeping a rigid distance from those involved in violence was that this State exercised little or no influence, other than a repressive one, on Republican thinking throughout the island. In co-operation with John Hume and a respected clergyman intermediary, shortly after becoming Taoiseach, I took up and carried forward efforts to get to grips with the professed reasons for the continued Republican violence, to see if ways could be found to satisfy principle, while dispensing with the need for violence.[18]

On 10 April 1993 Gerry Adams was seen visiting the home of John Hume in Derry. News of previous secret meetings was reported in an Irish newspaper the following day. Opinion was divided, although many unionists were appalled and accused Adams of trying to bolster support for Sinn Féin in advance of the local elections. The talks were welcomed by, amongst others, Cathal Daly, the Primate of Ireland, who said:

I greatly admire the courage of John Hume in continuing with his work for peace and being prepared to take political risks – quite considerable physical risks – in doing what he's doing.

I sincerely hope, and thousands hope with me, that it may lead to an end of violence and to peace.[19]

On 24 April Hume and Adams issued a joint statement. It proclaimed that: 'Everyone has a solemn duty to change the political climate away from conflict and towards a process of national reconciliation which sees the peaceful accommodation of the differences between the people of Britain and Ireland and the Irish people themselves.' While restating that Ireland had a right to self-determination, it admitted that, 'In striving for that end we accept that an internal settlement is not a solution because it obviously does not deal with all the relationships at the heart of the problem.' However, Hume and Adams acknowledged that there were differences of opinion about how to achieve peace, even within their own parties.[20]

Unionist opinion was outraged, the outcome being that both the UUP and the DUP refused to participate further in any talks in protest. Criticized by some within both the British and Irish parliaments, Hume responded defiantly that he did not care 'two balls of roasted snow' for their criticisms.[21] Following a deadly bombing in Shankill in October, unionists took delight in pillorying Hume for negotiating with terrorists. The governments in London and Dublin distanced themselves from both Hume and Adams and jointly said that they would not adopt or endorse any proposal made by them.[22] Nonetheless, negotiations between Hume and Adams continued and further joint statements followed, in September and November 1993, in September and October 1995, and two in July 1997.[23] Despite their differences, the two main nationalist parties in Northern Ireland were showing their commitment to find a peaceful solution, regardless of setbacks.

Unusually for a Conservative leader, John Major made Northern Ireland a priority.[24] By doing so, he made a significant, if sometimes overlooked, contribution to the eventual peace process. Publicly, though, his rhetoric was similar to Thatcher's. The appointment of Sir Patrick Mayhew as Northern Ireland Secretary suggested that the initiatives started by Brooke would be continued. In one of his first interviews, Mayhew stated that the Irish had 'a history which is horrific, extending over centuries, and memories that make elephants seem like amnesiacs'. He added: 'I resolutely refuse to believe that any Englishman arriving in Ireland has the answer. But there is a huge prize for Ireland if hatreds and suspicions can be mitigated and togetherness can be engendered slowly, for reasons that don't need spelling out.'[25]

While public attempts were being made to bring the constitutional parties together, multiple talks were also taking place less publicly between the various nationalist groups, between republicans and British officials, and, far more tentatively, with some Protestant groups. The British government continued to deny this, but although the general public may have believed the denials, those closely involved with Northern Ireland politics no longer did. A telling insight into the doublespeak came in the early 1990s when Ian Paisley stated that he had more faith in the republican version of what was happening than that provided by the British government.[26] He, like many others, was unaware at that stage that secret links between the IRA/Sinn Féin and the British government had been first established in 1973, although used only intermittently.[27]

On 15 November 1993 the *Belfast Telegraph* revealed that the British government had been involved in secret talks with Sinn Féin. As rumours of negotiations with the IRA became rife, Major responded by informing the House of Commons that talking to the IRA would 'turn my stomach. We will not do it' – an assertion that was repeated by British officials over the subsequent days.[28] Given the reality of what was happening, it was a disingenuous overstatement. The Conservative Party was in a politically vulnerable position. Their parliamentary majority had long eroded, which made Major dependent on the support of nine unionist MPs in order to maintain a majority. In the United States, many sections of the media had come to believe that talking to the IRA and Sinn Féin was a way to stop the violence, and the *New York Times* urged the British government to 'Tell the Truth About the IRA'.[29]

A few weeks following Major's declaration, an 'exclusive' appeared in *The Observer* that opened with:

> A secret communication chain has been running between the Government and the IRA with the Prime Minister's approval, an authoritative British source has told *The Observer*.

The contacts have been in place for many months. Confirming that there had been contacts, the Northern Ireland Office said in a statement to *The Observer* last night: 'The IRA have not delivered the ending of violence envisaged in their original approach'.[30]

The article claimed that Albert Reynolds had not been informed of these talks. The following day Sir Patrick Mayhew revealed that contact had been made with the IRA, but only since February, when a serious offer of a ceasefire had been made. Justifying their response he claimed, 'The Government had a duty to respond to that message. Peace properly attained is a prize worth risks.'[31] Paisley responded by calling the Prime Minister 'a liar'.[32]

The revelations came only a few days before the Anglo-Irish Summit. This meeting was to prove to be historic because on 15 December 1993 Major and Reynolds announced the Joint Declaration on Peace, better known as the Downing Street Declaration. To a large extent, this document was the work of John Hume and Albert Reynolds, who had been working together for months to put together a framework for peace. It also followed an intensive period of negotiations between Hume and Sinn Féin, and so seemed to augur an IRA ceasefire.[33] The Declaration commenced:

> The Taoiseach, Mr Albert Reynolds TD, and the Prime Minister, the Rt. Hon. John Major MP, acknowledge that the most urgent and important issue facing the people of Ireland, North and South, and the British and Irish Governments together, is to remove the conflict, to overcome the legacy of history and to heal the divisions which have resulted, recognising the absence of a lasting and satisfactory settlement of relationships between the peoples of both islands has contributed to continuing tragedy and suffering.[34]

It continued: 'It is their aim to foster agreement and reconciliation, leading to a new political framework founded on consent and encompassing arrangements within Northern Ireland, for the whole island, and between these islands.'[35] The Declaration guaranteed the constitutional status of Northern Ireland and said that any change to partition could only come about with the consent of those who lived in the North. While reassuring unionists that a united Ireland would never be imposed on them, it guaranteed to nationalists that Britain would not stand in the way of a united Ireland achieved through consent. The Declaration emphatically called on the IRA to end its violence. Unusually, also, a large portion of the Declaration was concerned with the anxieties of unionists. This type of initiative was necessary because many unionists had felt excluded from the Anglo-Irish Agreement, despite attempts by Peter Brooke and others to include them.[36] When introducing the Declaration, Reynolds explained that:

> Due to the efforts I have had to make to bring republicans in from the cold – I have also had useful contacts through an intermediary with loyalist organisations who also tend to be politically ignored – I have been subject to sustained political attack in recent times from some Unionist politicians.[37]

He paid particular tribute to James Molyneaux for assisting him in the process and for dampening any 'hysteria' within the unionist community. However, he made reference to:

> the wholly destructive policies of another brand of Unionism which in the past has tried to do everything in its power to sabotage any reasonable prospects of peace. Some of the attitudes that have been adopted have undoubtedly fuelled the violence of the past 25 years.[38]

As a gesture of goodwill toward the IRA and Sin Fein, the Republic's broadcasting ban was allowed to lapse in January 1994.

Reaction to the Declaration within the British House of Commons was mixed, with opposition coming from unionist members of the Conservative Party. Before John Major made his statement, Patrick Mayhew convened a meeting to reassure them that the safeguards for the unionist position were 'cast-iron'.[39] The document was welcomed by the Labour Opposition and, more cautiously, by the Ulster Unionist Party. It also bolstered support for John Major within his own party.[40]

The Downing Street Declaration had enshrined the principle of consent into the peace process, but consent was far from the response of hardline unionists and opponents of the IRA. Conor Cruise O'Brien, former Labour Party Minister in the Republic and entrenched anti-republican, described the document as indicative of 'the rising influence of the Provisional IRA, through its trusted political intermediaries'. He lambasted the Dublin and London governments for 'dancing to the IRA's tune' and warned that 'only the gunmen have benefitted'.[41] Paisley and Robinson, both of the DUP, condemned the Declaration. Paisley was furious that Dublin was to have any formal role in the future of Northern Ireland and predicted that the document would be viewed as 'a sell-out act of treachery'.[42] He regarded it as a cover for a pan-nationalist agreement, which had the goal of a united Ireland. In a protest letter to Major, Paisley accused the Prime Minister of having 'sold Ulster to buy off the fiendish Republican scum'.[43]

The fear expressed by Paisley and others that a pan-nationalist agreement could deliver a united Ireland was far from the political reality of the early 1990s. A survey in the Republic in 1988–9 had suggested that a majority of Irish people felt closer to British people that to those in the North from either community: 49 per cent regarded Northern Ireland and the Republic as two separate nations; 35 per cent agreed with the statement that 'Northerners on all sides tend to be extreme and unreasonable'.[44] While the distance between peoples in the North and South appeared to be growing, people in the Republic appeared to be developing an affinity with their traditional enemy. A survey from September 1993 placed Britain at the top of a list of favourable counties – 4 per cent ahead of the USA.[45] Surveys carried out in the North over the same years revealed that Catholic support for a united Ireland was substantial but not overwhelming, with 53 per cent of Catholics saying they would like Northern Ireland to be part of a united Ireland. Protestants were more in agreement on this issue with 78 per cent opposing a united Ireland.[46] Pan-nationalism was not as unified as its opponents made it appear.

Following the Joint Declaration, the initiative passed to the IRA and Sinn Féin. Neither the IRA Army Council nor Sinn Féin rejected the Declaration, but actually declaring a ceasefire was a far larger step. The dynamics changed in February 1994 when President Bill Clinton, at the request of Senators Edward Kennedy and Daniel Moynihan, agreed to grant Gerry Adams a 48-hour visa to attend a conference on Northern Ireland in New York. Both the American

Embassy in London and the State Department had recommended that the visa be denied, but Clinton had overruled them.[47] Less well known was the role of four businessmen in the US (Niall O'Dowd, Bruce Morrison, Charles Feeney and William Flynn) in promoting American involvement in the affairs of the six counties. These men were known as the Connolly House Group. Despite having a less public profile than the 'Four Horsemen', they played a pivotal role in ensuring that Sinn Féin would have a voice in the embryonic peace talks.[48] Bringing Adams to the States, effectively bringing him in from the wilderness, was an essential part of this process.

The *Daily Mirror* claimed that, when Adams boarded the plane, the special relationship between Britain and America had ended.[49] The British government was furious and summoned the American Ambassador to Downing Street, where the Prime Minister and the Foreign Secretary, Douglas Hurd, gave him a 'harsh lecture'.[50] They were particularly galled to see Adams feted and admired, and not merely by the Irish American community.[51] They accused the American media of not asking sufficiently tough questions. Hurd also informed the House of Commons that 'It would be quite wrong if he were given some special treatment simply because he has used the bomb and the bullet to disguise the fact that electorally he has not been successful.'[52] The *New York Times* accused the British government of being hypocritical, pointing out that 'Apparently Mr Major considers it appropriate to talk to Mr Adams in secret, but inappropriate for the United States to allow him to talk to its people in public.'[53] On the eve of Adams's visit, Edna O'Brien had travelled to Belfast to meet him and she wrote a flattering editorial about him in the *New York Times*, describing him as 'thoughtful and reserved, a lithe, handsome man with a native formality'. Nonetheless, she claimed, 'When Prime Minister John Major utters his name in the House of Commons, he cannot conceal his loathing, and on television and in newspapers Mr Adams is depicted as a chilling and inscrutable figure.'[54]

Despite years of being banned from speaking on Irish and British television, Adams proved to be an adept interviewee, even when appearing on high-profile shows such as *Larry King Live*. A portion of the show was transmitted in Britain, but in it Adams's voice was dubbed.[55] During his brief stay in the USA Adams made only one public speech, during which he said, 'I come here with a message of peace.'[56] In the space of two days, he came, he charmed, and he conquered. At this point it seemed that Gerry Adams, so long a media pariah, had single-handedly won the propaganda war. Despite the fact that he had lost his parliamentary seat in the 1992 general election, for a number of years Adams became 'the most-profiled non-elected politician in Europe'.[57] Inevitably Sinn Féin's dominance of the media marginalized and isolated the unionist community even further.

Peace?

Following Adams's visit to the USA, a ceasefire seemed a possibility. Throughout the summer intense negotiations were taking place between Adams and Reynolds, using Reid and Mansergh as the intermediaries. Little was achieved.[58] Hope was revived by a US delegation to Northern Ireland in mid-August, although nobody was sure what the outcome would be.[59] Frustrated by the uncertainty, the poet Michael Longley sent a poem to the *Irish Times* entitled 'Ceasefire'. He hoped that 'it might change the mind of one ditherer on the IRA council'.[60] It was based on the episode in the *Iliad* when Priam visits Achilles in his tent at night in order to plead for the body of his son Hector. Thus two historical enemies meet for the sake of a dead son's body. For the sake of peace, the father of the dead boy got down on his knees and kissed the hand of his son's killer. He performed this act because he understood that it 'must be done'.[61] The two final lines of the poem were quoted by Senator Edward Kennedy when speaking in Derry some years later. He reminded his audience, 'The two communities in Northern Ireland must reach out and do what must be done – and join hands across centuries and chasms of killing and pain.'[62]

On 31 August 1994 the IRA declared a complete and unconditional ceasefire. This brought to an end 25 years of sustained conflict – the longest in Irish history. The IRA announced that they were willing to participate in talks concerning the future of Northern Ireland. No reference was made to what they would do with their weapons. Despite rumours and counter-rumours, when the ceasefire came it was unexpected and promised more than had generally been expected. According to Adams, it could not have happened a year or even a month earlier. The communiqué was 'on a typewritten piece of paper so small that it looked, according to one Irish diplomat, as if it had been smuggled out of Long Kesh in a cigarette box'.[63] At the time of the ceasefire, 3,168 lives had been lost since 1969 as a result of the conflict.[64]

The ceasefire was warmly accepted by many in the nationalist community. It was also welcomed in the Republic. The Irish government responded by promising to recognize the electoral mandate of Sinn Féin. Reynolds informed the Dáil:

> Every Irish person at home and abroad will welcome with relief and thanksgiving the decision announced today of an end to the 25-year-old IRA campaign. It is a day that many had begun to fear they might never see . . .
>
> Today's announcement presents us with a great opportunity to break free from the stagnation and demoralisation caused by the prolonged violence of the past 25 years. We expect to see the complete cessation of violence implemented fully. It is on that understanding that Northern Republicans will be fully incorporated into the democratic process. Political and other progress will depend on confidence-building measures on all sides.[65]

John Bruton, the leader of the Opposition, responded enthusiastically by saying: 'I heartily welcome the cessation of violence by the IRA. I am absolutely delighted this has happened. It is a historic day for Ireland, the world and the Irish community spread throughout the world.'[66]

The ceasefire was also welcomed in Britain, including by the new leader of the Labour Party, Tony Blair. The words of Seamus Heaney, from the poem 'The Cure at Troy', although written in 1990, were frequently quoted. It pointed out that an opportunity to bring about peace only came 'once in a lifetime'.[67]

Response to the ceasefire within the unionist community was more muted, with many viewing the agreement as a betrayal and fearing that concessions had secretly been made. Reynolds tried to reassure unionists by saying, 'I would urge that nobody should be afraid of peace and the whole new vista of opportunities which can now open up for the benefit and economic prosperity of all the people of Ireland.'[68] James Molyneaux, of the UUP, however, warned that there should be no talks with the IRA until they had added the word 'permanent' to the ceasefire declaration.[69] His fellow MP, William Ross, suggested that, 'If they are really renouncing violence, let them hand in their Semtex and all their weapons, because they won't need them any longer.'[70] John Alderdice of the Alliance Party cautioned, 'This is an historic moment for Ireland, but I have to say that most people here feel they judge the I.R.A. by their actions and not by their words. So everyone will be watching very closely to see what happens.'[71] Predictably, Paisley's response was less temperate. He averred: 'The vast majority of people in Northern Ireland don't want civil war but they are being compelled into a civil war situation by what the Government is doing. What the Unionists have been told has been a tissue of lies from Whitehall.'[72]

Although the Dublin and London governments took credit for the ceasefire, American involvement had been crucial in bringing about the announcement.[73] When it finally came, according to one British newspaper, London had 'lost control of the peace process. In the final stages, Washington and Dublin were making all the running.'[74] In his speech to the Dáil, however, while Reynolds paid tribute to the British and American governments he suggested that most of the credit for the ceasefire lay with the Joint Declaration that he and John Hume had prepared in the previous year.[75] Adams was personally praised for his role in bringing the ceasefire about – although less so in Britain than elsewhere. The *New York Times* declared, 'Mr Adams has shown once again that he is a major catalyst in the Northern Ireland strife and its politics and that he can deliver a ceasefire.'[76]

In the weeks following the ceasefire, a number of gestures were made that were largely symbolic rather than substantial: the Taoiseach allowed himself to be photographed shaking Gerry Adams's hand; the British Army started to wear berets rather than metal helmets; a number of border roads were reopened; the BBC lifted its ban on broadcasting the voices of republicans; political prisoners were released or transferred to Northern Ireland; Adams was granted a second visa to visit the United States. Together, these changes suggested a new era in Irish politics. Pressure was mounting for a loyalist response. It came on 13 October when a number of loyalist groups declared their own ceasefire. Before doing so, the Combined Loyalist Military Command had sought reassurance that the IRA ceasefire was permanent and that no deal had been done with them. The statement opened:

> After a widespread consultative process initiated by representations from the Ulster Democratic and Progressive

Unionist Parties, and after having received confirmation and guarantees in relation to Northern Ireland's constitutional position within the United Kingdom, as well as other assurances, and, in the belief that the democratically expressed wishes of the greater number of people in Northern Ireland will be respected and upheld, the CLMC will universally cease all operational hostilities as from 12 midnight on Thursday 13th October 1994.

It went on to warn, 'The permanence of our ceasefire will be completely dependent upon the continued cessation of all nationalist/republican violence, the sole responsibility for a return to War lies with them.' After congratulating all those who had fought and given their lives, it promised, 'They did not die in vain. The Union is safe.'[77] Not all loyalists were happy. The ceasefire was condemned in the *Ulster News* as a 'grovelling defeatist diatribe' that had been written by 'paid collaborators'. 'True' loyalists were called on to form a new army to smash the IRA and the Joint Agreement.[78] In the Dáil, Reynolds declared that, 'This decision effectively signifies the end of twenty-five years of violence, and the closure of a tragic chapter in our history.'[79] Peace, it seemed, had finally come to Ireland.

For a few months it appeared that real breakthroughs were being made. On 9 December 1994 British officials met with Sinn Féin representatives – their first official talks in 22 years. In February 1995 two Framework Documents were published, outlining proposals for a new single-chamber assembly, and for institutions to facilitate North-South cooperation. Reassurances to unionists were made by both the Dublin and London governments.[80] An assault was led by the DUP leader, Ian Paisley, who described the documents as 'a one way street to Dublin' and warned that his supporters would 'break this conspiracy you have hatched against them'. His deputy, Peter Robinson, warned that 'when you lick away the sugar coating [it] leads to a united Ireland'.[81]

The honeymoon period was short-lived. Increasingly, decommissioning of IRA weapons was made a precondition for further progress. Albert Reynolds, who had resigned as Taoiseach in November 1994, argued that this demand was unreasonable at this stage. His successor, John Bruton, adopted a similar line, suggesting that this single issue should not be allowed to disrupt the peace process.[82] For unionists, this issue provided an important mechanism for attacking the IRA ceasefire and pointing to its lack of permanence. In March 1995, while in Washington, Patrick Mayhew laid out steps for a decommissioning of arms by the IRA; moreover, decommissioning was now to be a precondition for Sinn Féin to enter into political talks. The IRA was furious and regarded this as a betrayal, accusing the British government of acting in 'bad faith'.[83] When pressed on this issue in the Dáil, the new Taoiseach stated, 'Nobody is suggesting that all arms should be dumped before talks take place.' The leader of the Opposition, Bertie Ahern, further pointed out that the British government was not insisting that the loyalists decommission as a precondition of talks with unionist parties.[84]

Mayhew's preconditions signalled a period of deadlock in the discussions. Moreover, relations between Britain and the United States deteriorated when President Clinton invited Adams to the White House for St Patrick's Day. Clinton had hoped that this would nudge the peace process forward, but it had the opposite effect and resulted in British-American relations reaching their lowest point in years.[85] Although Major and Clinton publicly patched their quarrel, it was a reminder that American involvement could be a double-edged sword. On 24 May 1995 Mayhew held an 'informal' meeting with Adams in Washington. It marked the highest level of contact between the British government and Sinn Féin.[86] It was a historical moment, but the peace process was foundering with no progress made. Some things had not changed. In June the British Parliament renewed the Prevention of Terrorism Act for a further year. Mayhew repeated his demand for decommissioning. Sinn Féin refused, Adams pointing out that the ceasefire was a sufficient indication of their commitment to peace. In July it was announced that President Clinton intended to visit Ireland and Britain later in the year and US envoys urged Sinn Féin to reconsider as a way of moving the peace process forward.[87] Adams was firm; decommissioning was not part of the ceasefire agreement. Moreover, there was a growing feeling among the IRA's followers that they had been tricked into calling a ceasefire.[88] Adams's off-the-cuff comment during a rally in Belfast, when he said that the IRA 'haven't gone away, you know', seemed an ominous portent of things to come.[89] Although Adams held meetings with British and Irish politicians over the next few months to find a way out of the impasse, the issue of decommissioning had created a new barrier to progress.

In the summer of 1995 attention became focused on the response of unionists to the peace process, in particular that of the Orange Order. The lead-up to the annual 12 July parade became a focus for expressing their frustration and discontent with years of being ignored and marginalized in various political talks and agreements. According to Dominic Bryan, 'The disputes were not reflecting the enmities of 1690, but the dynamic politics of 1995.'[90] Drumcree in County Armagh was the flashpoint for these tensions. As 12 July approached, there was disagreement between the local Orange Order and the RUC when the latter refused to allow the Orangemen to march down the Garvaghy Road, a predominantly nationalist area. The stand-off lasted for a number of days, attracting international media attention. The RUC sought to end the situation by allowing 500 Orangemen, without their accompanying bands, to march down the road, despite protests by the inhabitants. Drumcree provided an opportunity for David Trimble of the UUP and Ian Paisley to demonstrate, albeit briefly, a united Protestant front. Trimble and Paisley led the parade hand-in-hand. The residents of the Garvaghy Road were incensed as, yet again, the police had given in to pressure from the Orange Order. Paisley further inflamed nationalist feeling when he described what had happened in Drumcree as 'one of the greatest victories during the past 25 years for Protestantism in Northern Ireland'.[91] Over the next few years, the annual Orange parades, and Drumcree in particular, became the focus of unionists' objections to the peace process. In the short term it boosted the popularity of Trimble, who took over the leadership of the Ulster Unionist Party a few months later, defeating the UUP veteran John Taylor; cleverly, 'at Drumcree, Trimble had touched the sacred hem of unionism in a way that brought out all the old atavism of the party faithful'.[92] Trimble brought fresh energy to the position as leader of the largest unionist party. Within weeks of coming to power, he had held meetings with John Major and Patrick Mayhew, with Dick Spring, the deputy Taoiseach, and with President Clinton. He made it clear, however, that he would not compromise on the issue of decommissioning.

What had proved to be a frustrating year, politically, ended on a high note. On 28 November 1995 it was announced that George Mitchell, a former US Senator, was to lead a body to look at decommissioning. His presence indicated that America had become a crucial part of the peace process. He was not a popular choice with the main unionist parties: Trimble claimed that his chairmanship would be 'the equivalent of an American Serb presiding over talks on the future of Croatia'. Meanwhile Paisley described Mitchell as 'a Catholic Irish-American from the same stable as the Kennedys'.[93] Mitchell was not an Irish American Catholic, but a Maronite Christian. He did have Irish grandparents, but his father had been adopted. It was an inauspicious start. Mitchell later recalled his first encounter with Ian Paisley:

> There was a noisy commotion. Paisley was standing and saying in a loud voice, 'No. No. No. No.' He repeated it over and over again. I was extremely uncomfortable. Although I had read and heard a lot about Paisley and his tactics, this was my first direct exposure to them, and it was shocking. I was accustomed to rough-and-tumble political debate but I'd never experienced anything like this.[94]

The role of America was confirmed when, on 30 November, President Bill Clinton and his First Lady, Hillary Clinton, visited Northern Ireland. He was the first serving President of the USA to visit the province. The two Clintons met with groups representing all shades of political opinion in Belfast and Derry. The President's overall message was that the ceasefire should hold and dialogue should continue. In the evening, he lit the Christmas tree lights in Belfast as a symbol of a new beginning.[95] The Clintons then travelled to Dublin, where the welcome was just as rapturous. Like President Kennedy in 1963 and President Reagan in 1984, Clinton was invited to address the Dáil. Sean Tracy, the Speaker of the House, who introduced him, said:

> You have come to us from your historic visit to Northern Ireland at a time, the first in 25 years, when the country as a whole has experienced peace for over the past 16 months. You, Mr. President have taken upon yourself the role of peacemaker, not alone in Ireland but in many other parts of the world, and you have done so with great success. Your herculean endeavours have won for you the praise and gratitude of all civilised people.[96]

Clinton commenced his Address by quoting both Seamus Heaney and George Bernard Shaw, the latter having said, 'peace is not only better than war but infinitely more arduous'.[97] His speech received a standing ovation. For the most part the Clintons' visit was a resounding success.

The good feelings quickly dissipated. Part of the framework for discussion in the peace process was the recognition of three 'Strands': the internal dimension; the relationship between Northern Ireland and the Republic; and the British-Irish dimension. The Ulster Unionist Party had been uncomfortable discussing Strand One issues with the Irish government, and Trimble showed that he was willing to take a harder line than his predecessor. In early December, Trimble turned down an invitation to talks with the Dublin government, whom he described as a 'foreign government' and 'impudent' for assuming they had a role to play. Bertie Ahern, the leader of the Opposition, pointed out that, despite being a lawyer, Trimble's comment was legally incorrect and described his outburst as 'simply childish'. The Taoiseach took a more temperate view, pointing out that:

> It would be the easiest thing in the world for Members of this House to criticise statements made by the Ulster Unionist Party, pointing to flaws and how it is inconsistent with internationally recognised law and so on. I would make the point to Members that in the past 70 years we in this House have engaged in this type of dialogue with unionism, when we have been able, at least to our own satisfaction, to 'win the argument' with them. That type of argument, which frequently involves the two traditions on this island talking past one another rather than talking to one another, is not particularly constructive.

Showing his determination to be conciliatory, he added:

> While I would not quarrel with any of the points Deputy Bertie Ahern has made, in terms of their strict truth, they are not ones that advance the position we seek to advance at this time. We should concentrate on expanding the area of agreement rather than accentuating disagreements which undoubtedly exist.[98]

The incident suggested that under Trimble's leadership unionism was retreating from some of the compromises made in the preceding months.

Although the peace process held throughout 1995, a different type of violence was evident on the streets of Northern Ireland as punishment beatings and drug-related killings took place. The latter were carried out by Direct Action Against Drugs, which was believed to be a cover-name used by the IRA. Between April and December 1995, six men were killed for allegedly being involved in drug trafficking.[99] The new year had started as the last one had ended: with the murder of a Catholic suspected of drug pushing.[100] Political dialogue continued to be dominated by decommissioning. In late January the Mitchell Report on Decommissioning was made public. It suggested that the process of decommissioning should take place during, rather than before or after, the talks. Effectively, the Commission was recommending that the British government drop its demand that the IRA decommission as a precondition to talks.[101] It was welcomed by the main nationalist parties, including by Sinn Féin, but neither the UUP nor the DUP accepted its recommendations.[102] Privately Mayhew described the report as 'a load of bollocks'.[103] At this stage the Conservatives had already decided that they did not want to push the unionists too far and so lose their parliamentary support. Ignoring most of the report's recommendations, the British government announced that it would proceed with the electoral process. They realized that a return to IRA violence was the likely outcome but, in the words of Mayhew, 'if they do, we have got to throw all the blame on them'.[104] Moreover, the all-party talks were in jeopardy as the UUP continued to refuse to meet with the Irish government. At the beginning of February 1996, Dick Spring travelled to the USA to meet with President Clinton.[105] Clearly, the peace process was in crisis.

A few days after Spring's meeting with Clinton, RTÉ received a statement saying that 'with great reluctance', the leadership of the IRA 'announces that the complete cessation of military operations will end at six o'clock'.[106] On the evening of 9 February 1996 the IRA planted a huge bomb at Canary Wharf in London's Docklands. Coded warnings had been given in advance of the explosion, but the buildings had not been fully cleared. Two men were killed, more than 100 people were injured and there was more than £85 million of damage. The Docklands bomb marked the end of a seventeen-month ceasefire. News of the bombing was greeted with shock, dismay and anger. In interviews given after the bombing, it appeared that Gerry Adams had not known about it, and he urged that the peace process continue.[107] It seemed, however, that the Army Council of the IRA, disillusioned with lack of political progress, was again setting the agenda for the republican movement. In the following months, there were further bombs in London and Manchester. Clinton's quotation, that peace was more arduous than war, had proved to be a self-fulfilling prophecy.

At the Crossroads

As predicted, the declaration of a ceasefire by the IRA contributed to an increase in inward investment to Northern Ireland. In December 1994 the European Commission agreed the funding of a £230 million aid programme for the six Northern counties and the border counties in the Republic.[108] In the same month, John Major announced a £73 million investment package for the province, which would create up to 300 new jobs.[109] At the same time, he cautioned, 'The peace process that is now unfolding is not yet certain, but it is developing in a way few people would have envisaged just a few months ago.' He introduced a further caveat by insisting that 'huge progress' would have to be made towards the destruction of IRA weapons before Sinn Féin would be allowed to enter formal talks.[110] Regardless of political posturing, the peace process proved to be an enormous boost to economic regeneration and to tourism. Unemployment in Northern Ireland in March 1995 was recorded as 89,600, but within a month it had fallen further, to 88,700 (11.8 per cent), which was the lowest it had been since December 1981.[111] The increased prosperity evident in Northern Ireland was outstripped by economic changes in the Republic. For decades the country had been associated with declining population, poor living standards and economic stagnation, but between 1990 and 2005 employment soared from 1.1 million to 1.9 million. Economic growth, low inflation and more jobs resulted in rising standards of living, for most people, and falling emigration.[112] Not only did emigration rates drop, but a feature of the economic revival was a high level of returned emigrants, especially of the highly educated generation that had left in the 1980s. In 1988 the *Economist* had referred to the Republic as the 'Poorest of the Rich'; ten years later it featured an article entitled 'Europe's Shining Light'.[113] Economic growth was unequal, however, with the cities benefiting most. This, in turn, put pressure on the infrastructure. The increased demand for housing, especially social housing, led to a rapid rise in house prices, which took them out of the range of many first-time buyers. The housing boom witnessed after 1994 made many house owners rich, but it also exposed the deep-rooted inequalities within Irish society.[114]

Even as negotiations were in place for a ceasefire, sensitivities regarding the place of culture in Northern politics continued to run high. This was evident in Derry in 1993 at the end of a production by Galway's Druid Theatre Company of *At the Black Pig's Dyke* by Vincent Woods. The play, set on the border of Northern Ireland and the Republic of Ireland, chronicled how the anger and frustration of three generations of a family is unleashed by the arrival of a group of Irish mummers, who traditionally roamed the countryside at Christmas. The performance by the mummers mirrors some of the tensions between nationalists and unionists, and that night protestors jumped on the stage to voice their displeasure at the play's alleged unionist overtones. The protest was widely condemned in the media, where it was referred to as a 'riot'.[115] The protest demonstrated that political sensibilities remained profound.

Sensitivities also continued to exercise the BBC in regard to songs about Ireland. Although the Simple Minds song 'Belfast Child' was banned by the BBC in 1989, it still reached the number one place in the British charts. 'Belfast Child' was set to the melody of the classic Irish folk song 'She Moves through the Fair' and made use of instruments such as the penny whistle and the *bodhrán*, all of which gave it a haunting air. The band said it was 'inspired by pictures coming out of Ireland at that time'.[116] Marxman's debut single, 'Sad Affair', enjoyed less popular success, but was nevertheless banned by most Irish and UK radio stations, including the BBC. It protested against the presence of British troops in Northern Ireland.[117] Its lyrics spoke of a dream that one day orange would simply refer to the sun in summer and not a knife 'that cuts apart a nation's soul, a nation's heart'.[118]

The song contained the Irish phrase '*Tiocfaidh Ar La*' ('Our day will come'), a phrase associated with Irish republicans. The band, whose members were predominantly Irish, described their influences as 'Marx, Engels, Lenin, Rosa Luxemburg, Bobby Sands . . . and all those who have devoted themselves to the overthrow of the bourgeoisie'. Their failure to make much of an impact in the music world was because, in the words of one critic, 'In the final analysis, there was simply too much analysis.'[119] 'Belfast Child' and 'Sad Affair' were at the opposite ends of the musical spectrum, but they both demonstrated a frustration with the ongoing war in Northern Ireland and the failure to resolve it. The fact they were both banned confirmed that discussing Northern Ireland politics in a popular arena continued to be feared.

A very different type of musical experience was provided through the medium of the Eurovision Song Contest, a competition in which Ireland did exceptionally well, winning in 1979 (Dana), 1980 and 1987 (Johnny Logan) and, uniquely, consecutively in 1992, 1993 and 1994 (Linda Martin, Niamh Kavanagh, and Paul Hattigan and Charlie McGettigan). A further win came in 1996 (Eimer Quinn). When hosting the 1994 competition in Dublin, a seven-minute dance sequence was used to fill the interval, loosely based on traditional Irish step dancing. It went on to become an international phenomenon. In the process, it made both the Eurovision Song Contest and Irish dancing appear to be cutting edge and sexy, attributes that had rarely been associated with either before. Tellingly, the two main dancers, Jean Butler and Michael Flatley, were Irish American, not Irish – but even this fact was rendered in a positive way, suggesting that Ireland was 'embracing the talents of the diaspora'.[120] Despite criticism of *Riverdance*'s invented Celticism, the show proved to be an enduring international success, even performing in China in 2004. By that time the company had toured 30 countries on four continents and been seen live by more than fifteen million people.[121] Moreover, *Riverdance* 'not only reclaimed the hidden folk and pagan elements in Irish dancing before it had been purified by church and prudish middle-class revivalists, but it recognised the Irish contribution to the Broadway musical genre'.[122] It suggested that Ireland was not only comfortable with its own cultural heritage, but was willing to show how it had both borrowed from and played a part in the cultural development of other countries. Overall, *Riverdance* was one indicator that the Republic was increasingly at ease with its history and heritage.

A further indication of Ireland's willingness to face its past was evident in the treatment of the 150th anniversary of the appearance of potato blight in Ireland, an event that had triggered the tragedy known as the Great Famine (or Hunger). Despite the significance of the Famine in Irish history, relatively little had been written on it, yet it continued to be a disputed area among historians, with those known collectively as 'revisionists' denying that it was an event of importance. Moreover, in an effort to dint the nationalist interpretation of the Famine, revisionists claimed that the British government had done all that it could to alleviate the suffering.[123] As the sesquicentenary approached, the release of a rap song by Sinéad O'Connor, in which she accused the British government of deliberately exporting food while the Irish poor starved, showed that talking about this topic continued to be controversial. She denied the fact that there had been a famine in Ireland, on the grounds that massive amounts of foodstuffs had continued to be exported to England 'while the Irish people starved'.[124] O'Connor, who was no stranger to controversy and opprobrium, was attacked by revisionist historians and by the media alike.[125] In fact, O'Connor was echoing the same sentiments expressed by George Bernard Shaw in 1903, in his play *Man and Superman*:

> 'Me father died of starvation in the black '47. Maybe you've heard of it?'
> 'The famine?'
> 'No, the starvation. When a country is full of food and exporting it there can be no famine. Me father was starved dead and I was starved out to America in me mother's arms.'[126]

The Irish government became involved in the commemoration, appointing a committee to oversee a number of events, and allocating £250,000 for this purpose. The new political situation – the ceasefire and the improved relationship with Britain – were highlighted as factors in the decision to host official commemorations. The Famine Commemoration Programme stated:

> The Peace Process allows us all the more freely to explore the truth. The relations between the two islands have now reached a maturity that allows us to look at our history objectively and tell the story as it was . . . After all, the Famine was not just an Irish event, it was just as much a British event, a shared experience.[127]

New research on the Famine was commissioned, but emphasis was to be placed on highlighting the problem of contemporary famines.[128] The Famine commemorations revealed deep differences about the interpretation, memory and legacy of the Great Hunger, not only in Ireland but also in Britain. In 1994 the leader of the Opposition, Bertie Ahern, called for the British government to apologize for the events of 150 years earlier.[129] John Major's government, however, distanced itself from what was going on, and refused to participate in the various famine-related events taking place in Britain, suggesting that the Dublin concept of a 'shared history' was not shared in London. Clearly, though, the commemorations touched a rare nerve. These tensions were evident in the United States, when New York decided to make a study of the Irish Famine part of the school curriculum. Strenuous objections were made by the British Ambassador in the United States.[130] In London *The Times* even claimed that those supporting the curriculum were imbued with 'the Fenian propaganda version which ambitious American politicians tend to prefer'.[131] In 1996 the peace process was in crisis. The way in which the Famine commemorations were approached provided a microcosm of the deep-rooted antagonisms and prejudices that made the task of bringing peace to Ireland so difficult. History, and the memory of the past, were to continue to play a part in the attempts to sustain the peace process in the following years.

NINE

Endgame

In the wake of the ending of the IRA ceasefire in February 1996, further bombs were planted in London. Additional troops were flown into Northern Ireland. Old patterns seemed to resume. Some things had changed, however. Peace rallies were held in Ireland and Britain on 25 February, the largest being in Dublin and Belfast. Despite the cold, an estimated 20,000 gathered outside City Hall in Belfast.[1] Many of the younger participants, who had grown up knowing only war, wanted a return to the peace that had proved to be so short-lived.

Despite the IRA bombing of Canary Wharf, the general consensus was that the peace process should continue, but should Sinn Féin be involved? The ending of the ceasefire had exacerbated fault lines regarding the peace talks, and had strained relationships between the Dublin and London governments. Within the Irish Republic, a poll showed that the majority of people (61 per cent) blamed the British government rather than the republicans for the breakdown of the IRA ceasefire. Even more tellingly, 84 per cent of people believed that both the Dublin and London governments should continue to meet with Sinn Féin.[2]

Although talks continued between the two governments, as did talks between them and the main unionist parties, the Irish government broke off official contact with Sinn Féin. A joint communiqué issued at the end of February by the two governments referred to their 'utter repudiation' of the use of violence for political ends. John Major also made it clear that Sinn Féin would not be admitted to any future talks unless they agreed to 'the principles of democracy and non-violence set out in the Mitchell report'.[3] In contrast, John Hume offered to meet with Gerry Adams and with the Army Council of the IRA. The White House, despite an appeal being made from

Trimble to Clinton, said they were 'keeping the door open' to further talks with Sinn Féin.[4]

A date was set for all-party negotiations – 10 June 1996 – in advance of which an election was to be held. To prepare for this, intense 'multi-lateral consultations', or 'proximity' talks, were to be held between 4 and 13 March. These talks would decide whether:

> there might be advantage in holding a referendum in Northern Ireland with a parallel referendum held by the Irish Government in its own jurisdiction on the same day as in Northern Ireland. The purpose of such a referendum would be to mandate support for a process to create lasting stability, based on the repudiation of violence for any political purpose.

The need for 'confidence-building' was viewed as essential and this was to take the form of making a commitment to non-violence and to decommissioning. The message to republicans was clear, and an appeal was made 'upon Sinn Féin and the IRA to make Sinn Féin's participation in the process of such negotiations possible'.[5] Sinn Féin, while anxious not to be held responsible for the actions of the IRA, at the same time had to convince the other parties that they could deliver IRA support for peace.

The IRA's response demonstrated their autonomy from Sinn Féin, while blaming the British government for the return to armed struggle:

> We pointed out to Mr Hume and Mr Adams that the failure by the British government to put in place inclusive negotiations free from preconditions, the abuse of the peace process by the British over 18 months and the absence of an effective and democratic approach capable of providing an irrevocable momentum towards a just and lasting peace in Ireland, were the critical elements which led to the failure, thus far, of the Irish peace process. We repeat that we are prepared to face up to our responsibilities; others need to do likewise.[6]

Elections took place on 30 May to choose delegates to the peace talks and to elect members of the Northern Ireland Forum. The voting system chosen was complicated, each of the ten parties with the most votes being allowed to elect another two representatives. Although the UUP won over 24 per cent of the vote, and the SDLP won over 21 per cent, they both regarded this as a disappointing result. Although the DUP received fewer votes than the SDLP overall, because of the geographical distribution of the voting, they ended up with more seats: 24 compared with the SDLP's 21.[7]

What the election did reveal was a move to the more hard-line parties on both sides: the DUP won almost 19 per cent of the votes and Sinn Féin won over 15 per cent. The traditional divisions had been challenged, however, by the newly formed Northern Ireland Women's Coalition, which drew support from women across the political and social spectrum. It won 1 per cent of the vote, and was ensured two seats at the talks.[8] For a while, the Women's Coalition became the darling of the media, not least because they offered a fresh perspective to an entrenched problem. The women argued that for the talks to be meaningful, they needed to be inclusive, and that this meant allowing Sinn Féin to join them. This stance drew the wrath of unionists.[9]

John Bruton and John Major attended the opening day of the June peace talks. Nine political parties took part. Because the IRA had not declared a fresh ceasefire, Sinn Féin was not allowed to participate, although they could attend. They decided not to. The PUP and UDP were allowed into the talks because the ceasefire called by the CLMC was still in place. In answer to the criticism that little progress had been made since the 1994 ceasefire, Major explained:

> It has taken us a long time to get to the beginning of these negotiations. Some may feel it took too long. It was a frustrating process. But there was no point launching talks when it was clear that the basis of confidence, and the prospect of broad participation, simply did not exist. A huge amount of preparatory work had to be done.[10]

The mood was generally pessimistic that anything could be achieved, a belief not helped by the fact that both the British and Irish governments were in the run-up period to a General Election, and both governing parties were relatively weak.[11] John Major was particularly vulnerable because he had a majority of only one in Parliament and therefore had to try to keep the unionists, who had nine votes, on his side.[12]

George Mitchell had been invited to chair the talks. For republicans, this signalled that the talks would be fair and open.[13] But his appointment was disliked by some unionists who refused to enter the talks until Mitchell's role was agreed. David Trimble took on the role of peacemaker when he supported a compromise allowing Mitchell to remain as chairman, although his role was to be modified. Ian Paisley proved less accommodating when told of the compromise, and threatened, 'I will dedicate my life to overturning the dastardly deed', and warned that he would boycott the plenary sessions.[14] As usual, the rift between the two main unionist parties was just as much about public posturing as principle. They quickly found common ground in attacking the Women's Coalition. Ian Paisley Jr described the women's understanding of politics as 'outrageous' and 'naive'.[15] The 'undisguised hatred' with which the women were treated was: 'more directed at the fact that, as women, they have dared to enter the political sanctum up to now dominated by men than at the fact that they argue for the inclusion of Sinn Féin'.[16]

While the peace talks limped along, the campaign of violence continued. Since February the IRA had resumed its bombing campaign, predominantly in England. On 15 June 1996 a massive bomb was detonated in the centre of Manchester. Although a warning had been given and 75,000 people had been evacuated, 200 were injured. The planning appeared to have been hasty, which Ed Moloney suggests was due to the fact that IRA cells in Britain had been penetrated and they knew they were under surveillance.[17] Following the attack, John Major stated that 'We shall not rest until those responsible have been brought to justice.' In 1999, though, the investigation was effectively closed, with no arrests having been made.[18]

IRA activities continued in the Republic. On 7 June 1996, Garda Jerry McCabe was killed during a bank robbery in Adare, County Limerick. Initially, the IRA denied any involvement. This position was later revised by a public statement:

> Our investigations have now established that individual volunteers were party to what happened in Adare. We wish to make our position clear. The shootings at Adare were in direct contravention of IRA orders. Such shootings were not – nor cannot be – sanctioned by the IRA leadership. Those who carried out these shootings did so to the detriment of the republican cause.[19]

McCabe's murder caused outrage throughout the Republic, with 40,000 attending his funeral.[20] Anger against the IRA increased when, only two weeks later, a bomb factory was found in Clonasee, County Laois. Following this find, the Taoiseach, John Bruton, called on Sinn Féin to condemn publicly the actions of the IRA in Adare, Manchester and Laois, and suggested that until this happened he would break off formal contacts with them. Bertie Ahern criticized this approach on the grounds that:

> In demanding that Sinn Féin condemns the recent actions of the IRA is the Government effectively creating a split in the Republican movement? Does the Taoiseach consider this is helpful to peace?
>
> The Taoiseach stated today and on other occasions that he would like the next ceasefire to be durable; so would I. Does he not consider it more important that Sinn Féin persuades the IRA to bring the movement which has been involved in the troubles during the past 25 years with it into the peace process rather than leaving a section behind that will continue to engage in violence?[21]

The peace talks and the ongoing violence took place against the backdrop of the 'marching' season, and the approach of the show-case annual march to commemorate the Battle of the Boyne. In the previous year, Drumcree in County Armagh had emerged as a flash-point for wider anxieties within the Protestant community. In 1996 concern turned to anger when, in early July, the RUC announced that the march would be re-routed to avoid the Catholic Garvaghy Road. Unionists were furious, seeing this decision as a further attack on their traditions and rights. The DUP, the UUP and the United Kingdom Unionists all withdrew from the talks in Belfast in protest. The Orange Order responded by re-routing many of its marches closer to Catholic areas in order to put pressure on the security forces. In the days leading up to 12 July, roadblocks were set up by supporters of the Orange Order and rioting became widespread.[22] On 7 July a Catholic taxi driver, Michael McGoldrick, was shot dead in Lurgan, not far from Drumcree. He had been working part-time to finance his degree at Queen's University. A maverick commander in the UVF, Billy Wright, known to the media as 'King Rat', was thought to be responsible. The RUC refused to describe the murder as sectarian because they did not want to inflame already existing tensions.[23] Nonetheless, rioting and sectarian attacks increased as 12 July approached. In the space of only four days, there were 156 arrests, more than 100 instances of intimidation, 90 civilian and 50 RUC injuries, 758 attacks on police and 662 baton rounds fired.[24] Although the British government provided 1,000 additional troops, the security forces were stretched and losing control of the situation. On 11 July, as thousands of Orangemen descended on Drumcree, the RUC did a volte-face and announced that they could march down the Garvaghy Road. Nationalists were furious; Orangemen were jubilant. The energies of the RUC were now focused on containing the local Catholic residents. The unionists had triumphed with the threat of physical force. When challenged about his U-turn, the Chief Constable, Sir Hugh Annersley, explained:

> I found it one of the most difficult decisions of my profes-
> sional career . . . I was faced with a serious and deteriorat-
> ing public order situation, not only in Drumcree where we
> might have anticipated some protest, but across the pro-
> vince. My resources were stretched . . . Neither side would
> give an inch . . . There was a potentially violent and dis-
> orderly crowd who were intent on making their protest and
> we did not and could not, even with 3,000 policemen and
> soldiers, have contained that . . . It had to be a back-off
> situation . . . that patch of road [Garvaghy Road] is not
> worth one human life.[25]

Yet violence did continue and more lives were lost. The decision at Drumcree precipitated riots in many nationalist areas. In Derry a protestor was killed when hit by an armoured car.[26] The peace talks in Belfast seemed far removed from the violence being played out on the streets of Drumcree and elsewhere. However, even the negotiations seemed in jeopardy. Bruton accused the British government of reneging on its promises and not protecting all citizens equally during the marching season. The SDLP protested at the events in Drumcree by withdrawing from the talks.[27] Belatedly, at the end of August, the British government announced the appointment of an Independent Review on Parades and Marches in Northern Ireland.[28] But much damage had been done. Some Presbyterian church leaders referred to what had happened in Drumcree in 1996 as 'Northern Ireland's Chernobyl', on the grounds that:

> it produced a meltdown in community relationships and widespread fallout . . . the deep bitterness stirred by both sides would not abate and, indeed, would continue to flare up each year, further poisoning relationships in Portadown and inhibiting efforts for a final and lasting settlement of the political differences in Northern Ireland.[29]

In other ways, it was obvious that sectarianism had not disappeared from Northern Ireland. A new element was injected into the politics of hate when, in 1996, the Loyalist Volunteer Force was formed. This followed the expulsion from the Ulster Volunteer Force of Billy Wright, the commander of the Mid-Ulster unit, and his associates. Wright was a divisive figure even within loyalist circles. The backdrop to his expulsion was the continuing stand-off at Drumcree. Wright and his supporters believed that they could inflame sectarian tensions further by murdering Catholics. As a 'birthday present' to Wright, his followers carried out the murder of Michael McGoldrick, even though, by doing so, they were putting the loyalist ceasefire in jeopardy. Wright's popularity amongst disaffected loyalists, however, meant that he presented a real threat to the peace process.[30] His blatant sectarianism resulted in the Combined Loyalist Military Command ordering him and one of his associates, Alex Kerr, to leave Northern Ireland or face 'summary justice'. His controversial actions led one senior police officer to say, 'It's really a question of who gets to him first – the IRA, the UVF or us.'[31] However, Wright had friends in high places. Rev. William McCrea, a leading member of the DUP, appeared on a platform with Wright in September 1996, thus giving tacit support to his aims and tactics.[32] In 1997 Wright was shot dead by three members of the INLA while inside the Maze. It was his first time in prison, even though he was believed to have been personally responsible for the deaths of at least 30 people.[33] Thousands attended his funeral and his death sparked a spate of sectarian killings by the LVF.[34]

A further disturbing event occurred during the 1996 marching season. In Harryville, near Ballymena, local loyalists responded to a decision to ban a local Apprentice Boys' march by picketing the Catholic Church of Our Lady. The parishioners were verbally and physically abused when attending church services, despite a large RUC presence.[35] On average, 180 policemen each week had to be deployed to protect the church, and ten of them were injured in the first six months of the protest.[36] The protest continued intermittently for more than four years.[37] In 2000, even though the protest had officially ended, there was an arson attack on the church.[38]

Against this backdrop of violence, in early September John Bruton claimed that a settlement was 'within reach'. He also suggested that the IRA was considering a reintroduction of the ceasefire. Some political commentators, including the seasoned journalist Tim Pat Coogan, denied that this was the case. He believed that the IRA was waiting for the results of the British General Election in the following spring. Bruton's optimism seemed misplaced when, on 23 September, the British police uncovered a massive cache of arms and weapons in London, which suggested that the IRA was not contemplating ending its campaign. During the raids, one IRA suspect was shot dead.[39] Following this, David Ervine, the PUP representative at the talks, declared that 'there is no peace process', while one official admitted that 'things are in a mess'.[40] The IRA responded to the infiltration of their cells in England by moving the campaign back to Northern Ireland, commencing with the bombing of the Thiepval Barracks in Lisburn, the headquarters of the British Army. Thirty-two people were injured, one of whom died a few days later. When the IRA admitted responsibility they apologized for injuries to civilians. They added that their actions were intended to 'enhance the democratic peace process', blaming the British government for 'squandering that historic opportunity in a vain attempt to defeat the IRA'.[41] The propaganda value of having infiltrated the heart of the British Army was immense. Ironically, this violent act, by demonstrating the potential of the IRA, allowed both they and Gerry Adams to contemplate peace once more, but from a position of strength, rather than weakness.[42]

In the final months of 1996 both the peace talks and the loyalist ceasefire appeared to have stalled again. Mo Mowlam, the British Labour Party spokesperson on Northern Ireland, visited the Maze Prison in October to speak to loyalist prisoners. At the same time, she was having secret talks with Sinn Féin, using Ken Livingstone as an intermediary.[43] In the following months other political leaders visited the Maze, which indicated the power of paramilitary prisoners in the peace talks. Also at this time, despite public distancing, there had been intermittent contact between the IRA and the Irish government following the ending of the ceasefire. When Dick Spring suggested in November that Sinn Féin should be admitted into the all-party talks, he was attacked by Trimble and accused of being 'a cheerleader for a terrorist gang'. Spring, inured to such personal assaults, shrugged it off.[44] Some political commentators suggested that despite official denials, the British government had also been holding secret meetings with Sinn Féin.[45]

At the end of 1996 the arrest of Roisín McAliskey, the 25-year-old daughter of Bernadette McAliskey (formerly Devlin), cast doubts on the probity of the British government when it came to dealing with Irish republicans. Roisín was arrested on an extradition warrant, issued by the German government, that accused her of involvement with a failed mortar attack on an army barracks in that country, thought to have been carried out by the IRA. The evidence was flimsy and she denied any involvement. She was four months pregnant at the time of her arrest. During the extradition hearings, Roisín was initially detained in Castlereagh in Belfast, and then flown to England, where she was placed in Belmarsh and Holloway Prisons, where she gave birth to a daughter. Amnesty International objected to the 'cruel and degrading' way in which she was being detained, especially the fact that she was being frequently strip-searched.[46] Under pressure from the Labour MP Kevin McNamara, it was revealed that no contraband been had been found during any of these searches.[47] McNamara's request for Roisín to be released on bail was refused. By March 1997, when strip-searching was ended, she had been searched in this way more than 70 times.[48] In May 1998 the Labour Home Secretary, Jack Straw, released Roisín on medical grounds, arguing that extradition would be 'unjust and oppressive'.[49] She was not extradited at that time, but in 2006, utilizing new legislation, the German government again demanded her detention.[50] In May of the following year she was arrested at her home in Northern Ireland and put on bail. In November a Belfast court refused to extradite her, using the 'passage of time' as the justification.[51] The treatment in 1996 and 1997 of Roisín McAliskey, who had not been convicted of any offence, indicated the limits of British justice when it came to dealing with those suspected of having republican leanings.

A New Dawn?

Behind the public political posturing and apparent logjam that marked most of 1996, things were moving. A presidential election in the US at the end of the year had returned Bill Clinton to office, and 1997 General Elections in both the Irish Republic and the United Kingdom were to have a momentous impact on the faltering peace process. Less significant politically, but important nonetheless, was the election of a new President in the Republic following the premature departure of Mary Robinson to take up a post as UN High Commissioner for Human Rights.

It seemed finally that some contentious issues were being addressed, if not resolved. At the end of January the Independent Review on Parades and Marches in Northern Ireland made its report. Its most important recommendation was that there should be an independent Parades Commission – an acknowledgement that the issue was far more complex than could be addressed in a three-month inquiry. But even holding this initial review had been regarded with suspicion by some unionists. The DUP had refused to make a submission to it, and the Grand Orange Lodge of Ireland had issued a press release unfavourable to its findings.[52] The continuation of traditional political fault lines was further shown when, in February, the UUP complained to the British government that President Mary Robinson had visited Northern Ireland too often, and that she had not sufficiently observed the differences between official and private visits. The President seemed undaunted. Before leaving office in September 1997, she returned to the North and pointed out that she had visited there on only nineteen occasions – even though she had received four times as many invitations. Her parting message was for peace on the island.[53]

In the early months of 1997, however, peace seemed as elusive as ever. The IRA's military campaign continued. Although they did not claim responsibility, some of the bombings were thought to be the work of loyalists. This suspicion was confirmed at the beginning of 1997 by Sir Ronnie Flanagan,[54] whose statement contradicted Sir Patrick Mayhew's earlier assertion that the loyalist ceasefire was holding up. The dispute exposed the desperation of the Conservative government, as a General Election approached, to demonstrate that the peace talks were successful. It also revealed the party's double standards in allowing political representatives of the loyalist paramilitary groups to attend the talks, but not those who represented republican paramilitary groups. The government's actions brought together traditional adversaries in their condemnation. Mitchel McLaughlin of Sinn Féin pointed out: 'Mr Mayhew's remarks completely ignore the assertion of his own Chief Constable that the loyalist ceasefire is over, and show his determination to operate a policy of unilateral exclusion against Sinn Féin.' A similar analysis was provided by the UK Unionist Party leader, Robert McCartney, who asked, with withering sarcasm: 'Do you think it was the tooth fairy that's planted the bombs? Do you think it is a band of tooth fairies that are breaking legs and crucifying people throughout Northern Ireland?'[55] In trying to appease extreme loyalists, Mayhew had brought together republicans and hard-line unionists. His refusal to condemn loyalist actions meant that the destruction of Catholic churches, attacks on the offices of Sinn Féin, and the beating and murder of Catholics continued.[56] In April a young Catholic man, Robert Hamill, was viciously beaten by a gang of loyalists in Portadown, while an RUC patrol looked on. He died of head injuries eleven days later. An inquiry into the circumstances of his death was not opened until 2005.[57]

Loyalist activities were not exclusively directed against Catholics. On 25 March 1997 David Templeton, a Presbyterian minister in Belfast, died as a result of injuries inflicted on him six weeks earlier by loyalist paramilitaries. Both his legs had been broken and his skull fractured. The reason for his attack was thought to be that, eighteen months earlier, he had been discovered with a pornographic homosexual videotape. Templeton was not the only victim of a punishment beating, although his death made it unusual and newsworthy. According to the RUC, in the first three months of 1997 there had been 25 loyalist beatings, fourteen loyalist shootings, and 33 republican beatings and one shooting. In the previous year loyalists had carried out 150 beatings and shootings, while republicans had been responsible for 170.[58] It was clear that a fresh approach to the peace process was required, that could heal both traditional and newly created political divisions.

As the British General Election approached, there were rumours of an SDLP/Sinn Féin electoral alliance. Sinn Féin argued that the justification for such a pact was that: 'The peace process needs a British government which can act without any dependence on either unionist parties. It also demands the election of the maximum number of nationalist representatives committed to the achievement of a lasting peace on this island.'[59] Hume, however, publicly refused to agree to an alliance without an IRA ceasefire, to which Mitchel McLaughlin of Sinn Féin responded:

> The election of 7 or 8 non unionist MPs and the consequent reduction in unionist representation, would transform the political landscape here. It would send a timely message to the unionist leadership after their disgraceful antics at Drumcree last summer. It would send a clear message to the next British government. It would greatly enhance the demand for an inclusive, credible and effective peace process.[60]

Nonetheless, Sinn Féin believed that the British elections really could change the political landscape in Ireland. At the Easter Commemorations in County Derry, Martin McGuinness urged the people to vote tactically to ensure a maximum number of nationalist candidates were returned – both Sinn Féin and SDLP. He explained:

> I am convinced that if Tony Blair – now almost certainly the next British Prime Minister – is prepared to display the courage required to rebuild a new, vibrant and meaningful peace process, then we can, all of us, working together, create a dynamic opportunity to bring to an end all the injustice and conflict and put in place a comprehensive, just and deeply rooted peace settlement. It is said that the performance of other Labour governments in the past were hopeless. That is indeed the case. But we must not allow ourselves to be put off by that . . .
>
> So where do we in Sinn Féin stand now? We stand ready for peace, ready for peace negotiations. Real, credible and meaningful peace negotiations. For the past two and a half years, those peace negotiations were denied us because the John Major government refused to subscribe to the need for inclusive negotiations, refused to clearly answer simple and straight forward proposals put to it by Gerry Adams and John Hume last October.[61]

The overall message provided by McGuinness was that change was coming and that Sinn Féin desired to be part of the negotiations.[62]

Regardless of the imminence of an IRA ceasefire, in the early months of 1997 its campaign of bombings, rocket and mortar attacks continued in Northern Ireland and in England. The targets were generally railways or businesses, but this was not always the case. An incident that caused both international interest and outrage was a warning that the IRA had planted a bomb at Aintree racecourse before the annual Grand National steeplechase. It turned out to be a hoax but the race, usually watched by 100 million TV viewers throughout the world, had to be abandoned. Sixty thousand racegoers, many of whom were stranded without their cars, were evacuated from the racecourse.[63] British public opinion was outraged, but it showed the ability of the IRA to disrupt everyday life, even without using actual violence.[64]

The IRA, however, was facing new challenges, but this time from their former allies. In 1986 supporters of Sinn Féin who disliked the move to electoral politics had broken away to form Republican Sinn Féin, matched in the same year by the creation of a Continuity Army Council and the Continuity IRA. Republican Sinn Féin's President was Ruairí Ó Bradaigh and its head office was in Dublin. Like Sinn Féin, it claimed to be the true heir of the movement founded by Arthur Griffith in 1905.[65] The Provisional IRA ceasefire in 1994 and the possibility of a renewal in 1997 created, in its view, the need for 'true' republicans to continue with the armed struggle.[66] Although the membership of the Continuity IRA was less than 50, they blew up a hotel in Enniskillen in 1996 and were responsible for other bombing and shooting incidents.[67]

Further divisions were apparent within Irish nationalism when, in early April, the Taoiseach, John Bruton, called on nationalists not to vote for Sinn Féin, saying it would be a vote for the IRA's 'campaign of murder'.[68] As the election approached, dissident loyalist groups also attempted to inflame nationalist anger against republicans by carrying out attacks that they blamed on the IRA. This included the burning of Mountpottinger Baptist Tabernacle in East Belfast – an attack that David Ervine of the PUP later admitted had been carried out by loyalists and not the IRA, as the UUP had claimed.[69]

The divisions within nationalism were overshadowed by the deepening conflicts within unionism. In the weeks that preceded the British General Election, a war of words was being carried out between the two main unionist parties, with Trimble referring to other unionists as 'loudmouths'. In turn, the DUP accused the UUP of 'double dealing' and not putting the interests of the Union first. During a TV programme that brought the two deputy leaders together less than a week before the election, John Taylor of the UUP accused the DUP of extremism, while Peter Robinson of the DUP accused Taylor of arrogance.[70] Shortly before the election, however, Paisley announced that he would withdraw some candidates in an attempt to help the UUP defeat Sinn Féin. He claimed that, by doing so, he was 'putting Ulster before the DUP'.[71] Against this backdrop of accusation and counter-accusation, General Elections were held in the United Kingdom in May and in the Republic in June.

The British General Election resulted in an outstanding victory for the Labour Party, bringing to an end eighteen years of Conservative government. Labour won with a 179-seat majority, which meant that they were not dependent on unionist support. Furthermore, they had a strong mandate for change. In total, Sinn Féin won 16 per cent of the votes in Northern Ireland, making it the third largest party, ahead of the DUP. Both Adams and McGuinness won seats in Westminster. The Ulster Unionist Party also gained a seat, bringing its total to ten – eight more than the DUP. The fact that the UUP had won 70 per cent of the total unionist vote appeared to suggest a rejection of the negative tactics of Paisley and his followers, although seasoned political commentators rejected the suggestion.[72] Following the election, President Clinton and others made a renewed call for an IRA ceasefire. Sinn Féin's electoral victory strengthened the argument that political involvement was preferable to violence. If Adams and McGuinness were unable to bring about a ceasefire, however, it would demonstrate that they had no real influence over the IRA, which, in turn, could weaken their position.[73] Trimble had stated he would only meet with Sinn Féin if the IRA announced a fresh ceasefire.

As expected, Mo Mowlam was appointed Secretary of State for Northern Ireland, the first woman to hold this position. Tony Blair and his new Secretary of State needed to balance the conflicting and opposing demands of Northern Irish politics. The approach of the 1997 marching season, which had done so much to damage the peace talks in the previous two years, rendered the task of the new Labour government even more fraught. Mowlam immediately travelled to Belfast to meet the local people. She proclaimed that unless there was an IRA ceasefire, there would be no talks with Sinn Féin.[74] The new Prime Minister's views became apparent when he flew to Northern Ireland two weeks after the election and urged Sinn Féin to get on board 'the settlement train'. In advance of this, though, he stated he was willing to meet with representatives of Sinn Féin. He also warned, probably to assuage unionist concerns, 'My agenda is not a united Ireland – and I wonder just how many see it as a realistic possibility in the foreseeable future.'[75]

The new government's honeymoon period was brief, even by Northern Ireland standards. At the beginning of June Paisley attacked Mowlam, saying that, while 'driving around Ulster, like a headless chicken, may endear her to certain sections of the community and gain praise from republican residents groups . . . it will do little, in real terms, to achieve anything of significance for the ordinary Ulster people'.[76] He was not her only critic, for she was heckled the following day when she addressed the annual conference of the Northern Ireland Police Confederation.[77] Worse was to follow. As the annual stand-off at Drumcree approached, Mowlam attempted to meet with all the interested parties and bring about some agreement. None was forthcoming. In the days that led up to the Boyne parade there was expectation on both sides that the police would not allow it to go ahead.[78] At the last moment, however, the police announced that the parade could march down the Garvaghy Road. Mowlam was 'livid' at the decision, as were nationalists.[79] Flanagan defended his decision on the grounds of wanting to avert loyalist violence.[80] In the long term, as some nationalists and republicans realized, the sight of people being dragged and beaten by the RUC in order that Orangemen could march down their road was a propaganda triumph.[81] In the short term, the decision indicated that the new Labour government, like its predecessors, was not willing to stand up to the Orangemen, no matter how violent their behaviour.

Within days of coming to power, there had been rumours that Labour had been in secret talks with Sinn Féin in an attempt to bring about a renewed ceasefire.[82] Sinn Féin refused to comment, but when in Belfast Blair insisted, 'Since the IRA ceasefire collapsed with the Canary Wharf bombing in February last year, there has been no Government contact with republicans.'[83] Unionists, however, remained suspicious, demanding to know full details of any contact.[84] Unionists were further upset when Adams and McGuinness announced that they would use their offices at Westminster and take the associated financial and other benefits, although, by refusing to take the oath of allegiance, they could not draw a salary as an MP. It was not only unionists who were outraged. Tom King, a former Northern Ireland Secretary, said their presence would be 'a gross affront to democracy' in the absence of a ceasefire.[85] The new Speaker of the House, Betty Boothroyd, ruled that the Sinn Féin members could not use any of the House of Commons facilities unless they swore an oath. This decision was challenged successfully by McGuinness.[86]

Unionists, dismayed by the General Election results, pinned their hopes on the local elections to reinvigorate their supporters, but further disappointment followed. Due to a poor turnout by traditional unionist voters, a number of long-held seats were lost. The low turnout was attributed to the negative image of unionist leaders caused by their constant internecine bickering, and to the belief that unionists' wishes would be ignored, no matter how they voted.[87] A further blow for hard-line unionism occurred at the beginning of June when Mowlam declared the Loyalist Volunteer Force to be illegal. On the same day, she also proscribed the Continuity Army Council.[88]

Talks resumed in Belfast on 3 June. Gerry Adams attempted to join them, but was refused admission. The mood of the meetings remained pessimistic, following an increase in bombings and attacks in the province in the preceding days. There was also a widespread fear that George Mitchell might resign from his role as chairperson. A few months earlier he had referred to the 'twin demons of Northern Ireland, violence and intransigence' and, despite the election of a Labour government, little seemed to have changed.[89] Additionally, there was a concern that time was running out, leading Mo Mowlam to warn that 'if the Republican movement fails to grasp the opportunity the talks will proceed without Sinn Féin. The ball is in their court.'[90]

The General Election held in the Republic on 6 June resulted in a defeat for the Coalition government led by John Bruton. Despite the high profile maintained by Dick Spring in the peace talks, his Labour Party halved its vote.[91] Fianna Fáil emerged as the largest party, although it did not have an overall majority, and was able to form a Coalition government together with the Progressive Democrats and some Independents. The new Taoiseach was Bertie Ahern, who, aged 45, was the youngest person ever to hold this office. Although it was public knowledge that his marriage had broken down, this had not damaged his climb to power. Ahern had been mentored by Charles Haughey, who had referred to the younger man as 'the best, the most skilful, the most devious and the most cunning' of all his would-be successors.[92] The single seat that Sinn Féin won, when Caoimhghin Ó Caoláin topped the poll for the border constituency of Cavan Monaghan, was their first since they changed their electoral policy in 1986.[93] Sinn Féin's electoral success put pressure on the new government to seek talks with the party, since its fortunes appeared to be on the rise on both sides of the border.[94] Ahern announced almost immediately that he would be meeting with Gerry Adams to urge a further IRA ceasefire.[95]

Towards Good Friday

The IRA had been given a deadline of 4 August to call a ceasefire, thus allowing Sinn Féin to enter the talks in September. For Trimble, a ceasefire alone was insufficient grounds for admission, and he appealed to the British government to toughen its stand on decommissioning and to insist that weapons be handed over as soon as talks began.[96] Months of speculation came to an end on 18 July when Adams and McGuinness called for a renewed IRA ceasefire, which was widely regarded as the harbinger of a formal announcement. The following day the IRA issued a statement that it was going to renew its 1994 ceasefire.

Two more people were killed before the IRA ceasefire was declared: both were teenagers, both Catholic and both killed by loyalists. Eighteen-year-old Bernadette Martin was shot in the head four times by the Loyalist Volunteer Force on 15 July while she lay sleeping in her Protestant boyfriend's arms at his home in the village of Aghalee. Police regarded it as a sectarian killing, possibly 'motivated by sheer hatred of a Catholic young woman with a Protestant boyfriend'. *The Independent* contended that the cold-blooded murder was shocking 'even by the recent grim standards of the Province'.[97] But violence continued to get grimmer. On 27 July the badly mutilated body of sixteen-year-old James Morgan, from Annesborough, County Down, was found in an animal carcass pit. He had been abducted three days earlier and tortured by loyalists. He had been chosen because he was a Catholic, yet the RUC refused to describe the murder as sectarian.[98] Despite the continuing loyalist ceasefire, it seemed that sectarian attacks were to continue.

The two governments, under their new leaders, were anxious to show that they were doing something to ensure that this ceasefire was permanent. Over the summer, they signed an agreement on decommissioning. It created an independent international body to look at this contentious issue.[99] Three days after the announcement of the IRA ceasefire, Sinn Féin representatives were admitted to Stormont to sort out administrative matters before the talks ended for the summer. Their entrance resulted in the departure of both the DUP and the United Kingdom Unionist Party, who urged the Ulster Unionist Party to join them. When Trimble stayed, a furious Paisley told reporters, 'He says he's digging in . . . He looks as if he's digging his own grave, of political leadership.'[100] In contrast to the divisions evident within unionism, Ahern, Adams and Hume issued a joint statement at the end of July, affirming their commitment to peace and seeking the cooperation of unionists to achieve it.[101] Unionist fears of a renewed pan-nationalist front appeared to be confirmed, but the unionist leadership seemed increasingly divided and fractious.

At the beginning of August, Mo Mowlam formally invited Sinn Féin to participate in the talks, which were to commence the following month. She knew that she would anger unionists by this decision, but explained how, 'In reaching it I have considered carefully all of the evidence available to me about the restoration of the I.R.A. cease-fire and about Sinn Féin's commitment to exclusively peaceful methods and their wish to abide by the democratic process'.[102] The next day Ian Paisley and Peter Robinson of the DUP flew to London to meet with Mowlam. They accused her of helping to promote a 'republican agenda' and urged her not to bend on the issue of decommissioning.[103] The UUP responded to Mowlam's actions by asking for proximity talks that would permit the different parties to be in separate rooms, with intermediaries conveying information as a way of avoiding face-to-face talks with Sinn Féin.[104] The two parties did come face to face on television, however. In August the UUP MP Ken Maginnis appeared in a BBC *Newsnight* debate involving Martin McGuinness of Sinn Féin, also an MP. It was the first time the UUP had appeared alongside Sinn Féin on British television. Inevitably the debate was heated: Maginnis described his opponent as the 'Godfather of Godfathers', responsible for the 'killing of hundreds of innocent people' through his involvement with the IRA – an assertion that was denied by McGuinness.[105]

Despite the political difficulties, for many the ceasefire brought hope that peace could finally come to Northern Ireland. On 26 August U2 played their first performance in Belfast for over a decade, giving up their holiday to add this show to their world tour. More than 40,000 attended, making it the largest concert in the city's history. In advance, Bono had said that he would leave 'politics to the politicians', although he dedicated one song to 'Tony Blair, Mo Mowlam, Gerry Adams, Paisley and everyone involved in Northern politics'.[106] Significantly, the songs performed did not include one of their biggest hits, 'Bloody Sunday'.[107] U2's latest single, 'Please', was released in Belfast on 23 September. If there were any doubts about its covert political message, the cover – on which the band's faces had been replaced by punk versions of Trimble, Paisley, Hume and Adams – confirmed the meaning of the song.[108] A few months later, on the eve of elections to endorse the latest peace agreement, U2 again played in Belfast at the newly opened Waterfront Hall. This time Bono's political message was upfront:

> We're here to try to convince some of the people who have real concerns, genuine concerns, about the peace agreement still to vote yes, because to vote no is to play into the hands of the extremists who've had their day. Their day is over as far as we're concerned. We're on to the next century here.[109]

On 9 September Sinn Féin signed the Mitchell Principles, which, amongst other things, provided for a process of decommissioning. Multi-party talks were to commence on 15 September. The ultimate aim was to establish a devolved assembly.[110] Despite a 'charm offensive' by Tony Blair, the main unionist parties refused to be part of round-table talks at Stormont.[111] Although the UUP, the PUP and the UDP had agreed to attend the talks, they refused to be in the same room as Sinn Féin.[112] Various reasons were given, among the most commonly used ones being decommissioning and the continuation of articles 2 and 3 of the Irish Constitution. Robert McCartney of the UKUP refused to attend, along with the DUP, on the grounds that: 'The two governments, in concert with the forces of pan-nationalism, had already predetermined the outcome and that, within the present talks' structure, no possible result could preserve the Union.'[113]

The talks were under threat almost as soon as they commenced when, only a day after officially meeting with Adams, the UUP decided to leave. Before doing so, Maginnis accused the new Labour government of having 'elevated an evil Mafia to a status that would shame any other country in Western Europe' and of 'bringing murderers to the table of democracy'. The main reason for Maginnis's anger was a bombing that he blamed on the Provisional IRA; shortly after the attack, however, Continuity IRA claimed responsibility.[114] It was not until 23 September, coincidentally the day that U2's single 'Please' was released, that the UUP and Sinn Féin gathered in the same room in Stormont. Trimble did not speak but Maginnis gave a 30-minute speech in which he attacked both Sinn Féin and the government's handling of republicanism. He avoided all eye contact with his opponents and admitted that he had agreed to the encounter 'with a heavy heart'.[115] Nonetheless, it was a groundbreaking meeting.

The following day the UUP consented to sit at a table with Sinn Féin and agreed on a framework for future talks. It was the first time that unionists and republicans had sat together. Both the DUP and the United Kingdom Unionist Party continued to boycott the proceedings, although they demanded that they should be given the minutes of all discussions.[116] Divisions within unionism were not unusual, but the fact that the main unionist party was talking to republicans was a new development. Paisley and McCartney framed Trimble's action not simply as an act of political betrayal, but as religious heresy. At a meeting in the Ulster Hall in Belfast, Paisley urged the audience to pray for deliverance from 'the powers of darkness, the demon from the pits of hell'.[117] This meeting marked the beginning of a 'road show' during which Paisley would take his message to the unionists throughout the province.

It was not only unionists who were divided. Some leading members of the IRA disapproved of the ceasefire and the ending of the armed struggle. A number left and formed a new paramilitary group that they called 'the Real IRA'.[118] This meant that there were now three republican paramilitary groups – the INLA, the Continuity IRA and the Real IRA – that had not agreed to a ceasefire. Further splits that became evident within Sinn Féin in October over the leadership's signing of the Mitchell Principles led to media speculation that Adams's leadership was under threat and the talks were in jeopardy.[119] Reports of divisions and departures from the IRA followed.[120]

At a Sinn Féin rally held in the Europa Hotel, Belfast, at the end of November various speakers denied that splits were occurring.[121]

The final months of 1997 were dominated by political wranglings, similar to those that had preceded the July ceasefire. They were frequently acrimonious, with both sides believing they were losing out in the latest round of talks. While the talks in Stormont staggered along, intercommunal violence continued to be widespread, showing the fragility of the peace talks. Bombings, punishment beatings, attacks on churches, loyalist parades, petrol bombs, sectarian attacks, street riots and arrests had not ceased. A violent feud between the UVF and the UFF (the front name for the UDA) not only increased the carnage but was a further indication of divisions within loyalism. Increasingly, the cause of the deadly intra-loyalist feuding was control of the drugs trade, rather than ideological differences.[122] Allegations of police collusion with the loyalist paramilitaries also continued. Many of these accusations subsequently proved to be true.[123] The appointment in October of a Parades Commission with extended powers confirmed how difficult it was to find a compromise. To ensure that Orangemen did not feel that they were being targeted exclusively, Trimble had insisted that the remit of the Commission be broadened to look at all cultural activities, a development that alarmed some nationalists. He had argued:

It is essential that before next year's marching season the Government and the Commission demonstrate that they are even-handed and that they show it's not something targeted only on the loyalist community and that cultural expressions in the nationalist community, including the disgracefully provocative way that the GAA [Gaelic Athletic Association] behave, are brought within the ambit of the legislation.

Nigel Dodds of the DUP claimed that the bill was 'Another concession to the pan-nationalist front, by giving powers to an unelected and unaccountable body to ban or re-route traditional lawful parades'.[124] Unionist anger increased when, on 11 December, Gerry Adams led a Sinn Féin delegation to Downing Street to meet with Tony Blair. Prior to this, Sinn Féin had not been invited to Downing Street since 1921, at the time of the treaty negotiations. Once inside, McGuinness was alleged to have remarked, 'So this is where all the damage was done . . . this was where Michael Collins signed the Treaty in 1921.'[125]

On 23 December the multi-party talks ended for the Christmas holiday. In reality little had been achieved. The year ended as it had started – violently. On 27 December three members of the INLA shot dead Billy Wright, founder of the LVF, while he was a prisoner in the Maze. Loyalists claimed collusion in the murder.[126] On the last day of the year, six men were shot, one killed while drinking in a bar in north Belfast. The LVF, although still supposed to be observing a ceasefire, claimed responsibility, saying it was retaliation for the murder of Wright. Other attacks on Catholics followed.[127] At the beginning of 1998, peace appeared as elusive as ever, despite an IRA ceasefire.

The New Year commenced much as the previous year had ended, with inter- and intra-community violence. To keep the peace talks moving, Mo Mowlam again visited loyalist prisoners in the Maze and the Irish and British governments issued a joint statement in an effort to re-energize the peace talks.[128] Despite the ceasefire, sectarian killings continued, mostly perpetrated by loyalist groups. On 23 January the UFF issued a reaffirmation of their ceasefire, in which they admitted that the violence of the IRA and INLA had 'made a measured military response unavoidable'.[129] It was a public admission that loyalist paramilitaries had been killing with impunity, and it exposed the double standards attached to paramilitary ceasefires. The UDP, who were associated with the UDA, were expelled from the talks, although told they could be readmitted if the new ceasefire held. Violent activities continued. In the first six months of 1998 an estimated twelve Catholic civilians were killed by loyalists. During this period, murders were also carried out by the INLA and the Continuity IRA.[130] Violence cast a deep shadow over the talks.

The multi-party talks commenced on 12 January 1998. To keep up the momentum, the two governments issued the 'Propositions on Heads of Agreement', which provided a framework for future negotiations. It was welcomed by the unionist parties and the SDLP, although Adams criticized it for emphasizing partition over the development of all-Ireland institutions. The IRA rejected the Heads of Agreement, describing it as a 'pro-Unionist document' that had 'created a crisis in the peace process'. They blamed Tony Blair, describing him as 'yet another British Prime Minister [who] has succumbed to the Orange Card'.[131] When Blair responded by producing a document to outline cross-border cooperation, it was rejected by the UUP, with Jeffrey Donaldson ripping up the document during the talks and drawing laughter from his colleague, David Trimble.[132] The zero-sum nature of unionist and nationalist politics was showing that, regardless of the paramilitary ceasefires, making constitutional progress would be a slow, tortuous process.

Traditional divisions became more marked as the anniversary of Bloody Sunday approached. On 29 January 1998 Blair announced that there would be a new independent judicial inquiry, something that the nationalist community had been demanding since the debacle of the Widgery report. It seemed that, at last, some long-running grievances were being confronted. To assuage any concerns about the inquiry by the British Army, Blair assured them that his faith in their professionalism was 'unshakeable'. He explained, 'We must wish it had never happened. Our concern now is simply to establish the truth, and close this painful chapter once and for all.' His announcement was criticized in the House of Commons by unionists and some Conservative MPs. Trimble warned, 'I think the hope expressed that this will be part of the healing process is likely to be misplaced. Opening old wounds like this is likely to do more harm than good.' Gregory Campbell, a DUP councillor, took the opportunity to make a larger political point: 'I hope that those who were condemning people like me who said the treadmill of concessions would not end are listening now.'[133] In the context of Northern Irish politics, the quest for truth and justice was made secondary to political point scoring.

As a gesture of openness, the talks moved between Belfast, Dublin and London. But a change of locations could not disguise the fact that they were faltering and ever more acrimonious. Trimble continued to refuse to talk directly to Sinn Féin, but negotiated through intermediaries; at official functions, they sat at separate tables.[134] The frustration of the main nationalist participants was also apparent. In mid-February, when Bertie Ahern gave his support to the British government, who were considering expelling Sinn Féin owing to the alleged involvement of the IRA in two recent killings, the usually restrained Gerry Adams publicly declared that he was 'pissed off' at trying to make the peace process work.[135] A compromise was reached when Sinn Féin was banned from the talks for just six days.[136] St Patrick's Day provided both relief and release from the talks when the annual pilgrimage to Washington took place: those who held meetings with President Clinton included not only Adams and Trimble, but also John Hume, Gary McMichael of the UDP and John Alderdice of the Alliance Party. Clinton was upbeat, urging them all to 'grab the chance of a lifetime'. Mitchell cautioned against expecting a swift breakthrough, believing: 'Their tribal instincts are too strong. They're not used to talking. They're not used to compromise. That's the understatement of the twentieth century.'[137] Nonetheless, a few weeks later he set a deadline for when talking was to stop and an agreement was to be reached: 9 April 1998.

In the days before the deadline, divisions were as wide as ever, with even the two governments failing to find consensus. On 7 April Trimble told Blair that he rejected the agreement, his main, but not only, objection being in regard to cross-border bodies and the amount of space that the Agreement devoted to them.[138] When Blair arrived in Hillsborough Castle later that day, he warned, in an uncharacteristically unprepared soundbite, 'A day like today is not a day for soundbites, we can leave those at home, but I feel the hand of history upon our shoulder with respect to this, I really do.'[139] Blair then held a two-hour meeting with Trimble. When Ahern arrived at Hillsborough the following morning, having spent the night keeping watch over his dead mother's body, Blair told him that the north-south part of the agreement had to be completely rewritten. The Taoiseach agreed. Despite this hurdle being overcome, Blair and his advisers did not believe that they could reach a settlement.[140] Blair then joined the parties involved at Stormont, for what proved to be two days of intense and fraught negotiations.

In advance of his arrival in Northern Ireland, Blair had been advised by Mitchell and Mowlam that: 'If the media mini-Olympic village start reporting one side is winning, expect the other to start demanding meetings with you. None of it will bear much relation to the true state of the negotiations.'[141] He was also warned not to make the final agreement 'the son of Sunningdale', with an equally rapid demise. As the talks progressed, they provided drama and spectacle to the watching world, but for those involved they represented hope, despair, frustration and exhaustion as almost 30 years of conflict were crystallized into a few days of talks. Aware that Sinn Féin believed they were being taken for granted, Blair made a concession regarding the early release of prisoners. During discussions, Adams had pointed out to the Prime Minister, 'released prisoners are the best ambassadors for the peace process'. Blair verbally conceded this point – although following the talks the release time reverted to two years.[142]

Despite the cold and the rain, local schoolchildren arrived outside the gates of Stormont with messages of peace. All the politicians were anxious to be photographed with them, but Adams showed the most acumen – when he provided them with drinks.[143] In the midst of the negotiations, Trimble returned to his party's headquarters in the centre of Belfast, where he was greeted by a cheering crowd. Turning to wave to them, he realized 'He need not have bothered – the screams were for teenage heart-throb Ronan Keating of Boyzone, who had just arrived for the Irish Rock and Pop Awards.'[144]

The deadline for the talks' completion was midnight on Thursday 9 April, but they continued afterwards, with mixed and contrary messages coming out of them. Significantly, Paisley was booed as he led protests against the talks and then tried to enter them. His lack of popularity extended to the journalists, one English paper reporting: 'Paisley, who was 72 on Monday, was pushed on to the defensive at this extraordinary press conference. As he ranted, on the stroke of midnight, the deadline, the press started to drift away. He seemed, for the moment at least, an anachronism, irrelevant to history in the making.'[145]

In the early hours of 10 April, Good Friday, there was a mood of celebration when Blair was informed that the deal was coming together. Two hours later, the mood became one of desolation, when a fresh 'hitch' was mentioned: unionists had asked for more assurances, particularly in regard to decommissioning. Blair, encouraged by President Clinton by phone, was determined that having come so far the talks should not founder. He gave a letter to Trimble reassuring him on two critical points: that politicians connected with paramilitary organizations that refused to hand over weapons would not hold office in any Northern Ireland government; and that the process of decommissioning would have to begin immediately after the Assembly came into being.[146] It was not until late afternoon that an agreement was confirmed – seventeen hours after the deadline had passed. At 5.36 pm George Mitchell told journalists, 'I am pleased to announce that the two governments and the political parties in Northern Ireland have reached agreement.'[147] At the news conference later in the day, Blair said, 'Today I hope that the burden of history can at long last start to be lifted from our shoulders.'[148]

The Agreement, which was referred to as the Good Friday, or Belfast, Agreement, opened with a Declaration of Support that stated: 'We, the participants in the multi-party negotiations, believe that the agreement that we have negotiated offers a truly historic opportunity for a new beginning.'[149] It proposed repealing the Government of Ireland Act of 1920, which had provided for the partition of Ireland. Two principles underpinning the new agreement were that the constitutional status of Northern Ireland could change only following the agreement of a majority vote of its citizens, and that all parties remained committed to 'exclusively peaceful and democratic means'. The Agreement provided for three interconnected groups of institutions that would evolve from the three 'strands' of relationships: within Northern Ireland, between Northern Ireland and the Republic, and between the UK and the Republic. The agreement also provided for a Northern Ireland Assembly, with 108 members to be elected by proportional representation. A British-Irish Council was also created, as was an Equality Commission and a Human Rights Commission. In addition, there was to be a comprehensive review of criminal justice and policing arrangements, and money was allocated to help victims of violence.[150] A copy of the proposals was to be posted to every household in Northern Ireland and the Irish Republic, and then voted on by referendum in May.

Regardless of the Agreement marking a historic political breakthrough, initial reaction on the streets of Northern Ireland was described as 'lukewarm'. Nonetheless, the *Belfast Telegraph* concluded:

> At this Easter weekend, with all its powerful symbolism, hope has conquered despair.
>
> TODAY Northern Ireland stands on the threshold of a bright new era. Prayers have been answered and after a predictably tense and fraught climax to the negotiations at Stormont, agreement has been reached. The people of this province, who had scarcely dared to believe that such an accommodation would be possible, can look to the future.[151]

A different form of praise for the Agreement came from the poet, Michael Longley: 'In its language the Good Friday Agreement depended on an almost poetic precision and suggestiveness to get its complicated message across. The good poetry that has emanated from here is like that too, and for exactly the same reasons.'[152] In the days that followed, the participants clarified their expectations of what the agreement meant to them. Mowlam warned that the Agreement was not a peace settlement, but a 'staging post' on the way to one.[153] Similarly, Adams described it as a 'transitional stage towards a democratic peace settlement', adding, 'And it could become a transitional stage towards reunification.'[154]

The referenda, held on both sides of the border on 22 May 1998, returned resounding 'yes' votes for the Good Friday Agreement. In the Republic, the referendum was a vote to amend articles 2, 3 and 29 of the Constitution. The implementation of the Agreement was contingent on these being removed. The vote was decisive, receiving 94 per cent approval, although the turnout was only 56 per cent. John Coakley has suggested that the amendment 'marked a significant evolution in public opinion, reflecting a recognition of unionist sensitivities, a revulsion towards IRA methods, and a readiness to see Irish unity as a relatively remote aspiration'.[155] In the North, 71 per cent of voters were in favour of the agreement, with 29 per cent opposed. Trimble claimed that the 'yes' vote 'provided the opportunity of a lifetime to create a new and representative government'.[156] A few days after the referendum, Elton John played a concert in the grounds of Stormont Castle that, although not linked to the referendum, 'acted as an unofficial celebration for the massive Yes vote last weekend'.[157] His coming was also part of Mowlam's attempts to encourage 'civic social normality' within Northern Ireland.[158] One English newspaper said that the two-and-a-half hour show was 'electric' and described it as 'the most extraordinary concert in Sir Elton's amazing career'.[159] Although it was described as a 'Peace Concert', Elton John made no political comments during the show. Both he and the show's promoter donated the profits towards building education facilities in the Castle's parkland.[160] Paisley, however, used the concert to criticize both Mowlam and Elton John by saying, 'And now she is bringing in the Sodomites.'[161]

The success of the referenda paved the way for elections to the new Assembly on 25 June. The UUP won 28 seats; the SDLP, 24 seats; the DUP, twenty seats; Sinn Féin, eighteen seats; the Alliance Party, six seats; the UKUP, five seats; the PUP, two seats; the Women's Coalition, two seats, and other parties, three seats. The new Assembly met on 1 July 1998. David Trimble and Seamus Mallon were elected as First and Second Minister, respectively. Inevitably, given the time of year, the marching season was starting to occupy political attention. Unionist ire was inflamed when, on 29 June, the Parades Commission announced that, unless a local agreement was reached, the Orangemen could not parade down the Garvaghy Road. For those opposed to the Good Friday Agreement, Drumcree had come to symbolize a last stand against encroachments on the Union. The decision served to further exacerbate these grievances. On 2 July ten churches in Northern Ireland were attacked by petrol bombs. Orange Halls were attacked in retaliation. As the week progressed, violence at Drumcree intensified. It was no longer simply a conflict of Catholic against Protestant, but was marked by open fighting between sections of the Orangemen and the police.[162]

Mowlam urged Orangemen not to view Drumcree as their 'last stand', because if they did, 'only the people of Northern Ireland will suffer'.[163] On this occasion, it was three children who were to pay the price for this intransigence. On 11 July, as tensions raged over the march in Drumcree, an arson attack was made on the home in Ballymoney, County Antrim, of a Catholic woman who had a Protestant boyfriend. Her three sons, Richard Quinn aged eleven, Mark aged nine, and eight-year-old Jason, perished in the fire as they slept in their beds. Blair described the arson attack as 'an absolutely heartbreaking act of barbarism'.[164] The attack was condemned by leading members of the Protestant churches and of the unionist parties. Even Trimble, whose own career had benefited from his militancy at Drumcree a few years earlier, called for the protest to end.[165] However, he insisted that the murders were not sectarian.[166]

Palpably, the peace process was in crisis. Blair and Ahern asked George Mitchell to join them for a meeting in Downing Street at the end of July. One newspaper suggested that the meeting:

> seemed to demonstrate that the Blairite magic which has been so effective in the peace process has vanished. The PM was seen to use every ounce of his political leverage on David Trimble, but all the persuasion and all the pressure were not enough to achieve a breakthrough.[167]

Mitchell's involvement was viewed as pivotal:

From the minute he first became involved in Northern Ireland in early 1995, then in the role of Bill Clinton's economic envoy, his American 'can do' manner generated both optimism and interest. His style was not that of brash and impatient hubris. Instead, it was obvious from the word go that this was a mature and seasoned statesman, a major player with abilities far in excess of those normally seen in Northern Ireland. In the years that followed it was often embarrassing to watch the mismatch between his consummate skills and some of Belfast's political pygmies.[168]

Hopes of progress were destroyed by the Omagh bombing on 15 August 1998. It was planted by the Real IRA, who opposed the involvement of the Provisional IRA in the peace process.[169] Twenty-nine people died and hundreds of others were seriously injured. It represented the largest single atrocity since 1969. There had been a warning, but the RUC had directed people towards, rather than away from, the bomb. The atrocity shocked opinion not just in Ireland but worldwide. The scale of the carnage led George Mitchell to hope 'that history will record that the troubles ended in Omagh'.[170] The Irish Taoiseach warned that:

> This vicious attack was intended to undermine the right of the people to decide on their own future.
>
> The Government is sending a clear message to those responsible for this atrocity. You will not succeed and you will not defeat the will of the people. If you continue to choose to ignore the will of the people of Ireland and continue on the path of violence, fear and intimidation, be in no doubt that this Government will crush you.[171]

The republican newspaper *An Phoblacht* carried a harsh message for former colleagues whom they now referred to as 'dissidents':

> Omagh was our bomb . . .
>
> It had nothing to do with republicanism, true, but it had everything to do with republicans. It had everything to do with republicans because a number of republicans planned and planted a big commercial bomb, one among many, because they thought they could reverse a tide and also blow

a Sinn Féin-led settlement strategy into smithereens . . .

But ordinary republicans who cannot face up to a future without armed struggle must claim this bomb as their own also, however much we do not want to touch it.[172]

A few days later, the Real IRA and the INLA called a ceasefire.

Not surprisingly, the republican and loyalist violence meant that the next phase of implementing the peace process was slow and controversial. The decision by President Clinton to visit Ireland on 3 September appeared to be a direct attempt to keep the process moving. During an address in the Waterfront Hall in Belfast, he said:

> The Latin word for assembly 'concilium' is the root of the word 'reconciliation'. The spirit of reconciliation must be rooted in all you do.
>
> There is another quality you will need, too. Our only Irish Catholic president, John Kennedy, loved to quote a certain British Protestant prime minister. 'Courage', Winston Churchill said, 'is rightly at the first of all qualities because it is the quality that guarantees all the others'.
>
> Courage and reconciliation were the heart of your commitment to peace.[173]

Following Clinton's visit it was announced that Martin McGuinness of Sinn Féin was to act as the liaison officer with the body overseeing decommissioning. This paved the way for the UUP to meet Sinn Féin.[174] On 10 September Adams and Trimble held a meeting: they did not shake hands and nothing was decided in their 35 minutes alone, but it was a historic moment: 'One, a former academic lawyer; the other, a one-time barman. Today, they lead Ulster Unionism and Irish republicanism, and this was the first time those incumbents had met in three-quarters of a century.'[175] When Seamus Mallon of the SDLP was asked if he felt 'the hand of history' on his shoulder, he responded, 'I have had the hand of history on my shoulder so many times, I don't notice any more.'[176] Following the meeting, Adams told the press that he had made it clear that he could not deliver IRA decommissioning.[177]

Four days later, the Assembly met for the first time since July. The formation of an Executive was postponed, however, with Trimble arguing that decommissioning was still an obstacle. The IRA accused Trimble of using this demand, which had not been part of the Good Friday Agreement, as an excuse.[178] While the internal wrangling continued, external attempts were made to boost the peace process. On 17 October 1998 it was announced that David Trimble and John Hume were to be awarded the Nobel Prize for Peace, 'for their efforts to find a peaceful solution to the conflict in Northern Ireland'. In his acceptance speech Trimble quoted extensively from Edmund Burke, the eighteenth-century Irish-born political philosopher, and also from Eoghan Harris, a former member of the anti-republican Workers' Party.[179] Regarding the £300,000 prize money, Trimble said he had no plans as to what to do with it.[180] Hume announced that he was giving his to charity, including the Vincent de Paul Society and the Salvation Army.[181] Not everyone approved of Trimble receiving the award: in the previous year he had been accused in a book, which expanded on a 1991 documentary originally shown on Channel Four, 'of complicity in the government-sanctioned murder of innocent people'. Trimble denounced these claims as absurd.[182]

Despite the international approbation given to the Irish peace process, in reality little progress was being made. The institutions outlined in the Agreement were supposed to be up and running by 31 October 1998, but this date was not met.[183] Moreover, the spectre of decommissioning, once raised, proved difficult to vanquish and was to haunt and hamper the peace process for years. The calls to demilitarize were directed at the IRA, who regarded this demand not only as a betrayal of the terms of the original Agreement, but also as a way of demeaning them by suggesting that they had been defeated.[184] Adams repeatedly called on Blair and Trimble to implement the agreement they had signed up to on 10 April.[185] He was not the only one frustrated with the lack of progress. An article in the *Washington Post* lamented the 'too-hasty faith in the Good Friday peace agreement'.[186] Although Trimble accused the government of considering dropping its insistence on decommissioning, it was not dropped, although the terms of the Agreement were being re-cast.[187] By 1999 the British government was suggesting, 'The position is that, in the Good Friday Agreement, decommissioning is not a precondition; nevertheless, it is an obligation.'[188] For republicans, allowing Trimble to use the issue of decommissioning as a 'test' of the sincerity of the IRA's commitment to the GFA was, in effect, allowing a unionist veto on the whole process. For McGuinness and his colleagues, 'The test for the two governments and for the Agreement itself is whether these democratic rights will be defended and acted upon.'[189]

Although the establishment of an Assembly had been part of the GFA, the Assembly did not meet in the early months of 1999, whereas the issue of IRA decommissioning – which that had not been part of the Agreement – remained a stumbling block to progress. On 16 February the British government set a deadline of 10 March by which to establish the Executive. When this date arrived, the deadline was extended to 2 April – symbolically Good Friday. In March, however, the Independent International Commission on Decommissioning, chaired by General John de Chastelain, revealed that no progress had been made in this area either. Following his announcement, a joint statement was issued by President Bill Clinton, Tony Blair and Bertie Ahern, stating that decommissioning had to be completed within the two-year framework.[190]

In the midst of these prevarications the death of Rosemary Nelson on 15 March 1999 suggested that little had changed. Nelson, a prominent human rights solicitor with three young children, was killed by a car bomb near her home in Lurgan. She had represented a number of republicans and Catholics, including Robert Hamill. After he was beaten to death by loyalists in 1997, she continued to represent his family, who had been subject to harassment by the RUC.[191] Increasingly, though, it was Nelson herself who faced harassment and death threats. Her complaints were ignored, as the RUC refused to give her protection. Responsibility for her death was claimed by the Red Hand Commandos, but there was press speculation that the UDA was involved.[192] The local RUC was also suspected of deliberate incompetence and possible collusion.[193] The Taoiseach marked her death by saying: 'I have noted the unique arrangements that have been put in place for the investigation and I hope it delivers the just outcome that we all want. It is absolutely essential that the investigation should not be only independent and transparent but be seen to be such.'[194] Nelson's death was condemned by human rights groups throughout the world. Governments as far away as Australia demanded that a full, independent inquiry be put in place.[195] In 2009 it was revealed that MI5 and the security services had been spying on Nelson before her death: in the summer of 1998 Mo Mowlam had sanctioned, apparently reluctantly, an application for a warrant to plant a bugging device in Nelson's property.[196] Nelson was yet another victim of dirty tricks and cover-up, a fact made even more tragic because her death occurred during the 'peace' process.

The continued failure to implement the Agreement resulted in April 1999 in the founding of a lobby group in Britain, The Friends of the GFA. It had the support of 90 MPS, eleven Peers and a number of trade unions, celebrities, writers and lawyers. Mo Mowlam also endorsed it. It called on the British people to 'assist in maintaining the momentum for peace and reconciliation'.[197] On 20 May 1999 Blair set a new – and absolute – deadline of 30 June for agreement on the formation of an Executive, warning that otherwise the Assembly would be suspended. According to Trimble, Blair had privately explored the possibility of excluding Sinn Féin from the Assembly, but decided on suspension instead, 'because moderate nationalists made it clear that they would not serve in an administration without the inclusion of republicans'.[198] The deadline passed on 30 June without agreement. During the intervening months, Sinn Féin had made a number of offers in regard to decommissioning – suggestions that Blair referred to as a 'seismic shift' – but the Ulster Unionist Party stuck to its 'no guns, no government' stance, maintaining they did not believe the republicans were serious.[199] Mowlam later blamed Trimble's repeated rebuttals on the Conservatives for not supporting the Good Friday Agreement.[200] Blair responded to the latest deadlock by issuing a new joint proposal with the Irish government. It was an attempt to allow Sinn Féin to enter government, while reassuring the unionists. According to Blair, 'All sides have legislative safeguards to ensure that commitments entered into are met. This is an historic opportunity.'[201] Again the Unionist Party refused to deviate from its hard-line stand. Mowlam's replacement as Secretary of State in October was regarded by some commentators as a way of appeasing unionists and moving the process along. Moreover, Peter Mandelson, who replaced her, had been suggested by Trimble.[202]

In late October and early November, the British media carried accusations by Michael Oatley, former director of MI6, that the arms decommissioning issue was irrelevant to the peace process. He accused unionists of using it to prevent political progress, to bring down the Good Friday Agreement and to provoke the IRA. In a damning attack on the right-wing media in Britain he said:

the issue has never been presented in a balanced way to the British electorate. Among others, the editors of *The Times* and *The Daily Telegraph*, together with a powerful element on the right wing of the Conservative party, are determined to portray the deadlock on decommissioning as proof that Sinn Féin is cynically insincere about its level of commitment to political action.

This tactic might be described as the picador approach to introducing a terrorist organisation to the attractions of the political arena. No doubt, if sufficient barbs are thrust into its flanks, the animal will eventually, with reluctance, charge. The picadors can then claim the beast was always a ravening monster.[203]

In other interviews he insisted that Sinn Féin was committed to peace and he criticized the British media for not paying attention to the actions of loyalist paramilitaries.[204] Oatley's comments not only suggested that Sinn Féin had been honest brokers in the peace process, they implied that, ultimately, the power to move things on remained in the hands of the Unionist Party, who continued to hold the political veto. It seemed little had changed since the 1960s.

In mid-November George Mitchell revealed details of a plan to rescue the peace process and allow the setting up of a power-sharing government. It provided for decommissioning to start 'a very short time' after the Assembly met. Both Trimble and Adams supported this new deal. The IRA also agreed to it.[205] Mitchell explained that his unusual method for finally brokering a deal was 'persuading the parties to have dinner together – without talking politics'.[206] Getting his party to support the Assembly, however, presented a considerable political risk for Trimble. Although he was praised by Tony Blair for his courage, he was accused by some of his followers of selling out the Union.[207] On 27 November the Ulster Unionist Council backed the Mitchell Deal by 480 votes to 349. In the days leading up to this meeting, 'a hothouse atmosphere pervaded the unionist community and the rest of Northern Ireland'. Trimble had published an article in the *News Letter* explaining his shift from a 'no guns, no government' policy, and reassuring readers that the Union would be safe. Nonetheless, the outcome of the vote was uncertain.[208] The acceptance of the deal paved the way for devolution. Only two days later the Northern Ireland Assembly met and ten ministers were nominated to the Executive. On 2 December 1999, more than nineteen months after the GFA had been agreed, power was passed from Westminster to Belfast, and the new Northern Ireland Executive met for the first time. At the same time, the IRA announced that it had appointed a representative to the body on decommissioning. Other significant steps were taken. In mid-December Blair and Ahern launched a British-Irish Council in London. Trimble described it as ending the 'cold war' between Britain and Ireland.[209] The DUP remained critical of these developments, describing the Council as a 'smokescreen'. While complaining that they had not been invited to its inaugural meeting, they also explained that they would not have attended anyway, because Sinn Féin was there.[210] The establishment of an Assembly had not ended traditional divides, but its setting up had created new ones.

The Assembly was immediately beset with controversy and contention. The suggestion that Martin McGuinness should be Minister for Education led to protests not only at Stormont, but within some Protestant schools. Just before the Christmas break it was revealed that 'Protestant pupils from five County Armagh schools have formed an "action committee" to co-ordinate their protest'.[211] The new millennium came, but old political fault lines remained. The issue of decommissioning did not go away, but continued to be used to show the bad faith of the republicans. Decommissioning was also a weapon that could be directed against Trimble by unionists for having accepted the Mitchell plan.[212] Lack of progress meant that on 11 February 2000 Peter Mandelson suspended political institutions in Northern Ireland and transferred power back to Westminster. The life of the Assembly had proved to be short and inglorious. An unforeseen consequence of the creation of the Assembly in 1999 was the implosion of the Unionist Party, and the concurrent rise of the DUP. Hard-line unionism was the immediate beneficiary. The failure of power-sharing was again linked with the failure of moderate unionism. The challenge of the new millennium, therefore, was to create a peace process that was inclusive and permanent, and could learn from four decades of failures.

Economy and Culture

Throughout the final years of the 1990s, as the peace process forged its rocky path, the Troubles and their background proved to be of interest to moviegoers in Ireland, Britain, the US and even further afield. The 1993 film *In the Name of the Father*, which starred Daniel

Day-Lewis and Pete Postlethwaite, told the story of Gerry Conlon, one of the 'Guildford Four' who had been wrongly convicted for planting IRA bombs in 1994. By the time the film was made, their imprisonment was known to be a miscarriage of justice, but this did not prevent politically motivated criticisms:

> Attacking a film for its standard of journalism, accusing it of distortion, was a deliberately inappropriate, indeed, pre-emptive strike by a hostile British news media. The power of the underlying truths portrayed in the film required damage-limitation strategies. Most of the British government, press and legal establishment disliked the film because it rekindled the outrage felt by the Irish community in Britain at an appalling miscarriage of justice.[213]

The film was nominated, however, for seven Oscars and for numerous other international film awards.[214]

The production team who made *In the Name of the Father*, Jim Sheridan (born in Dublin) and Terry George (born in Belfast), made two further films concerned with Irish politics, *Some Mother's Son* (1996) and *The Boxer* (1998). *Some Mother's Son*, which starred Helen Mirren and Fionnula Flanagan, showed the 1981 hunger strike through the eyes of two Catholic mothers at different ends of the social and political spectrum. Despite its subject matter – one critic described it as 'high-minded and as depressing as hell' – it won critical acclaim, but mostly outside Ireland and Britain.[215] Showing divisions within a community that outsiders generally regarded as monolithic brought it some criticisms from nationalists. The most vehement criticism, however, came from those who objected to presenting any view of republicanism that could be sympathetic. Like *In the Name of the Father*, *Some Mother's Son* was attacked through insinuations that it was pro-IRA, a distortion of the message in both films.[216] *The Boxer*, the final film in the trilogy, which also starred Daniel Day-Lewis, proved to be the most controversial within Ireland. Day-Lewis, himself the son of the Irish poet Cecil Day-Lewis, played the eponymous hero who spends fourteen years in jail for IRA activities. Following his release, he wants to avoid contact with his former republican colleagues but, as a result of his love for a married woman, is forced to re-enter that world. A review in *An Phoblacht* lamented:

This is supposed to be Belfast in the '90s but it seems more like the '70s – the '70s, that is, of the director's imagination, with all its false and outmoded notions of life in nationalist districts and of the IRA. This has nothing to do with the communities that we know. In this film they are sullen, broken and derelict like their crumbling environment.

It concluded that the film was 'an utter travesty'.[217]

Of all the films made in these years the one that attracted most attention was a historical look at the life of Michael Collins, a signatory of the 1921 Treaty. It went into production during the IRA ceasefire of 1994–6 and was directed by the Sligo-born Neil Jordan. He had established his reputation as an international director through films such as *Angel* (1982), *Mona Lisa* (1986), *We're No Angels* (1989), *The Crying Game* (1992) and *Interview with the Vampire* (1994). Collins was played by Liam Neeson, who had been involved in some of the early Field Day productions. The film's reception was mixed. It was a box-office success in Ireland, largely ignored in Britain, and had poor box-office receipts in the United States.[218] Nonetheless, its timing and its content meant that '*Michael Collins* demonstrated that film had become the pre-eminent medium through which Ireland both examines itself and projects its image to the wider world.'[219] In 2000 the small town of Ballymena, where Neeson had grown up, decided to offer him the Freedom of the Borough. Councillors from the DUP, however, objected to the proposal, citing allegedly derogatory remarks that Neeson had made about growing up in the town and feeling like a second-class citizen because he was Catholic.[220]

Outside the hype and glamour of Hollywood, two films that won awards and praise from republicans were *A Further Gesture*, which was premiered in Dublin in 1997, and *Bogwoman* (1998), which won the new director's award at the St Louis Film Festival. *A Further Gesture* depicts the escape of IRA prisoners from Long Kesh. The main character, played by Stephen Rea, makes his way to New York where he becomes involved in helping a group of South American revolutionaries. The script was written by Ronan Bennett, himself a former prisoner in Long Kesh.[221] Unusually, the action in *Bogwoman* is shown through the eyes of a woman who had moved from County Donegal to Derry in the late 1950s. According to *An Phoblacht*, 'the film is as much a feminist as a republican story'. It ends with the eponymous heroine, Maureen, on the barricades during the Battle of the Bogside.[222]

Unionists had traditionally claimed that they were both under-represented and misrepresented in films and in the media in general. The concentration on the IRA had led to a misleading view that all violence in the conflict had been perpetrated by republicans, but two small-budget films dealt, unusually, with loyalist paramilitary experiences.[223] *Nothing Personal* (1995) looked at the short-lived loyalist and republican truce of 1975. It was directed by Thaddeus O'Sullivan, who made a conscious decision to give a screen presence to Southern and Northern Irish Protestants.[224] *Resurrection Man* (1998) was based on the killings carried out by the loyalist Shankill Butchers. The main protagonist is depicted as having an Oedipal relationship with his parents, which explains his gratuitous use of violence, rather than the politics of Northern Ireland being responsible.[225] The film's graphic depiction of brutality resulted in criticism from both Irish and British critics, some of whom walked out during its premiere.[226] Predictably, some critics in the conservative press described it as pro-IRA propaganda, to which the producer Andrew Eaton responded, 'My father was killed by the IRA. Murdered. I'm hardly likely to have forgotten that. So why would I be apologising for them?' These criticisms provoked a review in *The Independent*:

> There are things about Northern Ireland that critics can't face, or become pious or pompous over, not realising how laughable, how irritating, their ignorance can be to those of us born and bred in the cauldron. They stand outside the situation as if it's nothing to do with them, and deliver judgement.[227]

The Irish presence in Hollywood was consolidated by the success of a number of actors – predominantly men, though mention should be made of Brenda Fricker – who starred in both Irish and non-Irish lead roles. The previous generation, which included Peter O'Toole and Richard Harris, had helped to break down the long-standing stereotypes and discrimination against Irish actors.[228] Amongst the next generation were Gabriel Byrne, whose films included *Into the West* (1992) and *The Usual Suspects* (1995); Liam Neeson, who was nominated for an Oscar in *Schindler's List* (1993);

Meath-born Pierce Brosnan, who played the quintessential English-man, James Bond; Stephen Rea, who worked closely with both Brian Friel and Neil Jordan, and whose films included *The Crying Game* (1992) and *Bloom* (2003); the Belfast-born Kenneth Branagh, best known for modern depictions of Shakespeare's classics; and Ciarán Hinds, also from Belfast, whose diverse films have included *Some Mother's Son* (1996) and *Munich* (2005). At the beginning of the twenty-first century, a new generation of Irish male actors was emerging, fronted by Colin Farrell, Jonathan Rhys Meyers, Stuart Townsend and Cillian Murphy.[229]

The final years of the 1990s brought relative economic prosperity and stability, both sides of the border. In the North, unemployment briefly benefited from the 1994 IRA ceasefire, but by mid-1996 had increased again.[230] The renewal of the ceasefire brought increased investment in the North, particularly from Britain, the Irish Republic and the United States. Tourism also benefited. In summer 1996 Prince Charles, who was then undergoing a messy divorce from Princess Diana, visited Northern Ireland amidst tight security. He was pictured walking, stick in hand, against the backdrop of the Giant's Causeway. The purpose, according to local newspapers, was to show that, despite the political uncertainty, the province was almost back to normal.[231] It could also be regarded as a healing measure, given his close relationship with Lord Mountbatten. Prince Charles returned in May 1997 to attend the gala opening of the new Waterfront Hall in Belfast, which was intended to be 'the jewel in the crown' of a regenerated Belfast. The concert was attended by 2,500 people. Even a bomb scare, and the actual blowing up of a flower van, could not dampen spirits on this symbolic occasion.[232]

The creation of a North-South Council as a result of the GFA provided for the establishment of an all-Ireland tourist initiative. This resulted in the creation of Tourism Ireland Limited, which was responsible for marketing the entire island overseas as a tourist destination. Politicians in the Republic regarded this scheme as providing a vital boost to their tourist industry.[233] The early signs were positive, with an increasing number of visitors travelling to Northern Ireland.[234] During 1999 alone, the number of visitors increased by 19 per cent to 1.65 million, with revenues increasing to £265 million.[235]

Overall, throughout the 1990s the Northern Irish economy grew 1 per cent faster than any other part of the United Kingdom.[236] This was due partly to the rapid expansion of the economy of the Republic, but also to the so-called 'peace dividend', the Good Friday Agreement having made investment more attractive. Despite the revival of the economy, inequalities remained. At the beginning of 1998 a report entitled *Employment Equality: Building for the Future* examined the effectiveness of fair employment legislation and the impact of government policy. Figures on unemployment showed that Catholics continued to be twice as likely to be unemployed as Protestants. Moreover, Northern Ireland continued to have the greatest levels of poverty and health and social inequalities in the United Kingdom.[237] One case of discrimination attracted especial attention. In 1998 Rhonda Paisley, daughter of Ian Paisley, took a case to the Fair Employment Tribunal in Belfast claiming that she had been turned down for the post of Arts Co-operation Officer on the grounds of her religious beliefs and political opinions. The position was jointly funded by the Arts Council of Northern Ireland and the Arts Council in the Republic, to promote cross-border links. She won and was awarded £24,249. More unexpectedly, in 2005 Ms Paisley announced that she was taking the DUP to court for gender discrimination in not employing her when she applied for a job in the previous year.[238] She won both an out of court settlement and an apology from the DUP.[239]

Economic progress in the North was overshadowed by the financial phenomenon that was widely referred to as the Celtic Tiger. The Republic's profile of high emigration, declining population, poor living standards and economic stagnation changed in the 1990s. By the end of the decade, the Republic had the second highest gross domestic product per capita within the European Union, second only to Luxembourg. One of the major successes of the Irish economy has been new job creation. A Labour Force Survey in October 1997 showed that the workforce stood at 1.3 million, which was the highest level in the history of the state. Economic growth, more jobs and rising living standards contributed to a reversal in emigration trends.[240]

Critics of the Celtic Tiger argued that the real, if hidden, cost of the rapid economic growth lay in 'wider social inequality, declining community life, too much emphasis on work and competition, a more selfish, [and a] materialist approach to life'. This negative view was challenged by others who pointed out that the Celtic Tiger had brought important social gains as well as economic growth, notably in a decline in poverty, increasing marriage and birth rates, and high national morale.[241] Economic well-being and prosperity had also benefited from the concurrent peace process and a cultural revival on both sides of the border.

Below the facade of increasing prosperity, however, there were social problems that were not addressed, particularly in the areas of social housing and health and social welfare provision. Less palatably, part of the underbelly of the economic miracle was an increase in crime, especially violent drug-related crime. In particular, increased affluence had contributed to the demand for cocaine.[242] A horrific and high-profile killing that shocked people in Ireland was the murder in June 1996 of the Dublin journalist Veronica Guerin, who was shot as punishment for her investigations into the activities of Irish drug barons. When the Taoiseach made a statement to the Dáil, he was fulsome in his praise for the young woman who had written:

> about the unacceptable face of life, about murders, drug dealing and crime. She did so with care and compassion. In doing so she made an important contribution to public life. Without the work she did, much of the recent public debate on crime would not have been as well informed as it was.[243]

Her high profile, however, had not saved her life.

The dramatic events in the North overshadowed political developments in the South, but the early departure of Mary Robinson as President in 1997 meant that an election had to take place for her successor. During the contest, various names were put forward, including that of John Hume, although it was officially confirmed in June that he would not be in the race. If Hume had entered, he would have had to resign as an MP and an MEP, and many feared that this could leave both positions open to a Sinn Féin gain.[244] The incident demonstrated how intertwined and complex politics within Ireland had become. Four of the five candidates who eventually stood for President were women – a tribute to Robinson's skill in making the office both accessible and relevant. The Fianna Fáil candidate, Mary McAleese, won the election with an unprecedented 59 per cent of the vote. Her victory meant that for the first time, anywhere in the world, a female head of state replaced another female head of state. Moreover, McAleese had been born in Belfast and so brought an all-Ireland, inclusive dimension to the position. Ian Paisley, however, greeted her victory by describing her as a 'bigoted and intolerant nationalist'.[245] McAleese paid her first official visit to Northern Ireland in December 1997. When visiting her former school on the Falls Road, she met and shook hands with Gerry Adams, an action that was condemned by unionists and by some in the Republic. Despite her controversial stand on the North, her popularity remained high.[246] The success of women in the Presidency races, however, contrasted with their long-term performance in electoral politics overall. Between 1922 and 1997, only 61 individual women were elected to the Dáil.[247] In 1997 Marie Geoghan Quinn, the first woman member of the Irish Cabinet since Countess Markievicz in the 1920s, resigned, citing 'family pressures' as the reason.[248] Women politicians in the North had an even tougher time. The members of the Women's Coalition were frequently attacked, both verbally and physically. Attacks by the DUP were so vicious that Monica McWilliams referred to them as 'ritual humiliation'. She believed: 'The animosity has been directed not only at their ideas but at them, for violating the custom that men rule politics and women confine themselves to children and kitchen.'[249]

A further consequence of the Celtic Tiger was the secularization of Irish society. One manifestation of this was the decline in religious vocations. An unpalatable side of the Catholic Church that had been covered up for decades was the abuse inflicted on those entrusted to their care by some in religious orders. It coincided with cases of alleged abuses elsewhere in the world, but in Ireland, where the position of the Catholic Church had been so powerful, accusations were particularly numerous. In 1994 the Irish Government collapsed over the mishandling of the case of a paedophile priest, Brendan Smyth. Belfast-born Smyth served four years at Magilligan Prison for sex offences against children over a period of twenty years while he was a priest in the Falls Road area of Belfast.[250] In July 1997 he was sentenced to a further twelve years by Dublin Circuit Criminal Court after admitting 74 charges of indecent and sexual assault on children in the Republic over a 35-year period up to 1993.[251] At this stage, several out-of-court settlements had already been made in other cases of alleged abuse involving priests. As more were revealed, pressure on the government to intervene intensified. On 11 May 1999 the Taoiseach, Bertie Ahern, apologized to victims of child abuse: 'On behalf of the State and of all citizens of the State, the Government wishes to make a sincere and long overdue apology to the victims of childhood abuse for our collective failure to intervene, to detect their pain, to come to their rescue.' He also announced the establishment of a commission of inquiry and other measures to help the victims.[252] The Catholic Church, which had been an integral part of the Southern state since its creation, was shrouded in shame and opprobrium as the century closed.

The Catholic Church was not the only institution under investigation. The Flood Tribunal was appointed in 1997 to investigate accusations of planning corruption in North Dublin. As it became clear that at least one high-ranking politician was involved, the investigation was broadened in 1998. Concurrently, the Moriarty Tribunal was established to investigate the financial dealings of Charles Haughey, the former Taoiseach, and some of his colleagues.[253] The twentieth century closed with the reputation of Irish political leaders in doubt.

The arrival of the new millennium was welcomed with concerts, fireworks and parties. There were celebrations throughout Northern Ireland, with an estimated 40,000 people attending the events in Belfast. John Hume summed up the mix of joy and sorrow when he said: 'It was very poignant and beautiful. It was a good time to stop and reflect on those people who were robbed of the chance to see the new millennium and to look forward to a better future for us all.'[254] In the Republic, the Millennium Committee marked the occasion by distributing a candle and a scroll to every household – 1.3 million in all. Symbolically, the candle was to be lit on the afternoon of New Year's Eve to coincide with the final sunset of the millennium. Also each baby born in the Republic on the first day of January was presented with a commemorative piece of silver and a presentation version of the new £1 millennium coin.[255]

In the 40 years since 1960, many aspects of Irish society had changed dramatically. As the new millennium dawned, and people throughout the country partied, it seemed that all parts of Ireland could face it with hopes of peace and prosperity.

Epilogue: Aftershock

The first day of 2000 was widely heralded as the beginning of the new millennium. Parties, fireworks and messages of a new beginning marked its commencement throughout Ireland. In Ireland and Britain, political stability seemed assured by the continuance of Bertie Ahern, Tony Blair and Bill Clinton in power. Clinton, however, was replaced by George W. Bush in January 2001.

The New Year was only a few days old when the traditional impasse over decommissioning reappeared. David Trimble had threatened to resign if the February deadline was not met. On 6 January the IRA issued a New Year Statement in which they criticized the UUP for imposing preconditions on political progress, the British government for permitting covert surveillance operations, and the RUC for trying to recruit informers in their war against republicans. They appealed to the British government to implement the Good Friday Agreement (GFA), adding, 'As we move into a new century there exists an unprecedented opportunity to leave behind the failures of the past.'[1] Before leaving office, President Clinton had met with Gerry Adams and urged him to apply pressure on the IRA; so too, did the SDLP.[2] Clearly, IRA decommissioning was being used as the barrier to progress and to lasting peace. In the following weeks frantic attempts were made to reach a compromise. On 5 February Trimble met with Adams in an attempt not only to save the Assembly, but also Trimble's premiership of it.[3] Failure to reach an accommodation resulted in the suspension of the Assembly on 11 February 2000. It had sat for 72 days. Following his decision, Peter Mandelson issued a statement saying: 'Today is a sad day for Northern Ireland but it will not stop the peace process and it will not prevent us putting the devolved Government back on track again.'[4] Immediately all sides blamed the other, while the DUP attempted to stamp their authority on unionist anger by calling for the resignation of Trimble.[5] A few days later the IRA withdrew from decommissioning talks.

The stalemate was broken on 6 May when, in a surprise move, the IRA undertook to initiate a process that would 'completely and verifiably' put their arms beyond use. In the wake of this announcement, Adams declared that it was up to Blair and Ahern to keep the peace process moving. He praised the IRA for taking the initiative and thus ending the stalemate. Almost immediately, Mandelson declared that the number of troops in Northern Ireland would be reduced.[6] Three years after the GFA, things finally seemed to be moving.

Two weeks after the statement, the Ulster Unionist Council narrowly supported Trimble in his decision to re-enter the Executive with Sinn Féin. Trimble, however, offended Sinn Féin by suggesting that they still needed to be 'house-trained' before they could become authentic democrats.[7] On 30 May the power-sharing Assembly was restored. In the months that followed, the IRA allowed an official inspection of their arms dumps. Trimble was again First Minister, but he had lost support in the process.

President Clinton and his wife Hillary had visited Ireland on 12 December 2000 for the third and final time in his official role, and the following day they travelled to Northern Ireland. The main purpose of the visit was to encourage the participants to keep the peace process moving.[8] He delivered the most unequivocal message that he had ever made during his presidency, offering a blueprint for progress. The *Belfast Telegraph* wrote:

> A simple, fond farewell it wasn't. By the time Air Force One turned over the Antrim Plateau for London last night, Bill Clinton had belied all ideas that he had come to Northern Ireland for nothing more than a final grand sightseeing tour.
>
> Mr Clinton used his last dose of official influence to make the most obvious political intervention of his time in office. The several hours spent in talks at Stormont and his speech at the Odyssey Arena will have a direct effect on the future direction of the peace process.
>
> With this passage of his speech, Mr Clinton effectively called on the British Government and the IRA to move – in that order – to unclog the peace process.[9]

At the beginning of 2001 President Clinton was replaced by a Republican administration led by George W. Bush. In Clinton the peace process had found a champion, whose determination and vision had helped to break a number of seeming impasses. Bush proved to be less interested in the affairs of Ireland.

On 24 January 2001 Peter Mandelson resigned as Secretary of State and was replaced by John Reid. The peace process was at a delicate stage requiring intense negotiations by the British and Irish governments to keep all sides involved.[10] At the beginning of May, Martin McGuinness officially confirmed that he had been second-in-command of the Irish Republican Army in Derry at the time of Bloody Sunday in 1972. His admission came following the submission of a draft statement to the Bloody Sunday Inquiry.[11] A sign of the changing times came in September 2001 when McGuinness was publicly made Chief of Staff of the IRA. Rather than this being a threatening move, it was widely regarded as beneficial to the peace process. McGuinness, who was Minister for Education at the time, demonstrated a willingness to admit his past and in doing so signified a shift towards a period of more openness in the republican movement.[12]

By mid-2001 the peace process, however, was faltering – again. The United Kingdom was also facing a General Election. Clinton, no longer President, visited Northern Ireland in May, starting in Derry. His enduring popularity was clear. He attended a dinner at Queen's University in Belfast, where tickets sold for up to £15,000 a table. His political message was clear: 'I came here to reaffirm my belief in the Good Friday Agreement because it is still the right path to the future for peace, reconciliation, and fairness.'[13]

In the election of 7 June, both Sinn Féin and the DUP made significant gains, with corresponding losses by the SDLP and the UUP. Ironically, it seemed the more extreme parties were the beneficiaries of the peace process. Lady Sylvia Hermon of the UPP, and widow of John, was elected the first woman MP from Northern Ireland for almost 30 years. Iris Robinson of the DUP was elected to Westminster in the same election. In the spirit of Northern Ireland politics, they refused to have a joint press conference.[14]

The first casualty of the election appeared to be David Trimble, who resigned as First Minister of the Executive on 1 July 2001. When doing so, he called on the British Prime Minister to suspend the Assembly. Blair and Ahern again entered intensive talks to save not just the Assembly, but the peace process.[15] As the marching season was reaching its climax at Drumcree, the *Belfast Telegraph* suggested:

> Do you ever get a feeling that Northern Ireland is stuck in a time-warp, doomed to repeat the mistakes that have always been made, since time immemorial? Welcome to ground-hog day.
>
> Back we go to Drumcree, to see if the Orange Order have lost any of their marching anger and if the Garvaghy Road residents are just as hostile to British feet polluting their ultra-Irish road.[16]

Political alliances, however, were again shifting. Trimble, whose involvement in the Assembly had lost him support in his party, rejected the IRA's moves towards decommissioning. He also negotiated with the anti-Assembly DUP on matters such as policing and excluding Sinn Féin from the Assembly. One politician in the Alliance Party appealed to him to 'put the GFA first for the first time'.[17] On 18 October the UUP and the DUP withdrew from the Assembly. It seemed they wanted to force the hands of both governments and of Sinn Féin.[18] Again the peace process was in crisis. It seemed militant unionists were holding democracy to ransom. Again Sinn Féin and the IRA had been forced into the role of peacemakers. On 22 October Adams made a speech in Belfast asking the IRA to decommission.[19] The following day, IRA decommissioning commenced – an event verified by the International Commission. But this was insufficient for both the UUP and the DUP. The former described what had happened as 'a confidence trick', while the DUP stated that the IRA's actions did 'not even scratch the surface of the arms issue'.[20] Nonetheless, the unionists returned to the Assembly. Trimble sought re-election as First Minister, but was unsuccessful after failing to gain the support of the DUP. After days of intense negotiation, followed by a fresh vote four days later, on 6 November, Trimble was elected with the support of the Alliance Party. When Trimble attempted to speak to the press he was jostled and pushed, and members of the DUP jeered him and called him 'traitor'.[21] The Assembly recommenced its business, but divisions amongst its elected members were as bitter as ever.

The succeeding months were filled with more calls for decommissioning by unionists, further suspensions of the Assembly and attempts by the two governments to make it work, all of which was set against a background of continued activities by the Real IRA and Continuity IRA, and widespread community violence, including rioting, shootings, the use of pipe bombs and punishment shootings.[22] There were also some sectarian murders. In September 2001 Martin O'Hagan, a Catholic journalist, was shot by loyalists. He was the first working journalist to have been killed since the outbreak of violence in 1969.[23] John Reid had considered officially declaring the UDA ceasefire to have ended, but he decided not to do so, based on their promises that the violence would cease.[24] The violence continued and, only two weeks later, Reid proscribed the main loyalist groups.[25]

As attempts were made to re-energize the peace process, a protest was taking place in Belfast that placed children – some born after the GFA – at the heart of underlying and unresolved tensions. The peace process and the high profile ascribed to the IRA had left some working-class Protestants feeling that they had got nothing from the GFA. Moreover, territories that they once occupied were being encroached on, while their traditional avenues of employment had disappeared.[26] This tension came to a head at Holy Cross Catholic School in North Belfast, which, like Drumcree, represented a microcosm of Protestant fears. For some months in 2001 the RUC, supported by the British Army, had had to protect the young children (aged four to eleven) attending the primary school. The school was situated next to a Protestant enclave and the residents did not like the fact that, due to changing housing patterns, the children passed their homes to get to school.[27] Since June the children had been attacked by loyalists, who hurled verbal abuse (including 'Fenian whores'), blew whistles and banged bin-lids, but their actions became more violent, with stones and other missiles being thrown at the children. When school recommenced the girls had to be protected by a cordon of police dressed in body armour. The police suggested that a more circuitous route should be used, but some parents and Father Aidan Troy, a school governor, insisted that they had to make a stand. On 4 September a pipe bomb was thrown, injuring a police officer.[28] Within days of the new school year in September a local doctor reported that fifteen pupils were on sedatives, as they were unable to sleep, were having nightmares or were bed-wetting.[29]

Events at Holy Cross were starting to attract international attention when attacks on the World Trade Center on 11 September

2001 displaced all other news items.[30] In tribute to the close relationship between Ireland and America, a three-minute silence was
observed in Northern Ireland on 14 September, while the Republic
declared a day of national mourning. The daily attacks on the Holy
Cross schoolchildren continued until late November 2001, when a
deal with the loyalists was brokered by Trimble and Mark Durkan,
who had replaced John Hume as leader of the SDLP. It was revealed
that the loyalists had been allowed to put forward a 'wish list' of
their demands.[31] Two years later the mother of one of the pupils
sued the RUC, which in November 2001 had been renamed the Police
Service of Northern Ireland. She argued that the way in which the
dispute had been handled was 'passive and discriminatory compared
to the way similar nationalist protests have been policed'. [32] The case
was rejected by the Law Lords in 2008.[33] Children, who should
have been the main beneficiaries of the peace process, were instead
forced into the vanguard of the continuing violence. As a headline
in the *New York Times* observed on 8 September 2001, 'A cycle of
hatred is visited on a new generation in Northern Ireland'.[34]

The bickering, posturing, double-dealings, accusations and
counter-accusations, fear and loathing that had been part of the
Assembly's short history continued into 2002. Unionists continued
to be resistant to progress being made on cross-border institutions.
The depth of dislike became evident in a speech made by David
Trimble to the Ulster Unionist Council in March, when asked by
those present to contrast the United Kingdom, 'a vibrant multi-
ethnic, multi-national liberal democracy – the fourth largest economy in the world – the most reliable ally of the United States in the
fight against international terrorism – with the pathetic, sectarian,
mono-ethnic, mono-cultural state to our south'.[35] His comments
not only offended nationalists and inhabitants of the Republic, but
some unionists were shocked by it as well. Despite these tensions,
real progress was made by the Assembly on issues relating to health,
education, job creation and housing. On 14 October, however, the
Assembly was again suspended by the Secretary of State, following
'a DUP motion expressing concern at the implications of a search of
the Sinn Féin offices at Parliament Buildings on 4 October 2002 and
the subsequent arrest of three Sinn Féin party members on spying
charges'.[36] The suspension provided an indictment of the fragile
democracy in Northern Ireland. Ahern and Blair issued a joint statement saying how saddened they were by this development, but their

decision was widely criticized. Monica McWilliams of the Women's Coalition described it as a 'disgrace', pointing out, 'The collapse of the Assembly is not a price worth paying for the problems we have and offers no constructive way out of those problems.'[37] Only the DUP appeared pleased, believing that the GFA was finally dead.[38] Shortly afterwards, Blair made a speech in Belfast in which he singled out the IRA for criticism and called on them to disband.[39] In the past, when there had been a logjam in the peace process, President Clinton had intervened. In April 2003 his successor, George W. Bush, arrived in Northern Ireland for discussions with Tony Blair. He also met Ahern and the leaders of the pro-agreement parties. One of his declared aims was to help bring 'a definite end to the paramilitary dimension'.[40] Bush's visit, unlike those of Clinton, was relatively muted, not helped by the unpopularity of the Iraq War.[41] Nonetheless, the Irish government believed that his visit would help to 'bring the current political uncertainty to an end and to facilitate a strong and credible pro-Agreement platform for the Assembly elections on 29 May'.[42]

On 8 December 2004 the so-called 'Stormont-gate Three' were acquitted on charges of spying. Initially no reason was given for the acquittal. But, out of the blue, it was revealed that the man at the centre of the spy ring allegations, Denis Donaldson, had been a paid British agent for twenty years. No prosecution could have been successful.[43] Clearly, the peace process had not brought an end to dirty tricks. Donaldson was murdered on 4 April 2006 in County Donegal. The Real IRA later claimed responsibility.[44]

Elections to the Assembly had been scheduled for May 2003, but the Secretary of State chose to suspend them until November. The outcome changed the balance of power in the Assembly, with the DUP overtaking the UUP as the largest party: the DUP won 32 seats (this included three members elected as Ulster Unionists who defected to the DUP); Sinn Féin, 24 seats; Ulster Unionists, 24 seats; and SDLP, eighteen seats.[45] *The Independent* offered a British perspective on the election result:

> Some of the papers have referred to the result as a crisis. Others argue that the peace process is 'on the brink of collapse'. And context changed. The present US administration has shown little or no interest in the problem. Things in Europe have moved on, and in Britain most people feel

that the problem was substantially solved with the agreement, and do not understand the constant ongoing disputes
between the parties.[46]

In recognition of the fragility of the situation, the Assembly was
not reconvened, but, in the words of the government, 'was restored
to a state of suspension', while political parties were 'engaged in a
review of the Belfast Agreement aimed at restoring the devolved
institutions'.[47] This situation reflected the difficulty of finding a compromise when so much of the political middle ground had been lost,
with both the Unionist Party and the SDLP being the main losers in
electoral terms.

A bank raid in December 2004 changed the political landscape
yet again. The raid on the Northern Bank in central Belfast was one
of the largest bank heists in British history. The professional way in
which £26.5 million was taken immediately raised suspicions that
the IRA had been involved. On 26 December an Irish journalist,
known for his anti-republican views, openly stated in a British newspaper that the IRA had been responsible and posed the question, 'is
not breaking the law, and in utterly spectacular ways, what the IRA
does?'[48] At the beginning of 2005 Hugh Orde, the Chief Police Commissioner in Northern Ireland, publicly announced that the IRA had
carried out the raid. He did not, however, reveal his intelligence
sources.[49] Nonetheless, both the Irish and British governments
claimed to be 100 per cent sure that the IRA was responsible, and for
a time they refused to meet with Sinn Féin while they considered
what sanctions to impose.[50] Shortly afterwards the IRA issued a public statement saying that they were not involved. The police and the
main political parties refused to believe them.[51] The political ping-
pong continued. The murder of a Catholic, Robert McCartney, at
the end of January 2005 by the IRA, following a fracas in a bar, and the
subsequent cover-up, weakened the republican position enormously.
McCartney's sisters mounted an effective publicity campaign to
expose the murderers, which even took them to the White House
at the invitation of George Bush.[52] Following the bank raid and
McCartney's murder some political commentators predicted that
the peace process was finally dead.[53] In contrast, officials in the
Labour Party believed that 'We had to use the crime to drive the
process into endgame'.[54] The consequence was evident a few
months later.

In the short term, the activities of the IRA did little damage to Sinn Féin electorally. The DUP and Sinn Féin again emerged as the largest parties after the General Election in May 2005, and this pattern was repeated in the local elections. The UUP suffered its worst ever General Election defeat, returning only one MP to Westminster. Trimble resigned three days later, blaming Blair's 'indulgence' of the IRA for his downfall.[55] At this stage, the IRA was adapting to the changing political context. On 28 July 2005 the IRA announced that it was ending its armed campaign. The Irish and British governments were delighted. Blair described the announcement as 'a step of unparalleled magnitude', while Ahern referred to it as 'momentous, historic and unprecedented'.[56] Gerry Adams regarded it as 'a truly momentous and defining point in the search for a lasting peace with justice', and said there was no reason for the two governments not to implement the GFA fully.[57] One British newspaper commented that the majority of British people had lost interest in what was going on in Northern Ireland.[58]

On 1 November 2005 it was revealed that the Loyalist Volunteer Force, which the *Guardian* described as 'one of Northern Ireland's most reviled and ruthless paramilitary splinter groups', was also considering decommissioning. Although this move was welcomed by unionists, there was scepticism as to whether the LVF would really give up its racketeering and drug dealing.[59] The LVF announcement put pressure, however, on loyalism's two main paramilitary groups, the Ulster Volunteer Force and the Ulster Defence Association, both of which were bigger than they had been at the time of the 1994 ceasefires. In October 2005 the government's ceasefire watchdog, the Independent Monitoring Commission, had found that loyalist violence, including shootings and assaults, had increased over the past six months.[60] In fact, following the second IRA ceasefire in 1997, loyalist violence had been greater than that of the republicans. Despite this, they continued to claim that they acted only in response to IRA activities.[61] Pressure by the Independent Monitoring Commission, who gave them a final deadline of February 2009 to put their weapons out of use, resulted in some movement in June 2008 by the UDA. It was later revealed that this had only been partial.[62] In January 2009, when the process had still not been completed, the deadline was again extended.[63] The UVF formally decommissioned their weapons in June 2009; the UDA decommissioning was confirmed on 6 January 2010.

A solution to the political impasse finally came at the end of 2006. Similar to the Good Friday Agreement, it required crisis talks that involved both Bertie Ahern and Tony Blair, only this time in St Andrews in Scotland rather than in Belfast. Power-sharing and policing were the main issues of contention. Mark Durkan of the SDLP summed it up as, 'Are the DUP ready to sign on for inclusive democracy and are Sinn Féin ready to sign on for the requirements of a lawful society?' Little progress was made on the first day and the DUP hinted that, even if Sinn Féin agreed to support policing, they would still be looking for 'verification'.[64] The mood was briefly lifted when the Taoiseach gave Paisley and his wife, who were celebrating their fiftieth wedding anniversary, a walnut bowl carved from a fallen tree in County Meath, near to the site of the Battle of the Boyne.[65] Agreement was reached on 13 October 2006. It allowed for the creation of a Transitional Assembly and a timetable to restore devolution in Northern Ireland, which included new elections to take place in March 2007. The Northern Ireland Secretary, Peter Hain, described the agreement as 'genuinely historic'.[66] Sir Reg Empey, who had replaced David Trimble as leader of the Ulster Unionist Party in 2005, said that the St Andrews proposals were 'the Belfast Agreement for slow learners'.[67] In doing so, he mirrored the rhetoric of Seamus Mallon of the SDLP in 1998, that the GFA was 'Sunningdale for slow learners'.[68] Unfortunately, it had taken 30 years and thousands of deaths and injuries to get to this point; as Empey's comments suggested, the politics of exclusion was no longer the preserve of the republicans.

There was also a feeling by some republicans that the peace process had been imposed on them by Sinn Féin and that not enough negotiation had taken place with the people who had suffered most. The seasoned political activist Bernadette McAliskey explained:

> There are two peace processes here, one top down and one bottom up. One which makes all the soundbites and gener-ates all the headlines and one which has been very much overshadowed by the other. There's the Peace Process that everybody sees – the all-singing, all-dancing one. That's the big process.[69]

Furthermore, the republican paramilitary groups, referred to as 'dissidents', had not agreed to the ceasefire and continued to see the GFA as a sell-out.

The election took place in March 2007 and the DUP and Sinn Féin were again the largest parties. It appeared to be another false start as the deadline for devolution came and went. The Assembly was not restored on 26 March, but a 'historic meeting' took place between Paisley and Adams.[70] Adams described it as 'marking the beginning of a new era of politics on this island'.[71] John Hume, former leader of the SDLP, welcomed the meetings, but lamented that this type of progress had not taken place at Sunningdale.[72]

On 7 May, power was devolved. Ian Paisley was elected First Minister and Martin McGuinness, Deputy First Minister. They were sworn in on 8 May. Edward Kennedy, the US Senator and long-time champion of peace, was present for what some in the media were labelling 'the joining of Ian Paisley and Martin McGuinness in political matrimony',[73] although Paisley had warned in advance that he would not be shaking McGuinness's hand.[74] Nonetheless, Paisley and McGuinness worked well together, despite previous animosities – so well that the media labelled them the 'Chuckle Brothers'.[75] Other gestures of reconciliation followed. On 11 May Ian Paisley, as the guest of the Taoiseach, visited the site of the Battle of the Boyne and together they toured a multi-million euro restoration project at Oldbridge House and planted a walnut tree. The DUP leader said the symbolic gesture was an indicator of a good future. Paisley also presented the Taoiseach with a musket from 1685, used at both the Battle of the Boyne and during the siege of Derry.[76] History had come full circle: Paisley, who had protested so vehemently in 1965 against the contact between Seán Lemass and Terence O'Neill, was now First Minister and a guest of the Irish Taoiseach. It seemed that the man who had preached hatred for so many decades, and said no to so many peace initiatives, had been fully rehabilitated.[77]

Paisley had said no to power-sharing for decades, and when he finally agreed to it, his time in power was short. Throughout the latter part of 2007 there were rumours that Ian Paisley Jr had been lobbying on behalf of a land deal in his constituency. Although he was cleared by the Ombudsman, innuendoes continued and he resigned as a minister in February 2008.[78] Paisley Jr's resignation left his father bereft of his right-hand man and his key political ally. Ian Paisley announced his own resignation on 4 March. There was a widespread belief that he had become a political liability and the DUP had ditched him.[79] Even as his political career came to an end, he remained a controversial figure, with letters to the local press oscillating between congratulating him for his long successful career, some saying he had sold out unionism, and others referring to his '50 years of negativism and destruction followed by 50 weeks of accepting the 1973 Sunningdale proposition'.[80] Some of the bitterest criticisms came from his former allies. Clifford Smyth, Paisley's biographer and onetime supporter, wrote:

> Ian Paisley appeared this week as a tragic figure, sustained only by the dwindling reserves of his super-ego and the affection of his family . . .
>
> For a generation Mr Paisley bestrode the province and the world as a Protestant protagonist without equal . . .
>
> Now, I wonder whether Ian Paisley's career was always about a grab for power at whatever the cost – fellowship, loyalty, political principle and, perhaps some years from now, the Union itself.[81]

It was also revealed that, despite Paisley's condemnation of those who had talked to republicans, he had been doing so himself for years. According to one of Tony Blair's close advisers, as early as 2003 'back channel' meetings had taken place. It was kept secret because the IRA had not decommissioned, therefore it would have contradicted Paisley's uncompromising rhetoric and lost him support. Paisley and Adams had never met or spoken, however, until they sat down for a photo-opportunity in March 2007.[82]

Paisley was replaced as First Minister by Peter Robinson. His retirement was regarded as marking the end of an era. In some areas, little had changed. Peter Robinson's wife, Iris, who was also an MP and a member of the Assembly (MPA), proved to be controversial in some of her views: in a 2008 radio interview she described homosexuality as an 'abomination' and said she was happy to put any homosexual in touch with a psychiatrist with a Christian background, who 'tries to help homosexuals – trying to turn away from what they are engaged in'. Although her views were widely condemned, she insisted that she stood by them. She also claimed that she was the victim of a witch-hunt against Christians.[83] Her husband endorsed her views, saying on a television show, 'It wasn't Iris

Robinson who determined that homosexuality was an abomination, it was the Almighty.'[84] Iris Robinson was named 'Bigot of the Year' at the Stonewall Awards in London in November 2008.[85] In the 1960s Ian Paisley had organized a campaign against 'sodomy'; attitudes did not seem to have changed within the DUP by 2008. At the beginning of 2010, Iris Robinson was again in the news – both national and international. Revelations about an affair and alleged financial impropriety not only led her to resign from the House of Commons, the Assembly and the DUP, but also seemed that they might damage her husband's career. The DUP's golden couple had lost their patina.

The disastrous performance of the DUP in the European elections in June 2009, where they ran a negative campaign based on attacking Sinn Féin, suggested to some that they were simply 'a party of protest, not power'.[86] Unionism, for so long the dominant power, seemed to be in crisis. Sinn Féin, in contrast, topped the poll.[87] The election offered an insight into the continued influence of religion in Northern politics – ironically, a charge that unionists had frequently levelled at the Republic. Counting took place on the following Sunday in every part of the European Union except Northern Ireland where, in deference to the sabbatarian ideals of traditional Protestantism, counting had to wait until Monday.

In contrast to the instability of politics in the North, in the Republic there was unusual continuity when a Fianna Fáil-Progressive Democrat coalition was re-elected in May 2002. Its success was helped by a fast-growing economy, the continuation of the peace process and Bertie Ahern's personal popularity. There was also continuity of the office of President. In November 2004 Mary McAleese was inaugurated to her second term in office. The election was uncontested.[88] There had been rumours that Dana Rosemary Scallon – better known as Dana, who had won the Eurovision Song Contest for Ireland in 1970 – would run for this position. In the 1997 presidential election Dana, who had campaigned for family values, had come a surprising third. Encouraged by this, she had stood for, and won, a seat in the European Parliament in 1999. In the 2004 presidential race, rather than presenting herself as a custodian of family values, she stood as guardian of the Irish Constitution. She failed to secure a nomination.[89]

In the new millennium, the Republic's relationship with Europe moved closer in a number of ways. On the first day of 2002, the euro replaced the Irish pound as the unit of currency. Since the United Kingdom had decided not to join the eurozone, it was consequently in Brussels and not in Belfast that the gulf between Britain and Ireland was becoming increasingly obvious. The border towns in the North, such as Derry and Newry, made it clear that they welcomed both currencies.[90]

The people in the Republic were traditionally regarded as good Europeans. On 1 January 2004 Ireland took over the Presidency of the European Commission. On 1 May celebrations to mark the enlargement of the EU were held in Dublin.[91] When the six-month presidency came to an end, the Republic was congratulated on 'one of the most successful presidencies ever'. Ahern was singled out for especial praise for his skills as a negotiator, as was the fact that he had 'shuttled among 24 capitals to help resolve myriad arguments over the proposed constitution'.[92] On a number of occasions, however, the Irish did not conform to the view of them as being pro-Europe. Involvement in the EU was made possible by the fact that any change in the Constitution had to be ratified by referendum, which gave the population a voice in determining European policy, unlike people in the United Kingdom. In 2001 a referendum was held in the Republic on whether to accept the Treaty of Nice, which allowed for an enlarged EU. On this occasion the Treaty was rejected, partly on the grounds that it might affect Ireland's neutrality. A further referendum was held on 19 October 2002. Ireland was now the last country to vote to ratify the Treaty and there were some concerns, both within Europe and among the main parties in the Republic, that she might vote 'no' again. The size of the 'no' vote remained the same, but this time more people (63 per cent) decided to vote in favour of the Treaty.[93] Bertie Ahern responded to the result by saying: 'This decision shows above all that, as a nation, we want to welcome the people of the applicant countries into the union with open hearts as well as open minds. It ensures that Ireland remains at the heart of Europe, where we belong.'[94]

In 2008 the people of the Republic again showed themselves to be out of step with the rest of the EU when 53 per cent of the votes cast rejected the Treaty of Lisbon, which sought to change the internal workings of the EU and centralize some of its functions.[95] Opponents believed that the proposals would weaken democracy by reducing the power of nation governments. As Ireland was the only country of the 27 member states allowed to vote on this Treaty, effectively one million people were deciding on behalf of the half billion who did not get this opportunity. Sinn Féin was one of the parties opposed to it.[96] Again the outcome of the vote was against the wishes of the main political parties: 'The electorate was threatened, cajoled, blackmailed and bullied. They were told their economy would collapse and their country would be ostracised, and still they voted "No".'[97] The result brought criticism from elsewhere in Europe, 'that a country that had benefited so mightily and visibly from EU largesse should bite the hand that fed it'.[98] This sentiment was echoed by President Nicolas Sarkozy of France, who exploded with anger, declaring that the Irish were 'bloody fools' who had been 'filling their faces at our expense for years'.[99] The Irish government responded to this democratic decision by organizing a second referendum for October 2009. The outcome was to accept the Treaty.

Ahern called a surprise General Election at the end of April 2007. His sliding personal popularity was not helped by his handling of a strike by nurses. His critics accused him and his party of complacency after ten years of economic prosperity.[100] During the election campaign the spotlight was increasingly focused on Ahern's personal finances. The expectation was that Fianna Fáil would fare badly, but they performed well enough on 24 May for Ahern to consider entering into another coalition with the Progressive Democrats. In contrast, Sinn Féin did less well than expected, losing one of its four seats in the Dáil.[101] Speculation and rumours about Ahern's financial dealings continued over the succeeding months, and in April 2008 he announced he would be resigning as Taoiseach. Inevitably, comparisons were being drawn between his behaviour and that of his mentor, Charles Haughey.[102] Unlike Haughey, he had presided over Ireland at a period of unprecedented peace and prosperity. His charm and hard work had won many friends for Ireland in Europe, while his personal life – taking office as a divorced man – had heralded that the Republic had changed. Ahern was replaced by Brian Cowen, who inherited a collapsing economy and a faltering peace process.

Economy

The early years of the new millennium were marked by increased economic prosperity on both sides of the border. Growth in the Northern Ireland economy outstripped that of the rest of the

United Kingdom. In the ten years that followed the start of the peace process in 1995, unemployment had almost halved. By 2001 unemployment was at its lowest level since records began. It had fallen from a peak of 17.2 per cent in 1986 to 6.2 per cent in June 2001.[103] Moreover, between 1999 and 2004 employment had grown by 8.3 per cent, which was over twice the UK average rate. Although there was a move to a knowledge-led economy, manufacturing output performed well, increasing by 24 per cent. This contrasted with a corresponding fall of 1.6 per cent in the United Kingdom as a whole during the same period.[104] An indication of how things had changed was evident when, in 2003, a European-wide survey voted Belfast the best place to live in the United Kingdom.[105] The peace process had also been important in attracting tourists: tourism revenue in the North in 2004 rose over 7 per cent to £325 million, following a rise of 4 per cent in total visits in the year. This was at a time when tourism revenue in Europe grew by 2 per cent.[106]

The economy of the Republic attracted worldwide attention after 1995, when it became one of the fastest growing and most prosperous economies in the world, the phenomenon known as the Celtic Tiger. Tourism had traditionally been an important part of the Southern economy and, in the decade after 1990, the industry enjoyed uninterrupted growth. The impact on the Irish economy was considerable. Visitor numbers in those ten years doubled, reaching six million in 2001. This had generated €4 billion in annual foreign revenue earnings while employment in the industry was estimated at 150,000. In 2001, however, the appearance of foot-and-mouth disease and the aftermath of 11 September in the United States had a negative impact on tourism.[107] The Special Olympics World Summer Games, held in Dublin in June 2003, gave a boost to Irish tourism and its reputation. It was the first time the event had been held outside the United States. It was also the biggest sporting event of the year, bringing 7,000 athletes, their coaches and their families to the city. Nelson Mandela attended the lavish opening ceremony and other celebrities who were present included Bono, Muhammad Ali, Colin Farrell, Arnold Schwarzenegger, Severiano Ballesteros and Roy Keane.[108] The Special Olympics was estimated to have provided a €30 million spending boost to the city.[109]

The GFA had provided for a new, 32-county tourism marketing company, Tourism Ireland Ltd, which in 2002 undertook promotional campaigns in the US and Britain. This meant that there were three tourist boards in Ireland. Tourism showed consecutive growth in each of the six years that followed this all-island initiative. During these years, Dublin remained the most popular destination, especially for weekend visits. The country's favourable reputation was helped by a European-wide survey in 2003 that judged the Irish Republic to be the 'most content' country in Europe, with Dublin being voted best capital city.[110] In both 2007 and 2009, Dublin was voted the friendliest city in Europe.[111] By 2008, 20 per cent of tourists to Ireland visited Northern Ireland, while 14 per cent chose it as their sole destination.[112] From that year, however, tourist numbers started to decline, partly as a result of the international recession. In February 2008 the Northern Ireland Tourist Board launched an initiative 'to educate Republic of Ireland residents about what there is to see and do in Northern Ireland, motivating them to visit'.[113] The early signs seemed auspicious. In the first three months of 2009, the number of tourists from the Republic to the North doubled over the previous year, giving a boost of a £14.3 million to the economy. This surge helped to counter the impact of the overall decline in tourist numbers to Ireland.[114]

Peace and prosperity meant that the all parts of Ireland experienced inward migration. This trend was in stark contrast to decades of large-scale emigration. By 2002, 6 per cent of the Republic's 3.9 million population were not Irish-born.[115] There was then an increase of immigrants after 2004 coming from the ten countries that had been allowed to join the EU. Overall, between 2002 and 2006 the Republic's population grew by 8.2 per cent, adding greatly to the cultural diversity of the state.[116] The great majority of immigrants were Polish: by 2007 there were an estimated 200,000 Poles in Ireland, representing 5 per cent of the population. Irish supermarkets began to stock Polish food, and the influx of such a large number of Catholics revitalized the Church in Ireland.[117] Under the Irish Constitution, every child born in the Republic had the right to Irish citizenship. There were accusations that some pregnant women were travelling to Ireland to avail of this provision, which, in turn, would give them the right to an EU passport – so-called 'citizenship tourism'. Politicians who promoted these ideas were accused of playing the race card. A referendum on tightening up the state's immigration regulations, held in June 2004, showed that 80 per cent of voters wanted to end the right to automatic citizenship for all babies born in Ireland. A poll published in the *Irish Times* in November 2009 revealed that attitudes to immigrants were hardening as people in the Republic searched for somebody to blame for the worsening economic situation. The poll showed that 72 per cent of respondents wanted non-Irish immigration reduced.[118] Ireland, who had sent so many millions of her population overseas, was closing a door on immigrants.

By 2009 Northern Ireland had the fastest growing and youngest population of all of the constituent parts of the UK. This was largely due to increased immigration and birth rates, both of which had been affected by the inflow of immigrants. As in the Republic, many were from Eastern Europe. In 2008, 2.4 per cent of births in Northern Ireland were to mothers who themselves had been born in a different country.[119] These demographic changes caused some concern amongst natives of Northern Ireland. A letter to the *Belfast Telegraph* expressed anxiety about the influx of 'foreigners and immigrants' and asked:

> having been on the NI housing list for the past six years and living in an area where there is mass unemployment, could someone from the local government please tell me where all this influx of people is going to be 'housed' and how can they possibly find employment?[120]

As economic growth slowed down in 2008 and 2009, owing to the worldwide recession, there was a sharp increase in unemployment, which was particularly severe in some of the rural areas. Mid-Ulster experienced some of the highest percentage increases in unemployment reported anywhere in the UK.[121] Immigrants became subject to racist attacks: some Polish immigrants, for example, were forced from their homes in March 2009 following an international football match against Poland. A more sustained attack was carried out over the summer against Romanians living in Belfast. The attacks became so violent that 100 people had to be moved to emergency shelters, the location of which was kept secret.[122] These attacks were reported in the international press and caused outrage, but between 2006 and 2007 there had been 125 racist incidents in Belfast, which had been largely unreported.[123] Many of the Roma families decided to leave Northern Ireland in the wake of this episode. Margaret Ritchie, the Northern Ireland Social Development Minister, responded to the news by saying:

Northern Ireland is still deeply divided, deeply segregated. People in urban areas here in Belfast live in divided communities.

All of this raises very fundamental questions about the type of society we want to develop and create in Northern Ireland some 15 years after the ceasefire.[124]

Loyalist groups were thought to have been involved in many of the attacks, which led some to suggest that, while Northern Ireland was 'post-conflict', it was not 'post-intolerant'.[125]

The meteoric growth of the Irish economy after 1995 was mirrored by its collapse after 2007. At the beginning of 2009 the Irish government predicted that GDP would fall more than 10 per cent, which some economists regarded as an admission that the economy was crossing the line from a recession into a depression. The official response was to increase taxes and cut government spending. In April 2009 a *New York Times* article entitled 'Erin Go Broke', written by the Nobel prize-winning economist Paul Krugman, identified Ireland as a model for the worst-case scenario for the global economy. The 2009 Budget, announced in December, was the most draconian in the history of the state. In the preceding twelve months the GDP had fallen by 7.5 per cent. An aim of the Budget was to 'plug' the €12 billion hole in public finances over three years.[126] Opposition parties in the Republic blamed Fianna Fáil for mishandling the economy.[127] Public disillusionment with Fianna Fáil had been evident when its share of the vote fell in both the European and the local elections on 5 June 2009: the party lost one seat in Europe and approximately 80 council seats. There were some calls for the Taoiseach to resign. In contrast to its success in the North, Sinn Féin lost its only MEP from the Republic.[128]

Search for Truth

The peace process had paved the way for a number of inquiries and investigations into past wrongs. Many of these concerned the thorny issue of collusion between loyalist paramilitaries and the security forces. This led to claims that republicans and their supporters were highly skilled at ensuring killings involving accusations of collusion were reinvestigated, but not those that had been carried out by republicans.[129] The issue of killings by the state (between 1970 and 2000, one-tenth of fatalities had been killed by state forces) remained a source of contention and controversy for decades. Appeals for investigations continued to be hampered after a peace process was in place.[130] Moreover, some of the inquiries were partial, deliberately obstructed, had limited terms of reference, or were repeatedly delayed, suggesting that the search for truth and justice was still something that was feared.

On 15 February 2000 Bertie Ahern issued the terms of reference for a Commission of Inquiry into the 1974 Dublin and Monaghan bombings. Two previous inquiries had been set up, but their findings had been deemed inadequate. An interim report by Mr Justice Barron was published on 10 December 2003, with a final one in November 2004.[131] During this time, additional investigations were entrusted to the Commission, including various bomb attacks in Dublin, a car bomb at Belturbet in County Cavan in December, bomb attacks in Clones, County Monaghan, and a number of murders in County Donegal.

Barron's initial report concluded that loyalist paramilitaries were responsible for the Dublin and Monaghan bombing and that they did this as a reaction to the Sunningdale Agreement. To say the security forces were involved was 'neither fanciful nor absurd', but evidence was insufficient to be conclusive. Emphatically, though, the report said that these concerns had to be taken seriously. Both the Fine Gael-Labour Coalition, which was then in power, and the Garda were criticized for failing to follow leads and investigate them fully. Damningly, Liam Cosgrave's Cabinet was castigated for failing 'to show the concern expected of it' – such criticisms had frequently been made by the families of the victims. Lack of cooperation by the RUC was also criticized. Despite the passage of time, however, it seemed that not everybody wanted the full story to be made public: files had gone missing from the Department of Justice and remained unaccounted for.[132]

These findings caused public outrage in the Republic.[133] Some of the families had stormed out during the launch of the report, claiming it contained nothing they did not already know. A solicitor for one family described it as 'a complete and utter waste of time and expense and my clients are severely disappointed'.[134] In the report published in November 2004, Justice Barron said he was surprised and disappointed at the lack of cooperation from officials in the UK. He also 'strenuously' criticized the way the Fine Gael-Labour government of the day handled the investigation.[135]

Following the investigation by Barron, the Irish government decided in May 2005 to establish a Commission of Investigation into the Dublin and Monaghan bombings, headed by Patrick MacEntee SC. The Commission, which was to cost €2,632,702, reported in April 2007.[136] It found that police intelligence failed 'to meet an adequate and proper standard' and 'The commission considers that it is probable that this serious organisational deficit provided an inadequate standard of support to those Gardaí involved in the criminal investigations.'

Photograph albums of suspects were missing, as were records of the contents. Garda notebooks were 'presumed lost, abandoned or destroyed'. Although the Commissioner had not been able to confirm why the information was missing, he did not rule out 'unauthorised removal of the documents'.[137] Like Barron, MacEntee had been hampered by lack of cooperation by the British government. He pointed out that the terms of reference had been too limited to allow further comment on some issues. This led to further criticisms in Ireland that, despite these investigations, a number of questions still remained unanswered, especially in relation to the role of the Irish Garda and the British government.[138] In a debate in the Dáil in October 2007, when pressed, the Taoiseach admitted:

> If the Deputy asked if I believe that all the information that is available in the British establishment has been given to us, I certainly would not answer 'yes' to that question. If the Deputy asked whether we have we all the information we are going to get from the British authorities, I would answer 'yes' to that question. After the considerable efforts of Mr Justice Hamilton, Mr Justice Barron and Mr MacEntee, we are unlikely to see any further information. With the help of numerous Secretaries of State they did ultimately change their position and gave far more information than they were giving in the first place. They moved substantially from their position. Any other information is probably in the hands of MI5 or MI6 and I do not see how we will get it.[139]

The death of fourteen people in Derry in January 1972 had been a source of grievance within the nationalist community, which had been inflamed by the belligerent Widgery Inquiry in the same year. The murders had been kept in the public eye through intermittent revelations. On 17 January 1997, 'Channel Four News', a British early evening news programme, carried a report presenting evidence that soldiers, other than those of the Parachute Regiment, had opened fire on those taking part in the civil rights march in Derry on 30 January 1972. It was suggested that members of the Royal Anglian Regiment could have been responsible for the deaths of three of the fourteen victims. Relatives of the victims renewed their call for a fresh inquiry into the events of 'Bloody Sunday'.[140] On 27 February 2000 the Saville Inquiry began its hearings into the events of Bloody Sunday. By the time it came to a close on 20 December 2004 the Saville Inquiry had cost almost £200 million, making it the most expensive inquiry in British legal history. Altogether it interviewed 900 witnesses.[141] Even before Martin McGuinness gave evidence in 2001, there were reports that he would admit to the Inquiry that he was an IRA commander in Derry when British paratroopers killed the fourteen men, and that the IRA had not opened fire on that day.[142] The Saville Inquiry was due to report in November 2008, though in that month it was revealed that it would be delayed for a further year. There were more false starts. In September 2009 a further delay was announced, with suggestions that there were technical difficulties relating to the printing of the 4,500-page document. The families were again disappointed, however, believing that they would not get a report in advance of the British General Election, which was expected to take place between March and June 2010.[143] In response to the pleas of the families that the report be made public, Saville explained: 'We have always found it difficult, given the scale and complexity of the material with which we are dealing, to predict accurately how long it will take us to complete our task.' His words were apposite. A further delay was announced in March 2010. The families travelled to Downing Street to protest, although their frustrations and uncertainties seemed, yet again, to be of little importance.[144]

Progress was also slow concerning investigations into the alleged shoot-to-kill policy in 1982. A breakthrough appeared to come in September 2009 when the Belfast Coroner said that the PSNI Chief Constable must hand over the Stalker and Sampson reports into the killings. He gave them seven weeks to hand over the documents, even if they were in 'redacted form'. This move was welcomed by Sinn Féin and the SDLP.[145] In November 2009, police in

Northern Ireland were told to comply with a court order to hand over top secret documents relating to shoot-to-kill. The PSNI continued to seek clarification about how many documents they were to disclose. Clearly, the police hierarchy remained unwilling to be held up to public scrutiny.

The investigation into the Omagh bombing proved similarly controversial. In 2001 the Northern Ireland Police Ombudsman, Nuala O'Loan, was highly critical of the police's handling of the investigations: 'The victims, their families, the people of Omagh and officers of the RUC were let down by defective leadership, poor judgement and a lack of urgency.'[146]

The Chief Constable threatened to take legal action to have the report quashed, but the families called for a public inquiry. Although a man was tried and convicted for the bombing at a special non-jury Criminal Court in Dublin in 2002, he was released three years later when it was shown that the Gardai had forged some of the evidence.[147] On 7 February 2008 the Northern Ireland Policing Board decided to appoint a panel of independent experts to review the police's investigation of the bombing. Some of the relatives of the victims criticized the decision, demanding an international public inquiry that was cross-border.[148] Nobody was convicted as a result of the police investigation, and the former head of the inquiry later claimed that elements within the intelligence services might have 'effectively sabotaged' the investigation.[149]

In 2008, ten years after the bombing, new evidence was uncovered by a BBC 'Panorama' team suggesting that Britain's electronic intelligence agency, GCHQ, recorded the bombers' conversations as they made their way to the scene. If these men had been intercepted, the bombing could have been prevented, or so it appeared. The families, who had been campaigning for an independent public enquiry since 2002, hoped that this new evidence would persuade the government to grant one.[150] Shortly afterwards the British Prime Minister, Gordon Brown, ordered a full-scale review of all the intelligence material gathered in the hours before the atrocity.[151] The Northern Ireland Secretary, Shaun Woodward, commented: 'Everybody feels terribly badly for the families of the victims. You have to be struck by the sense of injustice. Given the information that was put into the public domain by Panorama, it is absolutely right that the Prime Minister has said there should be a review.'[152] Not for the first time in the Northern Ireland conflict, it had taken a television investigation team to reveal the shortcomings of Irish policing and British justice.

The question of collusion in killings in Northern Ireland proved to be sensitive. It was apparent that the opening of inquiries as far back as Samuel Devenney in 1969 proved to be futile due to a conspiracy of silence by the RUC and others.[153] These difficulties became evident during a 2007 investigation into the circumstances surrounding the death of Raymond McCord Jr, a Protestant and a former RAF man who had been beaten to death with a breeze block in 1997; his face had been so badly beaten that he was unrecognizable. It seemed that the UVF had ordered his death in order to protect their drug-dealing activities. The inquiry resulted from the sustained efforts of McCord's father to seek justice for his son.[154] When reporting the investigation, the Police Ombudsman's office revealed that they had encountered difficulties. Some documents, including murder files, decision logs and intelligence documents, had been either missing, lost or destroyed. This meant that senior officers could not be held to account. Nonetheless, 'Mrs O'Loan has concluded that her investigation has established collusion between certain officers within Special Branch and a UVF unit in North Belfast and Newtownabbey.'[155] Just as damningly, police informants were linked to ten murders and 72 instances of other crime, including ten attempted murders, ten 'punishment' shootings, thirteen punishment attacks, a bomb attack in Monaghan, seventeen instances of drug dealing, and criminal damage, extortion and intimidation.[156]

In 2009 it was revealed that the Police Ombudsman, Al Hutchinson, had postponed publishing a report on the police investigation into the deaths of six Catholic men from Loughinisland, County Down, who were shot in 1994 as they watched football on television. The delay was despite reported interim findings that were critical of the police. No one had been convicted over the killings. In September 2009 it was revealed that RUC informers knew that the UVF were planning the massacre.[157] The families asked the Police Ombudsman to investigate. Caitríona Ruane, the Sinn Féin MLA for South Down, pointed out that a number of very serious questions remained unanswered about the UVF killings: 'Most worryingly, it appears they would have remained unanswered unless the families had put the necessary pressure for a full investigation into the atrocity.'[158]

The difficulties of trying to seek redress for what happened in the past led the Northern Ireland Secretary, Peter Hain, to establish an independent consultative group in 2007 to seek a consensus across the community in Northern Ireland on the best way to deal with the legacy of the past.[159] One of the most controversial suggestions was to give £12,000 each to the victims of the war, including those of paramilitary groups. However, concern with the past was not universally welcomed. In 2009, for example one British newspaper criticized the fact that:

> The pompously named Consultative Group on the Past, set up by Tony Blair in one of his touchy-feely moments, has come up with a £300m plan to finally resolve the years of violence.
> Why? . . .
> Peace was prevailing and Belfast seemed like a modern European city until the Consultative Group on the Past started sticking in their silly snouts.[160]

As a search for the 'truth' to the violence engendered by the conflict in Ireland unfolded, concurrently a search for the truth to the role of the Catholic Church took place. Accusations of the abuse of children in their care had been a running sore throughout the 1980s and '90s. These accusations seemed substantiated when, on 29 March 1998, the Irish Christian Brothers made a public apology to those who had been abused in any of their institutions. The apology was published in newspapers both north and south of the border. It stated:

> We, the Christian Brothers in Ireland, wish to express our deep regret to anyone who suffered ill-treatment in our care. And we say to you who have experienced physical or sexual abuse by a Christian Brother, and to you who complained of abuse and were not listened to, we are deeply sorry.
> We want to do more than say we are sorry. As an initial step, we have already put in place a range of services to offer a practical response. Further services will be provided as needs become clearer.[161]

Details of help lines and help centres were provided, with promises that the help would be both independent and confidential. What followed amounted to the biggest sex scandal ever exposed in the

Irish Republic. Most of the male victims had been aged between ten and sixteen. The reports showed that abuse had been systematic and systemic, rather than sporadic and isolated. A can of worms had been opened that the apology and its aftermath did not resolve. Consequently, on 11 May 1999, Bertie Ahern issued a public statement: 'On behalf of the State and of all citizens of the State, the Government wishes to make a sincere and long overdue apology to the victims of childhood abuse for our collective failure to intervene, to detect their pain, to come to their rescue.'[162]

The issue did not end there. In May 1999 the *Irish Times* published a letter from Brian Quinn, former editor of the *Evening Herald*, which revealed how the Christian Brothers had tried to make the paper suppress stories about child abuse in Artane Industrial School.[163] The statement suggested earlier collusion between successive governments and the Catholic Church that, it appeared, was now at an end. Only a few days later it was announced that a Commission into Child Abuse would be established, chaired by Justice Mary Laffoy. More was to follow in 2002, when the Residential Institutions Redress Board was established to inquire into child abuse. Despite their public statements, the Christian Brothers remained on the defensive, even legally challenging the validity of the Commission on the grounds that the alleged abuses had occurred decades earlier. Nonetheless, they offered to pay €128 million as compensation into a State Sexual Abuse Fund, but only on condition that, in return, they were granted immunity from any civil actions against religious orders accused of abusing children in institutions. At the same time, the claimants were accused of being money-grabbing and attention-seeking.[164] The work of the Commission continued, although most of its enquiries were held in private. Those accused were reported to be adversarial, and to have cooperated only at the most minimal level.[165] Having been repeatedly delayed by church lawsuits, missing documentation and alleged government obstruction, the report was finally released in May 2009. It showed that thousands of children suffered sexual abuse, beatings, malnutrition and emotional abuse for decades in the Irish institutions where they were raised.[166] This long-awaited report made gruelling reading as it recounted how beatings and humiliation by nuns and priests were common at institutions that together held up to 30,000 children.[167] Before its publication there had been widespread denial about the existence of abuse. However, the Pope had urged the Irish bishops, 'to establish the truth of what has happened; ensure that justice is done for all; put in place the measures that will prevent these abuses happening again; [and] with a view to healing the hurt suffered by survivors'. Following the report's release, Archbishop Diarmuid Martin of Dublin added, 'Let's listen and learn . . . and do a little bit of soul searching about what way the church in Ireland will look in years to come.' The issue did not go away, however, even following a much-publicized intervention by the Pope. In March 2010 Benedict XVI issued a pastoral letter to Irish Catholics castigating Irish bishops for 'grave errors of judgment' in handling the paedophilia scandal. For many though, it was too little and too late.[168] The road travelled by the Catholic Church since 1960 had ended in ignominy some 40 years later. Nevertheless, it had contributed to a realignment of the relationship between the Church and the people and by doing so paved the way for a more secular society that could be inclusive of the various traditions that resided in Ireland.

On 28 January 2009 a report was launched in Belfast about how Northern Ireland could handle the hurts of the past. A suggestion had been made that the families of victims of the Troubles should each be given £12,000 in compensation. Before the meeting some of the families formed what one called a 'guard of dishonour' outside the hotel, holding up placards that read 'Sale Here today: Truth and Justice on offer for £12,000' and 'The wages of murder is £12,000', as guests arrived for the official presentation. Some later stormed onto the stage, their actions suggesting how deep and raw their pain continued to be.[169] Overall, the ten years that followed the Good Friday Agreement were marked by many false starts and unfilled expectations. Progress was made, but past grievances and enmities proved hard to shake off.

Cultural Crossings

In the early years of the twenty-first century, Ireland continued to produce artists of international stature. In 2003 the Antrim-born poet, Paul Muldoon, was awarded the Pulitzer Prize for Poetry for his collection, *Moy Sand and Gravel*.[170] John Boyne's award-winning novel about the Holocaust, *The Boy in Striped Pyjamas* (2006), demonstrated that Irish authors were not only concerned with national issues. The book was made into a film in 2008.[171] Wexford-born author John Banville won the 2005 Man Booker Prize for Fiction for his novel *The Sea*.[172] Three Irish authors – William Trevor, Colm Tóibín and Ed O'Loughlin – were among the thirteen contenders for the 2009 Man Booker Prize.[173] Interest in the Irish conflict continued to intrigue audiences. In 2009 the Northern Ireland-based drama *Five Minutes of Heaven*, directed by Oliver Hirschbiegel and starring Liam Neeson and James Nesbitt, won two awards at the Sundance Film Festival. The film dramatized the story of Alistair Little, a UVF man who spent thirteen years in prison for the 1975 murder of a nineteen-year-old Lurgan man, and of the televised meeting with his victim's brother.[174]

Even political art, however, was incorporated into the peace process. In 2008 the Arts Council announced an allocation of £505,469 to eighteen community-based projects across Northern Ireland as part of the £3.3 million 'Re-imaging Communities Programme'. This programme placed artists in divided communities to work with local people in tackling visible signs of sectarianism and racism. Wall murals were an obvious target of this change.[175]

The peace process, however, did not mean a total cessation of violence. Feuds continued between various factions of loyalism. While for some republicans the GFA marked the end of a 30-year period of war, for others it marked the start of a different phase of conflict. On 12 February 1997 the Provisional IRA had shot dead Lance Bombardier Stephen Restorick in Bessbrook, County Armagh. He was often referred to as the last British soldier to be killed in the Northern Ireland conflict. This changed on 7 March 2009 when two soldiers were killed by the Real IRA in Antrim as they took delivery of some pizzas immediately before they were deployed to Afghanistan. The deaths not only shocked public opinion, but revealed the divisions within republicanism. Gerry Adams described the attack as 'wrong and counter-productive' and, more revealingly, said that his party had a 'responsibility to be consistent . . . the logic of this is that we support the police in the apprehension of those involved in last night's attack'.[176]

There were other signs that achieving peace and an end to sectarian hatred would not be easy. In 2009 the end of the British football season ended tragically for one Catholic family in Northern Ireland. The two leading Glasgow teams in the Scottish Premier League are Rangers, traditionally supported by Protestants, and Celtic, the Catholic team. It was a tense season. Early on the

Rangers fans adopted a new song about the Irish Famine, which included the lyrics:

From Ireland they came.
Brought us nothing but trouble and shame.
Well the famine is over.
Why don't they go home?[177]

The Irish government made diplomatic representations to the Scottish government asking that they intervene. However, the Northern Ireland Sports Minister, Gregory Campbell, a member of the DUP, used the controversy as an opportunity to suggest that Celtic should stop its fans from singing pro-IRA chants.[178] One Rangers fan who continued to sing it was put on probation for eighteen months and given a football banning order. His appeal was defended by Donald Findlay QC, who himself had resigned as Rangers' vice-chairman in 1999 after he was secretly filmed singing sectarian songs.[179] The 2008/9 Scottish football season ended on 24 May, with Rangers fans in both Scotland and Northern Ireland celebrating winning the league title. In County Derry this resulted in some disturbances and attacks on Catholics. In Coleraine, Kevin McDaid, a Catholic community worker and 49-year-old father of four, was killed by 'a loyalist mob'. Detective Chief Inspector Frankie Taylor confirmed that the motive had been sectarian. Northern Ireland politicians from all parties, including Gregory Campbell of the DUP, condemned the murder. However, no members of the unionist parties attended the funeral.[180] Clearly, the continuing violence placed the future of the Northern Ireland peace process in doubt.

A survey of political attitudes carried out in 2007 by the Economic and Social Research Council, which had asked the question 'Generally speaking, do you think of yourself as a unionist, a nationalist or neither?', revealed that 36 per cent identified themselves as unionist, 24 per cent as nationalist, 40 per cent as neither.[181] When given a choice of completing the question, 'Do you think the long-term policy for Northern Ireland should be for it . . .', 55 per cent of respondents wanted 'to remain part of the United Kingdom with devolved government'. In contrast, only 23 per cent wished 'to reunify with the rest of Ireland'.[182] The reverberations of the partition of Ireland proved that reunification was not easy. A partition that was less than 100 years old had become deeply embedded in the psyche of the Irish people. Finding a vision for the future was difficult – especially finding an inclusive, consensual future. Political changes, however, were not only taking place in Ireland, but also in Britain. Moreover, the impact of nationalism, in the form of the Scottish National Party and the British National Party, were redefining the political landscape of Britain.

As 2009 drew to a close, there was widespread pessimism on both sides of the border. In November, the Murphy Report into sexual abuse in the Archdiocese of Dublin had been published. It made shocking reading, demonstrating that the Catholic Church in Ireland was 'rotten to the core', while the evidence of collusion illustrated 'the Catholic Church's iron grip on Irish society and the machinery of the state'.[183] The economies in both the North and South remained weak and the December budget in the Republic suggested that the situation would get worse before it got better. Following the budget there were to be wage cuts in the public sector, rising to 15 per cent for the highest paid. On 29 December, however, the Department of Finance revealed that, in fact, the cuts to the salaries of those on higher incomes would not be as large as had initially been suggested.[184] The implication was that those with fewest resources would proportionately be carrying the largest burden of the reductions.[185]

The political situation in the six counties gave little cause for optimism as the main unionist parties appeared to be returning to their traditional stance of negative posturing. When Ian Paisley had left politics early in 2008 he had been replaced by his long-time ally, Peter Robinson. In his new capacity, Robinson would be forced to work closely with Martin McGuinness of Sinn Féin – one of the people he had once advocated hanging.[186] The press speculation was that the warm public relationship that Paisley and McGuinness had enjoyed would be replaced by a businesslike one – or as one commentator put it, 'Ulster's Chuckle Brothers will now give way to Brothers Grimm'.[187] In the following months, there seemed no reason to find a new sobriquet as the reports in the press, and comments by both men, demonstrated their impatience and anger with the other.

The Ulster Unionist Party, which had been reduced to only one minister in parliament, was clearly searching for a new role, not only within the Assembly, but within the United Kingdom. This came in the form of an electoral pact with the British Conservative Party, led by David Cameron. In July 2008 Reg Empey, leader of the UUP, and Cameron had issued a joint statement which outlined their desire for closer co-operation, and pointed out:

> The links between our parties have been long and intimate, stretching back to the 1880s. But as Northern Ireland has now entered a new era and entered it as an unambiguous partner within the wider United Kingdom family, the time now seems right for both parties to take stock and to consider how best to take forward our shared values of support for the Union, support for the family, respect for hard-work, self-reliance, law and order, public service and our obligations to others within society.[188]

The benefits for the Conservative Party, which desired to extend its support out of the heartland of England, were clear. Empey and his party would also benefit from a strengthened United Kingdom. But the question remained as to why the Conservatives had chosen to ally with the UUP, which had only one MP, in preference to the DUP, with nine MPs. The answer, it seemed, was Iris Robinson. Her frequently expressed views on homosexuality were regarded as out of keeping with the inclusive, modern party that Cameron was trying to create.[189]

The tensions within unionism came to a head over the issue of the devolution of policing and justice powers to the Assembly. The decision to devolve these powers, with the approval of the political parties, had been part of the Good Friday Agreement. The matter had been put on hold during the tumultuous early years of the Assembly. During the 2006 St Andrews Agreement, however, it was agreed that these powers would be transferred by May 2008. One consequence of this agreement was that in January 2007 Sinn Féin voted to support policing in Northern Ireland, for the first time in the history of the state. However, in February 2008 the DUP, then led by Paisley, announced that the deadline agreed at St Andrews would not be met.

The newly appointed Robinson, as First Minister, repeatedly delayed agreeing to this matter. McGuinness, his Deputy, set a final deadline of Christmas 2009 but, on 4 December, Robinson made known that this deadline would not be met either. Robinson also tried to make the sensitive issue of parading a precondition for his agreement. The differences between Robinson and McGuinness became obvious during a tense North/South Ministerial meeting in Limavady on 14 December, at which Brian Cowen, the Taoiseach, was present.[190] Yet again, the future of the Assembly appeared to be in doubt. However, as 2009 ended, the personal lives of two prominent politicians pushed the issue of policing and justice into the background.

In December it was revealed that Liam Adams, brother of Gerry, had, a year earlier, failed to appear at a preliminary court hearing to answer questions about alleged sexual offences against his daughter, Áine. These revelations had become known during an 'Insight' programme, broadcast on UTV. Gerry Adams described the matter as being 'hugely difficult', but urged his brother to turn himself in.[191] Although Adams insisted that this was a personal matter, his opponents used it to damage his political credibility. Ian Paisley Jr of the DUP asked an Assembly committee to investigate if Adams had breached its rules by failing to act in respect of his brother's alleged sex abuse.[192] Gerry's niece also accused him of not doing enough to stop Liam working with children.[193] At the beginning of March 2010 Liam Adams gave himself up in Dublin, where he was arrested. He was shortly afterwards released on bail – part of which was put up by another daughter.[194]

Peter Robinson and his wife Iris had been the first husband and wife team from Northern Ireland to sit simultaneously in the Commons. Shortly before Christmas, it was revealed that Iris Robinson was claiming to be suffering from depression. Following the holiday, it was announced that she would be resigning from politics. It was then revealed that she had been having a relationship with a man thirty years her junior. Accusations of financial improbity followed. On 7 January Peter Robinson issued a statement in which he stated that he had known of the affair since the previous March. He admitted that he felt 'betrayed after almost forty years of being happily and closely bonded together'. He also pledged that he would continue to perform his role as First Minister.[195] Later that day, BBC Northern Ireland's *Spotlight* programme confirmed details of Iris Robinson's affair and suggested that she had broken the law in acquiring money for her lover.[196] Following these revelations, her membership of the DUP was terminated, and it was announced that she was stepping down from the Assembly. This was followed by resignation from Westminster. On 11 January Peter Robinson announced that he would be taking a leave of absence for six weeks.[197] Arlene Foster took over as acting First Minister during this period.

Despite his personal problems, Robinson remained involved with the negotiations over devolution of policing and justice. At the beginning of January, when the future of the Assembly seemed in doubt, he made an unequivocal statement defending devolution and the record of the Executive. In a warning to his fellow dissident unionists he cautioned, 'Those who argue for a return to direct rule need to remember the powerlessness and isolation that such a situation meant for our community'.[198] Nonetheless, the issue remained at an impasse. At the end of January, following talks at Downing Street, the Prime Minister, Gordon Brown, and the Taoiseach, Brian Cowen, announced that they would fly to Northern Ireland to meet the leaders of the Assembly. By 27 January no deal had been made, but a 48-hour deadline had been given for an agreement to be reached.[199] It was not, however, until 4 February that the DUP revealed that they had agreed unanimously to the devolution of policing and justice.

The vote on the devolution of policing and justice was due to take place on Tuesday, 9 March. The UUP, led by Sir Reg Empey, appeared opposed to the agreement, but stated that they would only make a final decision the day before the vote. The future of the Northern Ireland Assembly and even that of the peace process seemed in jeopardy. The British Secretary of State, Shaun Woodward, warned that a cross-community vote would be 'nothing less than a vote for the future of Northern Ireland'. He went on to say:

> The responsibility on all MLAS next Tuesday cannot be over-estimated. By voting to complete devolution they will be doing so much more that voting for the transfer of policing and justice powers from Westminster to Stormont, important as that is.
>
> They will be voting for the hopes and aspirations of future generations who do not want to relive the past.[200]

Again, the politics of Northern Ireland were played out on the world stage, with Hillary Clinton, the United States Secretary of State, phoning both McGuinness and Empey. A more unexpected intervention came from the former American President, George W.

Bush, who asked the Tory Party leader, Cameron, to urge the UUP to support the deal.[201] These interventions did not persuade the UUP, who voted against the agreement. The overall result was that, out of the 105 votes cast, a total of 88 supported devolution of these powers, with seventeen against. Despite the opposition of the UUP, not for the first time in Northern Ireland politics, the outcome of the vote was described as 'historic' by a British Prime Minister. Brown went on to say that it 'sends the most powerful message to those who would return to violence: that democracy and tolerance will prevail'. He also predicted that this vote would mark the end to decades of strife.[202] The UUP countered by saying that the DUP had 'caved in to NIO [Northern Ireland Office] and SF pressure'.[203] A truly historic event took place on 24 March 2010 when Ian Paisley addressed the British House of Commons for the last time. Paisley's parliamentary career had commenced in 1970 and for decades he had dominated and shaped unionist thought, often in a negative way. Ironically, perhaps, his final message was one of peace – although he was referring to the situation in Afghanistan not Northern Ireland. Paisley's notoriety for saying 'no' was forgotten. Instead, his belated contribution to the peace process was lauded, with the Prime Minister praising him for 'the part you played in bringing the unionist community together – indeed bringing the whole community together in Northern Ireland – to ensure that we have devolution of power, and to ensure now that we have completed the process of devolution of power'. Brown also predicted that Paisley's role would 'adorn the history books in many decades and centuries to come'.[204] In the short-term though, unionism has lost its most famous, controversial and colourful figurehead. On the eve of the 2010 British General Election, unionism seemed fractured and fragmented, searching for a role within a United Kingdom that was itself searching for an identity.

In August 2009 Mary Robinson, former President of Ireland, attended a commemoration to mark the death of Michael Collins, the man who had signed a treaty agreeing to the partition of Ireland. As the first female President she had already cut across gender and political boundaries, and when United Nations Commissioner for Human Rights she proved that her view of social justice transcended national boundaries. During her speech in County Cork she said:

Every generation faces its own challenges which call for particular qualities of vision and leadership. That is as true today as it was in Collins's time, even if the island that Michael Collins lived in and died for is a very different place from the modern Ireland – and the responses needed are also very different.[205]

Since 1960 Ireland has changed enormously, but for some the quest for social justice remains at the forefront of the Irish struggle, both north and south of the border.

References

1 Population statistics are provided on the website of Conflict Archive on the Internet (CAIN); www.cain.ulst.ac.uk. Accessed 3 May 2008.

2 Department of Commerce, US Bureau of the Census; www.infoplease.com/ipa/A0108355.html. Accessed 4 May 2008.

3 An Act to provide for the Better Government of Ireland, enacted 23 December 1920 (1920) s 10 & 11 Geo. 5 c. 67.

4 Constitution of Council of Ireland, Government of Ireland Act 1920.

5 Adjournment Motion, Dáil Éireann, vol. 63, 13 August 1936; www.oireachtas.gov.ie. Accessed 4 May 2009.

6 'BUNREACHT NA HÉIREANN, Constitution of Ireland. Enacted by the People, 1st July, 1937. In operation as from 29th December, 1937'.

7 Stormont Papers, vol. 19 (1936, 37), pp. 1283–4; stormontpapers.ahds.ac.uk. Accessed 6 May 2009.

8 *Belfast Telegraph*, 25 January 1964.

9 For example, Alec Cairncross, *The British Economy since 1945: Economic Policy and Performance, 1945–1995*, 2nd edn (Oxford, 1995), does not refer to Northern Ireland, demonstrating how distinct the economies had become.

10 Adjournment Motion, Dáil Éireann, vol. 63, 13 August 1936; www.oireachtas.gov.ie. Accessed 4 May 2009.

11 Peter Rose, *How the Troubles Came to Northern Ireland* (Basingstoke, 2001), p. xiii.

12 Peter Berresford Ellis, 'Lest we forget: Life in Northern Ireland before "the Troubles"', *Irish Democrat* (April/May 2002); www.irishdemocrat.co.uk/features/lbefore-the-troubles/. Accessed 14 July 2009.

13 The transatlantic cable, completed in 1866 and running from County Kerry to Newfoundland, is a modern example of this.

14 Christine Kinealy, *Repeal and Revolution: 1848 in Ireland* (Manchester, 2009).

15 *Washington Post*, 13 May 2007.

16 Pamphlet issued by the Irish Department of Foreign Affairs on the EEC and Irish agriculture, December 1971 (Dublin, 1971).

17 *Sunday Tribune*, 4 October 2009.

18 Equality Commission for Northern Ireland; www.equalityni.org/sections/default.asp?secid=5. Accessed 19 July 2009.

19 Michael Parker, *The Hurt World: Short Stories of the Troubles* (Belfast, 1995).

20 *Washington Post,* 13 May 2007.

21 Michael Cox, 'Northern Ireland: The War that Came in from the Cold', *International Affairs,* LXXIII/4 (1997), pp. 671–93.

22 *The Times,* 10 November 1990.

23 Martin Mansergh, 'The Early Stages of the Irish Peace Process', *Conciliation Resources* (December 1999); www.c-r.org/our-work/accord/northern-ireland/early-stages.php. Accessed 13 May 2009.

1 FAULT LINES

1 Lance Pettitt, *Screening Ireland* (Manchester, 2000), pp. 81–2.

2 *Irish Independent,* 12 March 2006.

3 Quoted on 'The Fame of Tipperary Group', http://homepage.eircom.net/~tipperaryfame/the_fotg.htm. Accessed 20 March 2008.

4 Tim Pat Coogan, *The Troubles: Ireland's Ordeal, 1969–96, and the Search for Peace* (London, 1996), pp. 58–9.

5 Censorship of Publications: 'That, in the opinion of *Seánad Éireann,* the Censorship of Publications Board appointed by the Minister for Justice under the Censorship of Publications Act, 1929, has ceased to retain public confidence, and that steps should be taken by the Minister to reconstitute the board' (Senator Sir John Keane). Debates of Seánad Éireann, vol. 27, 9 December 1942: http://historical-debates.oireachtas.ie/S/0027/S.0027.194212090003.html. Accessed 15 January 2008.

6 Ibid.

7 Literary Chat with Edna O'Brien: www.salon.com/02dec1995/departments/litchat.html. Accessed 4 August 2008.

8 Julia Carlson, *Banned in Ireland: Censorship and the Irish Writer* (Athens, GA, 1990), p. 69.

9 Quoted in Susan Cannon Harris, *Gender and Modern Irish Drama* (Bloomington, IN, 2002), p. 268.

10 Carlson, *Banned in Ireland,* pp. 4–5.

11 Pettitt, *Screening Ireland,* pp. 149–50.

12 History of RTÉ, RTÉ Archives: www.rte.ie/laweb/brc/brc_1960s.html. Accessed 20 March 2008.

13 RTÉ Entertainment, 11 May 2009: www.rte.ie/arts/2009/0511/latelateshow.html. Accessed 4 February 2008.

14 RTÉ Libraries and Archive: www.rte.ie/laweb/ll/ll_to2_main.html. Accessed 4 February 2008.

15 'A Journey Home: John F. Kennedy in Ireland, John F Kennedy Presidential Library and Museum': www.jfklibrary.org/JFK+Library+and+Museum/Visit+the+Library+and+Museum/Museum+Exhibits/JFK+in+Ireland+Exhibit. Accessed 1 May 2008.

16 'Warm Welcome for JFK in Ireland', BBC News, 27 June 1963: http://news.bbc.co.uk/. Accessed 1 May 2008.

17 Address by President Kennedy, Seánad Éireann, vol. 56, 20 June 1963: http://historical-debates.oireachtas.ie/S/0056/S.0056.196306200010.html. Accessed 2 May 2008.

18 Sylvia A. Ellis, 'The Historical Significance of President Kennedy's Visit to Ireland in June 1963', *Irish Studies Review*, XVI/2 (2008), pp. 113–30.

19 'Death of the President of the United States of America, John Fitzgerald Kennedy', Dáil Éireann, vol. 206, 26 November 1963.

20 Frank Pakenham, *Éamon De Valera* (London, 1970), p. 296.

21 Mark Callanan, ed., *Foundations of an Ever Closer Union: An Irish Perspective on Fifty Years since the Treaty of Rome* (Dublin, 2007), p. 28.

22 Melissa Wilde, 'Who Wanted What and Why at the Second Vatican Council? Toward a General Theory of Religious Change', *Sociologica*, no. 1 (2007); www.sociologica.mulino.it/journal/articlefulltext/index/Article/Journal: ARTICLE: 33. Accessed 3 March 2009.

23 Francis Xavier Carty, *Hold Firm: John Charles McQuaid and the Second Vatican Council* (Dublin, 2007).

24 Richard Finnegan and Edward McCarron, *Ireland: The Challenge of Conflict and Change* (Boulder, CO, 1983), p. 211.

25 David Quinn, quoted in 'Catholic Church faces new crisis – Ireland is running out of priests', 27 February 2008; http://rentapriest.blogspot.com/2008/02/catholic-church-faces-new-crisis.html. Accessed 4 March 2009.

26 Allegations of abuse, when finally investigated, culminated in the Ryan report, 2009.

27 'Irish Public Service Broadcasting – 1950s: Broadcast of the Angelus', A History of Irish Broadcasting (RTÉ Libraries and Archives); www.rte.ie/laweb/brc/brc_1950s_a.html. Accessed 4 March 2008.

28 'Meeting with Northern Ireland Premier', Dáil Éireann, vol. 214, 10 February 1965; www.oireachtas.gov.ie. Accessed 3 February 2008.

29 Ibid.

30 'Visit of An Taoiseach', 3 February 1965, Stormont Papers, vol. 59 (1965), pp. 271–2; http://stormontpapers.ahds.ac.uk. Accessed 20 August 2008.

31 Joseph Lee, *Ireland, 1912–1985: Politics and Society* (Cambridge, 1990), p. 366.

32 Callanan, *Foundations of an Ever Closer Union*, p. 28.

33 Michael Kennedy, *Division and Consensus: The Politics of Cross-border Relations in Ireland, 1925–1969* (Dublin, 2000), p. 256.

34 Stewart Parker, quoted in John P. Harrington and Elizabeth J. Mitchell, *Politics and Performance in Contemporary Northern Ireland* (Amherst, MA, 1999), p. 14.

35 Andrew J. Wilson, 'Maintaining the Cause in the Land of the Free: Ulster Unionists and US Involvement in the Northern Ireland Conflict, 1968–72', *Éire-Ireland*, XL/3–4 (2005), pp. 212–39.

36 'Visit of An Taoiseach', Stormont Papers, 3 February 1965.

37 It was not until 2007 that the Irish Football Association lifted the ban on Sunday games, Bay Ledger News Zone at www.blnz.com/news/2008/05/10/Irish_scraps_60-year-old_Sunday_matches_8/_1.html.

38 James McAleavy, 'Sam Thompson, 1916–65' in Bernice Schrank and William W. Demastes, eds, *Irish Playwrights, 1880–1995* (Westport, CT, 1997), p. 367.

39 Harrington and Mitchell, *Politics and Performance in Contemporary Northern Ireland*, pp. 14–15.

40 McAleavey, 'Sam Thompson', p. 267.

41 Michael Parker, *Northern Irish Literature, 1956–1975* (Basingstoke, 2007), p. 7.

42 Malcolm Anderson *et al.*, *The Irish Border: History, Politics, Culture* (Liverpool, 1999), p. 123.

43 'Visit of An Taoiseach', Stormont Papers, pp. 271–4.

44 Ibid., p. 273.

45 Ibid., p. 295.

46 Ibid., pp. 283–91.

47 *Irish Independent*, 16 January 1965.

48 Graham Walker, *A History of the Ulster Unionist Party: Protest, Pragmatism and Pessimism* (Manchester, 2004), p. 174.

49 'The European Theological Seminary', British Centre for Science Education; www.bcseweb.org.uk/index.php/Main/EuropeanTheologicalSeminary. Accessed 4 June 2008.

50 'Ian Paisley', BBC News, http://news.bbc.co.uk/2/hi/uk_news/northern_ireland/6289827.stm. Accessed 10 July 2009.

51 Coogan, *The Troubles*, p. 58.

52 *Irish Independent*, 16 June 1966.

53 'Ulster Volunteer Force', 6 October 1966, Stormont Papers, vol. 64 (1966), pp. 1213–14; http://stormontpapers.ahds.ac.uk. Accessed 1 January 2009.

54 'Seamus Justin Heaney' at the Poet's Corner, www.gale.cengage.com/free_resources/poets/bio/heaney_s.htm. Accessed 4 February 2009.

55 *The Observer*, 2 November 2008.

56 Official website of James Galway, www.jamesgalway.com/. Accessed 1 January 2008.

57 Alan Webber, 'Maradona Good; Pelé Better; George Best', at Articlebase, www.articlesbase.com/soccer-articles/maradona-good-pel-better-george-best-380803.html. Accessed 3 June 2009.

58 'Profile: Ian Paisley', BBC News, 1 February 2007; http://news.bbc.co.uk/2/hi/uk_news/northern_ireland/6289827.stm.

59 Henry Patterson, 'Party versus Order: Ulster Unionism and the Flags and Emblems Act', *Contemporary British History*, XIII/4 (1999), pp. 105–29.

60 'Housing Trust Report', 1 December 1964, Stormont Papers, vol. 58 (1964), pp. 997–8; http://stormontpapers.ahds.ac.uk.

61 Angela Bourke, *The Field Day Anthology of Irish Writing: Irish Women's Writing and Tradition* (Cork, 2005), p. 380.

62 Bob Purdie, Civil Rights at: http://cain.ulst.ac.uk/events/crights/purdie.htm#nicra. Accessed 3 June 2009.

63 *An Phoblacht*, 5 June 2008.

64 Michael Farrell, 'Historical Reflections on the Civil Rights Movement', paper presented to the Desmond Greaves Summer School, 30 August 2008; www.nicivilrights.org/?p=127. Accessed 3 June 2009.

65 'Youths Go on a Rampage in Protest in Londonderry', *New York Times*, 7 October 1968.

66 *Irish Times*, 13 October 1968.

67 Purdie, chapter 4; http://cain.ulst.ac.uk/events/crights/purdie.htm#nicra.

68 Farrell, 'Historical Reflections'.

69 Jonathan Moore, *Ulster Unionism and the British Conservative Party: A Study of a Failed Marriage* (London, 1997), p. 10.

70 *New York Times*, 6 December 1968.

71 Moore, *Ulster Unionism*, p. 11.

72 Dáil Éireann, vol. 236, 23 October 1968; http://historical-debates.oireachtas.ie/D/0236/D.0236.196810230003.html. Accessed 4 December 2008.

73 *New York Times*, 29 November 1968.

74 Ibid., 10 December 1968.

75 Moore, *Ulster Unionism*, pp. 9–10.

2 TROUBLES

1 *Disturbances in Northern Ireland: Report of the Commission appointed by the Governor of Northern Ireland*. Chairman: The Honourable Lord Cameron, D.S.C. Presented to Parliament by Command of His Excellency the Governor of Northern Ireland, September 1969 (Belfast, 1969).

2 Bowes Egan and Vincent McCormack, 'To Antrim: From Pantomime to Near-pogrom', *Burntollet* (London, 1969); http://cain.ulst.ac.uk/events/pdmarch/egan.htm. Accessed 14 July 2009.

3 Malachi O'Doherty, 'Lord Bew on Burntollet', Interview, 8 August 2008; http://malachi.podcastpeople.com/posts/25628. Accessed 14 January 2009.

4 Richard English, *Armed Struggle: The History of the IRA* (Oxford, 2003), p. 97.

5 Ibid.

6 *Irish News*, 4 and 6 January 1969.

7 Michael Kennedy, *Division and Consensus: the Politics of Cross-border Relations in Ireland, 1925–1969* (Dublin, 2000), p. 318.

8 George Cross, 'History of the B Specials'; www.royalulsterconstabulary.org/history3.htm. Accessed 4 January 2009.

9 Ibid.

10 Kennedy, *Division and Consensus*, pp. 318–19.

11 'Young Lions into Old Guards', in NICRA, '"We Shall Overcome": The History of the Struggle for Civil Rights in Northern Ireland 1968–1978 by NICRA (1978)'. Accessed 14 July 2009.

12 Ibid., 'PD gets "Pushy"'.

13 *New York Times*, 23 April 1969.

14 'What is the UVF?', BBC News, 3 May 2007; http://news.bbc.co.uk/2/hi/uk_news/northern_ireland/6619417.stm. Accessed 14 December 2008.

15 'Meeting with British Prime Minister', Dáil Éireann, vol. 241, 15 July 1969: www.oireachtas.gov.ie. Accessed 19 December 2008.

16 Kennedy, *Division and Consensus*, p. 324.

17 Ibid., p. 327.

18 Quoted in NICRA, '"We Shall Overcome"'.

19 *Irish News*, 29 January 2007.

20 'Samuel Devenny's Death', in NICRA, '"We Shall Overcome"'.

21 *Belfast Telegraph*, 10 May 1969.

22 NICRA, '"We Shall Overcome"'.

23 BBC News, 17 April 1969; http://news.bbc.co.uk/onthisday/hi/dates/stories/april/17/newsid_2524000/2524881.stm. Accessed 11 August 2008.

24　*New York Times*, 23 April 1969.

25　Ibid.

26　NICRA, '"We Shall Overcome"'.

27　'Police Use Tear Gas in Bogside', BBC News, 12 August 1969; http://news.
bbc.co.uk/onthisday/hi/dates/stories/august/12/newsid_3829000/3829219.
stm. Accessed 12 February 2008.

28　'British Troops Sent to Northern Ireland', BBC News, 14 August 1969; http://
news.bbc.co.uk/onthisday/hi/dates/stories/august/14/newsid_4075000/
4075437.stm. Accessed 12 February 2008.

29　Kennedy, *Division and Consensus*, p. 311.

30　Page compiled by Fionnuala McKenna, CAIN website; http://cain.ulst.ac.uk/
issues/politics/docs/jl13869.htm. Accessed 15 February 2008.

31　'British Troops Sent to Northern Ireland', BBC News, 14 August 1969.

32　Tim Pat Coogan, *The Troubles: Ireland's Ordeal, 1969–96, and the Search for Peace*
(London, 1996), p. 118–19.

33　Obituary of Charles Haughey, *Irish Times*, 13 June 2006.

34　Ibid.

35　This information had been closed under the 30-year closure rule. The *Irish
Independent* published the correspondence, but for the full controversy, see
Niall Meehan, 'A Little Subversion in Ireland', *Spinwatch*, 16 September 2005;
www.spinwatch.org/-articles-by-category-mainmenu-8/52-northern-ireland/
182-a-little-subversion-in-ireland. Accessed 20 December 2009.

36　Malcolm Sutton, 'An Index of Deaths from the Conflict in Ireland'; http://
cain.ulst.ac.uk/sutton/chron/1970.html. Accessed 20 December 2009.

37　Coogan, *The Troubles*, p. 120.

38　Haughey Obituary.

39　'Francis Bacon, 1909–92'; www.visual-arts-cork.com/irish-artists/francis-
bacon.htm. Accessed 3 December 2008.

40　Iain McCalman, *Making Culture Bloom* (Canberra, 2004), p. 12.

41　Lance Pettitt, *Screening Ireland* (Manchester, 2000), pp. 178–9.

42　'Ireland Wins the Eurovision Song Contest', 21 March 1970, RTÉ Libraries and
Archives; www.rte.ie/laweb/brc/brc_1970s.html. Accessed 14 March 2009.

43　John Kennedy O'Connor, *The Eurovision Song Contest: The Official History*
(Glasgow, 2005).

44　Remarks made by President Nixon on his arrival at Shannon Airport, 3 October 1979, American Presidency Project; www.presidency.ucsb.edu/ws/index.
php?pid=2695. Accessed 4 January 2009.

45　Ibid.

46　*New York Times*, 5 October 1970.

47　Arthur P. Williamson, 'Policy for Higher Education in Northern Ireland: The
New University of Ulster and the Origins of the University of Ulster', *Irish
Educational Studies*, XII/1 (1993), pp. 285–301.

48　Quoted in Coogan, *The Troubles*, p. 136.

49　Ibid.

50　*The Times*, 17 August 1969.

51　Kennedy, *Division and Consensus*, p. 348.

52　Aogán Mulcahy, *Policing Northern Ireland* (Cullompton, Devon, 2005), pp. 17–18;

Report of the Advisory Committee on Police in Northern Ireland [Hunt Report] (Belfast, 1969).

53 *Disturbances in Northern Ireland* [Cameron Commission], vol. 74, para. 6; http://stormontpapers.ahds.ac.uk. Accessed 5 April 2008.

54 Ibid., para 9.

55 Ibid., para. 11.

56 Ibid., paras 224–6.

57 Ibid., pp. 7–8.

58 Ibid., pp. 10–12.

59 Ibid., p. 31.

60 Ibid., pp. 33–4.

61 Ibid., pp. 747–8.

62 Graham Ellison and Jim Smyth, *The Crowned Harp: Policing in Northern Ireland* (London, 2000), p. 65.

63 *Report of the Advisory Committee on Police in Northern Ireland*, Chairman: Baron Hunt [Hunt Report] (Belfast, 1969), para. 10.

64 Ibid., para. 13.

65 Ibid., para. 14.

66 Ibid., point 176.

67 Ellison and Smyth, *The Crowned Harp*, p. 65.

68 BBC News, 10 October 1969; http://news.bbc.co.uk. Accessed 1 February 2008.

69 *Review Body on Local Government in Northern Ireland*, Chairman: Patrick A. Macrory [Macrory Report] (Belfast, 1970), paras 5 and 14.

70 Coogan, *The Troubles*, p. 121.

71 Ibid.

72 'Paisley Victory Rattles NI Parliament', BBC News, 16 April 1970; http://news.bbc.co.uk. Accessed 5 February 2008.

73 Ibid.

74 Disorders in Belfast, 1 July 1970, Stormont Papers, vol. 76 (1970), pp. 2005–6; http://stormontpapers.ahds.ac.uk. Accessed 2 April 2009.

75 Ibid.

76 CAIN Chronology of the Troubles; http://cain.ulst.ac.uk/othelem/chron. Accessed 11 December 2008.

77 *A Better Tomorrow* [Conservative Party Manifesto] (1970); www.psr.keele.ac.uk/area/uk/m an/con70.htm. Accessed 4 January 2009.

78 'Violence Flares as Devlin is Arrested', BBC News, 26 June 1970; http://news.bbc.co.uk. Accessed 6 January 2008.

79 English, *Armed Struggle*, p. 135.

80 CAIN Chronology of the Troubles.

81 *Irish News*, 6 July 1970.

82 Quoted in English, *Armed Struggle*, pp. 135–6.

83 'Change in Plastic Bullet Rule', BBC News, 1 August 1999; http://news.bbc.co.uk/2/hi/special_report/regions/wales/409215.stm.

84 Interview with Eric Stewart of 10cc, *Bandfacts*, www.songfacts.com/detail.php?id=8523.

85 Coogan, *The Troubles*, pp. 111–13.

86 Ibid., pp. 112–13.

87 Ibid., p. 114.

88 SDLP History at www.sdlp.ie/about_us.php. Accessed 4 June 2008.

89 English, *Armed Struggle*, p. 132.

90 Joseph Ruane and Jennifer Todd, 'Irish Nationalism and the Conflict in Northern Ireland' in David Miller, ed., *Rethinking Northern Ireland* (Harlow, 1998), p. 62.

91 Orange Loyalist Songbook, *Over the Bridge*; http://overthebridgeni.wordpress.com/2009/04/08/orange-loyalist-songbook-1971/.

92 Coogan, *The Troubles*, p. 154.

93 Ibid., p. 154.

94 Shaun Ley, 'The Westminster Hour', BBC News, 19 February 2006; http://news.bbc.co.uk/2/hi/programmes/the_westminster_hour/4674264.stm. Accessed 4 March 2009.

95 Toby Harnden, *Daily Telegraph*, 2 July 1998.

96 Bernadette Hayes and Ian McAllister, 'Religious Independents in Northern Ireland: Origins, Attitudes and Significance', *Review of Religious Research*, XXXVII/1 (1995), pp. 65–8.

97 Orange Loyalist Songbook, *Over the Bridge*.

98 Ronan Bennett, 'Don't Mention the War: Culture in Northern Ireland', in Miller, ed., *Rethinking Northern Ireland*, p. 199.

99 In 1974 he was imprisoned in Long Kesh. He escaped in 1975 and was immediately recaptured. 'Love in a Cage', interview with Ronan Bennett by David Bowman, 16 November 1999; www.salon.com/books/int/1999/11/16/bennett/. Accessed 5 March 2009.

100 Miller, ed., *Rethinking Northern Ireland*, p. 200.

101 Quoted in Michael Parker, *Northern Irish Literature, 1956–1975* (Basingstoke, 2007), p. 176.

102 Jeanne Colleran and Jenny S. Spencer, *Staging Resistance: Essays on Political Theater* (Ann Arbor, MI, 1998), p. 214.

103 Ibid., p. 20.

104 Coogan, *The Troubles*, p. 144.

105 Ibid., p. 143.

106 Frank Kitson, *Low Intensity Operations: Subversion, Insurgency, Peacekeeping* (London, 1971), p. 200.

107 Ibid., pp. 126–7.

108 Martin Dillon, *The Dirty War: Covert Strategies and Tactics Used in Political Conflicts* (Oxford, 1999), pp. 25–6.

109 Liz Curtis, *Ireland. The Propaganda War: The Media and the 'Battle for Hearts and Minds'* (London, 1983), p. 229.

110 Dillon, *The Dirty War*, pp. 25–6.

111 Ibid., pp. 179–80.

112 Fred Holroyd and Nick Burbridge, *War without Honour* (London, 1989).

113 Response by The Minister of State for the Armed Forces (Mr Archie Hamilton), Regarding Captain Fred Holroyd, House of Commons (HC) Deb 29, November 1989, vol. 162 cc.811–8.

114 Sutton, 'An Index of Deaths from the Conflict in Ireland'.

3 WAR

1 Ed Moloney, *A Secret History of the IRA* (London, 2003), p. 95.

2 Richard English, *Armed Struggle: The History of the IRA* (Oxford, 2003), p. 137.

3 Paul Bew, *Ireland: The Politics of Enmity, 1789–2006* (Oxford, 2009), p. 502.

4 Graham Walker, *A History of the Ulster Unionist Party* (Manchester, 2004), p. 189.

5 Obituary of Lord Moyola, *New York Times*, 20 May 2002.

6 *The Guardian*, 20 May 2002.

7 Ibid.

8 Walker, *History of the Ulster Unionist Party*, p. 190.

9 *Sunday Times*, 26 March 1972, quoted in Jonathan Moore, *Ulster Unionism and the British Conservative Party: A Study of a Failed Marriage* (London, 1997), p. 19.

10 Eric P. Kaufmann, *The Orange Order: A Contemporary Northern Irish History* (Oxford, 2009), p. 69.

11 'British Troops Shot Londonderry Rioters', BBC News, 8 July 1971; http://news.bbc.co.uk. Accessed 8 April 2008.

12 'Preface', *Inquiry into the Circumstances Surrounding the Deaths of Seamus Cussack and George Desmond Beattie*, Chairman: Lord Gifford (Belfast, 1971).

13 Tim Pat Coogan, *The Troubles: Ireland's Ordeal, 1969–96, and the Search for Peace* (London, 1996), p. 126.

14 This information was based on Cabinet Papers released 30 years later, see 'Army Warned against Internment', BBC News, 1 January 2002; http://news.bbc.co.uk. Accessed 10 September 2008.

15 'NI Activates Internment Law', BBC News, 9 August 1971; http://news.bbc.co.uk. Accessed 12 September 2008.

16 Ibid.

17 Michael J. Cunningham, *British Government Policy in Northern Ireland, 1969–1989: Its Nature and Execution* (Manchester, 1991), p. 9.

18 Bew, *Ireland*, p. 503. The Scarman Tribunal in 1969 estimated the number of refugees to be far lower. During a debate in the Dáil, the Taoiseach referred to 'the thousands' of Catholics who had sought refuge in the South: 'Adjournment Debate: Northern Ireland Situation', Dáil Éireann, vol. 256, 20 October 1971; www.oireachtas.gov.ie. Accessed 3 January 2008.

19 Bew, *Ireland*, p. 503.

20 Moloney, *Secret History of the IRA*, p. 98.

21 Moore, *Ulster Unionism*, p. 19.

22 This information is based on Cabinet Papers released 30 years later, see 'Army Warned against Internment', BBC News, 1 January 2002; http://news.bbc.co.uk. Accessed 5 May 2008.

23 '1971 Internment Killings in Ballymurphy – Campaign Launches Demands', *An Phoblacht*, 19 June 2008.

24 Bew, *Ireland*, p. 503.

25 'Border Infringements', Dáil Éireann, vol. 256, 27 October 1971.

26 'Northern Ireland Situation', Dáil Éireann, vol. 256, 20 October 1971.

27 Ibid.

28 This is referred to in Michael Parker, *Northern Irish Literature, 1956–1975* (Basingstoke, 2007), p. 283, n. 138.

29 Moloney, *Secret History of the IRA*, p. 176.

30 Dave Harper, *Psychology and the 'War on Terror'*; www.davidsmail.freeuk. com/harper.htm. Accessed 4 May 2008.

31 Martin Dillon, *The Dirty War: Covert Strategies and Tactics Used in Political Conflicts* (Oxford, 1999), p. xxvii.

32 *Daily Mail*, 6 December 2008.

33 Number One singles in 1972: wapedia.mobi/en/Number-one_singles_ of_1972_(Ireland). Accessed 19 February 2009.

34 Barleycorn, *Live in New York*, 1979; www.theballadeers.com/bc_do6_ny.htm.

35 History of UDA 'Scottish Loyalists', www.scottishloyalists.com/paramilitaries/uda.htm. Accessed 20 February 2009.

36 CAIN chronology, http://cain.ulst.ac.uk/othelem/chron/ch71.htm. Accessed 7 March 2008.

37 Peter Taylor, *Loyalists* (London, 2000), p. 87.

38 CAIN chronology.

39 'Bomb Explodes in Post Office Tower', BBC News, 31 Oct 1971; http://news.bbc. co.uk. Accessed 9 November 2008.

40 *Irish Democrat*, 28 January 2008.

41 'We shall overcome', http://cain.ulst.ac.uk/events/crights/nicra/nicra785. htm. Accessed 14 June 2009.

42 *Report of the inquiry into allegations against the Security Forces of physical brutality in Northern Ireland arising out of events on the 9th August, 1971, Chairman, Sir Edmund Compton, GCB, KBE* [Compton Report] (London, 1971); http://cain.ulst.ac.uk/hmso/compton.htm.

43 *New York Times*, 21 March 1972.

44 John McGarry and Brendan O'Leary, *The Northern Ireland Conflict: Consociational Engagements* (Oxford, 2004), p. 196.

45 'On this Day', BBC News, 4 December 1971; http://news.bbc.co.uk. Accessed 5 April 2008.

46 Vanderbilt Television Archive, 23 December 1971; http://tvnews.vanderbilt. edu/program.pl?ID=455517. Accessed 9 May 2008.

47 Bew, *Ireland*, p. 503.

48 'Acceptable Violence?', *Time*, 27 December 1971; www.time.com/time/magazine/article/0,9171,905596,00.html. Accessed 10 October 2008.

49 *Irish News*, 29 November 2000.

50 'We shall overcome', http://cain.ulst.ac.uk/events/crights/nicra/nicra785. htm. Accessed 5 May 2009.

51 Paul Bew, *Ireland: The Politics of Enmity, 1789–2006* (Oxford, 2007), p. 503.

52 'The Bitter Road from Bloody Sunday', *Time*, 14 February 1972; www. time. com/time/magazine/article/0,9171,903280-3,00.html. Accessed 4 October 208.

53 'Statements on Northern Ireland Situation', Dáil Éireann, vol. 258, 1 February, 1972; www.oireachtas.gov.ie. Accessed 12 November 2008.

54 'British Embassy on Dublin Burned', BBC News, 2 February 1972; http://news. bbc.co.uk. Accessed 4 November 2008.

55 *New York Times*, 29 February 1972.

56 Mr McQuade, *Tribunal of Inquiry*, House of Commons (Northern Ireland),

Stormont Papers, vol. 84 (1972), pp. 67–8; http://stormontpapers.ahds.ac.uk. Accessed 5 October 2008.

57 Ibid., Ian Paisley, pp. 61–2.

58 *The Guardian*, 10 November 1995.

59 Debate in Dáil, Dáil Éireann, vol. 258, 10 February 1972; www.oireachtas.gov.ie. Accessed 4 December 2008.

60 Michael Parker, *Seamus Heaney: The Making of the Poet* (Basingstoke, 1994), p. 118.

61 *The Times*, 27 February 1972.

62 'IRA Bomb Kills Six at Aldershot Barracks', BBC News, 22 February 1972; http://news.bbc.co.uk.

63 J. Bowyer Bell, *The IRA, 1968–2000: An Analysis of a Secret Army* (London, 2000), p. 229.

64 'Return of the Roaring Girl: Interview with Bernadette McAliskey', *Sunday Independent*, 5 October 2008.

65 Parker, *Seamus Heaney*, p. 188.

66 Neil Spencer, 'The 10 Most X-rated Records', *Sunday Observer Music Monthly*, 22 May 2005.

67 Taylor Parkes, 'In Defence of Paul McCartney and Wings', *The Quietus*, 22 June 2009; http://thequietus.com/articles/01922-paul-mccartney-the-beatles-wings-the-best-of. Accessed 8 May 2009.

68 Seán Mac Mathúna, 'John Lennon and the Irish Question', *Flame*, www.fantom powa.net/Flame/john_lennon_irish_roots.htm. Accessed 8 May 2009; *Guardian*, 17 February 1972.

69 Ibid.

70 *Sunday Times*, 22 February 2000.

71 U2, 'Sunday Bloody Sunday', on www.youtube.com/watch?v=JFM7Ty1EEvs. Accessed 4 November 2008.

72 *Irish Times*, 19 March 1972.

73 Northern Ireland Office; www.nio.gov.uk/index/about-the-nio.htm. Accessed 19 October 2008.

74 'Heath was Direct Rule Architect', BBC News on the death of Heath, 18 July 2005; http://news.bbc.co.uk. Accessed 4 August 2008.

75 P. Johnson *et al.*, '1972: the Year of Bloody Sunday, Direct Rule from London and a Humiliating Miners' Strike', *Daily Telegraph*, 1 January 2003.

76 *New York Times*, 25 March 1972.

77 *Northern Ireland. The Scarman Report*, House of Lords Debate, 7 March 1972, *Hansard*, vol. 329, cc. 6–7; http://hansard.millbanksystems.com/lords/1972/mar/07/northern-ireland-the-scarman-report. Accessed 4 November 2008.

78 *Government of Northern Ireland. Violence and Civil Disturbances in Northern Ireland in 1969. Report of Tribunal of Inquiry*, Chairman: The Hon. Mr Justice Scarman (Belfast, 1972), para. 1.5.

79 Ibid., 1.13.

80 Ibid., 2.4.

81 Ibid., 2.9.

82 Ibid., 2.15.

83 Ibid., 3.8.

84 *The Guardian*, 10 November 1995.

85 Reaction to the Widgery Report: http://library.thinkquest.org/18666/history/widgeryreact.htm. Accessed 10 October 2008.

86 'Butcher's Dozen: A Lesson for the Octave at Widgery'. Available at http://cain.ulst.ac.uk/events/bsunday/kinsella.htm. Accessed 14 March 2010.

87 'IRA Ceasefire', BBC News; http://news.bbc.co.uk/hi/english/static/in_depth/northern_ireland/2001/provisional_ira/1972.stm. Accessed 12 October 2008.

88 Ibid.

89 Obituary of Joe Cahill, *The Times*, 26 July 2004.

90 *Belfast Telegraph*, 31 August 2007.

91 Northern Ireland: Draft Rules of Engagement, Top Secret – Perimeter, 26 July 1972, Document reference: PREM 15/1011; http://cain.ulst.ac.uk/publicrecords/1972/index.html#220772. Accessed 4 January 2009.

92 *Towards a New Ireland*, 1972.

93 Letter from R. A. Curtis, Ministry of Defence, to the Prime Minister's Office, 29 November 1972, National Archives, England (NAE), PREM 15/1016: http://cain.ulst.ac.uk/publicrecords/1972/index.html#291172. Accessed 4 October 2008.

94 This and other secret conversations became available 30 years later, see Rory Rapple, 'Painful Secrets of 1972', *Sunday Business Post*, 5 January 2003.

95 'Redrawing the Border and Population Transfer', 22 July 1972 (NAE), PREM 15/1010; http://cain.ulst.ac.uk/publicrecords/1972/index.html#220772. Accessed 14 November 2008.

96 Ibid.

97 House of Commons Debates, *Hansard*, 16 November 1972, vol. 846, c.188W, c. 31–42.

98 Dillon, *Dirty War*, p. 179.

99 Ibid., p. 180.

100 Evidence of Colin Wallace given before Public Hearings on the Barron Report on 17 February 2004; www.gov.ie/oireachtas/Committees. Accessed 17 November 2008.

101 Bew, *Ireland*, p. 510

102 Evidence of Colin Wallace at Barron Hearing.

103 Dillon, *Dirty War*, p. 181.

104 Ibid., p. 184.

105 Paul Foot, *Who Framed Colin Wallace?* (London, 1990).

106 Lance Pettitt, *Screening Ireland* (Manchester, 2000), p. 149.

107 Ibid.

108 Ibid., p. 208.

109 CAIN chronology.

110 'Amendment of Constitution', Dáil Éireann, vol. 263, 25 October 1972; www.gov.ie/oireachtas. Accessed 4 September 2008.

111 Ibid.

112 Brian Girvin, 'Church, State, and Society in Ireland since 1960', *Éire-Ireland*, XLIII/1–2 (2008), pp. 74–98.

113 Yvonne Galligan, *Women and Politics in Contemporary Ireland: From Margins to the Mainstream* (London, 1998), p. 146.

114 Anne Stopper, *Mondays at Gaj's: The Story of the Irish Women's Liberation Movement* (Dublin, 2006).

115 Mary Kenny, 'The Day we Drove the Condom Train Straight through de Valera's Ireland', *Sunday Independent*, 13 May 2001.

116 Galligan, *Women and Politics*, p. 148.

117 Tourist Industry, Dáil Éireann, vol. 264, 12 December 1972; www.oireachtas. gov.ie. Accessed 13 December 2008.

118 John Coakley and Michael Gallagher, *Politics in the Republic of Ireland* (London, 2009), p. 59.

119 Bowyer Bell, *The IRA, 1968–2000*, pp. 229–30.

120 Paul O'Mahony, *Criminal Justice in Ireland* (Dublin, 2002), p. 81.

121 This irony was pointed out by Mr L'Estrange TD, in a debate on tourism, Dáil Éireann, vol. 264, 12 December 1972.

122 Houses of the *Oireachas*, Interim Report on the Report of the Independent Commission of Inquiry into the Dublin Bombings of 1972 and 1973 (Dublin, 2004), p. 24; www.dublinmonaghanbombings.org/DubInterim.pdf. Accessed 6 November 2008.

123 Mr Justice Barron, quoted in 'Joint Committee on Justice, Equality, Defence and Women's Rights: Sub-Committee on the Barron Report', Dé Máirt, 25 Eanáir 2005 [25 January 2005], *Public Hearing on the Barron Report*; www. seanad. net/documents/op/Deco4/Business/op141204. Accessed 11 October 2008.

124 Their deaths were the subjects of an award-winning documentary on the atrocity, *The Forgotten Bomb*, made by Fran McNulty (2004).

125 Dillon, *Dirty War*, pp. 100–101.

126 Following an article in *Asia Times*, 13 June 2003, this issue was raised in the House of Commons by Dr Martha Mundy; www.publications.parliament. uk/pa/cm200203/cmselect/cmfaff/813/813we16.htm. Accessed 4 December 2008.

127 Ibid.

128 Pettitt, *Screening Ireland*, p. 148.

129 'History of Irish Public Service Broadcasting', RTÉ Libraries and Archives; www.rte.ie/laweb/brc/brc_timeline.html. Accessed 17 November 2008.

130 Brian Hanley and Scott Millar, 'The Story of the Revolutionaries Working inside RTÉ', *Sunday Times*, 30 August 2009; extracted from Hanley and Millar, *The Lost Revolution: The Story of the Official IRA and Workers' Party* (Dublin, 2009).

131 'Ex-Prime Minister Averts Party Clash in Northern Ireland', *New York Times*, 12 December 1972.

4 IMPLOSION

1 Eamon Phoenix, 'Whitelaw Thought UDA "Less Vicious" than the IRA', *Irish News*, 3 June 2004.

2 Ian S. Wood, *Crimes of Loyalty: A History of the UDA* (Edinburgh, 2006), p. 359.

3 'A Talk with "King Billy" of Ulster', *Time*, 10 June 1974.

4 'Ulster Loyalist Leader, William Craig', *New York Times*, 27 March 1972.

5 Ibid.

6 'Northern Ireland: Belfast Strike Violence', debate in House of Lords, *Hansard*, 8 February 1973, vol. 338, cc. 1148–51.

7 William Craig, *The Future of Northern Ireland* (1972); http://cain.ulst.ac.uk/ othelem/organ/docs/craig.htm.

8　Ibid.

9　Ibid.

10　Ibid.

11　Ibid.

12　'A Talk with "King Billy" of Ulster', *Time*, 10 June 1974.

13　'Ulster: One Man's Solution', *New York Times*, 18 February 1973.

14　'Northern Ireland Votes for Union', BBC News, 9 March 1973; http://news. bbc.co.uk. Accessed 4 August 2008.

15　HMSO, *Northern Ireland Constitutional Proposals* (London, 1973).

16　Eric P. Kaufmann, *The Orange Order: A Contemporary Northern Irish History* (Oxford, 2009), p. 90.

17　This was raised by Caoimhghín Ó Caoláin TD, the Sinn Féin leader in the Dáil, on 31 January 2008; www.sinnfein.ie/contents/11376. Accessed 4 March 2009.

18　'Liam Cosgrave', *Brittanica Online*; www.britannica.com/EBchecked/topic/ 139136/Liam-Cosgrave. Accessed 9 January 2009.

19　Telegram from Edward Heath to Liam Cosgrave, 2 April 1973, National Archives, England (NAE), FCO 87/247; www.nationalarchives.gov.uk/releases/ 2004/nyo/prem_15_1689.htm. Accessed 12 May 2009.

20　'British White Paper on Northern Ireland: Motion', Dáil Éireann, vol. 265, 8 May 1973; historical-debates.oireachtas.ie. Accessed 3 December 2008.

21　Ibid.

22　*Coleraine Times*, 14 June 2007.

23　Wood, *Crimes of Loyalty*, p. 22.

24　Ibid., p. 360.

25　'Murdered Senators to be Honoured', BBC News, 22 November 2001; http:// news.bbc.co.uk/2/hi/uk_news/northern_ireland/1670470.stm. Accessed 15 November 2008.

26　Wood, *Crimes of Loyalty*, p. 22.

27　'Subversion in the UDR', document found in the Public Record Office, London (NAE) by researchers from the Pat Finucane Centre; http://cain.ulst.ac.uk/ publicrecords/1973/subversion_in_the_udr.htm. Accessed 19 May 2009.

28　Ibid.

29　Results of Assembly Election (NI), Thursday 28 June 1973; http://cain.ulst. ac.uk/issues/politics/election/ra1973.htm. Accessed 4 December 2008.

30　William Whitelaw to Prime Minister, 2 July 1973, NSE, PREM 15/1693; www. nationalarchives.gov.uk/releases/2004/nyo/prem_15_1689.htm.

31　'Chaotic Meeting of Belfast Assembly', BBC News, 31 July 1973; http://news. bbc.co.uk. Accessed 4 June 2008.

32　Paul Bew, 'Obituary of Sir Jamie Flanagan', *The Independent*, 20 April 1999.

33　Letter from A. W. Stephens to V.H.S. Benham, 16 November 1973, NAE, FCO 87/248; http://cain.ulst.ac.uk/publicrecords/1973/index.html. Accessed 19 November 2008.

34　'Bomb Blasts Rock Central London', BBC News, 10 September 1973; http:// news.bbc.co.uk. Accessed 7 June 2008.

35　*An Phoblacht*, 28 October 2004.

36　*New Musical Express*; www.nme.com/artists/wolfe-tones. Accessed 10 December 2008.

37 Telegram from Edward Heath to Liam Cosgrave, 2 April 1973, NAE, FCO 87/247; http://cain.ulst.ac.uk/publicrecords/1973/index.html#020473. Accessed 20 November 2008.

38 Letter from A. W. Stephens to W.K.K.White, 4 April 1973, FCO 87/247.

39 'State Papers on Libya Move Released', RTÉ News, 1 January 2004; www.rte.ie/news/2004/0101/state.html. Accessed 9 February 2009.

40 Ibid.

41 *Irish Times*, 18 and 19 September 1973.

42 Dr Richard Bourke, 'Heath Was Told Irish Ministers Were "Timorous"', *Irish Times*, 2 January 2004.

43 'Northern Ireland Situation', Dáil Éireann, vol. 268, 17 October 1973; www.historical-debates.oireachtas.ie. Accessed 2 January 2009.

44 Ibid.

45 Ibid.

46 Adjournment Debate: British Army Border Patrols', Dáil Éireann, vol. 268, 18 October 1973.

47 *Irish Times*, 2 January 2004.

48 Walker, *Ulster Unionist Party*, p. 219.

49 Obituary of Francis Pym, *Daily Telegraph*, 7 March 2006.

50 P. J. McLoughlin, '"Dublin is Just a Sunningdale Away"? The SDLP and the Failure of Northern Ireland's Sunningdale Experiment', in *Twentieth Century British History*, online, 23 September 2008; http://tcbh.oxfordjournals.org/cgi/content/abstract/hwn024v1. Accessed 10 May 2009.

51 Walker, *Ulster Unionist Party*, p. 219.

52 Ibid.

53 'Sunningdale Agreement Signed', BBC News, 9 December 1973; http://news.bbc.co.uk/onthisday/hi/dates/stories/december/9/newsid_2536000/2536767.stm. Accessed 19 August 2008.

54 Paul Bew, *Ireland: The Politics of Enmity, 1789–2006* (Oxford, 2007), p. 513.

55 'Council of Ireland. Northern Ireland', House of Commons Debates, 13 December 1973; www.theyworkforyou.com/debates/?id=1973-12-13a.619.8. Accessed 20 November 2008.

56 Stephen E. Atkins, *Encyclopedia of Modern Worldwide Extremists and Extremist Groups* (Santa Barbara, CA, 2004), p. 330.

57 'Department of the Taoiseach', Dáil Éireann, vol. 269, 12 December 1973; www.historical-debates.oireachtas.ie. Accessed 4 November 2008.

58 Bourke, 'Heath Was Told Irish Ministers were "Timorous"', *Irish Times*, 2 January 2004.

59 Alvin Jackson, *Home Rule: An Irish History, 1800–2000* (Oxford, 2004), p. 270.

60 Bew, *Ireland*, p. 72.

61 'Ulster Army Council', at *Encyclopaedia On-line*, Reference.com; www.reference.com/browse/Ulster+Army+Council. Accessed 9 December 2008.

62 Laurence C. Hunter, 'British Incomes Policy, 1972–1974' (1975); www.jstor.org/pss/2521851. Accessed 8 July 2008.

63 *Irish Times*, 16 February 1972.

64 Peter Dorey, *British Politics since 1945* (Chichester, 1995), p. 124.

65 Ministerial Conference, Stormont Castle. 19 December 1973, NAE, CJ 4/487; www.

nationalarchives.gov.uk/releases/2005/nyo/ni.htm. Accessed 10 May 2009.

66 Statement from the Northern Ireland Executive, 31 December 1973, CJ 4/487.

67 Statement by Secretary of State for Northern Ireland, 3 January 1974, CAB 128/53 74 (1).

68 Obituary of Harry West, *Daily Telegraph*, 7 February 2004.

69 Draft of a message from Edward Heath to Liam Cosgrave, 10 January 1974 (NAE) PREM 15/2142; www.nationalarchives.gov.uk/releases/2005/nyo/ni.htm. Accessed 10 May 2009.

70 Bew, *Ireland*, p. 513.

71 *Orange Standard* (February 1974).

72 Joseph Lee, *Ireland, 1912–1985: Politics and Society* (Cambridge, 1990), p. 448.

73 Garret Fitzgerald, 'The 1974–5 Threat of a British Withdrawal from Northern Ireland', *Irish Studies in International Affairs*, xvii (2006), p. 142.

74 Wood, *Crimes of Loyalty*, p. 34.

75 Martin Dillon, *The Shankill Butchers* (London, 1999), p. 38.

76 Confidential – Note for the Record – by F. Cooper, 5 March 1974 (NAE) FCO 87/334; www.nationalarchives.gov.uk/releases/2005/nyo/ni.htm. Accessed 4 February 2009.

77 Wood, *Crimes of Loyalty*, p. 33.

78 'Northern Ireland Policy', Dáil Éireann, vol. 271, 13 March 1974; www.historical-debates.oireachtas.ie. Accessed 6 February 2008.

79 Ibid.

80 Wood, *Crimes of Loyalty*, p. 35.

81 Ibid.

82 Cabinet Memo, marked 'Top Secret', Confidential Annex CC (74) 11th Conclusions, Minute 1, 10 April 1974 at 18:00pm (NAE) CAB 128/54; www.national archives.gov.uk/releases/2005/nyo/ni.htm. Accessed 5 February 2009.

83 Martin Reid to Mr Trevelyan after discussion between Rees and Faulkner, 8 April 1974, CJ 4/471.

84 Note of meeting between Harold Wilson and the Northern Ireland Executive, marked 'Secret', Thursday, 18 April 1974, PREM 16/145.

85 Wood, *Crimes of Loyalty*, p. 37.

86 Note of meeting between Stanley Orme and a UWC delegation on 15 May 1974, 16 May 1974 (NAE) FCO 87/341; www.nationalarchives.gov.uk/releases/2005/nyo/ni.htm. Accessed 5 February 2009.

87 Don Anderson, 'Fall of Sunningdale Recounted', BBC News, 12 May 2004; http://news.bbc.co.uk/2/low/uk_news/northern_ireland/3706449.stm.

88 Letter from F.E.R. Butler, marked 'Secret', Friday 17 May 1974 (NAE), PREM 16/146; www.nationalarchives.gov.uk/releases/2005/nyo/ni.htm. Accessed 6 February 2009.

89 Note of meeting held at Chequers, marked 'Secret', Friday 24 May 1974, PREM 16/147.

90 Fax from Harold Wilson to Liam Cosgrave, marked 'Confidential', Saturday 25 May 1974, FCO 87/336.

91 Memo from Merlyn Rees to Harold Wilson, marked 'Top Secret', Monday 27 May 1974, PREM 16/148.

92 Quoted in Wood, *Crimes of Loyalty*, p. 47.

93 Memo from Harold Wilson, marked 'Top Secret', Thursday 30 May 1974 (NAE), PREM 16/148; www.nationalarchives.gov.uk/releases/2005/nyo/ni.htm. Accessed 6 February 2009.

94 Fitzgerald, *British Withdrawal*, p. 143.

95 'Bombs Devastate Dublin and Monaghan', BBC News, 17 May 1974; http://news.bbc.co.uk/onthisday/hi/dates/stories/may/17/newsid_4311000/4311459.stm. Accessed 19 November 2008.

96 Justice for the Forgotten; www.dublinmonaghanbombings.org/may74.html. Accessed 20 November 2008.

97 'Barron Nails Myth of British Collusion', *The Independent*, 14 December 2003.

98 'Dublin and Monaghan Bombings: Statement by Taoiseach', Dáil Éireann, vol. 272, 21 May 1974; www.historical-debates.oireachtas.ie. Accessed 10 October 2008.

99 Ibid.

100 Ibid.

101 'The Truth Trickles Out', *Magill* (September 2002).

102 Fitzgerald, *British Withdrawal*, p. 141.

103 *The Northern Ireland Constitution* (London, 1974), para 45.

104 Prime Minister to Merlyn Rees, titled 'Northern Ireland: Extremist Groups' and marked 'Top Secret', 16 September 1974 (NAE) PREM 16/151; www.national archives.gov.uk/releases/2005/nyo/ni.htm. Accessed 7 February 2009.

105 Obituary of Merlyn Rees, *The Independent*, 7 January 2006.

106 *Irish Times*, 6 May 1974.

107 *An Phoblacht*, 3 June 2004.

108 'Repatriation of Irish Prisoners', Dáil Éireann, vol. 270, 6 February 1974; www.historical-debates.oireachtas.ie. Accessed 1 May 2008.

109 'Soldiers and Children Killed in Coach Bombing', BBC News, 4 February 1974; http://news.bbc.co.uk.

110 *Guardian*, 22 March 1991.

111 'Four Dead in Guildford Bomb Blast', BBC News, 5 October 1974; http://news.bbc.co.uk. Accessed 1 November 2008.

112 'Birmingham Pub Blasts Kill 19', BBC News, 21 November 1974; http://news.bbc.co.uk. Accessed 1 November 2008.

113 *Time*, 9 December 1974.

114 David Bonner, *Executive Measures, Terrorism and National Security* (Aldershot, 2007), p. 38.

115 *Time*, 9 December 1974.

116 On the thirtieth anniversary of the attacks in 2003, Gerry Adams, the President of the IRA's political wing, Sinn Féin, said he regretted the bombings had taken place.

117 Richard English, *Armed Struggle: The History of the IRA* (Oxford, 2003), p. 178.

118 T. P. Coogan, *The Troubles: Ireland's Ordeal 1969–96, and the Search for Peace* (London, 1996), p. 217.

119 'Heath's Home is Bombed', BBC News, 22 November 1974.

120 'Note of a meeting between British government officials and Protestant clergymen', 31 December 1974, marked 'Secret', (NAE), PREM 16/515/4.

121 'Note of a meeting between Harold Wilson and Church leaders from North-

ern Ireland', Wednesday 1 January 1975, (NAE), PREM 15/515/3.

122 Parker, *Northern Ireland*, vol. I, p. 222.

123 Interview with Michael Hewitt, *Thumbscrew*, 12 (Winter 1998/9); www.poetry magazines.org.uk/magazine/record.asp?id=12172.

124 Floyd Collins, *Seamus Heaney: The Crisis of Identity* (Cranbury, NJ, 2005), p. 105.

125 Quoted in Parker, *Northern Ireland*, vol. I, pp. 222–3.

126 David Miller, ed., *Rethinking Northern Ireland* (Harlow, 1998), pp. 2–6.

127 Ibid., p. 36.

128 Brendan Bradshaw, 'Nationalism and Historical Scholarship in Modern Ireland', *Irish Historical Studies*, XXVI (1989), pp. 329–51.

129 Christine Kinealy, *A Death-Dealing Famine: The Great Hunger in Ireland* (London, 1997), pp. 1–6.

130 Miller, *Rethinking Northern Ireland*, p. 36.

5 STALEMATE

1 Secretary of State for Northern Ireland to the Prime Minister, titled 'Northern Ireland Extremist Groups', 30 December 1974, (NAE), PREM 16/515; www.nationalarchives.gov.uk/releases/2005/nyo/ni.htm. Accessed 15 December 2008.

2 Alec Cairncross, *The British Economy since 1945: Economic Policy and Performance, 1945–1995* (Oxford, 1995), p. 184.

3 *Irish News*, 6 January 2008.

4 Telegram from Galsworthy, British Embassy, Dublin, to Harding, Foreign and Commonwealth Office, and Cooper, Northern Ireland Office, regarding Conversation with Taoiseach, the Irish Prime Minister [*sic*], 20 January 1975 (NAE), PREM 16/151; www.nationalarchives.gov.uk/releases/2005/highlights_december/december29/northernireland.htm. Accessed 14 January 2009.

5 Ibid.

6 'UK EYES. Top Secret. Terms for a Bi-Lateral Truce', 1 October 1975, PREM 16/521.

7 Richard English, *Armed Struggle: The History of the IRA* (Oxford, 2003), p. 177.

8 Note by Harold Wilson on letter re Harold Wilson from Treasury to Rees, 20 January 1975 (NAE), PREM 16/490; www.nationalarchives.gov.uk/releases/2005/highlights_december/december29/northernireland.htm. Accessed 14 January 2009.

9 Kieran Anthony Kennedy, Thomas Giblin and Deirdre McHugh, *The Economic Development of Ireland in the Twentieth Century* (London, 2001), p. 113.

10 Angelique Chrisafis, 'Bring me sunshine, bring me paramilitary surrender', *Guardian*, 29 December 2005.

11 Cudliff Memo to various officials looking for suggestions for 'Brightening Up Ulster', 18 March 1975 (NAE), PREM 16/490; www.nationalarchives.gov.uk/releases/2005/highlights_december/december29/northernireland.htm. Accessed 14 December 2008.

12 Chrisafis, 'Bring me sunshine'.

13 Ibid.

14 *Report of a Committee to consider, in the context of civil liberties and human rights, measures to deal with terrorism in Northern Ireland*, Chairman: Lord Gardiner

(London, 1975) [Gardiner report].

15 Ibid., para. 21.

16 Ibid., para. 11.

17 Ibid., para. 8, 'Terrorism and Subversion'.

18 Kieran McEvoy, *Paramilitary Imprisonment in Northern Ireland: Resistance, Management, and Release* (Oxford, 2001), p. 216.

19 Gardiner report, paras 100 and 108.

20 Report of Secretary of State, marked 'Confidential', 15 May 1975 (NAE), CAB 134/3921; www.nationalarchives.gov.uk/releases/2005/highlights_december/december29/northernireland.htm. Accessed 4 March 2009.

21 Northern Ireland Constitutional Convention Elections 1975, Northern Ireland Elections (Economic and Social Research Council); www.ark.ac.uk/elections/fc75.htm. Accessed 3 March 2008.

22 Memo regarding UUUC, marked 'Confidential', 19 September 1975 (NAE), CAB 134/3921; www.nationalarchives.gov.uk/releases/2005/highlights_december/december29/northernireland.htm. Accessed 6 March 2008.

23 Ibid.

24 Memo from a senior political adviser to Harold Wilson, 19 September 1975, PREM 16/520.

25 *New York Times*, 1 August 1975.

26 *Irish News*, 29 December 2006.

27 'IRA Kidnappers Release Hostage', BBC News, 7 November 1975; http://news.bbc.co.uk/onthisday/hi/dates/stories/november/7/newsid_2539000/2539461.stm. Accessed 19 December 2008.

28 *The Independent*, 25 December 2005.

29 'IRA Kidnappers Release Hostage', BBC News, 7 November 1975.

30 *Irish Examiner*, 19 October 2005.

31 'Bomb Blasts Rock Northern Ireland', BBC News, 22 September 1975; http://news.bbc.co.uk/onthisday/hi/dates/stories/september/22/newsid_2528000/2528435.stm. Accessed 19 March 2008.

32 *The Times*, 27 November 1975.

33 'The IRA Campaigns in England', BBC News, 4 March 2001; http://news.bbc.co.uk/2/hi/uk_news/1201738.stm. The 'Balcombe Street Gang' (Martin O'Connell, Edward Butler, Harry Duggan and Hugh Doherty) were freed under the terms of the Good Friday agreement.

34 Ibid.

35 *New York Times*, 2 September 1975.

36 Ibid., 18 December 1975.

37 Ibid., 23 December 1975.

38 Debate on Northern Ireland, *Hansard*, 18 March 1976; http://hansard.millbanksystems.com/commons/1976/mar/18/security

39 A similar claim was made in an article in the *Irish News* (a Belfast-based newspaper) on 2 May 2000.

40 Sutton index of deaths on CAIN; www.cain.ulst.ac.uk.

41 *New York Times*, 30 August 1975.

42 Ibid.

43 Dr Deirdre McMahon, Papers of Éamon de Valera (1882–1975), UCD archives;

www.ucd.ie/archives/html/collections/devalera-eamon.htm.

44 *Belfast Telegraph*, 29 December 2006.

45 'The SAS in Northern Ireland: a History', *Elite UK Forces*; www.eliteukforces. info/special-air-service/history/northern-ireland/. Accessed 15 December 2008.

46 Ronan Fanning, 'Year of Assassination and Resignation', *Irish Independent*, 31 December 2006.

47 Paul Bew, 'Obituary of Lord Lowry', *The Independent*, 18 January 1999.

48 Political Situation in Northern Ireland, *Hansard*, 27 May 1976, vol. 912, cc.609–12; http://hansard.millbanksystems.com/commons/1976/may/27/political-situation. Accessed 9 September 2008.

49 Fanning, 'Year of Assassination and Resignation'.

50 Ian S. Wood, *Crimes of Loyalty: A History of the UDA* (Edinburgh, 2006), p. 65.

51 Martin Dillon, *The Shankill Butchers* (London, 1999), pp. 142–9.

52 Michael Longley, 'The Butchers', quoted in Tim Kendall, *The Oxford Handbook of British and Irish War Poetry* (Oxford, 2009), p. 677.

53 Peter McDonald, 'An Interview with Michael Longley: "Au Revoir, Oeuvre"', *Thumbscrew*, 12 (Winter 1998/9).

54 *Dundalk Democrat*, 25 May 2005.

55 See, for example, Barron report, 15 December 2003.

56 Fanning, 'Year of Assassination and Resignation'.

57 National Emergency: Motion, Dáil Éireann, vol. 292, 31 August 1976; www.oireachtas-gov.ie.

58 Ibid., see, for example, comments by Deputy G. Collins.

59 Fanning, 'Year of Assassination and Resignation'.

60 'Garda Michael Clerkin', RTÉ, 9 February 2009; www.RTE.ie/tv/gardaarlar/09prog4.html. Accessed 3 June 2009.

61 Joseph Lee, *Ireland, 1912–1985: Politics and Society* (Cambridge, 1990), p. 482.

62 *An Phoblacht*, 13 October 2005.

63 'Portlaoise Hunger Strike', Dáil Éireann, vol. 456, 3 October 1995; www.oireachtas.gov.ie.

64 Ibid., 'Solitary Confinement'; Dáil Éireann, vol. 298, 21 April 1977.

65 *Sunday Post*, 30 December 2007.

66 Tim Pat Coogan, *The IRA* (Aldershot, 2002), p. 418.

67 Response of Mr Hattersley, Secretary of State for Foreign and Commonwealth Affairs, House of Commons, 28 November 1975, vol. 901, c.333W; http://hansard.millbanksystems.com. Accessed 4 November 2008.

68 Tony Geraghty, *The Irish War: The Hidden Conflict between the IRA and British Intelligence* (Baltimore, MD, 2002), pp. 119–21.

69 *Irish News*, 13 July 2006.

70 Maire Drumm was subsequently murdered by loyalist gunmen while a patient in hospital, *Belfast Telegraph*, 29 December 2006.

71 Question by Mr William Ross in House of Commons, 1 March 1976; http://hansard.millbanksystems.com/written_answers/1976/mar/01/frank-stagg. Accessed 4 December 2008.

72 Query – Frank Stagg, Dáil Éireann, vol. 290, 4 May 1976; www.oireachtas-debates.gov.ie. Accessed 16 September 2008.

73 Geraghty, *The Irish War*, p. 99.

74 McEvoy, *Paramilitary Imprisonment*, p. 233.

75 Yvonne Jewkes and Helen Johnston, eds, *Prison Readings: A Critical Introduction to Prisons and Imprisonment* (Cullompton, Devon, 2006), p. 138.

76 'Northern Ireland', *Hansard*, 18 March 1976; http://hansard.millbanksystems.com/commons/1976/mar/18/security. Accessed 4 June 2009.

77 'Northern Ireland (Temporary Provisions)', House of Commons, 2 July 1976; www.theyworkforyou.com/debates/?id=1976-07-02a.879.3. Accessed 24 May 2009.

78 Liz Curtis, *Ireland. The Propaganda War: The Media and the 'Battle for Hearts and Minds'* (London, 1983), p. 51.

79 Wood, *Crimes of Loyalty*, p. 64.

80 'Legacy of NI Peace Movement', BBC News, 11 August 2006; http://news.bbc.co.uk/1/hi/northern_ireland/4781091.stm. Accessed 2 September 2008.

81 'The Press and the Peace People', *The British Media and Ireland – Truth: the First Casualty*, ed. The Campaign for Free Speech on Ireland (Belfast, ?1979); available at http://cain.ulst.ac.uk/othelem/media/docs/freespeech.htm. Accessed 4 April 2008.

82 Sarah Buscher and Bettina Ling, *Máiread Corrigan and Betty Williams* (New York, 1999), pp. 85–90.

83 Geoffrey Wheatcroft, 'A Happy 80th Birthday to the IRA's Most Deadly Foe', *Daily Telegraph*, 18 April 2004.

84 Joseph Ruane and Jennifer Todd, *The Dynamics of Conflict in Northern Ireland: Power, Conflict and Emancipation* (Cambridge, 1996), p. 162.

85 David Miller, 'Colonialism and Academic Representations', in *Rethinking Northern Ireland*, ed. David Miller (Harlow, 1998), p. 23.

86 Éamon Phoenix, 'Stormont Secret Papers Released', BBC News, 28 December 2007; http://news.bbc.co.uk/1/hi/northern_ireland/7162727.stm.

87 Éamon Phoenix, 'Tough Response to Loyalist Strike', BBC News, 28 December 2007; http://news.bbc.co.uk/1/hi/northern_ireland/7162952.stm.

88 *The Times*, 13 September 1977; Buscher and Ling, *Máiread Corrigan*, p. 89.

89 'Tight Security for Queen's Irish Visit', BBC News, 10 August 1977; http://news.bbc.co.uk/onthisday/hi/dates/stories/august/10/newsid_2528000/2528727.stm.

90 J. Bowyer Bell, *The Secret Army: the IRA* (New Brunswick, NJ, 1997), p. 429.

91 Oliver Rafferty, *Catholicism in Ulster, 1603–1983: An Interpretive History* (Columbia, SC, 1995), p. 275.

92 Alvin Jackson, *Home Rule: An Irish History, 1800–2000* (Oxford, 2004), p. 286.

93 Jonathan Bardon, 'Pointless Verbal Fencing Hindered Attempts to Discuss a Settlement for the North', *Irish Times*, 30 December 2008.

94 P. J. McLoughlin, '"Humespeak": The SDLP, Political Discourse, and the Northern Ireland Peace Process', *Peace and Conflict Studies*, xv/1 (2008); www.ucd.ie/ibis/P.J.%20McLoughlin%20-%20Humespeak.pdf. Accessed 14 April 2009.

95 Wood, *Crimes of Loyalty*, p. 58.

96 Bardon, 'Pointless Verbal Fencing'.

97 'Belfast Bomb Suspects Rounded Up', BBC News, 18 February 1978; http://news.bbc.co.uk. Accessed 10 April 2008.

98 Quoted in Bardon, 'Pointless Verbal Fencing'.

99 Éamon Phoenix, 'Dirty Protest Escalates in 1978', BBC News, 29 December

2008; http://news.bbc.co.uk/1/hi/northern_ireland/7803409.stm. Accessed 3 June 2009.

100 E. Hannigan to Mason.

101 Aly Renwick, 'The Training Ground', *Oliver's Army* (2004); www.troopsout-movement.com/oliversarmychap10.htm. Accessed 4 November 2008.

102 'Britain Rejected Secret IRA Peace Talks Offer, 1978 Archives Reveal', *Irish Times*, 30 December 2008.

103 'The 1979 European Elections', Elections, Northern Ireland; www.ark.ac.uk/elections/fe79.htm. Accessed 4 November 2008.

104 'Ian Paisley', *New World Encyclopaedia*; www.newworldencyclopedia.org/entry/Ian_Paisley. Accessed 12 November 2008.

105 'Conservative Party, General Election Manifesto 1979, 11 April 1979', The History of the Conservative Party; www.conservatives.com/People/The_History_of_the_Conservatives/Key_Dates.aspx. Accessed 3 February 2009.

106 Martin Dillon, *The Dirty War: Covert Strategies and Tactics Used in Political Conflicts* (Oxford, 1999), p. 260.

107 *The Independent*, 22 February 2002.

108 Political Situation in Northern Ireland, House of Commons, House of Commons Debate, 24 May 1979, vol. 967, cc1213–5; http://hansard.millbank systems.com/commons/1979/may/24/political-situation#S5CV0967P0_19790524_HOC_84. Accessed 4 June 2008.

109 *New York Times*, 2 May 1979.

110 Irish Republican Army (Propaganda), House of Commons Debate, 15 June 1979, vol. 968, cc357–8W; http://hansard.millbanksystems.com/commons/1979/june/15/political-situation#S5CV0967P0_19790524_HOC_84. Accessed 4 June 2008.

111 *Ellensburg Daily Record*, 27 August 1979.

112 'IRA Bomb Kills Lord Mountbatten', BBC News, 27 August 1979; http://news.bbc.co.uk/onthisday/hi/dates/stories/august/27/newsid_2511000/2511545.stm.

113 *Time* Magazine, 10 September 1979.

114 Ibid.

115 'Lord Mountbatten', *Mountbatten History.Com Encyclopaedia*; www.history.com/this-day-in-history.do?action=Article&id=7002.

116 'Soldiers Die in Warrenpoint Massacre', BBC News, 27 August 1979; http://news.bbc.co.uk/onthisday/hi/dates/stories/august/27/newsid_3891000/3891055.stm. Accessed 4 August 2008.

117 'Pope Calls for Peace in Ireland', BBC News, 29 September 1979; http://news.bbc.co.uk/onthisday/hi/dates/stories/september/29/newsid_3926000/39267 55.stm. Accessed 4 August 2008.

118 Joe Carroll, 'A Visit that Inspired and Rallied Irish Catholics', *Irish Times* Archive; www.irishtimes.com/focus/papaldeath/article_p4a.htm. Accessed 13 December 2008.

119 Ibid.

120 Kennedy *et al.*, *Economic Development of Ireland*, p. 141.

121 Office for National Statistics, 'A Demographic Report of Northern Ireland', *Population Trends*, no. 135 (Spring 2009), pp. 91–2.

122 Kennedy et al., *Economic Development of Ireland*, p. 97.

123 *New York Times*, 25 August 1977.

124 Ibid., 31 August 1977.

125 Bardon, 'Pointless Verbal Fencing'.

126 Ivan Fallon, 'Obituary for John DeLorean', *The Independent*, 22 March 2005.

127 Seamus J. Sheehy, 'The Impact of EEC Membership on Irish Agriculture', *Journal of Agricultural Economics*, XXXI/3 (2008), pp. 297–310.

128 S. C. O'Cleireacain, 'Northern Ireland and Irish Integration: The Role of the European Communities', *Journal of Common Market Studies* (1983).

129 John Coakley and Michael Gallagher, *Politics in the Republic of Ireland* (London, 2009), p. 443.

130 Tom McGurk, 'A Victim of Disgraceful Political Funk', *Sunday Business Post*, 21 January 2001.

131 Niall Meehan, 'Historian, Politician, Censor. Conor Cruise O'Brien, 1917–2008', *Counterpunch*, 22 December 2008; www.counterpunch.org/meehan 12222008.html. Accessed 19 April 2009.

132 Farrel Corcoran, *RTÉ and the Globalisation of Irish Television* (Bristol, 2004), p. 37.

133 Niall Meehan, 'How RTÉ Censored its Censorship', *Sunday Business Post*, 20 April 2003.

134 Ibid.

135 Ruane and Todd, *The Dynamics of Conflict in Northern Ireland*, quoted in Coakley and Gallagher, *Politics in the Republic*, p. 52.

136 Philip Schlesinger, quoted in Miller, 'Colonialism and Academic Representations', in Miller, ed., *Rethinking Northern Ireland*, p. 32.

137 Ibid., p. 33.

138 Fr Raymond Murray, 'Censorship in the North of Ireland', *The British Media and Ireland – Truth: the First Casualty*, ed. The Campaign for Free Speech on Ireland (Belfast, ?1979); http://cain.ulst.ac.uk/othelem/media/docs/ freespeech. htm. Accessed 8 December 2008.

139 Ibid.

140 Ibid., Paul Madden, 'Banned, Censored and Delayed: A Chronology of Some TV Programmes Dealing with Northern Ireland'.

141 *Fermanagh Herald*, 31 December 2008.

142 Madden, 'Banned, Censored and Delayed'.

143 Northern Ireland (Bennett Report), House of Commons, *Hansard*, 16 March 1979, vol. 964, cc.961–84; http://hansard.millbanksystems.com/commons/ 1979/mar/16/northern-ireland-bennett-report.

144 Amnesty International, *Northern Ireland: Report of an Amnesty International Mission to Northern Ireland (28 November 1977–6 December 1977)* (London, 1978); http:// cain.ulst.ac.uk/issues/police/docs/amnesty78.htm. Accessed 6 February 2008.

145 *Fermanagh Herald*, 31 December 2008.

146 Madden, 'Banned, Censored and Delayed'.

147 John A. Andrews, ed., *Human Rights in Criminal Procedure* (The Hague, 1982), p. 157.

148 Aogán Mulcahy, 'The Impact of the Northern "Troubles" on Criminal Justice in the Irish Republic', *Criminal Justice in Ireland*, ed. Paul O'Mahony (Dublin, 2002), p. 288.

149 'State Papers 1977: Dublin Government's Duplicitous Role Exposed', *An*

Phoblacht, 10 January 2008.

150 Glenn Aylett, 'BBC under Fire – 80s Style'; www.transdiffusion.org/emc/aspidistra/bbcthatcher.php. Accessed 3 February 2009.

151 Michael Parker, *Northern Irish Literature, 1956–1975* (Basingstoke, 2007), p. 28.

152 Ibid., pp. 227–8.

153 Derek Mahon, E-Notes; www.enotes.com/poetry-criticism/mahon-derek. Accessed 18 January 2009.

154 Parker, *Northern Irish Literature, 1956–1975*, pp. 235–6.

155 Ibid., p.239.

156 Edna Longley ('Inner émigré or artful voyeur', p. 79) criticizes Heaney's Catholicism and suggests that his move south made him more Catholic. See Parker, *Northern Irish Literature, 1956–1975*, p. 250.

157 Neil Roberts, *A Companion to Twentieth-Century Poetry* (Oxford, 2003), p. 526.

158 Fran Brearton, *The Great War in Irish Poetry* (Oxford, 2000), p. 218.

159 'Keane on Longley', BBC NI interview with Longley by Fergal Keane, broadcast 22 January 2008; www.bbc.co.uk/northernireland/tv/programmes/longley/index.shtml. Accessed 4 January 2009.

160 Parker, *Northern Irish Literature, 1956–1975*, pp. 226–7.

161 Conor Cruise O'Brien, 'Politics and the Poet', *Irish Times*, 21 and 22 August 1975. Niall Meehan has written about this episode, e.g. *Irish Times*, 24 December 2008.

162 *New York Times*, 26 January 1975.

6 HUNGER

1 *Time*, 6 October 1980.

2 Paul Dekar, 'Máiréad Corrigan Maguire and the Northern Irish Peace People', *Peace Magazine* (July–August 1992), p. 7.

3 Sarah Buscher and Bettina Ling, *Máiread Corrigan and Betty Williams* (New York, 1999), pp. 90–93.

4 Questions by Mr McCluskey to Atkins, *Hansard*, 18 March 1980; http://hansard.millbanksystems.com/commons/1980/march/18. Accessed 14 December 2008.

5 Joseph Lee, *Ireland, 1912–1985: Politics and Society* (Cambridge, 1990), p. 504.

6 Joseph O'Malley, 'Flawed Pedigree but He Did Some Service', *The Independent*, 18 June 2006.

7 'Private Members' Business. *Magill* Magazine Allegations', Dáil Éireann, vol. 324, 25 November 1980; http://historical-debates.oireachtas.ie. Accessed 15 December 2008.

8 *Belfast Telegraph*, 14 June 2006.

9 *Guardian*, 13 June 2006.

10 Prime Minister (engagements), *Hansard*, 20 May 1980, vol. 985, cc. 247–51; http://hansard.millbanksystems.com/commons/1980/may/20/. Accessed 16 December 2008.

11 *Irish Times*, 21 May 1980.

12 Ibid., 22 May 1980.

13 Ibid., 16 June 2006.

14 HMSO, *The Government of Northern Ireland: Proposals for Further Discussion* (London, 1980).

15 'Meeting of Taoiseach and British Prime Minister: Motion', Dáil Éireann, vol. 325, 11 December 1980; http://historical-debates.oireachtas.ie. Accessed 30 October 2008.

16 'Press Conference after Anglo-Irish Summit', Margaret Thatcher Foundation, 8 December 1980; www.margaretthatcher.org/speeches/displaydocument.asp?docid=104456. Accessed 3 March 2009.

17 Ibid.

18 Lee, *Ireland*, pp. 504–5.

19 'Supplementary Estimates, 1979. Vote 24: Garda Síochána', Dáil Éireann, vol. 316, 21 November 1979; http://historical-debates.oireachtas.ie. Accessed 19 August 2008.

20 *Time*, 6 October 1980.

21 Martin Dillon, *The Dirty War: Covert Strategies and Tactics Used in Political Conflicts* (Oxford, 1999), p. 182.

22 'Kincora Boys' Home', House of Commons, *Hansard*, 1 March 1990, vol. 168, c.370; http://hansard.millbanksystems.com. Accessed 22 August 2008.

23 *Belfast Telegraph*, 15 September 2002.

24 Ibid.

25 'Kincora Boys' Home', House of Commons, 1 March 1990.

26 'Kincora Boys' Home', House of Commons, 9 March 1989, vol. 148, cc. 1024–5; http://hansard.millbanksystems.com. Accessed 23 August 2008.

27 Dillon, *The Dirty War*, p. 183.

28 'Kincora Boys' Home', House of Commons, *Hansard*, 6 November 1989, vol. 159, cc. 670–71; http://hansard.millbanksystems.com. Accessed 24 August 2008.

29 'Kincora Boys' Home', House of Commons, *Hansard*, 22 January 1991, vol. 184, cc. 125–6W; http://hansard.millbanksystems.com. Accessed 14 November 2008.

30 'Meeting of Taoiseach and British Prime Minister', Dáil Éireann, vol. 325, 11 December 1980; http://historical-debates.oireachtas.ie. Accessed 16 November 2008.

31 'Background to Hunger Strikes', Bobby Sands Trust; www.bobbysands trust.com/hungerstrikers/history. Accessed 3 February 2008.

32 Quoted in Sean O'Hagan, *The Observer*, 19 October 2008.

33 Margaret Thatcher to Senators Kennedy and Moynihan, Congressman O'Neill and Governor Carey (Northern Ireland), 14 May 1981 (MTF); www.margaretthatcher.org/speeches/displaydocument.asp?docid=104648. Accessed 11 March 2009.

34 'The 1980 Hunger Strike', Hunger Strike commemorative webpage; http://larkspirit.com/hungerstrikes/1980.html. Accessed 4 April 2008.

35 Richard English, *Armed Struggle: The History of the IRA* (Oxford, 2003), pp. 193–4.

36 Margaret Thatcher, 20 November 1980 (MTF); www.margaretthatcher.org/speeches/displaydocument.asp?docid=104446. Accessed 12 March 2009.

37 Ibid.

38 D. M. Daugherty, 'The Women Hunger Strikers of Armagh Prison', *Ireland's*

Own (October 2002).

39 *An Phoblacht*, 22 November 1980; reprinted on 23 November 2000.

40 Margaret Thatcher, 'Press Conference after Anglo-Irish Summit', 8 December 1980 (MTF); www.margaretthatcher.org/speeches/displaydocument.asp? docid=104456. Accessed 12 March 2009.

41 Margaret Thatcher, 'Radio Interview (Anglo-Irish Summit)', 8 December 1980; www.margaretthatcher.org/speeches/displaydocument.asp?docid=104458. Accessed 12 March 2009.

42 English, *Armed Struggle*, pp. 194–5.

43 Daugherty, 'The Women Hunger Strikers'.

44 *An Phoblacht*, 10 January 1981.

45 'The 1980 Hunger Strike', Hunger Strike commemorative webpage.

46 Daugherty, 'The Women Hunger Strikers'.

47 Sands's diary is available at www.irishhungerstrike.com/bobbysdiary.html. Accessed 10 October 2008.

48 Sean O'Hagan, *The Observer*, 19 October 2008.

49 English, *Armed Struggle*, p. 199.

50 *Chicago Tribune*, 29 April 1981.

51 *Pittsburgh Post-Gazette*, 7 May 1981.

52 Margaret Thatcher, 'Speech to Scottish Conservative Conference' (MTF), 8 May 1981; www.margaretthatcher.org/speeches/displaydocument.asp?docid= 104644. Accessed 3 May 2009.

53 Margaret Thatcher, 'Letter to Senators Kennedy and Moynihan, Congressman O'Neill and Governor Carey (Northern Ireland)', 14 May 1981; www. margaretthatcher.org/speeches/displaydocument.asp?docid=104648. Accessed 11 March 2009.

54 'Order of Business'. Dáil Éireann, vol. 328, 13 May 1981; www.oireachtas.gov.ie. Accessed 6 June 2008.

55 Margaret Thatcher, 'TV Interview for ITN (Ulster visit)' (MTF), 28 May 1981; www.margaretthatcher.org/speeches/displaydocument.asp?docid=104658. Accessed 10 June 2009.

56 *An Phoblacht*, 15 June 2006.

57 Representation of the People Act, 1981 (c.34)

58 English, *Armed Struggle*, pp. 204–5.

59 *The Times*, 1 July 1981.

60 'Extract from a letter dated 8 July 1981 from 10 Downing Street to the Northern Ireland Office' (MTF); www.margaretthatcher.org/archive/display document. asp?docid=111766. Accessed 1 August 2009.

61 'Death of Hungerstriker: Statement by Taoiseach', Dáil Éireann, vol. 329, 8 July 1981; www.oireachtas.gov.ie. Accessed 4 August 2008.

62 Ibid.

63 *Courier*, 9 August 1981.

64 Ibid.

65 *Irish Times*, 10 August 1981.

66 'Expressions of Sympathy', Dáil Éireann, vol. 330, 20 October 1981; www. oireachtas.gov.ie. Accessed 4 August 2008.

67 English, *Armed Struggle*, p. 202.

68 Sean O'Hagan, 'Interview with Pat Sheehan', *The Observer*, 19 October 2008.

69 David Beresford, *Ten Men Dead: The Story of the 1981 Irish Hunger Strike* (New York, 1987), p. 332.

70 'IRA Maze Hunger Strikes at End', BBC News, 3 October 1981; http://news.bbc.co.uk/onthisday/hi/dates/stories/october/3/newsid_2451000/2451503.stm. Accessed 5 August 2008.

71 Ian McAllister, '"The Armalite and the Ballot Box": Sinn Féin's Electoral Strategy in Northern Ireland', *Electoral Studies*, XXIII (2004), pp. 123–42.

72 Laurence White, 'Richard O'Rawe, Blanketman: Will we ever uncover full truth about hunger strike?', *Belfast Telegraph*, 15 June 2009.

73 Interview by Professor Padraig O'Malle with Sir John Blelloch, a member of MI5 who had been seconded to the NIO as a Deputy Secretary in 1980 and 1981, Bobby Sands Trust; www.bobbysandstrust.com/archives/1069. Accessed 13 December 2008.

74 '2006 RTÉ interview with Gerry Adams', quoted in *Sunday Times*, 5 April 2009.

75 White, 'Richard O'Rawe'.

76 'Extract from a letter dated 8 July 1981, from 10 Downing Street to the Northern Ireland Office' (MTF); www.margaretthatcher.org/archive/displaydocument.asp?docid=111766. Accessed at 3 July 2009.

77 Liam Clarke, 'Was Gerry Adams Complicit over Hunger Strikers?', *Sunday Times*, 5 April 2009.

78 *Irish News*, 28 September 2009.

79 Liam Clarke, 'Why Adams Sticks to his Maze Myth', *Sunday Times*, 12 April 2009.

80 *Belfast Telegraph*, 4 June 2009.

81 'Hunger Strikes Movie Cleans Up at Irish Film and TV Awards Night', *Belfast Telegraph*, 16 February 2009.

82 Denis O'Hearn, *Nothing but an Unfinished Song: Bobbie Sands the Hunger Striker who Ignited a Generation* (New York, 2006), p. 377.

83 This song was quoted in Alex Massie, 'Could You Go a Chicken Supper, Bobby Sands'; www.spectator.co.uk/alexmassie/3242016/could-you-go-a-chicken-supper-bobby-sands.thtml. Accessed 5 January 2008.

84 Kieran McEvoy, *Paramilitary Imprisonment in Northern Ireland: Resistance, Management, and Release* (Oxford, 2001), p. 101.

85 Begoña Aretxaga and Joseba Zulaika, *States of Terror: Begoña Aretxaga's Essays* (Reno, 2005), pp. 109–10.

86 'Six Counties Deaths', Dáil Éireann, vol. 331, 24 November 1981; www.oireachtas.gov.ie. Accessed 12 October 2008; 'History of Plastic Bullets', *Relatives for Justice*; web.archive.org/web/20060110022317/www.relativesforjustice.com/plastic/plastic_history.htm. Accessed 2 February 2009.

87 Ken Simons, *Peace Magazine*, July to Sept 2001, p. 13.

88 'Britain: Terror on a Summer's Day', in *Time* Magazine, 2 August 1982.

89 House of Commons, *Hansard*, HC vol. 33, 7 December 1982 cc. 708–12; http://hansard.millbanksystems.com. Accessed 3 October 2008.

90 Ibid.

91 Ken Livingstone, *Our Campaigns*; www.ourcampaigns.com/CandidateDetail.html?CandidateID=46190. Accessed 3 February 2009.

92 'Harrods (Bomb Incident)', House of Commons, *Hansard*, HC Deb, 19

December 1983, vol. 51, cc. 19–27; http://hansard.millbanksystems.com. Accessed 4 December 2008.

93 'Tory Cabinet in Brighton Bomb Blast', BBC News, 12 October 1984; http://news.bbc.co.uk. Accessed 6 December 2008.

94 Ibid.

95 'IRA members jailed for 4000 Years', BBC News, 5 August 1983; http://news.bbc.co.uk. Accessed 7 December 2008.

96 'Northern Ireland Supergrass Trials', Dáil Éireann, vol. 354, 4 December 1984; www.oireachtas.gov.ie. Accessed 3 November 2008.

97 Ibid.

98 Ibid.

99 Ibid.

100 Lord Gifford, *Supergrasses: The Use of Accomplice Evidence in Northern Ireland* (London, 1984).

101 'Northern Ireland: The I.R.A.'s Great Escape', *Time*, 10 October 1983.

102 HMSO, *Report of an Inquiry by HM Chief Inspector of Prisons into the Security Arrangements at HM Prison, Maze Relative to the Escape on Sunday 25th September 1983, including Relevant Recommendations for the Improvement of Security at HM Prison, Maze* (London, 1984).

103 Obituary of John Herman, *The Guardian*, 8 November 2008.

104 'UK Condemned over IRA Deaths', BBC News, 4 May 2001, http://news.bbc.co.uk/2/hi/uk_news/northern_ireland/1311724.stm. Accessed 7 November 2008.

105 Debate in House of Commons, *Hansard*, HC [130/1271-76], 31 March 2008.

106 Margaret Thatcher, 'Press Conference in Brisbane' (MTF), 5 August 1988; www.margaretthatcher.org/speeches/displaydocument.asp?docid=107315. Accessed 8 March 2009.

107 Ibid., Margaret Thatcher, 'Speech to Conservative Party Conference', 14 October 1988; www.margaretthatcher.org/speeches/displaydocument.asp?docid=107352.

108 *An Phoblacht*, 28 September 1995.

109 *The Times*, 17 March 1988.

110 Gerry Adams, *A Farther Shore: Ireland's Long Road to Peace* (New York, 2003), p. 69.

111 Martin Dillon, *Stone Cold: The True Story of Michael Stone and the Milltown Massacre* (London, 1992).

112 'The Two Corporals' in *SAOIRSE 32*, 19 March 1988.

113 *The Independent*, 30 December 1992.

114 Margaret Thatcher, 'Letter to the Rev. Ian Paisley' (MTF), 10 December 1980; www.margaretthatcher.org/speeches/displaydocument.asp?docid=104285. Accessed 14 April 2009.

115 Martin Dillon, *God and the Gun: The Church and Irish Terrorism* (New York, 1999), p. 240.

116 *The Independent*, 30 November 1993.

117 *The Times*, 7 March 1981.

118 Ibid.

119 'Northern Ireland: Unleashing the *Third Force*', 7 December 1981.

120 Ibid.

121 *Florida Ledger*, 22 December 1981.

122 John Coakley and Michael Gallagher, *Politics in the Republic of Ireland* (London, 2009), p. 415.

123 *The Times*, 7 November 1981.

124 Thomas Hennessey, *The Northern Ireland Peace Process: Ending the Troubles?* (New York, 2001), p. 22.

125 Vernon Bogdanor, *Devolution in the United Kingdom* (Oxford, 1999), pp. 104–5.

126 Coakley and Gallagher, *Politics in the Republic*, pp. 236–7.

127 Ibid., p. 415.

128 Margaret Thatcher, 'Press Conference for American Correspondents in London' (MTF), 7 December 1984; www.margaretthatcher.org/speeches/display document.asp?docid=105810. Accessed 6 March 2009.

129 Anglo-Irish Agreement 1985 between the Government of Ireland and the Government of the United Kingdom; www.uhb.fr/langues/cei/agree85.htm. Accessed 2 December 2008.

130 *The Times*, 15 November 1995.

131 *Daily Telegraph*, 31 May 2003.

132 Meeting of Taoiseach and British Prime Minister, Dáil Éireann, vol. 325, 11 December 1980; http://historical-debates.oireachtas.ie/D/0325/D.0325. 19801211004.html. Accessed 26 October 2008.

133 John McGarry, ed., *Northern Ireland and the Divided World: Post-Agreement Northern Ireland* (Oxford, 2001), pp. 163–4.

134 Christians in Schools Trust, 'The Story of Gordon Wilson'; www.cist. org.uk/pv/em/er2521.htm. Accessed 2 February 2009.

135 Margaret Thatcher, Public Statement, 12 November 1987, House of Commons, *Hansard*, HC [122/547-52].

136 Peter Taylor, 'Who Knew about Enniskillen Plans?', BBC News, 21 April 2008; http://news.bbc.co.uk/2/hi/uk_news/7356159.stm. Accessed 4 March 2009.

137 *Irish News*, 5 November 2007.

138 Brian Feeney, *Sinn Féin: a Hundred Turbulent Years* (Dublin, 2002), pp. 354–5.

139 *The Times*, 21 August 1988.

140 *Belfast Telegraph*, 28 September 2008.

141 Thomas E. Hachey, Joseph M. Hernon and Lawrence John McCaffrey, *The Irish Experience: a Concise History* (New York, 1996), p. 227.

142 Text of speech in Ballyporeen, 3 June 1984; www.reagan.utexas.edu/ archives/speeches/1984/60384a.ht. Accessed 2 February 2009.

143 Kieran Anthony Kennedy, Thomas Giblin and Deirdre McHugh, *The Economic Development of Ireland in the Twentieth Century* (London, 2001), p. 77.

144 *The Independent*, 18 June 2006.

145 'European Council Meeting: Statement by Taoiseach', Dáil Éireann, vol. 341, 24 March 1983; www.oireachtas.gov.ie. Accessed 10 December 2008.

146 Thomas Friedman, 'Ireland: The End of the Rainbow', *New York Times*, 29 June 2005.

147 'How the Brain Drain Hit Ireland in the '80s', *The Independent*, 17 January 2009.

148 A. P. Lobo and J. J. Salvo, 'Resurgent Irish Immigration to the US in the 1980s and Early 1990s: A Socio-demographic Profile', *International Migration*,

xxxvi/2 (1998), pp. 257–80.

149 'How the Brain Drain Hit Ireland in the '80s', *The Independent*, 17 January 2009.

150 King and Shuttleworth, *Emigration and Employment*, pp. 2–5.

151 Thomas Friedman, 'Ireland: The End of the Rainbow', *New York Times*, 29 June 2005.

152 Peter Townroe and Ron Martin, *Regional Development in the 1990s: The British Isles in Transition* (London, 1992), p. 118.

153 English, *Armed Struggle*, p. 164.

154 *The Independent*, 29 June 2008.

155 Carrickfergus Borough Sixtieth Anniversary; www.carrickfergus.org/council/60th-anniversary.

156 'Obituary for John De Lorean', *Washington Post*, 21 March 2005.

157 Townroe and Martin, *Regional Development in the 1990s*, p. 118.

158 'How the Economy was Crippled by Adams' Marxist Terror Plan', *The Independent*, 29 June 2008.

159 Townroe and Martin, *Regional Development in the 1990s*, p. 118.

160 Lee, *Ireland*, p. 653.

161 'Chronology of the Abortion Debate in Ireland', News in Focus, *Irish Times*; www.irishtimes.com/focus/abortion/issues/chronology.htm. Accessed 3 January 2009.

162 'Abortion in Northern Ireland', BBC News, 13 June 2001; http://news.bbc.co.uk/2/hi/uk_news/northern_ireland/1386450.stm. Accessed 7 December 2008.

163 Lee, *Ireland*, p. 146.

164 Jennifer E. Spreng, *Abortion and Divorce Law in Ireland* (Jefferson, NC, 2004), pp. 95–6.

165 'Ireland – Yes on Divorce but Barely', CNN News, 26 November 1995; www.cnn.com/WORLD/9511/ireland_vote/index.html. Accessed 10 October 2008.

166 Coakley and Gallagher, *Politics in the Republic*, p. 364.

167 *Irish Independent*, 9 March 1983.

168 'Portrait of the Irish Senator as a Gay Activist', *OutSmart*, June 2004; www.outsmartmagazine.com/issue/i04-01/irish.html. Accessed 13 October 2008.

169 Council of Europe/Conseil de l'Europe, *Yearbook of the European Convention on Human Rights, 1987* (Strasbourg, 1992), p. 87.

170 Michael Farrell, 'Pink Power on the Emerald Isle', *The Colby Reader*; www.colby.edu/par/Spring%2099/emerald.htm. Accessed 5 April 2009.

171 Councillor Tim Attwood, in response to an article in *The Independent* (see reference 172).

172 'Paisley Gay Remarks are Dangerous', *The Independent*, 2 June 2007.

173 Coakley and Gallagher, *Politics in the Republic*, p. 42.

174 From the album *Mondo Bongo* (1979).

175 Bob Geldof website; www.bobgeldof.info/Charity/liveaid.html. Accessed 2 December 2008.

176 'Fight against Famine Put Geldof on World Stage', *Daily Mail*, 1 July 2005.

177 *Belfast Telegraph*, 10 September 1997.

178 Anne Flynn, 'Women in Irish Society. How Far have they Come?' (2005); www.rmu.edu/OnTheMove/findoutmore.open_page?ichap. Accessed 12 Decem-

ber 2008.

179 Declan Kiberd, *Inventing Ireland: The Literature of the Modern Nation* (London, 1995), p. 584.

180 Seamus Heaney, 'An Open Letter' (Derry, 1983).

181 'Interview with Seamus Heaney', *Daily Telegraph*, 2 January 2009.

182 'Profile of Medbh McGuckian', *Contemporary Writers*; www.contemporary writers.com/authors/?p=auth02D9P274512627448. Accessed 5 April 2009.

183 Michael Parker, *Northern Irish Literature, 1975–2006* (Basingstoke, 2007), p. 87.

184 *Guardian*, 21 December 2005.

185 Lance Pettitt, *Screening Ireland* (Manchester, 2000), pp. 235–6.

186 Anthony Roche, ed., *The Cambridge Companion to Brian Friel* (Cambridge, 2006), p. 123.

187 J. H. Andrews, 'Brian Friel: Making a Reply to Criticisms of *Translations*', in Scott Boltwood, *Brian Friel, Ireland, and The North* (Cambridge, 2007), pp. 159–66.

188 Ibid.

189 Paul Delaney, ed., *Brian Friel in Conversation* (Ann Arbor, MI, 2000), p. 175.

190 Boltwood, *Brian Friel*, pp. 1–2.

191 Csilla Bertha, 'Brian Friel as a Post-Colonial Playwright', in Roche, ed., *Cambridge Companion to Brian Friel*, p. 154.

192 Jeanne Colleran and Jenny S. Spencer, *Staging Resistance: Essays on Political Theater* (Ann Arbor, MI, 1998), pp. 24–5.

193 From the album 'Ghost in the Machine', BBC *Guide to the Police*; www.bbc. co.uk/dna/h2g2/A653375. Accessed 3 December 2008.

194 'Politics and Protest', *Guardian*, 18 March 2009.

195 Paul Mason, *Criminal Visions: Media Representations of Crime and Justice* (Uffculme, Devon, 2003), p. 136.

196 Pettitt, *Screening Ireland*, p. 211.

197 John Wilson, *Understanding Journalism* (London, 1996), p. 223.

7 OVERTURES

1 *The Times*, 23 September 1989.

2 Margaret Thatcher, 'Remarks Visiting Marine Barracks at Deal', Margaret Thatcher Foundation (MTF), 25 September 1989; www.margaretthatcher.org/ speeches/displaydocument.asp?docid=107782. Accessed 4 April 2009.

3 'Guildford Four Released after 15 Years', BBC News, 19 October 1989; http:// news.bbc.co.uk/onthisday/hi/dates/stories/october/19/newsid_2490000/24 90039.stm#. Accessed 19 August 2008.

4 Francis M. Carroll, *The American Presence in Ulster: a Diplomatic History, 1796– 1996* (Washington, DC, 2005), p. 211.

5 *Belfast Telegraph*, 29 May 2009.

6 Quoted in Graham Ellison and Jim Smyth, *The Crowned Harp: Policing Northern Ireland* (London, 2000), p. 146.

7 As late as 2004, John Hume asked the Prime Minister, Tony Blair, for an Inquiry, *Hansard*, col. 879, 28 April 2004: www.parliament.the-stationery-office.co.uk/pa/cm200304/cmhansrd/vo040428/debtext/40428-03.htm.

Accessed 5 January 2009.

8 'Stevens Inquiry: Key People', BBC News, 17 April 2003; http://news.bbc. co.uk/2/low/uk_news/northern_ireland/2956161.stm. Accessed 19 December 2008.

9 G. Ellison and J. Smyth, *The Crowned Harp: Policing in Northern Ireland* (London, 2000), p. 146.

10 'Obituary of Sir John Hermon', *Guardian*, 8 November 2008.

11 'Female FRU Operative Named', *An Phoblacht*, 15 February 2001.

12 'Journalist Pursued the Truth for 13 Years', *Irish News*, 19 June 2002.

13 'Channel Four Duped by Hoaxer, Claims RUC', *The Independent*, 2 August 1992.

14 *Irish Times*, 25 June 2002.

15 *Irish News*, 20 June 2002.

16 *Mirror*, 20 June 2002.

17 *New York Times*, 29 June 2002.

18 British Irish Rights Watch, for Peace, Justice and Human Rights; www.birw. org/. Accessed 3 January 2009.

19 'How Stakeknife Paved Way to Defeat for IRA', *The Times*, 12 May 2003.

20 Stevens Enquiry: Overview and Recommendations, 17 April 2003 (London, 2003), Chairman, Sir John Stevens, QPM, DL, Commissioner of the Metropolitan Police Service; http://cain.ulst.ac.uk/issues/collusion/stevens3/stevens3 summary.htm. Accessed 3 October 2008.

21 Kevin McNamara's speech on Stevens Enquiry in the House of Commons, 12 May 2003; http://hansard.millbanksystems.com. Accessed 10 October 2008.

22 *Belfast Telegraph*, 17 August 1996.

23 Even following the Peace Process, pressure had to be applied: in Britain, Labour MP Kevin McNamara repeatedly pressed for an inquiry, as did Aengus Ó Snodaigh, Sinn Féin TD, see Dáil Éireann, vol. 600, 13 April 2005.

24 'Stakeknife: Uncovering the Hidden War', BBC News, 11 May 2003; http://news. bbc.co.uk/2/hi/uk_news/northern_ireland/3018537.stm. Accessed 4 October 2008.

25 Section 3, 'Declaration Against Terrorism: Local Elections', Elected Authorities (Northern Ireland) Act 1989; www.opsi.gov.uk/ACTS/acts1989/ukpga_ 19890003_en_1. Accessed 19 December 2008.

26 Colin Knox, 'Sinn Féin and Local Elections: the Government's Response in Northern Ireland', *Parliamentary Affairs*, XLIII/4 (1990), pp. 448–63.

27 Northern Ireland and the European Parliament; www.ark.ac.uk/elections/ feo9.htm. Accessed 1 December 2008.

28 John Coakley and Michael Gallagher, *Politics in the Republic of Ireland* (London, 2009), Appendix 2e, p. 370.

29 Cees van der Eijk et al., 'European Election Study, 1989' (Amsterdam, 1993); www.ees-homepage.net/docs/ees_cdb_1989.pdf. Accessed 12 November 2008.

30 Coakley and Gallagher, *Politics in the Republic of Ireland*, pp. 25–6.

31 'Ulster Defence Regiment', House of Commons, *Hansard*, HC Deb 17 October 1989, vol. 158 c.24; http://hansard.millbanksystems.com/commons/1989/ oct/17/ulster-defence-regimen. Accessed 9 October 2008.

32 'Defence Estimates', *Hansard*, 19 October 1989, vol. 158 cc. 293–368.

33 'Anglo-Irish Relations', Mr Liam Kavanagh, Labour Party, Dáil Éireann, vol.

393, 23 November 1989; debates.oireachtas.ie/D/0393/D.0393.19891230081. html. Accessed 11 October 2008.

34 Mr Bobbie Molloy, Minister for Energy.

35 Chris Flood, Fianna Fáil.

36 Defence Estimates, House of Commons, *Hansard*, 19 October 1989, vol. 158 cc. 293–368; http://hansard.millbanksystems.commons/1989. Accessed 9 October 2008.

37 Ibid., quoted by Archibald Hamilton, Minister of State for the Armed Forces.

38 *The Times*, 4 November 1989.

39 *Irish Independent*, 4 November 1989.

40 Margaret Thatcher, interview with *The Times*, 22 November 1989.

41 *The Independent*, 4 September 1994.

42 *Boston Globe*, 19 November 1989.

43 *Irish Independent*, 22 November 1989.

44 *The Times*, 2 July 1990.

45 'No more Mr Nice Guy', *Guardian*, 19 September 2002.

46 *New York Times*, 15 May 1991.

47 Sidney Elliott and Paul Bew, 'The Prospects for Devolution' in *Studies: An Irish Quarterly Review*, LXXX, no. 138 (Summer 1991), pp. 124–32.

48 Joseph P. O'Grady, 'Forcing the Question of Northern Ireland: The Brooke-Mayhew Talks, 1990–1992', *New Hibernia Review*, V/4 (2001), pp. 73–92.

49 Paul Bew, *Ireland: The Politics of Enmity, 1789–2006* (Oxford, 2007), p. 542.

50 Feargal Cochrane, *Unionist Politics and the Politics of Unionism since the Anglo-Irish Agreement* (Cork, 1997), chapter 7.

51 Ian S. Wood, *Crimes of Loyalty: A History of the UDA* (Edinburgh, 2006), p. 148.

52 Ibid., pp. 149–50.

53 Ibid., p. 166.

54 Tim Pat Coogan, *The Troubles: Ireland's Ordeal, 1969–96, and the Search for Peace* (London, 1996), p. 240.

55 Bew, *Ireland*, p. 539.

56 *The Times*, 17 December 1992.

57 'Stories that have Put Newspapers in the Dock', *Daily Telegraph*, 10 April 2001.

58 'Faith in British Justice is Shaken by Forced Confessions and False Jailings', *New York Times*, 2 June 1991.

59 *New Scientist*, 18 May 1991.

60 'Ulster's Regiment: a Question of Loyalty?', *Panorama*, British Film Institute; http://ftvdb.bfi.org.uk/sift/title/449499. Accessed 4 October 2004.

61 Colin Worton, 'Guilty until Proven Innocent? British Irish Rights Watch'; www.birw.org/Colin.html. Accessed 10 October 2008.

62 Alan F. Parkinson, 'Ulster Loyalism and the British Media', Chapter 3 (1998); http://cain.ulst.ac.uk/othelem/media/parkinson/parkinson98.htm. Accessed 4 October 2008.

63 Ibid.

64 J. Bowyer Bell, *The IRA, 1968–2000: An Analysis of a Secret Army* (London, 2000), p. 626.

65 *The Independent*, 27 October 1992.

66 Margaret Thatcher, 'Remarks on the Murder of Ian Gow' (MTF), 30 July 1990;

www.margaretthatcher.org. Accessed 2 January 2009.

67 Kevin Toolis, *Rebel Hearts: Journeys within the IRA's Soul* (New York, 1995), pp. 197–9.

68 *The Times*, 8 February 1991.

69 *Irish Times*, 18 January 1992.

70 Coogan, *The Troubles*, p. 239.

71 *The Independent*, 12 July 1992.

72 Wood, *Crimes of Loyalty*, p. 166.

73 Tony Geraghty, *The Irish War: the Hidden Conflict between the IRA and British Intelligence* (Baltimore, MD, 2002), p. 217.

74 'Why are the IRA Bombing London?', *Ulster Nation*, February 1996; www. ulsternation.org.uk/why_are_the_ira_bombing_london.htm. Accessed 4 December 2008.

75 *Irish Times*, 29 March 1993.

76 'Warrington Tragedy', Dáil Éireann, vol. 428, 23 March 1993; www.oireachtas. gov.ie. Accessed 9 December 2008.

77 *New York Times*, 29 March 1993.

78 'Tim Parry', Jonathan Ball Foundation for Peace; www.foundation4peace.org. Accessed 10 October 2008.

79 'Gerry Adams Has Said Sorry . . .', BBC World News, 1 November 2007; http:// news.bbc.co.uk/2/hi/uk_news/northern_ireland/7071981.stm. Accessed 1 February 2009.

80 *The Independent*, 5 August 1996.

81 Jonathan Tonge, *Northern Ireland* (Cambridge, 2006), p. 78.

82 Wood, *Crimes of Loyalty*, p. 174.

83 'Bomb that Spells More Bloodshed: Republican attacks on Shankill Road's loyalist heartland are sure to mean retaliation against Catholics', *The Independent*, 24 October 1993.

84 Richard B. Finnegan and Edward McCarron, *Ireland: Historical Echoes, Contemporary Politics* (Boulder, CO, 2000), p. 344.

85 'Greysteel Loyalist Murderer was Shielded by RUC', *The Independent*, 7 February 2006.

86 *The Independent*, 8 November 1993.

87 Wood, *Crimes of Loyalty*, p. 150.

88 *The Independent*, 20 June 1994.

89 Wood, *Crimes of Loyalty*, p. 189.

90 'UVF's Catalogue of Atrocities', BBC News, 18 June 2009; http://news.bbc.co. uk/2/hi/uk_news/northern_ireland/6617329.stm. Accessed 1 August 2009.

91 *The Independent*, 20 June 1994.

92 'Police Ombudsman Postpones Loughinisland Murders' Report', *Irish Times*, 11 September 2009.

93 'IRA Attack Sparks Fears of Loyalist Retaliation: Cycle of violence in Ulster appears set to continue despite shock over pub murders', *The Independent*, 21 June 1994.

94 Tim Menzies, Review of Roddy Doyle's 'Barrytown Trilogy'; http://menzies. us/index.php?news=7015. Accessed 14 April 2009.

95 Lance Pettitt, *Screening Ireland* (Manchester, 2000), p. 126.

96 Obituary of Joseph O'Malley, *Sunday Independent*, 18 June 2006.

97 'Nomination of Taoiseach', Dáil Éireann, vol. 391, 29 June 1989; www. oireachtas-debates.gov.ie. Accessed 4 November 2008.

98 Michael Buckley [former Chief Executive of Allied Irish Bank], 'Haughey's Determination the Driving Force behind IFSC', *Irish Post*, 18 June 2006.

99 *The Times*, 13 June 2006.

100 *Sunday Business Post*, 14 September 2003.

101 'Economic Dependence, the Back Door to Dublin Rule', *Ulster Nation* (n.d.); www.ulsternation.org.uk/economic_dependence.htm. Accessed 9 December 2009.

102 'Resignation of Taoiseach', Dáil Éireann, vol. 415, 11 February 1992; www. oireachtas.gov.ie. Accessed 4 May 2008.

103 *Belfast Telegraph*, 22 February 2002.

104 'Half-baked Potato in Need of a Filling', *Daily Telegraph*, 6 March 2002.

105 *The Times*, 13 June 2006.

106 International Fund for Ireland; www.internationalfundforireland.com/about. html. Accessed 2 January 2009.

107 'International Fund for Ireland: Statements', Seanad Éireann, XXIX (April 1993); www.oireachtas.gov.ie. Accessed 4 December 2008.

108 Lee Alan Smithey, 'Strategic and Collective Action and Collective Identity Reconstruction: Parading Disputes and Two Northern Towns', PhD thesis, University of Texas at Austin, 2002, p. 287.

109 'European Funding'; www.dfpni.gov.uk/index/finance/european-funding. htm. Accessed 3 March 2009.

110 This point was made by Rev. William McCrea, the MP for the area, House of Commons, 30 January 1999; www.publications.parliament.uk/pa/cm199192/ cmhansrd/1992-01-30/Orals-1.html. Accessed 6 January 2009.

111 Ibid., Richard Needham.

112 Margaret Ward, *Unmanageable Revolutionaries: Women and Irish Nationalism* (London, 1995).

113 *Sunday Tribune*, 30 August 2009.

114 *Los Angeles Times*, 30 June 1991.

115 *The Independent*, 4 December 1993.

116 Flynn quoted in Fintan O'Toole, 'Profile: Mary Robinson: Mary, Quite Contrary', *The Independent*, 9 June 1996.

117 Coakley and Gallagher, *Politics in the Republic of Ireland*, p. 364.

118 'Battle of Maastricht: Ireland', *The Economist*, 29 February 1992.

119 'The Abortion Referendum', *Irish Times*; www.irishtimes.com/focus/ abortion/issues/chronology.htm. Accessed 15 January 2009.

120 Jennifer E. Spreng, *Abortion and Divorce Law in Ireland* (Jefferson, NC, 2004), pp. 148–9.

121 *Irish Times*, 2 December 1997.

122 Ibid., 11 December 1997.

123 'Irish Abortion "Journeys" Avoided in Election', *Women Enews*, 24 May 2007; www.womensenews.org/article.cfm/dyn/aid/3180/context/archive. Accessed 6 April 2009.

8 CEASEFIRE

1 Ed Moloney, *A Secret History of the IRA* (London, 2003), pp. 291–2.

2 Ibid., pp. 292–6.

3 Ibid., pp. 296–7.

4 *A Scenario for Peace*, Sinn Féin website; www.sinnfein.ie/contents/15210. Accessed 10 November 2008.

5 Ibid.

6 Richard English, *Armed Struggle: The History of the IRA* (Oxford, 2003), pp. 264–5.

7 Moloney, *Secret History of the IRA*, p. 281.

8 Ibid., pp. 254–60.

9 English, *Armed Struggle*, p. 265.

10 Moloney, *Secret History of the IRA*, pp. 394–5.

11 'Protestant Clergy Reveal Dialogue with Sinn Féin', *The Independent*, 22 April 1996.

12 Exceptions were the United Irishmen in the 1790s and Young Ireland in the 1840s, who both adopted an inclusive, non-sectarian approach. For more, see Christine Kinealy, *Repeal and Revolution: 1848 in Ireland* (Manchester, 2009).

13 *The Independent*, 22 April 1996.

14 *Irish Independent*, 31 December 2005.

15 *The Times*, 1 December 1990.

16 Moloney, *Secret History of the IRA*, pp. 387–8.

17 John Coakley and Michael Gallagher, *Politics in the Republic of Ireland* (London, 2009), p. 211.

18 'IRA Cessation of Violence in Northern Ireland', Dáil Éireann, vol. 445, 31 August 1994.

19 *The Independent*, 12 April 1993.

20 'First joint statement issued by Social Democratic and Labour Party (SDLP) leader Mr John Hume and Sinn Féin President, Mr Gerry Adams on Saturday 24 April, 1993', Sinn Féin website; www.sinnfein.ie/humes-adams-statements. Accessed 9 March 2009.

21 'John Hume – Ireland's Peacemaker', SDLP website; www.sdlp.ie/about_hume.php. Accessed 9 March 2009.

22 Richard B. Finnegan and Edward McCarron, *Ireland: Historical Echoes, Contemporary Politics* (Boulder, CO, 2000), p. 343.

23 'Humes Adams Statements', Sinn Féin website; www.sinnfein.ie/humes-adams-statements. Accessed 10 March 2008.

24 English, *Armed Struggle*, p. 268.

25 *The Independent*, 12 July 1992.

26 English, *Armed Struggle*, p. 268.

27 Nicholas Watt, 'Extent of Secret Links between Government and IRA revealed', *Guardian*, 11 March 2008.

28 *The Economist*, 4 December 1993.

29 *New York Times*, 30 November 1993.

30 Anthony Bevins, Eamonn Mallie and Mary Holland, 'Major's Secret Links with IRA Leadership Revealed', *The Observer*, 28 November 1993.

31 *The Times*, 30 November 1993.

32 *New York Times*, 30 November 1993.

33 *The Independent*, 16 December 1994.

34 Paragraph 1, 'Joint Declaration on Peace: The Downing Street Declaration', Wednesday 15 December 1993; http://cain.ulst.ac.uk/events/peace/docs/ dsd151293.htm. Accessed 10 February 2009.

35 Ibid., para. 2.

36 Sidney Elliott and Paul Bew, 'The Prospects for Devolution', *Studies: An Irish Quarterly Review*, LXXX, no. 138 (Summer 1991), pp. 124–32.

37 'IRA Cessation of Violence in Northern Ireland', Dáil Éireann, vol. 445, 31 August 1994; www.oireachtas.gov.ie. Accessed 19 November 2008.

38 Ibid.

39 *The Independent*, 16 December 1994.

40 Ibid., 16 December 1993.

41 Conor Cruise O'Brien, 'Lending Succour to the IRA: Dublin and London have agreed before. And only the gunmen have benefited, warns Conor Cruise O'Brien', *The Independent*, 16 December 1993.

42 'Ireland (Joint Declaration)', House of Commons, *Hansard*, 15 December 1993; www.publications.parliament.uk/pa/cm199394/cmhansrd/1993-12-15/Debate-1.html. Accessed 20 November 2008.

43 *The Independent*, 16 December 1993.

44 Coakley and Gallagher, *Politics in the Republic of Ireland*, p. 53.

45 Ibid., p. 54.

46 Niall O'Dochartaigh, 'Role of Government', in *Social Attitudes in Northern Ireland: the Seventh Report*, ed. Gillian Robinson, Deirdre Heenan, Ann Marie Gray and Kate Thompson (September 1998); http://cain.ulst.ac.uk/othelem/ research/nisas/rep7c1.htm. Accessed 5 February 2009.

47 *New York Times*, 2 February 1994.

48 Conor O'Clery, *Daring Diplomacy* (Boulder, CO, 1997).

49 Alan F. Parkinson, *Ulster Loyalism and the British Media* (Dublin, 1998), pp. 58–76.

50 *New York Times*, 5 February 1994.

51 Moloney, *Secret History of the IRA*, p. 420.

52 'IRA Ally's U.S. Success Riles London – Northern Ireland: Gerry Adams Packs Two Days in New York with Media Appearances', *Los Angeles Times*, 3 February 1994.

53 *New York Times*, 5 February 1994.

54 Edna O'Brien, in *New York Times*, 1 February 1994.

55 *New York Times*, 5 February 1994.

56 Moloney, *Secret History of the IRA*, pp. 420–21.

57 Parkinson, *Ulster Loyalism*, pp. 58–62.

58 Moloney, *Secret History of the IRA*, p. 422.

59 *The Independent*, 4 September 1994.

60 'Interview with Michael Longley'; www.teachnet.ie/ckelly/ceasefire.htm. Accessed 7 April 2009.

61 Ibid., Michael Longley, 'Ceasefire'.

62 Address of Senator Edward Kennedy, 'Northern Ireland – a View from America', Tip O'Neill Memorial Lecture, University of Ulster, Magee College. Delivered at the Guildhall, Derry, 9 January 1998; http://cain.ulst.ac.uk/events/ peace/docs/ek9198.htm. Accessed 29 November 2008.

63 *The Independent*, 4 September 1994.

64 *New York Times*, 1 September 1994.

65 'IRA Cessation of Violence in Northern Ireland', Dáil Éireann, vol. 445, 31 August 1994. www.oireachtas-debates.gov.ie. Accessed 2 December 2008.

66 Ibid.

67 Seamus Heaney, *The Cure at Troy: A Version of Sophocles' Philoctetes* (New York, 1991).

68 'IRA Cessation of Violence in Northern Ireland', Dáil Éireann.

69 *The Times*, 1 September 1994.

70 *Irish Times*, 1 September 1994.

71 Ibid.

72 'Paisley Warns of Civil War in Ulster: Major and Reynolds try to defuse tension over impending ceasefire', *The Independent*, 31 August 1994.

73 Marianne Elliott, *The Long Road to Peace in Northern Ireland* (Liverpool, 2002), p. 65.

74 *The Independent*, 4 September 1994.

75 'IRA Cessation of Violence in Northern Ireland', Dáil Éireann.

76 *New York Times*, 1 September 1994.

77 Combined Loyalist Military Command (CLMC) Ceasefire Statement, 13 October 1994; http://cain.ulst.ac.uk/events/peace/docs/clmc131094.htm. Accessed 5 April 2009.

78 Ian S. Wood, *Crimes of Loyalty: A History of the UDA* (Edinburgh, 2006), pp. 208–9.

79 'Framework Document on Northern Ireland', Dáil Éireann, vol. 449, 23 February 1995.

80 Ibid.

81 *The Times*, 23 February 1995.

82 *Sunday Tribune*, 18 December 1994.

83 English, *Armed Struggle*, pp. 289–90.

84 'Decommissioning of Weapons', Dáil Éireann, vol. 451, 28 March 1995.

85 *New York Times*, 5 April 1995.

86 *Washington Post*, 19 May 1995.

87 *New York Times*, 7 July 1995.

88 *Irish Times*, 14 July 1995.

89 *The Times*, 14 August 1995.

90 Dominic Bryan, *Orange Parades: The Politics of Ritual, Tradition and Control* (London, 2000), p. 170.

91 Quoted in Chris Ryder and Vincent Kearney, *Drumcree: The Orange Order's Last Stand* (London, 2001), p. 122.

92 'Apprentice for Peace. Profile: David Trimble', *The Independent*, 5 April 1998.

93 'George Mitchell: The Man to Bring Peace to Ulster?', *The Independent*, 18 July 1999.

94 Ibid.

95 *The Times*, 1 December 1995.

96 'Remarks by *An Ceann Comhairle* (Mr Seán Treacy)', Dáil Éireann, vol. 459, 1 December 1995.

97 'Address of President Clinton', Dáil Éireann, vol. 459, 1 December, 1995; www.oireachtas.gov.ie. Accessed 19 January 2009.

98 'Northern Ireland Peace Process', *ibid.*, 6 December, 1995.

99 Julia Hall, *To Serve Without Favour: Policing, Human Rights, and Accountability in Northern Ireland* (Helsinki, 1995), p. 115.

100 Ibid.

101 *New York Times*, 24 January 1996.

102 'George Mitchell: The Man to Bring Peace to Ulster?'.

103 Quoted in Julia Langdon, *Mo Mowlam: The Biography* (London, 2000), p. 275.

104 Ibid., pp. 275–6.

105 *Washington Post*, 12 February 1996.

106 *The Times*, 10 February 1996.

107 *The Independent*, 12 February 1996.

108 'Working Towards a New Europe: The Role and Achievements of Europe's Regional Policy, 2004–20009'; http://ec.europa.eu/regional_policy/policy/impact/pdf/legacy_2009_en.pdf. Accessed 19 August 2009.

109 *Los Angeles Times*, 15 December 1994.

110 Ibid.

111 'Northern Ireland's Economic Fears', BBC News, 22 June 2001; http://news.bbc.co.uk/2/hi/business/1402261.stm. Accessed 14 December 2008.

112 'How Ireland Became the Celtic Tiger', *The Heritage Foundation*, 23 June 2006; www.heritage.org/research/worldwidefreedom/bg1945.cfm. Accessed 12 December 2008.

113 Antoin E. Murphy, *The Celtic Tiger: An Analysis of Ireland's Economic Performance* (San Domenico di Fiesole, 2000).

114 Tony Fahey and David Duffy, *Quality of Life in Ireland: The Social Impact of Economic Boom* (Dordrecht, 2002), pp. 1–4.

115 Jeanne Colleran and Jenny S. Spencer, ed., *Staging Resistance: Essays on Political Theater* (Ann Arbor, MI, 1998), pp. 26–7.

116 'Interview with Jim Kerr: Travel Broadens the Mind', *Fair Play for Creators*; www.fairplayforcreators.com/Jim%20Kerr%20Ivor%20Essay%20FINAL.pdf. Accessed 12 July 2008.

117 'Troubles Tunes which Annoyed Auntie', BBC News, 20 June 2008; http://news.bbc.co.uk/1/hi/northern_ireland/7464668.stm. Accessed 3 January 2009.

118 'Sad Affair', from album *33 revolutions per minute* (1994).

119 'Replaying Marxman – and Very Much Appreciating Them', *Review*, 1 August 2005; http://nomorebigwheels.blogspot.com/2005/08/replaying-marxman-and-very-much.html. Accessed 4 January 2009.

120 Lance Pettitt, *Screening Ireland* (Manchester, 2000), p. 178.

121 '*Riverdance* Taps China', in *Invest in China*; http://en.invest.china.cn/english/travel/59459.htm. Accessed 6 January 2009.

122 Pettitt, *Screening Ireland*, p. 178.

123 See, for example, Roy Foster, 'We are All Revisionists Now', in *Irish Review* (Cork, 1986), pp. 1–6.

124 Sinéad O'Connor, 'Famine' from *Universal Mother* (1994).

125 *Dublin Evening Press*, 24 September 1994.

126 Quotation taken from W. R. Aykroyd, *The Conquest of Famine* (London, 1974), p. 45.

127 'Introduction by Minister of State, Avril Doyle T.D.', Famine Commemoration Programme, 27 June 1995 (Dublin, 1995).

128 Christine Kinealy, *The Great Irish Famine: Impact, Ideology and Rebellion* (London, 2002), pp. 1–30.

129 *Irish Independent*, 7 June 1997.

130 Kinealy, *Great Irish Famine*, p. 13.

131 *The Times*, 13 October 1996.

9 ENDGAME

1 *The Independent*, 26 February 1996.

2 Ibid., 19 February 1996.

3 John Major, House of Commons, *Hansard*, 21 March 1996; www.publications.parliament.uk/pa/cm199596/cmhansrd/vo960321/debtext/60321-05.htm. Accessed 9 December 2008.

4 *New York Times*, 13 February 1996.

5 'Communiqué following meeting between John Major and John Bruton', 28 February 1996; http://cain.ulst.ac.uk/events/peace/docs/com280296.htm. Accessed 7 December 2008.

6 P. O'Neill, Irish Republican Army (IRA) Statement, 29 February 1996, Irish Republican Publicity Bureau, Dublin.

7 'The 1996 Forum Elections and the Peace Process, Northern Ireland elections'; www.ark.ac.uk/elections/ff96.htm.

8 Kate Fearon, 'Northern Ireland Women's Coalition: institutionalizing a political voice and ensuring representation', 2002; www.c-r.org/our-work/accord/public-participation/ni-womens-coalition.php. Accessed 29 November 2008.

9 'Northern Ireland: Gender Agenda', BBC News, 23 February 2006; http://news.bbc.co.uk/2/hi/programmes/politics_show/4742540.stm. Accessed 12 November 2008.

10 'Speech by John Major at the Opening of All-Party Negotiations in Stormont, Belfast', 10 June 1996; http://cain.ulst.ac.uk/issues/politics/docs/pmo/jm100696.htm.

11 Barry White, 'An Irish Peace?', *Belfast Telegraph*, 14 June 1996.

12 The 1996 Forum Elections and the Peace Process, Northern Ireland Elections'.

13 Tim Pat Coogan, *The Troubles: Ireland's Ordeal, 1969–96, and the Search for Peace* (London, 1996), p. 507.

14 *The Times*, 13 June 1996.

15 *Belfast Telegraph*, 6 June 1997.

16 Carol Coulter, 'Feminism and Nationalism in Ireland', in *Rethinking Northern Ireland*, ed. David Miller (Harlow, 1998), pp. 176–7.

17 Ed Moloney, *A Secret History of the IRA* (London, 2003), p. 443.

18 *Manchester Evening News*, 13 June 1996.

19 'Plan to Set Garda Killers Free', BBC News, 11 May 2004; http://news.bbc.co.uk/2/hi/uk_news/northern_ireland/3694601.stm. Accessed 20 November 2008.

20 *Irish Examiner*, 7 June 2006.

21 'Northern Ireland Peace Process', Dáil Éireann, vol. 467, 25 June 1996; www.oireachtas.gov.ie. Accessed 1 December 2008.

22 Dominic Bryan, *Orange Parades: The Politics of Ritual, Tradition and Control* (London, 2000), pp. 4–5.

23 *The Independent*, 14 July 1996.

24 Bryan, *Orange Parades*, pp. 5–6.

25 Interviewed by Brian Cowan on Radio Ulster, 14 July 1996, quoted in Chris Ryder and Vincent Kearney, *Drumcree: The Orange Order's Last Stand* (London, 2001), pp. 172–4.

26 Ibid., p. 6.

27 Ibid., p. 175.

28 The North Report was published in January 1997.

29 Ryder and Kearney, *Drumcree*, p. 176.

30 Tim Pat Coogan, *The IRA* (Aldershot, 2002), p. 706.

31 *The Independent*, 8 March 1997.

32 Coogan, *The IRA*, p. 706.

33 Ibid.

34 *Guardian*, 1 November 2005.

35 *An Phoblacht*, 28 May 1998.

36 'Harryville Chapel Protest', House of Commons, *Hansard*, 18 March 1997, vol. 292 c.532W; http://hansard.millbanksystems.com. Accessed 13 December 2008.

37 *Irish Times*, 5 May 1999.

38 'Arson Attack on Protest Church', BBC News, 18 July 2000; http://news.bbc.co.uk/2/hi/uk_news/northern_ireland/839152.stm. Accessed 10 December 2008.

39 *The Times*, 24 September 1996.

40 *New York Times*, 25 September 1996.

41 'Irish Republican Army (IRA) Statement on the Bombing of British Army Headquarters in Lisburn, County Antrim', 8 October 1996; http://cain.ulst.ac.uk/events/peace/docs/ira81096.htm. Accessed 1 December 2008.

42 Moloney, *Secret History of the IRA*, p. 444.

43 Julia Langdon, *Mo Mowlam: the Biography* (London, 2000), p. 4.

44 *Irish News*, 11 November 1996.

45 *New York Times*, 11 November 1996.

46 'United Kingdom: Cruel, Inhuman or Degrading Treatment: Detention of Róisin McAliskey', Amnesty International; www.amnesty.org/en/library/info/EUR45/008/1997. Accessed 4 December 2008.

47 Written Answers, House of Commons, *Hansard*, 16 January 1997; http://hansard.millbanksystems.com. Accessed 6 December 2008.

48 *Guardian*, 22 August 2007.

49 *Irish News*, 10 March 1998.

50 *Guardian*, 2 August 2007.

51 Ibid., 24 November 2007.

52 'Parades and Marches – Independent Review of Parades and Marches in Northern Ireland, January 1997 (The North Report)'; http://cain.ulst.ac.uk/issues/parade/north.htm. Accessed 4 November 2008.

53 *Belfast Telegraph*, 9 September 1997.
54 'Loyalist Ceasefire is over, RUC chief says', *The Independent*, 14 January 1997.
55 Ibid.
56 *An Phoblacht*, 18 December 1997.
57 *Belfast Telegraph*, 21 May 2005.
58 *The Independent*, 26 March 1997.
59 'Sinn Féin Press Release', 19 February 1997; www.sinnfein.org/releases/ pr021997.html. Accessed 17 December 2008.
60 Mitchel McLaughlin interviewed in the *Irish News*, 19 February 1997.
61 'Easter Commemoration 1997', Address by Sinn Féin Chief Negotiator Martin McGuinness, The Loup, Co. Derry, 31 March 1997; www.sinnfein. org/releases/97eastermcguinness.html. Accessed 17 December 2008.
62 Gerry Kelly speaking in Dublin made the same point as Mitchel McLaughlin; www.sinnfein.org/releases/97eastermclaughlin.html. Accessed 17 December 2008.
63 *The Independent*, 6 April 1997.
64 *Daily Mail*, 6 May 1997; *The People*, 6 May 1997.
65 Republican Sinn Féin website; www.rsf.ie. Accessed 5 February 2009.
66 Sheldon Stryker, Timothy Joseph Owens, and Robert W. White, eds, *Self, Identity, and Social Movements* (Minneapolis, MN, 2000), pp. 323–4.
67 Richard English, *Armed Struggle: The History of the IRA* (Oxford, 2003), p. 316.
68 *The Economist*, 12 April 1997.
69 *An Phoblacht*, 24 April 1997.
70 *Belfast Telegraph*, 25 April 1997.
71 *The Independent*, 12 April 1997.
72 For example, Mark Simpson, 'Trimble Wins Unionist Battle: Paisley, Robinson, Can't be Discounted', *Belfast Telegraph*, 3 May 1997.
73 *New York Times*, 6 May 1997.
74 *Belfast Telegraph*, 3 May 1997.
75 Ibid., 16 May 1997.
76 Ibid., 3 June 1997.
77 Ibid., 4 June 1997.
78 Ryder and Kearney, *Drumcree*, pp. 218–20.
79 Ibid., pp. 221–2.
80 Ibid., pp. 222–3.
81 Bryan, *Orange Parades*, p. 173.
82 *Sunday Business Post*, 11 May 1997.
83 *Belfast Telegraph*, 16 May 1997.
84 Ibid., 12 May 1997.
85 Ibid.
86 Kieran McEvoy, *Paramilitary Imprisonment in Northern Ireland: Resistance, Management, and Release* (Oxford, 2001), p. 170.
87 *Belfast Telegraph*, 24 May 1997.
88 *Irish Times*, 4 June 1997.
89 *New York Times*, 4 June 1997.
90 Ibid.
91 John Coakley and Michael Gallagher, *Politics in the Republic of Ireland* (London,

2009), p. 97.

92 Moloney, *Secret History of the IRA*, p. 463.

93 *Irish Times*, 7 June 1997.

94 English, *Armed Struggle*, p. 294.

95 *Belfast Telegraph*, 9 June 1997.

96 Ibid., 16 July 1997.

97 *The Independent*, 18 July 1997.

98 *An Phoblacht*, 18 December 1997.

99 'Agreement on Independent International Commission on Decommissioning, 26 August 1997'; http://cain.ulst.ac.uk/events/peace/docs/dec26897.htm. Accessed 13 December 2008.

100 *Belfast Telegraph*, 24 July 1997.

101 Joint Statement issued by Bertie Ahern, John Hume and Gerry Adams, 25 July 1997; http://cain.ulst.ac.uk/events/peace/docs/js250797.htm. Accessed 10 December 2008.

102 *The Times*, 30 August 1997.

103 *Belfast Telegraph*, 7 August 1997.

104 Ibid.

105 *The Independent*, 29 November 2001; *Daily Telegraph*, 6 January 2001.

106 *Irish Times*, 27 August 1997.

107 U2 PopMart Tour, Europe, 26 August 1997, Botanic Gardens, Belfast, Northern Ireland; www.u2gigs.com/show645.html. Accessed 9 January 2009.

108 *Belfast Telegraph*, 24 September 1997.

109 *Washington Post*, 20 May 1998.

110 *Sunday Times*, 31 August 1997.

111 *Belfast Telegraph*, 15 September 1997.

112 Ibid.

113 Ibid., 25 September 1997.

114 *Irish Times*, 24 September 1997.

115 *Belfast Telegraph*, 24 September 1997.

116 Ibid., 26 September 1997.

117 *The Independent*, 1 October 1997.

118 English, *Armed Struggle*, p. 296.

119 *Boston Globe*, 8 November 1997.

120 *Irish Times*, 12 November 1997.

121 *Belfast Telegraph*, 24 November 1997.

122 Julie Hyland, 'Ulster Defence Association Leader Arrested after Intra-Loyalist Violence in Belfast', 24 August 2000; www.wsws.org/articles/2000/aug2000/ire-a24.shtml. Accessed 18 October 2008.

123 Public Statement by Mrs Nuala O'Loan on her investigation into the circumstances surrounding the death of Raymond McCord Junior and related matters (Operation Ballast), 22 January 2007; http://cain.ulst.ac.uk/issues/police/ombudsman/poni220107.htm. Accessed 19 October 2008.

124 *Belfast Telegraph*, 17 October 1997.

125 *The Independent*, 22 March 2008.

126 *Belfast News Letter*, 29 June 2008.

127 *Irish Times*, 29 December 1997.

128 Text of Joint Statement by the British and Irish Governments on 'Propositions on Heads of Agreement', 12 January 1998; http://cain.ulst.ac.uk/events/peace/docs/bi12198.htm. Accessed 22 October 2008.

129 Ulster Freedom Fighters (Ulster Defence Association) Statement, 23 January 1998; http://cain.ulst.ac.uk/events/peace/docs/uff23198.htm. Accessed 23 October 2008.

130 'Conflict Related Deaths in 1998', British Irish Rights Watch; www.birw.org/Deaths%20since%20ceasefire/deaths%2098.html. Accessed 26 October 2008.

131 *An Phoblacht*, 22 January 1998.

132 *Irish News*, 28 January 1998.

133 *Belfast Telegraph*, 31 January 1998.

134 *New York Times*, 18 March 1998.

135 *Irish Examiner*, 28 February 1998.

136 *The Times*, 28 February 1998.

137 *New York Times*, 18 March 1998.

138 *The Observer*, 12 April 1998.

139 *Irish Times*, 8 April 1998.

140 Based on Memoirs of Jonathan Powell, *Guardian*, 19 March 2008.

141 *The Observer*, 2 April 1998.

142 *Guardian*, 19 March 2008.

143 *The Observer*, 12 April 1998.

144 Ibid.

145 Ibid., 12 April 1998.

146 Jonathan Powell, *Guardian*, 19 March 2008.

147 *Irish Times*, 11 April 1998.

148 *The Times*, 11 April 1998.

149 The full text of the Agreement is available at www.nio.gov.uk/agreement.pdf. Accessed 7 December 2008.

150 Ibid.

151 *Belfast Telegraph*, 11 April 1998.

152 Interview with Michael Longley, *Thumbscrew*, 12 (Winter 1998/9); www.poetrymagazines.org.uk/magazine/record.asp?id=12172. Accessed 8 January 2009.

153 English, *Armed Struggle*, p. 300.

154 Ibid.

155 Coakley and Gallagher, *Politics in the Republic*, pp. 289–90.

156 *Belfast Telegraph*, 26 May 1998.

157 'Elton Rocks Stormont', BBC News, 30 May 1998; http://news.bbc.co.uk/2/hi/events/northern_ireland/latest_news/101413.stm. Accessed 19 September 2008.

158 Langdon, *Mo Mowlam*, p. 297.

159 *Daily Mirror*, 28 May 1998.

160 'Elton Rocks Stormont'.

161 Langdon, *Mo Mowlam*, p. 297.

162 Bryan, *Orange Parades*, p. 174.

163 Quoted in Ryder and Kearney, *Drumcree*, p. 272.

164 *Irish Times*, 13 July 1998.

165 Bryan, *Orange Parades*, p. 175.

166 *Irish News*, 14 July 1998.

167 *The Independent*, 18 July 1998.

168 Ibid.

169 English, *Armed Struggle*, p. 318.

170 Ibid.

171 'Omagh Tragedy: Statements', Seanad Éireann, vol. 156, 3 September 1998; www.oireachtas.gov.ie. Accessed 5 December 2008.

172 *An Phoblacht*, 27 August 1998.

173 Bill Clinton's keynote address at the Waterfront Hall, Belfast, Thursday, 3 September 1998; http://cain.ulst.ac.uk/events/peace/docs/bc3998.htm. Accessed 15 August 2008.

174 *The Observer*, 6 September 1998.

175 *Guardian*, 11 September 1998.

176 *Belfast Telegraph*, 11 September 1998.

177 Ibid., 10 September 1998.

178 *An Phoblacht*, 3 September 1998.

179 The full text of the speech is available at Nobel Lecture, Oslo, 10 December 1998; http://nobelprize.org/nobel_prizes/peace/laureates/1998/trimble-lecture.html. Accessed 7 January 2010. For the source of the reference to Eoghan Harris, see his 'The Necessity of Social Democracy', in Richard English and Joseph Morrison Skelly, eds, *Ideas Matter: Essays in Honour of Conor Cruise O'Brien* (Dublin, 1998), p. 333.

180 *Belfast News Letter*, 4 December 1998.

181 RTÉ News, 26 March 1999; www.rte.ie/news/1999/0326/hume.html. Accessed 30 May 2008.

182 The book was Sean McPhilemy, *The Committee: Political Assassination in Northern Ireland* (Boulder, CO, 1998). This was based on the TV documentary *The Committee* (1991), made by McPhilemy for Channel Four's 'Dispatches' series. See Michael McMenamin, 'Truth, Terror and David Trimble', *Reason* (October 1999); www.reason.com/news/show/31137.html. Accessed 15 December 2008.

183 Ibid., 26 November 1998.

184 *An Phoblacht*, 3 September 1998.

185 Ibid., 1 October 1998.

186 *Washington Post*, 15 November 1998.

187 'David Trimble, Agreeing to Differ', *Guardian*, 5 April 2008.

188 *The Independent*, 18 January 2000.

189 'The Agreement Must Stand', by Martin McGuinness MP, Sinn Féin Chief Negotiator, 28th October 1998; www.sinnfein.org/releases/9810mcgart.html. Accessed 4 December 2008.

190 *Belfast Telegraph*, 19 March 1999.

191 *An Phoblacht*, 12 February, 1998.

192 Ian S. Wood, *Crimes of Loyalty: A History of the UDA* (Edinburgh, 2006), p. 234.

193 *An Phoblacht*, 8 April 1999.

194 'Northern Ireland Issues', Dáil Éireann, vol. 502, 23 March 1999; www.oireachtas.gov.ie. Accessed 3 December 2008.

195 'Rosemary Nelson Murder', Parliament of New South Wales, 5 December 2007;

www.parliament.nsw.gov.au/prod/parlment/hansart.nsf/V3Key/LA20000810
009. Accessed 17 December 2008.

196 *Guardian*, 4 July 2009.

197 *An Phoblacht*, 8 April 1999.

198 'David Trimble, Agreeing to Differ'.

199 *Belfast Telegraph*, 3 July 1999.

200 *New Statesman*, 27 November 1999.

201 Ibid.

202 Coogan, *The IRA*, p. 731.

203 *Sunday Times*, 31 October 1999.

204 *Guardian*, 1 November 1999.

205 'IRA Statement', 17 November 1999, BBC News; http://usproxy.bbc.com/2/hi/
uk_news/northern_ireland/525098.stm. Accessed 5 October 2008.

206 *Belfast Telegraph*, 19 November 1999.

207 Ibid., 20 November 1999.

208 Feargal Cochrane, *Unionist Politics and the Politics of Unionism since the Anglo-
Irish Agreement* (London, 1997), p. 390.

209 *Belfast Telegraph*, 17 December 1999.

210 Ibid.

211 Ibid., December 1999.

212 Cochrane, *Unionist Politics*, pp. 392–3.

213 Lance Pettitt, *Screening Ireland* (Manchester, 2000), p. 259.

214 See www.imdb.com/title/tt0107207/awards. Accessed 5 March 2008.

215 Review, *Entertainment Weekly*, 17 January 1997; www.ew.com/ew/article/
0,,286488,00.html. Accessed 5 March 2008.

216 Pettitt, *Screening Ireland*, p. 260.

217 *An Phoblacht*, 5 February 1998.

218 Pettitt, *Screening Ireland*, pp. 256–7.

219 Ibid., p. 258.

220 'Dispute over Liam Neeson Honour', BBC News, 8 March 2000; http://news.
bbc.co.uk/2/hi/uk_news/northern_ireland/670076.stm.

221 *An Phoblacht*, 27 February 1997.

222 Ibid., 4 February 1999.

223 John David Slocum, ed., *Terrorism, Media, Liberation* (Piscataway, NJ, 2005), p.
226.

224 Pettitt, *Screening Ireland*, p. 262.

225 Slocum, *Terrorism, Media, Liberation*, p. 228.

226 Pettitt, *Screening Ireland*, p. 262.

227 'Film: Deafened by Ulster's Primal Scream', *The Independent*, 30 January 1998.

228 'Leading Men: The Hollywood Irish', *World of Hibernia*, 22 September 1997.

229 Rebecca Murray, 'Top 10 Irish Actors', *About Hollywood*; http://movies.about.
com/od/toppicks/tp/irishactro31506.htm. Accessed 15 April 2009.

230 *Belfast Telegraph*, 15 May 1996.

231 Ibid., 26 June 1996.

232 *Daily Mirror*, 7 May 1997.

233 'Remarks on the Northern Ireland peace process by Minister Cowen T.D.,
Limerick', 27 June 2001, Department of Foreign Affairs; www.dfa.ie/home/

index.aspx?id=26425. Accessed 3 December 2008.

234 David Leslie, 'Northern Ireland, Tourism and Peace', *Tourism Management*, XVII/1 (February 1996), pp. 51–5.

235 'Northern Ireland's Economic Fears', BBC News, 22 June 2001; http://news. bbc.co.uk/2/hi/business/1402261.stm. Accessed 11 February 2008.

236 Economic Development in Northern Ireland, NI Bureau; www.nibureau. com/index/ni-and-usa/economic-development.htm. Accessed 11 February 2008.

237 Anne Lazenbatt, Una Lynch and Eileen O'Neill, 'Revealing the Hidden "Troubles" in Northern Ireland: the Role of Participatory Rapid Appraisal', *Health Education Research*, XVI/5 (October 2001), pp. 567–78.

238 *The Independent*, 19 November 2005.

239 *Belfast News Letter*, 18 December 2005.

240 Sean Dorgan, 'How Ireland Became the Celtic Tiger', 23 June 2006; www. heritage.org/research/worldwidefreedom/bg1945.cfm. Accessed 15 February 2009.

241 Tony Fahey, Helen Russell and Christopher T. Whelan, eds, *Best of Times? The Social Impact of the Celtic Tiger in Ireland* (Dublin, 2007).

242 Mary Fitzgerald, 'The Celtic Tiger's Underbelly', *Prospect*, 20 January 2008; www.prospectmagazine.co.uk/2008/01/theceltictigersunderbelly/. Accessed 14 January 2009.

243 'Killing of Dublin Journalist: Statements', Dáil Éireann, vol. 467, 26 June 1996; www.oireachtas-debates.gov.ie. Accessed 2 February 2009.

244 *Belfast Telegraph*, 14 June 1997.

245 *New York Times*, 2 November 1997.

246 Coakley and Gallagher, *Politics in the Republic*, p. 311.

247 Ibid., p. 296.

248 Coulter, 'Feminism and Nationalism in Ireland', in Miller, ed., *Rethinking Northern Ireland*, p. 176.

249 *New York Times*, 20 April 1997.

250 *Belfast Telegraph*, 26 July 1997.

251 Ibid., 26 July 1997.

252 Establishment of the Commission to Inquire into Child Abuse (CICA); www. childabusecommission.ie/rpt/01-01.php. Accessed 3 February 2009.

253 Martin J. Bull and James L. Newell, *Corruption in Contemporary Politics* (London, 2003), p. 165.

254 *Belfast Telegraph*, 3 January 2000.

255 'Millennium Celebrations', Dáil Éireann, vol. 513, 26 January 2000; http:// historical-debates.oireachtas.ie. Accessed 12 October 2008.

EPILOGUE: AFTERSHOCK

1 Irish Republican Army (IRA) New Year Statement, 6 January 2000; www.cain. ulst.ac.uk. Accessed 3 March 2008.

2 *Belfast Telegraph*, 14 January 2000.

3 *The Independent*, 5 February 2000.

4 *Irish News*, 12 February 2000.

5 Ibid.

6 Ibid., 8 May 2000.

7 Ibid., 29 May 2000.

8 Ibid., 13 December 2000.

9 *Belfast Telegraph*, 14 December 2000.

10 *Irish News*, 25 January 2001.

11 *Belfast Telegraph*, 3 May 2001.

12 Ibid., 7 October 2001.

13 *Irish News*, 24 May 2001.

14 Ibid., 11 June 2001.

15 *Belfast Telegraph*, 5 July 2001.

16 Ibid., 7 July 2001.

17 Ibid., 4 September 2001.

18 *Irish News*, 19 October 2001.

19 'Looking to the Future', Text of a speech made by Gerry Adams, Sinn Féin President, Conway Mill, West Belfast, 22 October 2001.

20 *Irish News*, 24 October 2001.

21 Ibid., 7 November 2001.

22 This coincided with the publication of a report by Liam Kennedy *'They Shoot Children Don't They?'*, showing that, between 1990 and 2000, 372 teenagers had been beaten and 207 shot by loyalist and republican paramilitary groups in what is commonly termed 'punishment' attacks.

23 *Guardian*, 1 October 2001.

24 Statement by Secretary of State for Northern Ireland, John Reid, at Hillsborough, 28 September 2001.

25 Statement by Secretary of State for Northern Ireland, John Reid, at Hillsborough, 12 October 2001.

26 Ian S. Wood, *Crimes of Loyalty: A History of the UDA* (Edinburgh, 2006), p. 342.

27 *Guardian*, 4 September 2001.

28 *Irish News*, 5 September 2001.

29 Ibid., 7 September 2001.

30 *New York Times*, 5 September 2001.

31 *Belfast Telegraph*, 23 November 2001.

32 *Guardian*, 1 December 2001.

33 *Belfast Telegraph*, 13 November 2008.

34 *New York Times*, 8 September 2001.

35 *Irish News*, 11 March 2003.

36 Northern Ireland Assembly; www.niassembly.gov.uk/io/summary/new_summary.htm. Accessed 12 June 2009.

37 *Irish News*, 15 October 2002.

38 Ibid.

39 *Belfast Telegraph*, 17 October 2002.

40 *Irish News*, 7 April 2003.

41 'Humanitarian Aid for Iraq', Dáil Éireann, vol. 564, 1 April 2001; www.oireachtas.gov.ie. Accessed 4 January.

42 'Northern Ireland Issues', Dáil Éireann, vol. 565, 9 April 2003.

43 *Sunday Business Post*, 25 December 2005.

44 *Belfast Telegraph*, 13 April 2009.

45 Northern Ireland Assembly; www.niassembly.gov.uk/io/summary/new_ summary.htm. 5 November 2009.

46 *The Independent*, 30 November 2003; *Sunday Business Post*, 27 June 2004.

47 Northern Ireland Assembly; www.niassembly.gov.uk/io/summary/new_ summary.htm. Accessed 14 September 2008.

48 *Daily Telegraph*, 26 December 2004.

49 *Belfast Telegraph*, 20 January 2005.

50 Ibid., 18 January 2005.

51 Ibid., 19 January 2005.

52 *New York Times*, 18 March 2005.

53 *Daily Telegraph*, 26 December 2004.

54 *The Times*, 29 March 2009.

55 *Guardian*, 8 May 2005.

56 Ibid., 29 July 2005.

57 *Irish News*, 29 July 2005.

58 *Guardian*, 29 July 2005.

59 Ibid., 1 November 2005.

60 Ibid.

61 Wood, *Crimes of Loyalty*, p. 345.

62 *Belfast Telegraph*, 7 September 2009.

63 Ibid., 31 January 2009.

64 *Irish News*, 13 October 2006.

65 Ibid., 14 October 2006.

66 *Belfast Telegraph*, 15 October 2006.

67 *Irish News*, 14 October 2006.

68 *The Independent*, 1 April 2007.

69 Bernadette Devlin, 'I'm uniquely qualified to bring lasting peace to Northern Ireland', *The Independent*, 29 July 2007.

70 *The Independent*, 1 April 2007.

71 *Irish News*, 27 March 2007.

72 *Irish News*, 27 March 2007.

73 *Irish News*, 9 May 2007.

74 *Belfast Telegraph*, 1 May 2007.

75 'Martin McGuinness and Ian Paisley: Chuckle Brothers Photo Exhibition', *The Times*, 9 May 2008.

76 RTÉ News, 11 May 2007; www.rte.ie/news/2007/0511/paisley.html. Accessed 3 February 2009.

77 *Sunday Journal*, 11 March 2008; www.sundayjournal.ie/lisa-burkitt/DOctoberor-No.3864028.jp.

78 BBC News, 18 February 2008.

79 *Belfast Telegraph*, 6 March 2008.

80 Ibid., 10 March 2008.

81 'Paisley's Path, and How it Cost Him Close Friends', *Belfast Telegraph*, 6 March 2008.

82 *Guardian*, 18 March 2008.

83 *Belfast Telegraph*, 11 June 2008.

84 Ibid., 31 October 2008.

85 *Pink News*, 7 November 2008; www.pinknews.co.uk/news/articles/2005-9517. html. Accessed 20 January 2009.

86 Letter from Roberta Dunlop, North Down Councillor, *Belfast Telegraph*, 11 June 2009.

87 *Irish News*, 8 June 2009.

88 Presidential Elections: www.electionsireland.org. Accessed 3 January 2009.

89 *Sunday Business Post*, 27 June 2004.

90 *Irish Times*, 1 January 2002.

91 Ibid., 3 May 2004.

92 *Irish News*, 1 July 2004.

93 *Belfast Telegraph*, 21 October 2002.

94 *Irish Times*, 21 October 2002.

95 Ibid., 14 June 2008.

96 www.sinnfein.ie/no-2-lisbon. Accessed 12 February 2009.

97 *Daily Telegraph*, 14 June 2008.

98 Ibid.

99 *Irish Times*, 24 September 2009.

100 *Belfast Telegraph*, 30 April 2007.

101 *Irish News*, 28 May 2007.

102 *Daily Telegraph*, 2 April 2008.

103 'Northern Ireland's Economic Fears', BBC News, 22 June 2001; http://news. bbc.co.uk/2/hi/business/1402261.stm. Accessed 4 October 2009.

104 Economic Telegraph, NI Bureau; www.nibureau.com/index/ni-and-usa/ economic-development.htm. Accessed 4 January 2009.

105 'Belfast Best Place to Live', BBC Survey, 1 October 2003; http://news.bbc.co.uk/ 2/hi/uk_news/northern_ireland/3156680.stm. Accessed 17 December 2008.

106 NI Tourist Board Marketing Plan for 2006; www.nitb.com. Accessed December 2008.

107 'Statement on Tourism by Minister for Arts, Sport and Tourism, Mr. John O'Donoghue, TD in Seanad Éireann on Wednesday 13 November, 2002'; www. arts-sport-tourism.gov.ie/publications/release.asp?ID=152. Accessed 3 March 2008.

108 'Sun Shines on Special Olympics', BBC News, 26 June 2003; http://news.bbc. co.uk/2/hi/europe/3023148.stm. Accessed 5 November 2008.

109 'Pop Concerts and Special Olympics a Major Boost to Dublin's Tourism Industry', *Dublin Chamber of Commerce*, 7 August 2003; www.dublinchamber. ie/press_release.asp?article=369. Accessed 19 November 2008.

110 'Belfast Best Place to Live'.

111 *Irish Times*, 4 May 2009.

112 *Tourism Ireland*, 2008, p.7; www.tourismireland.com. Accessed 15 February 2009.

113 'Tourism Spotlight', *Northern Ireland Tourist Board*, Edition 37, February 2008; www.nitb.com. Accessed 1 July 2009.

114 *Irish Times*, 28 July 2009.

115 Anna Triandafyllidou and Ruby Gropas, eds, *European Immigration: a Sourcebook* (Aldershot, 2007), p. 169.

116 *Irish Times*, 24 September 2009.

117 *Newsweek*, 8 October 2007.

118 'Ireland Votes to End Birth Right', BBC News, 13 June 2004; http://news.bbc. co.uk/2/hi/europe/3801839.stm. Accessed 15 November 2008; *Irish Times*, 26 November 2009.

119 Office for National Statistics, 'A Demographic Report of Northern Ireland', *Population Trends*, no. 135 (Spring 2009), pp. 91–3.

120 *Belfast Telegraph*, 25 June 2004.

121 *Irish Times*, 28 July 2009.

122 *The Times*, 18 June 2009.

123 *Irish Times*, 18 June 2009.

124 *Belfast Telegraph*, 18 June 2009.

125 *Irish Times*, 18 June 2009.

126 Ibid., 21 April 2009.

127 Ibid., 3 April 2009; *Guardian*, 9 December 2009.

128 *Belfast Telegraph*, 9 June 2009.

129 Wood, *Crimes of Loyalty*, p. 315.

130 Bill Rolston, with Mairead Gilmartin, *Unfinished Business: State Killings and the Quest for Truth* (Belfast, 2000).

131 'Dublin and Monaghan Bombings', Justice for the Forgotten; www.dublin-monaghanbombings.org/publications.html. Accessed 3 February 2009.

132 'Interim Report on Dublin and Monaghan Bombing', *Oireachtas Nollaig*, 2003; www.oireachtas.gov.ie. Accessed 4 May 2008.

133 *The Independent*, 11 and 12 December 2003.

134 *Irish News*, 11 December 2003.

135 'Report on Dublin and Monaghan Bombings', RTÉ News, 17 November 2004; www.rte.ie/news/2004/1117/bombings.html. Accessed 18 November 2008.

136 'Dublin-Monaghan Bombings', Dáil Éireann, vol. 639, 10 October 2007; www. oireachtas.gov.ie. Accessed 4 May 2008.

137 *Belfast Telegraph*, 4 April 2007.

138 *Irish Independent*, 5 April 2007.

139 'Dublin-Monaghan Bombings', Dáil Éireann.

140 'Bloody Sunday', Channel Four News, 17 January 1997.

141 BBC News, 20 December 2004.

142 *The Independent*, 30 April 2001.

143 *Irish Independent*, 24 September 2009; UTV news, 5 November 2009.

144 *Irish Times*, 8 November 2008; *Irish Times*, 19 March 2010.

145 Ibid., 17 September 2009.

146 'Omagh Bomb Report "Grossly Unfair"', BBC News, 12 December 2001; http://news.bbc.co.uk/2/hi/uk_news/northern_ireland/1707299.stm. Accessed 4 March 2008.

147 'Move to Dismiss Omagh Bomb Case', BBC News, 14 November 2001; http://usproxy.bbc.com/2/hi/uk_news/northern_ireland/1656401.stm. Accessed 4 March 2008.

148 *Belfast Telegraph*, 8 February 2008.

149 *Guardian*, 26 January 2009.

150 *Daily Telegraph*, 15 September 2008.

151 *The Times*, 17 September 2008.

152 Ibid.

153 *Irish News*, 30 January 2007.

154 Raymond McCord, *Justice for Raymond* (Dublin, 2008).

155 'Public Statement by Mrs Nuala O'Loan on her investigation into the circumstances surrounding the death of Raymond McCord Junior and related matters (Operation Ballast)', 22 January 2007; www.cain.ulst.ac.uk/bibdbs/authorbib.htm. Accessed 15 May 2008.

156 Ibid.

157 'RUC Informers Knew about Loughinisland Shootings', UTV News, 13 September 2009; www.u.tv/news. Accessed 15 September 2009.

158 *Irish Times*, 11 September 2009.

159 'Hain Announces Group to Look at the Past', Media Centre Northern Ireland Office, Friday 22 June 2007; www.nio.gov.uk/hain-announces-group-to-look-at-the-past/media-detail.htm?newsID=14484. Accessed 5 February 2009.

160 *Daily Mirror*, 31 January 2009.

161 *The Times*, 29 March 1998.

162 *Irish Times*, 12 May 1999.

163 Ibid., 11 May 1999.

164 *Irish Independent*, 23 May 2006.

165 *Commission to Enquire into Child Abuse – Third Interim Report*, December 2003.

166 *The Times*, 20 May 2009.

167 'Endemic Rape and Abuse of Irish Children in Catholic Care, Inquiry Finds', *Guardian*, 20 May 2009.

168 *Irish Times*, 9 June 2009.

169 *Belfast Telegraph*, 29 January 2009; *Guardian*, 20 March 2010.

170 *Princeton Bulletin*, XCII/23 (14 April 2003).

171 'Boy in Striped Pyjamas', *Good Reads*; www.goodreads.com/book/show/39999.The_Boy_in_the_Striped_Pajamas. Accessed 7 April 2009.

172 Man Booker Prizes, www.themanbookerprize.com/prize/archive. Accessed 6 March 2009.

173 *Irish News*, 29 July 2009.

174 *Belfast Telegraph*, 27 January 2009.

175 'Re-imaging Programme Helps Communities to Take First Step to Transformation', *Reimaging Communities*, 7 March 2008; http://images.google.com. Accessed 14 December 2008.

176 *Guardian*, 19 March 2009.

177 *Belfast Telegraph*, 22 September 2008.

178 Ibid.

179 *Daily Express*, 16 May 2009.

180 *Irish Times*, 26 May 2009.

181 'Northern Ireland Life and Times', Economic and Social Research Council; www.ark.ac.uk/nilt/2007/Political_Attitudes/UNINATID.html. Accessed 10 March 2009.

182 Ibid.

183 *Times*, 29 November 2009.

184 *Irish Times*, 2 January 2010.

185 *Sunday Times*, 29 November 2009.

186 *Guardian*, 14 April 2008.

187 *Guardian*, 14 April 2008.

188 Joint statement by Sir Reg Empey and David Cameron MP, 24 July 2008, Official Website of the Ulster Unionist Party, http://www.uup.org/news/general/general-news-archive/joint-statement-by-sir-reg-empey-and-david-cameron-mp.php. Accessed 10 January 2010.

189 Paul Bew, *Guardian*, 24 July 2008.

190 BBC News, 14 December 2009. http://news.bbc.co.uk/1/hi/northern_ireland/8411353.stm. Accessed 19 March 2010.

191 BBC News, 18 December 2009, http://news.bbc.co.uk/1/hi/northern_ireland/8420275.stm. Accessed 16 March 2010.

192 BBC News, 4 January 2010, http://news.bbc.co.uk/1/hi/northern_ireland/8458972.stm. Accessed 14 March 2010.

193 BBC News, 25 January 2010. http://news.bbc.co.uk/1/hi/northern_ireland/8478237.stm. Accessed 15 March 2010.

194 BBC News, 4 March 2010. http://news.bbc.co.uk/1/hi/northern_ireland/8549939.stm. Accessed 14 March 2010.

195 *Irish Times*, 7 January 2010.

196 BBC News, 8 January 2010, http://news.bbc.co.uk/1/hi/northern_ireland/8447383.stm. Accessed 14 March 2010.

197 *Irish Times*, 12 January 2010.

198 *Irish Times*, 2 January, 2010.

199 *Guardian*, 27 January 2010.

200 BBC News, 5 March 2010, http://news.bbc.co.uk/1/hi/northern_ireland/8552699.stm. Accessed 19 March 2010.

201 *Guardian*, 5 March 2010.

202 BBC News, 9 March 2010, http://news.bbc.co.uk/1/hi/northern_ireland/8558466.stm. Accessed 20 March 2010.

203 Official Website of Ulster Unionist Party, 12 March 2010, http://www.uup.org/news/policing-justice/policing-and-justice-archive/dup-caved-to-nio-and-sf-pressure.php. Accessed 19 March 2010.

204 *Irish Times*, 25 March 2010.

205 *Sunday Tribune*, 30 August 2009.

Bibliography

PRIMARY SOURCES

Kennedy, E., 'Northern Ireland – a View from America', Tip O'Neill Memorial Lecture, University of Ulster, Magee College. Delivered at the Guildhall, Derry, 9 January 1998; http://cain.ulst.ac.uk/events/peace/docs/ek9198.htm

Conservative Party, *A Better Tomorrow* (1970) [manifesto]; www.conservativemanifesto. com/1970/1970-conservative-manifesto.shtml

Craig, W., *The Future of Northern Ireland* (n.p., 1972?); http://cain.ulst.ac.uk/othelem/ organ/docs/craig.htm

Famine Commemoration Programme (Dublin, 1995)

Pamphlet issued by the Irish Department of Foreign Affairs on the EEC and Irish Agriculture (Dublin, 1971)

'Working towards a New Europe: The Role and Achievements of Europe's Regional Policy, 2004–2009'; http://ec.europa.eu/regional_policy/policy/ impact/pdf/legacy_2009_en.pdf

LEGISLATION, REPORTS AND INQUIRIES

Anglo-Irish Agreement 1985 between the Government of Ireland and the Government of the United Kingdom; www.uhb.fr/langues/cei/agree85.htm

Bennett Report, *Report of the Committee of Inquiry into Police Interrogation Procedures in Northern Ireland*. Chairman: His Honour Judge H. G. Bennett, QC (London, 1979)

Cameron Report, *Disturbances in Northern Ireland: Report of the Commission Appointed by the Governor of Northern Ireland*. Chairman: The Honourable Lord Cameron, DSC. Presented to Parliament by Command of His Excellency the Governor of Northern Ireland, September 1969 (Belfast, 1969)

Compton Report, *Report of the Enquiry into Allegations against the Security Forces of Physical Brutality in Northern Ireland Arising out of Events on the 9th August, 1971*. Chairman: Sir Edmund Compton, GCB, KBE (London, 1971)

Gardiner Report, *Report of a Committee to Consider, in the Context of Civil Liberties and Human Rights, Measures to Deal with Terrorism in Northern Ireland*. Chairman: Lord Gardiner (London, 1975)

Government of Ireland Act (1920) (10 & 11 Geo. 5 c. 67)

389

HMSO, *Northern Ireland Constitutional Proposals* (London, 1973)

—, *The Northern Ireland Constitution: Presented to Parliament by the Secretary of State for Northern Ireland by Command of Her Majesty* (London, 1974)

—, *The Government of Northern Ireland: Proposals for Further Discussion* (London, 1980)

—, *Report of an Inquiry by HM Chief Inspector of Prisons into the Security Arrangements at HM Prison, Maze Relative to the Escape on Sunday 25th September 1983, including Relevant Recommendations for the Improvement of Security at HM Prison, Maze* (London, 1984)

Hunt Report, *Presented to Parliament by Command of His Excellency the Governor of Northern Ireland, October 1969* (Belfast, 1969)

Macrory Report, *Review Body on Local Government in Northern Ireland, Presented to Parliament by Command of His Excellency the Governor of Northern Ireland, June 1970* (Belfast, 1970)

North Report, *Parades and Marches: Independent Review of Parades and Marches in Northern Ireland, January 1997*. Chairman: Dr Peter North (London, 1997)

Patten Report, *Independent Commission on Policing for Northern Ireland*. Chairperson: Chris Patten (London, 1999)

Scarman Report, *Violence and Civil Disturbances in Northern Ireland in 1969: Report of Tribunal of Inquiry*. Chairman: The Hon. Mr Justice Scarman (Belfast, 1972)

Stevens Enquiry, *Overview and Recommendations, 17 April 2003*. Chairman: Sir John Stevens QPM, DL, Commissioner of the Metropolitan Police Service (London, 2003)

SECONDARY SOURCES

Adams, G., *A Farther Shore: Ireland's Long Road to Peace* (New York, 2003)

Anderson, M., et al., *The Irish Border: History, Politics, Culture* (Liverpool, 1999)

Andrews, J. A., ed., *Human Rights in Criminal Procedure* (The Hague, 1982)

Aretxaga, B., and J. Zulaika, *States of Terror: Begoña Aretxaga's Essays* (Reno, 2005)

Atkins, S. E., *Encyclopaedia of Modern Worldwide Extremists and Extremist Groups* (Santa Barbara, CA, 2004)

Aykroyd, W. R., *The Conquest of Famine* (London, 1974)

Beresford, D., *Ten Men Dead: The Story of the 1981 Irish Hunger Strike* (New York, 1987)

Bew, P., *Ideology and the Irish Question: Ulster Unionism and Irish Nationalism, 1912–1916* (Oxford, 1994)

—, *Ireland: The Politics of Enmity, 1789–2006* (Oxford, 2007)

Boltwood, S., *Brian Friel, Ireland, and The North* (Cambridge, 2007)

Bonner, D., *Executive Measures, Terrorism and National Security* (Aldershot, 2007)

Bourke, A., *The Field Day Anthology of Irish Writing, IV and V: Irish Women's Writing and Tradition* (Cork, 2005)

Bowyer Bell, J., *The IRA, 1968–2000: An Analysis of a Secret Army* (London, 2000)

Bradshaw, B., 'Nationalism and Historical Scholarship in Modern Ireland', *Irish Historical Studies*, XXVI (1989), pp. 329–51

Brearton, F., *The Great War in Irish Poetry* (Oxford, 2000)

Bryan, D., *Orange Parades: The Politics of Ritual, Tradition and Control* (London, 2000)

Bull, M. J., and J. L. Newell, *Corruption in Contemporary Politics* (London, 2003)

Buscher, S., and B. Ling, *Máiread Corrigan and Betty Williams* (New York, 1999)

Cairncross, A., *The British Economy since 1945: Economic Policy and Performance, 1945–1995* (Oxford, 1995)

Callanan, M., ed., *Foundations of an Ever Closer Union: An Irish Perspective on Fifty Years since the Treaty of Rome* (Dublin, 2007)

Cannon Harris, S., *Gender and Modern Irish Drama* (Bloomington, IN, 2002)

Carlson, J., *Banned in Ireland: Censorship and the Irish Writer* (London, 1990)

Carroll, F. M., *The American Presence in Ulster: a Diplomatic History, 1796–1996* (Washington, DC, 2005)

Carty, F. X., *Hold Firm: John Charles McQuaid and the Second Vatican Council* (Dublin, 2007)

Coakley, J., and M. Gallagher, *Politics in the Republic of Ireland* (London, 2009)

Cochrane, F., *Unionist Politics and the Politics of Unionism since the Anglo-Irish Agreement* (Cork, 1997)

Colleran, J., and J. S. Spencer, *Staging Resistance: Essays on Political Theater* (Ann Arbor, MI, 1998)

Collins, F., *Seamus Heaney: The Crisis of Identity* (Cranbury, NJ, 2005)

Coogan, T. P., *The Troubles: Ireland's Ordeal 1969–96, and the Search for Peace* (London, 1996)

——, *The IRA* (Aldershot, 2002)

Corcoran, F., *RTÉ and the Globalisation of Irish Television* (Bristol, 2004)

Council of Europe / Conseil de L'Europe, *Yearbook of the European Convention on Human Rights, 1987* (Strasbourg, 1992)

Cox, M., 'Northern Ireland; The War that Came in from the Cold', *International Affairs*, LXXIII/4 (1997), pp. 671–93

Craig, W., *The Future of Northern Ireland* (n.p., 1972?)

Cunningham, M. J., *British Government Policy in Northern Ireland, 1969–1989: Its Nature and Execution* (Manchester, 1991)

Curtis, L., *Ireland, The Propaganda War: The Media and the 'Battle for Hearts and Minds'* (London, 1983)

Delaney, P., ed., *Brian Friel in Conversation, Theatre: Theory, Text, Performance* (Ann Arbor, MI, 2000)

Dillon, M., *Stone Cold: The True Story of Michael Stone and the Milltown Massacre* (London, 1992)

——, *The Dirty War: Covert Strategies and Tactics Used in Political Conflicts* (Oxford, 1999)

——, *The Shankill Butchers* (London, 1999)

Dorey, P., *British Politics since 1945* (Chichester, 1995)

Elliott, M., *The Long Road to Peace in Northern Ireland* (Liverpool, 2002)

Elliott, S., and P. Bew, 'The Prospects for Devolution', *Studies: An Irish Quarterly Review*, LXXX (Summer 1991), pp. 124–32

Ellis, S. A., 'The Historical Significance of President Kennedy's Visit to Ireland in June 1963', *Irish Studies Review*, xvi/2 (2008), pp. 113–30

Ellison, G., and J. Smyth, *The Crowned Harp: Policing in Northern Ireland* (London, 2000)

English, R., *Armed Struggle: The History of the IRA* (Oxford, 2003)

English, R., and J. Morrison Skelly, eds, *Ideas Matter: Essays in Honour of Conor Cruise O'Brien* (Dublin, 1998)

Fahey, T., and D. Duffy, *Quality of Life in Ireland: The Social Impact of Economic Boom* (Dordrecht, 2002)

Fahey, T., H. Russell and C. T. Whelan, eds, *Best of Times? The Social Impact of the Celtic Tiger in Ireland* (Dublin, 2007)

Feeney, B., *Sinn Féin: a Hundred Turbulent Years* (Dublin, 2002)

Finnegan, R. B., and E. McCarron, *Ireland: The Challenge of Conflict and Change* (Boulder, CO, 1983)

——, *Ireland: Historical Echoes, Contemporary Politics* (Boulder, CO, 2000)

Fitzgerald, G., 'The 1974–5 Threat of a British Withdrawal from Northern Ireland', *Irish Studies in International Affairs*, XVII (2006), pp. 141–50

Foot, P., *Who Framed Colin Wallace?* (London, 1990)

Foster, R., 'We are All Revisionists Now', *Irish Review*, 1 (1986), pp. 1–6

Galligan, Y., *Women and Politics in Contemporary Ireland: From Margins to the Mainstream* (London, 1998)

Geraghty, T., *The Irish War: The Hidden Conflict between the IRA and British Intelligence* (Baltimore, MD, 2002)

Gifford, Lord, *Supergrasses: The Use of Accomplice Evidence in Northern Ireland* (London, 1984)

Girvin, B., 'Church, State, and Society in Ireland since 1960', *Éire-Ireland*, XLIII/1–2 (2008), pp. 74–98

Hachey, T. E., J. M. Hernon and L. J. McCaffrey, *The Irish Experience: a Concise History* (New York, 1996)

Hall, J., *To Serve without Favour: Policing, Human Rights, and Accountability in Northern Ireland* (Helsinki, 1995)

Harrington, J. P., and E. J. Mitchell, *Politics and Performance in Contemporary Northern Ireland* (Amherst, MA, 1999)

Hayes, B., and I. McAllister, 'Religious Independents in Northern Ireland: Origins, Attitudes and Significance', *Review of Religious Research*, XXXVII/1 (1995), pp. 65–83

Heaney, Seamus, *An Open Letter* (Derry, 1983)

——, *The Cure at Troy: A Version of Sophocles' Philoctetes* (New York, 1991)

Hennessey, T., *The Northern Ireland Peace Process: Ending the Troubles?* (New York, 2001)

Holroyd, F., and N. Burbridge, *War without Honour* (London, 1989)

Jackson, A., *Home Rule: An Irish History, 1800–2000* (Oxford, 2004)

Jewkes, Y., and H. Johnston, eds, *Prison Readings: A Critical Introduction to Prisons and Imprisonment* (Cullompton, Devon, 2006)

Kaufmann, E. P., *The Orange Order: A Contemporary Northern Irish History* (Oxford, 2009)

Kendall, T., *The Oxford Handbook of British and Irish War Poetry* (Oxford, 2009)

Kennedy, K., T. Giblin and D. McHugh, *The Economic Development of Ireland in the Twentieth Century* (London, 2001)

Kennedy, L., *'They Shoot Children Don't They?'* (Belfast, 2001)

Kennedy, M., *Division and Consensus: The Politics of Cross-border Relations in Ireland, 1925–1969* (Dublin, 2000)

Kennedy O'Connor, J., *The Eurovision Song Contest: The Official History* (Glasgow, 2005)

Kiberd, D., *Inventing Ireland: The Literature of the Modern Nation* (London, 1995)

Kinealy, C., *A Death-Dealing Famine: The Great Hunger in Ireland* (London, 1997)

——, *The Great Irish Famine: Impact, Ideology and Rebellion* (London, 2002)

——, *Repeal and Revolution: 1848 in Ireland* (Manchester, 2009)

King, Russell, and Ian Shuttleworth, 'The Emigration and Employment of Irish Graduates', in *European Urban and Regional Studies*, II/I (1995), pp. 21–40

Kitson, F., *Low Intensity Operations: Subversion, Insurgency, Peacekeeping* (London, 1971)

Langdon, J., *Mo Mowlam: The Biography* (London, 2000)

Lazenbatt, A., U. Lynch and E. O'Neill, 'Revealing the Hidden "Troubles" in Northern Ireland: the Role of Participatory Rapid Appraisal', *Health Education Research*, XVI/5 (2001), pp. 567–78

Lee, J., *Ireland, 1912–1985: Politics and Society* (Cambridge, 1990)

Leslie, D., 'Northern Ireland, Tourism and Peace', *Tourism Management*, XVII/I (1996), pp. 51–5

Lobo, A. P., and J. J. Salvo, 'Resurgent Irish Immigration to the US in the 1980s and early 1990s: A Socio-demographic Profile', *International Migration*, XXXVI/2 (1998), pp. 257–80

McCalman, I., *Making Culture Bloom* (Canberra, 2004)

McEvoy, K., *Paramilitary Imprisonment in Northern Ireland: Resistance, Management, and Release* (Oxford, 2001)

McGarry, J., ed., *Northern Ireland and the Divided World: Post-Agreement Northern Ireland* (Oxford, 2001)

McGarry, J., and B. O'Leary, *The Northern Ireland Conflict: Consociational Engagements* (Oxford, 2004)

McLoughlin, P. J., '"Dublin is Just a Sunningdale Away"? The SDLP and the Failure of Northern Ireland's Sunningdale Experiment', in *Twentieth Century British History*, XIX/4 (2008), pp. 74–96

——, '"Humespeak": The SDLP, Political Discourse, and the Northern Ireland Peace Process', *Peace and Conflict Studies*, XV/I (2008), pp. 95–114

McPhilemy, S., *The Committee: Political Assassination in Northern Ireland* (Boulder, CO, 1998)

Madden, P., 'Banned, Censored and Delayed: A Chronology of Some TV Programmes Dealing with Northern Ireland', *The British Media and Ireland – Truth: the First Casualty*, ed. The Campaign for Free Speech on Ireland (Belfast, 1979?)

Mansergh, M., 'The Early Stages of the Irish Peace Process', *Conciliation Resources*, December 1999; www.c-r.org/our-work/accord/northern-ireland/early-stages. php

Mason, P., ed., *Criminal Visions: Media Representations of Crime and Justice* (Uffculme, Devon, 2003)

Miller, D., ed., *Rethinking Northern Ireland: Culture, Ideology and Colonialism* (Harlow, 1998)

Moloney, E., *A Secret History of the IRA* (London, 2003)

Moore, J., *Ulster Unionism and the British Conservative Party: A Study of a Failed Marriage* (London, 1997)

393

Mulcahy, A., *Policing Northern Ireland* (Cullompton, Devon, 2005)

Murphy, A. E., *The Celtic Tiger: An Analysis of Ireland's Economic Performance* (San Domenico di Fiesole, 2000)

Murray, Fr Raymond, 'Censorship in the North of Ireland', *The British Media and Ireland – Truth: the First Casualty*, ed. The Campaign for Free Speech on Ireland (Belfast, 1979?)

O'Cleireacain, S.C.M., 'Northern Ireland and Irish Integration: The Role of the European Communities', *Journal of Common Market Studies*, XXII/2 (1983), pp. 107–24

O'Clery, Conor, *Daring Diplomacy* (Boulder, CO, 1997)

Office for National Statistics, 'A Demographic Report of Northern Ireland', *Population Trends*, no. 135 (Spring, 2009)

O'Mahony, P., *Criminal Justice in Ireland* (Dublin, 2002)

Parker, M., *The Hurt World: Short Stories of the Troubles* (Belfast, 1995)

——, *Seamus Heaney: The Making of the Poet* (Basingstoke, 1994)

——, *Northern Irish Literature, 1956–1975*, 2 vols (Basingstoke, 2007)

Parkinson, A. F., *Ulster Loyalism and the British Media* (Dublin, 1998)

Patterson, H., 'Party versus Order: Ulster Unionism and the Flags and Emblems Act', *Contemporary British History*, XIII/4 (1999), pp. 105–29

Pettitt, L., *Screening Ireland* (Manchester, 2000)

'The Press and the Peace People', *The British Media and Ireland – Truth: the First Casualty*, ed. The Campaign for Free Speech on Ireland (Belfast, 1979?)

Rafferty, O. P., *Catholicism in Ulster, 1603–1983: An Interpretative History* (Columbia, SC, 1995)

Roberts, N., *A Companion to Twentieth-Century Poetry* (Oxford, 2003)

Roche, A., ed., *The Cambridge Companion to Brian Friel* (Cambridge, 2006)

Rolston, B., with M. Gilmartin, *Unfinished Business: State Killings and the Quest for Truth* (Belfast, 2000)

Rose, P., *How the Troubles Came to Northern Ireland* (Basingstoke, 2001)

Ryder, C., and V. Kearney, *Drumcree: The Orange Order's Last Stand* (London, 2001)

Schrank, B., and W. W. Demastes, eds, *Irish Playwrights, 1880–1995* (Westport, CT, 1997)

Sheehy, S. J., 'The Impact of EEC Membership on Irish Agriculture', *Journal of Agricultural Economics*, XXXI/3 (2008), pp. 297–310

Slocum, J. D., ed., *Terrorism, Media, Liberation* (Piscataway, NJ, 2005)

Smithey, L. A., 'Strategic and Collective Action and Collective Identity Reconstruction: Parading Disputes and Two Northern Towns', PhD thesis, University of Texas at Austin, 2002

Spreng, J. E., *Abortion and Divorce Law in Ireland* (Jefferson, NC, 2004)

Stopper, A., *Mondays at Gaj's: The Story of the Irish Women's Liberation Movement* (Dublin, 2006)

Stryker, S., T. J. Owens and R. W. White, eds, *Self, Identity, and Social Movements* (Minneapolis, MN, 2000)

Taylor, P., 'Reporting Northern Ireland', *The British Media and Ireland – Truth: the First Casualty*, ed. The Campaign for Free Speech on Ireland (Belfast, 1979?)

——, *Loyalists* (London, 2000)

Tonge, J., *Northern Ireland* (Cambridge, 2006)

Toolis, K., *Rebel Hearts: Journeys within the IRA's Soul* (New York, 1995)

Townroe, P., and R. Martin, *Regional Development in the 1990s: The British Isles in Transition* (London, 1992)

Triandafyllidou, A., and R. Gropas, *European Immigration: a Sourcebook* (Aldershot, 2007)

Walker, G., *A History of the Ulster Unionist Party: Protest, Pragmatism and Pessimism* (Manchester, 2004)

Ward, M., *Unmanageable Revolutionaries: Women and Irish Nationalism* (London, 1995)

Whalen, L., *Contemporary Irish Republican Prison Writing: Writing and Resistance* (London, 2007)

Wilde, M., 'Who Wanted What and Why at the Second Vatican Council? Toward a General Theory of Religious Change', *Sociologica*, 1 (2007); www.sociologica.mulino.it/journal/articlefulltext/index/Article/Journal:ARTICLE:33

Williamson, A. P., 'Policy for Higher Education in Northern Ireland: The New University of Ulster and the Origins of the University of Ulster', *Irish Educational Studies*, xii/1 (1993), pp. 285–301

Wilson, A. J., 'Maintaining the Cause in the Land of the Free: Ulster Unionists and us Involvement in the Northern Ireland Conflict, 1968–72', *Éire-Ireland*, xl/3–4 (2005), pp. 212–39

Wilson, J., *Understanding Journalism* (London, 1996)

Wood, I., *Crimes of Loyalty: A History of the UDA* (Edinburgh, 2006).

Acknowledgements

The origins of this book lay in the long period of time that I lived, studied and worked in Dublin and Belfast. When I left Belfast in the early 1990s, a peace process seemed unlikely. That one is in place, however shaky, is a tribute to men and women of vision. Much more remains to be done to build a truly inclusive Ireland, however. During my frequent returns to Ireland, I am struck by how rapidly it is changing. An aim of this study is to place these changes in context, and to give a voice to some of the forgotten heroes, and victims, of the last fifty years.

I am grateful to various people who have read sections of this book. Particular thanks are due to Francine Sagar and Francine Becker, but also to Lauretta Farrell, Barry Quest and David Sexton.

I have benefited greatly from discussions with a number of people, including Bernadette Barrington, Niall Meehan, Carol Russell, Jim Cullen, Don Mullen, James Loughlin, Jim Larraghy, Owen Rodgers, Gerard MacAtasney, Seán Sexton, Michael Parker, Bill Rogers, Arthur Luke, Bernard Quinn and Stephen Butler. Collectively they represent Irish, British, French and American perspectives and they cover a multiplicity of religious and political views. I thank them for their time and their insights.

Teaching two classes on Northern Ireland (an undergraduate and a graduate one) at Drew University proved to be both challenging and rewarding. Special thanks are due to Alexander Wallick, Judith Campbell, Peggy Terry, Ronnie Stout-Kopp, James Wojkiewicz, Liz Ramella and the many other students who cared enough to keep asking questions, and ensure that the classes were full to over-flowing.

Over the years I have been fortunate to meet with various people involved in Irish politics, including Mary Robinson, Kevin McNamara, Mary McAleese, Tony Blair, Gerry Adams, John Hume, Ivan Copper, Ken Livingstone, David Trimble, Ian Paisley, Billy Hutchinson, the late Dave Ervine and Mo Mowlam. While the contribution of most of the aforementioned has been immense, there are many more people who have worked tirelessly behind the scenes to bring about social justice and peace in Ireland. They are mostly nameless, yet are a vital part of the story. I am grateful to Bonnie Lofton for drawing my attention to the wonderful work that has been carried out at Eastern Mennonite University in the US to bring about reconciliation in Northern Ireland. The full story of four peace-brokers in the US, known as the 'Connolly House Group', also remains to be told. I am grateful to Judy Campbell for sharing her research on these men. They and many others made a contribution that was vital, but easy to overlook in general histories of the period.

I have also benefited from conversation with people who remember Ireland before 1960, especially my dear Wexford friends Ella and Johnny; John, whose wonderful pub in Duncormick tells much of the recent history of the country on its walls; David from Belfast, a Protestant nationalist, who felt an outsider because of his politics; and Seán, who could not wait to leave Ireland and escape the repressive atmosphere of the 1950s, but who now laments the loss of Irish culture as he remembers it.

Finally, many thanks to the friends I have ignored in the final stages of writing this book, including Honora, Susan, Bernadette, Linda, Angela, Rita, David and Jean.

As always, my deepest gratitude is due to my children: Siobhán, who was born in Dublin, and Ciarán, who was born in Belfast. They are the best example of cross-border cooperation I know.

Responsibility for the contents and for any mistakes or omissions in this account are, of course, my own.

Index